D1253575

Florida A&M University, Tallahassee
Florida Atlantic University, Boca Raton
Florida Gulf Coast University, Ft. Myers
Florida International University, Miami
Florida State University, Tallahassee
University of Central Florida, Orlando
University of Florida, Gainesville
University of North Florida, Jacksonville
University of South Florida, Tampa
University of West Florida, Pensacola

Paddler's Guide
to the Sunshine State

Sandy Huff

With guest authors:

Arnie Diedrichs, Jean Faulk, Bryce Huff, John Phillips, Larry Reed, Nancy Scharmach, and Laurilee Thompson

University Press of Florida

Gainesville · Tallahassee · Tampa · Boca Raton
Pensacola · Orlando · Miami · Jacksonville · Ft. Myers

Library of Congress Cataloging-in-Publication Data
Huff, Sandy.
Paddler's guide to the Sunshine State / Sandy Huff ; with guest authors,
Arnie Diedrichs . . . [et al.].
p. cm.
Includes bibliographical references (p.) and index.
ISBN 0-8130-2282-7 (pbk. : alk. paper)
1. Canoes and canoeing—Florida—Guidebook. 2. Florida—Guidebooks. I. Title.
GV776.F56 H84 2001
797.1'22'09759—dc21   2001041578

The University Press of Florida is the scholarly publishing agency for the State University
System of Florida, comprising Florida A&M University, Florida Atlantic University, Florida
Gulf Coast University, Florida International University, Florida State University, University
of Central Florida, University of Florida, University of North Florida, University of South
Florida, and University of West Florida.

University Press of Florida
15 Northwest 15th Street
Gainesville, FL 32611-2079
http://www.upf.com

To my mom, Anna Holladay, who would meet a challenge with a whoop of glee, followed by a long packing list

Seize the moment, for this exact instant shall never come again.
Look around. Delight in the sunbeam. Savor the perfume. Feel the love.
Exult in your life. This moment shall never come again.

author unknown

Unfortunately, there is a tendency to go on some of these outdoor experiences as if it were work. Take time to smell the roses on your great escape from the rat race. Great things happen when paddlers, hikers, or even scuba divers sit still, and just enjoy the surroundings. Make a point on any adventure trip you make while paddling the various waters in Florida to break away from the hard-charging fellow adventurers, at least for a half-day of contemplative solitude. Smile at the wild world and it just might smile back at you!

John Phillips

Contents

Preface

Paddling in Florida is different.

We have few rapids, but we do have three different kinds of water: fresh, salt, and brackish. We don't have moose or elks, but we do have alligators—and you should know a few basic facts about these formidable aquatic lizards.

Sunburn, rain, mosquitoes, and logjams are all part of being outdoors, but a few simple precautions will keep you safe and comfortable.

Above all, paddling in Florida is FUN!

Where else can you silently glide among the giant tree trunks of a primordial swamp? Slip down a stream so clear you can count every blade of turtle grass under your keel? Paddle through miles of saw grass under a sky so huge you can see the horizon in every direction? Plunge through waves beside curious dolphins?

Along the way, you'll discover the beauty, history, and mysteries of America's subtropical wonderland.

Florida is a great place to paddle. Come join us!

How to Use This Book

The first two sections of this book are dedicated to information specific to Florida—avoiding sunburn, the best bug spray, coping with animals, plus a plethora of "good stuff."

The third and largest section lists places to go canoeing and kayaking. These destinations are a mixture of well-known and hidden spots, from one-hour jaunts to week-long expeditions.

Each destination chapter starts with information to help you prepare for your trip:

Length—The length of the trip is given either in miles or in the time an average paddler would take to complete the run.

Current—Florida river currents average two to three miles per hour, but there are wide fluctuations according to rainfall, wind, and season. At low water most rivers have almost imperceptible flows and you might have to portage over sandbars and other obstructions that are normally under water. At flood stage you might be rushed along through interlacing tree-tops, or be unable to find the main channel.

Skill level—Gauge your own paddling skills, which are a combination of experience, agility, upper body strength, and expertise in different strokes. The official Florida Canoe Trails lists almost every trail as "beginner" level, but I've found many of these destinations unsuited for first-timers, children, or nonfit paddlers. If you're a first-timer, choose a quiet backwater or pond, and save the strenuous wilderness expeditions for later.

Wind—The slightest breeze can be an enormous factor when you are on the open water. A strong wind will inexorably push you downwind, especially if you are paddling a canoe whose high sides act as sails. Consider the wind when you decide whether to paddle the narrow, protected upper reaches of a river or a wide, exposed marsh or waterway.

Emergency numbers—Listed are the local sheriff, police, or other appropriate numbers to call for help. It is prudent to carry a cell phone, GPS unit, or radio for long trips.

Rentals—When I could find them, I listed the canoe and kayak liveries that rent paddling gear for that specific waterway. New liveries pop up all the time, and a more up-to-date list is posted on several websites, including www.paddlefl.com.

DeLorme's atlas page numbers—Most Florida paddling clubs use DeLorme's oversized book of maps to give directions and plot courses, so the maps in this book are also keyed to that atlas. Copies sell for under twenty dollars at book, drug, and discount stores.

Official Florida canoe trail—Florida has thirty-nine official canoe trails, with several more scheduled to be added. These rivers have been kept in as natural a state as possible, which means you might encounter logjams, sandbars, and other obstructions.

As a service to you, this book will open flat, so that you can copy just the pages you'll use for each trip.

My best advice:

Make a phone call! Before you set off on any trip listed in this book, call ahead. Conditions change constantly. Ramps, roads, and liveries open and close. Rivers rise and fall. I've seen the Withlacoochee so high that we couldn't find the channel, and two years later watched kids bicycle down the middle of the same stream bed. A lake that was choked with hydrilla six months ago may be a dream to paddle today—or it may have gotten so bad that the fish are thumbing rides.

A number of people worked with me to make sure that the information in this book was correct at the time of publication. We checked and rechecked phone numbers, websites, and other details. But you know yourself that Internet sites, addresses, zip codes, area codes—in fact all of Florida is changing at a whopping rate. That's why there is plenty of room in the margins for you to make your own notes.

So before you pull out of your own driveway, make that phone call. It might make a difference.

Getting Started

Like tennis, swimming, or even ping-pong, paddling is a skill. Tiny steering strokes, applied at the right moment, are more effective than whacking the water with brute strength. Little kids and creaking grannies can easily maneuver a canoe or kayak. It's a matter of knowing how.

Should you take a course in canoeing or kayaking? If you're a do-it-yourselfer and prefer to learn on your own, check out the many books and videos available at your local library or bookstore. When you join the American Canoe Association, you receive an excellent text with clear illustrations of the skills and knowledge you'll need on the water. Even the little Canoeing Merit Badge book put out by your local Boy Scout council contains clear, well-illustrated material.

Still, the best way to learn to canoe or kayak is to enroll in a class. You learn water safety, how to recover from a capsize, and how to steer using seven or eight different strokes. The classes are also great fun.

To find such courses, check your Yellow Pages under "Canoes & Kayaks." Most of the shops that sell gear also arrange classes. Also call your local chapter of the American Red Cross, Girl Scout and Boy Scout councils, and community colleges and ask about classes in canoeing and kayaking.

The American Canoe Association arranges certified courses across the nation, announced in their newsletter *The American Canoeist*. Check out their website at www.acanet.org.

When you call a local paddling school, ask if they are ACA accredited. If not, go ahead and take the class (you'll learn a lot anyway), and suggest they get certified. Most classes concentrate on basic paddling and safety tips. If you want advanced training, such as Eskimo rolls, you can often arrange private lessons.

What's Your Canoe IQ?

This little quiz was designed for students who had completed the first day of my American Red Cross canoe course. See how you do.

1. According to law, must a personal flotation device (PFD) be available for every occupant of a canoe?
   A. yes
   B. no

2. You've fallen overboard in fast water. You should:
   A. float head downstream, face down
   B. float upright to get your footing
   C. try to stand up on a rock
   D. float on your back, feet downstream

3. The best length for a canoe paddle is:
   A. as tall as you are
   B. from the ground to your chin
   C. four inches taller than you are
   D. waist high

4. Your buddy is knocked unconscious when your canoe capsizes. You should:
   A. hold his wrists across the overturned keel
   B. push him in front of you as you swim
   C. hold him up from behind with both arms
   D. leave him and save yourself

5. If you capsize in open water, far from shore, you should:
   A. stay beside your boat
   B. start swimming for shore

6. You capsize in a narrow river. You are in current, but you can see both banks. The best way to swim is:
   A. upstream
   B. cross-current
   C. downstream at an angle

7. When you carry a canoe, it is less likely to be damaged by a drop if you carry it:

A. right side up

B. upside down

8. The safest paddling position in a canoe is:

   A. standing up so you can see

   B. sitting on a seat

   C. kneeling

   D. sitting flat on the bottom

9. You're in a canoe, approaching a tired swimmer. You should:

   A. extend your hand for a good grip

   B. extend your paddle

   C. throw her a rope

10. You're in the water, fully clothed. Your most efficient swimming stroke is:

    A. an underwater breast stroke

    B. an overhand crawl

11. For the best stability in a canoe in rough weather, keep your weight:

    A. high and at the bow

    B. low and centered

12. A properly equipped canoe has:

    A. a paddle for each person plus a spare

    B. painters or end lines

    C. a life vest for each person

    D. flashlight

13. When you're sitting in a boat, starboard is to your:

    A. right

    B. left

14. The term "freeboard" means:

    A. the length of the canoe

    B. the leading point

    C. from the waterline to the gunwales

    D. the underwater part of your canoe

15. When making a pivot turn, who makes the reverse sweep?

    A. stern paddler

    B. bow paddler

Answers

1. A. Yes, a Coast Guard approved life vest must be available for each person. Children under six in a boat less than 26 feet long must have theirs *on* at all times. This is not only the law, it's common sense.

2. D. In current, float face up, with your feet downstream. If the current rams you into a rock, which would you rather hit, your head or your toes?

3. B. The recommended paddle length is from your toes to your nose, or if you have the canoe paddle resting on the ground, up to your chin. Some racing paddlers are opting for shorter paddles now, and ultimately paddle selection is a personal choice.

4. A. Clutching his wrists over the keel is the safest way of holding on to an unconscious person. You can move slowly by kicking your feet.

5. A. A boat is easier to see than the small dot your head makes in the water. Also remember that the shore is always farther away than it looks.

6. C. Currents are powerful. Save your strength and let the river help you.

7. B. Carrying your boat upside down means you'll get a better hand grip too. The rule of thumb is, if you drop your boat, which would you rather get cracked, the gunwale or the keel? Kayaks with nice handles obviously should be carried upright.

8. C. Kneeling gives you the most control and flexibility, and keeps your weight low in the boat.

9. B. Extend your paddle, not your hand, so the swimmer won't capsize you beside her.

10. A. An underwater breast stroke produces less drag and is less tiring.

11. B. Keep your boat low and centered.

12. All the answers are correct, though you probably won't pack a flashlight for a short morning trip. On the other hand, remember *Gilligan's Island*?

13. A. For a mnemonic trick, remember that "starboard," "green," and "right" are all long words. "Port," "red," and "left" are all short words.

14. C. For safety, there should be at least six to ten inches of freeboard when your canoe is fully loaded. Kayaks are designed to sit low in the water, but overloading will make one unstable and heavy to paddle.

15. A. The stern paddler makes the reverse sweep.

Did you miss any? Were some of the terms unfamiliar? If you got 13 to 15 of the questions right, you win the golden paddle. Nine to 12 right, you might be safe in calm water, but beware of emergencies. Fewer than 9 right, you need some instruction. After all, there's no time to learn what you should do *after* you're in trouble.

Personal Gear and Clothing for Florida Paddling

Life Vest

Your most important piece of personal gear is the one item you'll be wearing for hours on end and which might just save your life—your life vest or PFD, meaning Personal Flotation Device.

A PFD is not an optional piece of equipment. You *must* have one. As an adult, you don't have to wear it at all times, but it must be right beside you in the boat. To quote the *Florida Boater's Guide* put out by the Department of Environmental Protection: "All boats must have a wearable type PFD for each person on board or being towed. Each PFD must be in good condition and readily available, and the proper size for the intended wearer."

"Readily available" means it isn't buried under a pile of gear or used as a sit-upon. It means that if you capsize, you can reach it in one motion and put it on in the water. In rough water or high winds, have it on, zipped and snapped.

Children under six must wear their PFDs the entire time they are in the boat. This is Florida law, and marine officers rightly have no sense of humor at all when they see a child without a life vest in a boat. It's a fast fifty-dollar ticket per kid. "Florida law requires every child under the age of six to wear a PFD while aboard any vessel less than 26 feet when it is underway." Smart parents require that their kids of all ages wear PFDs when they're around water.

Your life vest is your most important piece of equipment. Make sure it is comfortable and fits perfectly. Sandy Huff.

Personal Flotation Devices not only keep you floating when you end up in the drink, they provide insulation from both extreme cold and extreme heat. Types 1 and 3 keep your head above water if you are unconscious, and they cushion your back against the hard seat.

Throwable cushions are no longer legal. You must have a wearable PFD of type 1, 2, or 3, and it must be U.S. Coast Guard approved.

Type 2 are the old-fashioned horse-collar life vests, which run around $4.99 at discount stores. These make good spares, but they are uncomfortable and are not full-time wearable gear.

Type 5 is a hybrid device. There are some new types that consist of a set of suspenderlike straps attached to a waistband. These have a CO_2 cartridge rigged to a pull cord. When you need flotation, you yank the cord and the straps blow up into big fat floating pillows. These also have inflation tubes next to your chin so you can blow them up by mouth. They're lightweight and not binding, and make sense. However, the straps will not fit some women, and each CO_2 cartridge can be used only once.

A type-3 PFD is what most paddlers wear. These come in a variety of sizes, styles, shapes, colors, and closures. Most of them have handy pockets too. Since this is the type most Florida paddlers use, we'll briefly discuss a few points here.

First of all, wear a shirt under your PFD to cushion the tender skin under your arms. Even the best life vest has rough spots, seams, or bulges that your moving arms will brush constantly during the day. A simple T-shirt not only helps avoid sunburn but keeps chafing from ruining an otherwise wonderful trip.

Next, get one that fits you exactly. It should give you a full range of motion without riding up, be easy to snap or zip shut, have no loose straps or loops that will snag on branches and twigs, and just plain feel good. Swing your arms a couple of dozen times, and if anything rubs, try another brand.

For years full-figured women in PFDs designed for flat-chested men have felt like they were wearing corsets. Now some new brands such as LOA and Extra Sport are designed for women's shapes. They are a lot pricier than a bright orange horse-collar PFD, but worth it in comfort.

Test your PFD in the store before you buy. This is especially important for children. Put it on, then raise your hands high over your head. Now have a friend grab the bottom of the vest and push it up. Does the front of the neckline grab your throat and choke you? Does it try to cut off your nose? Worse, does it come completely off? The vest floats, remember, and this is the position it will be in once you're in the water.

If possible, try it in the water. I jump right in. If the vest stays on the surface while I plunge to the bottom, it was too big. Another factor is how it rides while you're both on the surface. It should stay in the general vicinity of your torso, not become a new hair ornament.

Proper fitting is vital for a child. Too often parents think their child is safe in a PFD, only to watch in horror as the kid slips completely out of the bottom of her life vest and sinks to the bottom. Children's life vests should have straps that go between their legs, and be snapped, buckled, and zipped shut at all times. Even then, stay close. Even the best life vest can get tangled, float upside down, or otherwise fail.

Now to other gear:

Shoes

Even here in Florida it's not a good idea to paddle barefoot. We have oysters, barnacles, crabs, stingrays, broken glass, sharp twigs, snapping turtles, old wire, and other hazards that lurk underwater.

Sneakers are the old standby. They're cheap, they're easy to tighten, and the canvas ones are self-draining. They're also a bit heavy and take a long time to dry.

Water sandals, such as Tevas, are best for fresh water. I formed this opinion the time I waded across an oyster bed and sliced the tops of my toes open when I didn't pick up my feet high enough. They do strap to your feet tightly and stay on in high surf and mud.

I personally think water shoes, such as Aquasox and Reef Walkers, are a great invention. They have soles sturdy enough to protect your foot, and they stay on, except in heavy surf and really deep mud. I go through three or four pair a year. Mine are worn out when the thin inner sole comes loose, and my big toes poke a hole through the fabric. Once, while a group of us were wading in the Homosassa River, a baby manatee came up to me and started sucking on my right toe, which was sticking out of the shoe.

Paddling shoes should be comfortable, dry quickly, and guard against sharp objects. Sandy Huff.

Gloves

Florida paddlers rarely have frostbite, but gloves feel good in winter in the north of the state, and they certainly protect your palms. Remember, all it takes to be miserable is one blister on your hand. Paddling gloves are excellent for holding a paddle all day, fending off rough tree bark on windfalls, hauling yourself and your boat across a logjam, pushing away thorny vines, and otherwise keeping your palms unbloodied.

In cold weather I use a pair of skin diver's neoprene gloves with the fingertips snipped off down to the first knuckle.

Most gloves don't float, so I've tried tying bits of floating material to the backs, such as little foam key-ring holders. These floats look tacky, but they keep a twenty-five-dollar pair of gloves from sinking if dropped.

Whistle

I've found a whistle essential several times: When that big yacht was adrift as her owner struggled to pull in a mackerel, and was sideslipping down on our group faster than we could paddle away. When a kid went overboard from a nearby bass boat and her parents didn't notice. When a friend paddled right past the camping spot and had to be called back.

Keep a rustproof whistle tied to your PFD. Make the cord tough, long enough to just reach your mouth, but short enough so it doesn't snag on anything. Tying it so it fits inside a pocket keeps it out of the way.

Use your whistle only when it is needed, not as a toy. Mariners use a whole system of sound signals you need to learn. For instance, the internationally recognized danger signal is five short blasts on a whistle or horn.

End Lines

A rope attached to the front and back of your kayak or canoe is a cheap and common sense bit of equipment. Whether you call it a painter, end line, or towrope, it's a vital handle. Make it ten to fifteen feet long. This will help you tow your boat, tie up at a stream bank, or tie down on a roof rack. You can also tie a slipknot to go around your waist so your boat will follow while you are snorkeling.

Bailer

Obviously, a wet-fanny sit-on-top kayak doesn't need a bailer. But in a closed-hull kayak or canoe, you will eventually need some way to bail out excess water.

Many people make a bailing scoop by cutting the bottom out of a bleach jug, saving the handle and putting the cap on really tight. Or they tie a cheap plastic cup with a handle to the thwarts.

I prefer a big sponge. This not only takes up a lot of water but wipes up mud, slime, spiders, crabs, Spanish moss, and a host of the little creepy and yucko things that end up in your bilge. I tie a three-foot length of red cord to mine, which makes it easy to find in the boat, ties the sponge to any thwart, and is an extra bit of rope when needed.

Kneeling Pads

Most of the time you'll be seated in your canoe. But if you're racing, or in rough water or high winds, you'll want to lower your center of gravity by kneeling on the bottom of the canoe and resting your rump on the seat. This is surprisingly comfortable—until your knees start to throb. Don't stick your PFD under your knees. It might compress the flotation chambers.

The best solution is to carry a little closed-cell foam pad from a garden shop, or invest five dollars in a pair of knee pads.

Water

Doesn't this belong in the chapter on food? Nope. Liquids are as essential as your PFD. Even when paddling in a wet bathing suit on a humid day, you'll lose a lot of moisture. Keep slurping. If you feel yourself suddenly weak and tired, try drinking something—you may be dehydrated. Plan on carrying, and drinking, a gallon of water per person per day.

The best drink for your body is plain water, called "Adam's ale." If your palate revolts, try mixing one-half orange soda and one-half water. Pure soda pop has so much sugar that it actually makes you thirstier. Diluting it gives your body the water it craves and soothes your taste buds.

Clothing

Sure, you can paddle in just a bathing suit. But you'll end up with a terrific sunburn, chafing from the suit, and frustration because you don't have pockets.

Serious paddlers have pet paddling outfits, usually consisting of a long-sleeved shirt and comfortable safari hat that they can leave on all day. I swim, snorkel, scuba dive, sail, and paddle in long-sleeved shirts. I like the western style with snaps and big handy pockets on the chest. A hip-length cotton or synthetic shirt blocks most of the sun, dries quickly, hides that dreaded cellulite, and looks fresh even when I'm worn out.

Cold-Weather Gear

For cold weather, dress in layers so you can strip up or down as the weather changes.

There are some new fabrics now available that wick moisture away from your skin, such as Polypro, Capilene, and Thermax.

On top of these, wear a sweatshirt-sized top made of pile, fleece, or wool. On the very outside, put on a rain suit or a paddling jacket.

For your head, bring a wind-cutting hat that covers at least the top of your ears. Wool socks or neoprene skin diver's booties will keep your feet warm, even when wet.

Paddling Jacket

Folks up in northern Florida wear paddling jackets. These are waterproof jackets with a high, velcro-shut turtleneck and cuffs, a tight waist, and usually a front pocket for gear. They're invaluable for keeping you warm and moderately dry in chilly weather.

Pants

Jeans are probably the worst thing you can wear while paddling. The thick denim takes forever to dry, the nonstretch fabric doesn't bend with you, and those hard metal studs invariably cut into either your boat or your body. The dark color also heats up in the sun.

One of the best paddling pants I ever found was a pair of biking shorts with a padded fanny. Boat seats get hard, and no matter how lazily you go down a river, you're shifting weight with each stroke.

I know another paddler who wears cotton pajama bottoms. He swears they're perfect—they are ultra lightweight, dry quickly, protect his knees from sun, twigs, and mosquitoes, and are cheap.

Do carry a spare set of duds in a waterproof container so when you get to shore you can take off that mud-encrusted, sopping outfit.

Hats

If you don't think the Florida sun is powerful, just walk around in the open for ten minutes, then feel the top of your head. It's hot!

A hat keeps the sun off the top of your head, thus preventing (or delaying) heatstroke. It shades your face and ears, which means you get an interesting "farmer's tan"—white forehead and tanned chin. If you wear glasses, a hat or visor is almost mandatory to keep glare and rain off the lenses.

A couple of hat styles don't work on our waterways. First, if you must have a huge, floppy-brimmed hat, be sure to carry a spare. The first gust of wind, overhanging branch, or high-reaching gesture will knock it off, and these hats always sink.

Men look dashing in an Australian bush hat. A nice feature on a breezy day or a tree-choked stream is a chin strap or a back clip that attaches to your collar. A ventilated crown lets air circulate to your scalp. I personally like visors, preferably with a whimsical flower or cute logo, and am always on the lookout for visors that float.

My sailing club has a yearly silly-hat contest. Like Jacques Cousteau's crew, we try to outdo each other in wild headgear. Wearing a really silly hat is a sure cure for stuffiness.

Bandannas

Did you know about the all-purpose bandanna? That's right, an old-timey cowboy's handkerchief. It can be a sweatband, bandage, sling, distress signal,

The amazing bandanna can be a sweatband, bandage, sling, distress signal, or protest flag. It can tie up a cracked paddle, wipe up goo, and hold all the fish you catch. Sandy Huff.

or racing protest flag. It can hold your collection of acorns, double as a fishing creel, fold into a compress, dampen a fevered brow, tie up a cracked paddle, make an emergency towrope, keep the sun off your camera, and wipe up goo. Keep a couple on hand.

If you're interested in fashion, you can try choosing a hull, PFD, hat, and clothing that are all color-coordinated, like some of the leisure-time motorcyclists who pay big money for helmets that match their hog and sidecar.

But remember, Florida paddling is a laid-back sport in a laid-back state. I can't think of *anyone* who is a serious Florida paddler who looks stylish. Or worries about it.

2

Packing Your Boat

Packing a boat is pretty standard in all the states, with a few refinements for Florida conditions.

First of all, remember the #1 rule: If you don't want it to get wet, don't bring it along.

Essentials

Even if you're only going on a two-hour day trip, take along the safety essentials: water, an extra paddle, a bailer or big sponge, and a PFD for each person. I usually take along a mesh bag to hold water, insect repellent, sunscreen, a spare bungee cord, and an extra hat. For a trip that might go past mealtime I toss in a couple of apples and a can of sardines.

If you're packing for a week-long jaunt down the Wilderness Waterway or the Suwannee, give a lot of thought to what you bring.

Gear should be loaded so your craft sits flat and handles easily. Plan to have at least eight inches of freeboard on a canoe; that's the distance from the waterline to the gunwales. Any less, and not only are you unstable, but the smallest wave can wash over your gunwales and fill the canoe.

Tie down everything. Murphy's Law predicts that if a thing can go bobbing away if it falls overboard, it will. Gear lost overboard will either sink, float into a spot where you cannot reach it, or zip downstream. Even if it just bobs alongside your boat, you have the inconvenience and even danger of maneuvering to pick it up.

Packing Gear

Bungee Cords

Bungee cords had to be made for paddlers. They come in all sizes, from tiny four-inch minis to giant four-foot cargo holders. They're cheap, take up little room, and are multipurpose.

Rope

Like bungee cords, rope has a hundred uses. First make sure that your canoe or kayak has ten- to fifteen-foot painters or end lines at bow and stern. Stick an extra twenty-five-foot coil of some type of rope in your day bag. Rentals often come with no painters, so insist the livery provide end lines before you push off.

I prefer an easy-to-hold ⅜" or ½" dacron braided line. It's worth a trip to the boating store or a large hardware store to stock up on a couple of lengths of this.

Tarps

For an overnight or longer trip in an open canoe, secure a tarp over your gear. It keeps the hot sun off your dry bags, sheds rain in case of an afternoon shower, keeps leaves out of your bilge, makes a nice mini-table on which to make a sandwich, and is useful when you get to shore as a sit-upon, rain flap, windbreak, and picnic table. Tarps come with built-in grommet holes, but it's useful to add another at the fold line so you can lash it down.

Luggage

Dry bags, which are waterproof plastic duffels that come in various sizes, are the luggage of choice among paddlers. However, they do sweat and build up heat in full sun, so it's a good idea to cover them loosely. To guard against punctures, I stick mine in contractor's garbage bags, which are a thicker mil than common kitchen trash bags and can double as extra trash, gear, and stinky-laundry bags if needed.

Mesh bags are good for diving and snorkeling gear. Many of them are designed to snap onto your belt so you can swim along with them.

Clear zip-shut plastic bags are invaluable for medicine, as an extra cover for the cell phone inside your dry bag, for extra film, loose food such as cereal, fruit, and cookies, and a dozen other uses. Freezer-weight bags are thicker and tougher than sandwich-weight bags.

The All-Purpose Pickle Barrel

Five-gallon pickle barrels and paint buckets make wonderful luggage for a canoe. These strong plastic cans come with fitted tops and big strong wire bales with a palm-sized handle. They're cheap, they're raccoon-proof, and they make excellent camp chairs.

You can get them for about a buck each at any fast-food outlet. Sometimes you must order these ahead, so give your local Burger King or paint store a call and tell them you'd like to buy a five-gallon bucket. When you get home, spend ten minutes to wash out the vinegar smell and cut all the little slits around the edge of the lid to make it easy to open.

To make a cushion for the lid, simply cut a circle of heavy cardboard or thin plywood to fit the top. Drill a hole down the center of this cardboard circle and through the lid. Now trim a piece of closed-cell foam into a circle just a hair bigger than the cardboard, and upholster it with a bit of sturdy cloth, such as canvas. Hot glue will hold the edges of the fabric underneath the cardboard circle. Hold the whole assemblage together with a nut, washer, and bolt through the hole you drilled in the middle. Voilà—there's your Florida all-purpose camp chair and suitcase.

3

Staying Healthy

Paddlers tend to be a healthy lot. Staying healthy even when you are out in the boondocks is a prime concern.

Keep your first-aid and CPR certifications current. These free or very cheap classes take only one evening each a year, and could literally save someone's life. Call your local fire station, night school, or Red Cross to find a class near you.

My dry bag holds a tiny fishing-tackle box that's stuffed with plastic bags of antihistamines, aspirin, a couple of Band-Aids, antidiarrhea medicine, a tiny folded Space Blanket, a bandanna, and assorted other goodies. On long trips I stick a small first-aid book in a zip-shut sandwich bag and bury it in a gear bag. Fortunately, I've only had to use the Band-Aids, usually for people who didn't use paddling gloves.

Stingray wounds, snakebites, dog bites, and other serious problems mean you have to get the victim to medical care fast. At least one person in your party should carry a cell phone or radio. Keep track of your approximate location so you can describe your position. Often you'll know more about the river than the dispatcher who answers 911. A good map and a GPS unit (that's Global Positioning System) help here. If nothing else, keep track of your left turns for a rough guide to where you are.

Here are a few of the more common problems:

Muscle Soreness

If I haven't paddled for a while, my arms ache after a few hours of paddling. I take one aspirin an hour. At bedtime, two aspirin calm those full-body aches long enough for me to drop off to sleep. A quick rubdown with Vicks Muscle Rub feels good, and even seems to keep a few mosquitoes away.

Sunburn

It's no accident that the number one health problem in the Sunshine State is too much sun. Tourists flock to the beaches by the thousands, determined to go home with a rich, golden tan. Unfortunately, some of them go home with raw, peeling skin, blisters, nausea, vomiting, or headaches, which are the result of sunburn.

You still don't think it's a problem? Every year, about three hundred people statewide are hospitalized with first- and second-degree burns. Two or three of them actually die. Doctors also warn that severe sunburns, even as a child, might trigger skin cancer later in life.

To see if you've had too much sun, push your finger against the affected skin. If the spot looks white and is slow to fade, you're already burned. Cover up *now*.

Dermatologists advise not going out in the Florida sun except when your shadow is longer than you are. That means the sun's rays should touch your bare skin only early in the morning and late in the afternoon. From 11 A.M. to 3 P.M. is the sunniest part of the day.

But since we all paddle in the daylight, and certainly between eleven and three, that means covering up, plus using a sunscreen with a high SPF (sun protection factor). Daub the backs of your hands and behind your ears too.

Heat Exhaustion and Sunstroke

It seems odd that you'd have to worry about getting overheated when you're surrounded by water. Prevention is fairly easy: paddle in the shade, hop overboard periodically to cool off, and keep splashing water onto your clothes to cool by evaporation. But I've seen paddlers who avoid getting wet at all costs. If you're around such a person on a hot day, watch for overheating.

A pale, sweating person has heat exhaustion. A red-faced, nonsweating person who feels like he's about to explode has heat stroke, and needs a doctor's care. In either case, get him out of the canoe and into the water to reduce his body heat, and give him plenty to drink. Gatorade is good if you have it.

Hypothermia

We were having lunch on a bank of the Alafia River when a teenage girl came drifting downstream in a half-swamped canoe. We found her friend upstream, stuck in a tree branch over the water.

I first thought they were drunk. One girl's lips were blue, her speech was slurred, and they both shivered constantly. Then I realized they were simply cold. It was hard to believe—here we were in Florida, on a delightfully breezy, cool day. But between their tiny bikinis, a beer each, and windchill, the young women were in the first stages of hypothermia.

Hypothermia does happen here in Florida, and is potentially dangerous. I'm not talking cold hands and feet. Hypothermia is torso cooling, when the internal temperature of your chest, belly, and hips goes below 95°F.

The symptoms are slurred speech, clumsiness, inability to add numbers, blue lips, violent shivering, and sleepiness. If the victim has also been drinking, he'll seem dead drunk. Victims of hypothermia also don't recognize their own symptoms.

Insulation is your first defense. Dressing in layers is a good idea, so you can add or subtract clothing as conditions change. A paddling jacket, with snug-fitting cuffs and collar, is ideal to keep in body heat. A raincoat or rain suit will stop the wind and hold in heat. A wet suit, including booties, gloves, and hat, is the best insulation of all.

What to Do If You're Suddenly in Cold Water

1. *Get out of the water,* especially if you're boating alone. Even the water in a swamped canoe is slightly warmer than open water. Get back into the boat, and *then* retrieve any lost gear.

Don't exercise if you're in open water. Movement increases circulation of cold water next to your skin. It's the underwater equivalent of windchill factor.

2. *Help your companions* get out of the water. If you can't decide which person to pull out first, go for the smaller or more tired person. Children, with a smaller body mass, cool off faster than adults.

Stay close to your capsized boat. It's a large surface to hang on to, and can be seen much more easily than the tiny dot your head makes in the water. The shore is always farther away than you think. Remember, you can get back inside and paddle a swamped canoe or kayak.

3. *Get warm* as soon as possible. That may mean going to shore and sitting in a warm car, exchanging shirts and a dry PFD with another boater, wrapping up in the Space Blanket in your emergency kit, whatever. Don't be ashamed to ask for help.

Lessen windchill by wrapping up in a blanket or paddling to the leeward side of a shore. However, if hypothermia has started, just wrapping yourself or another victim in blankets will not help. You need outside warmth, such as another person's body heat, a hot water bottle, or a chemical heat pad. Avoid alcohol completely.

4. *Work fast.* If you pull another boater out of the water, and she's unconscious, you may have only minutes before she lapses into a coma.

5. *Keep watching.* Even after the immediate symptoms have passed, a hypothermia victim is physically stressed and will act irritable.

Rashes

Poison ivy, oak, and sumac can cause symptoms as late as two weeks after contact. But here's the trick—the resin must bond to your skin for an hour or more for the toxins to penetrate. If you've brushed up against some three-leafed plants with fuzzy red stems, hop in the water and scrub off with a handful of sand. Scrub your clothes too, and hang them in the sun to oxidize any remaining resin.

If you do get itchy, first wash your skin thoroughly, then apply some kind of cream. Even suntan lotion helps relieve itching if you didn't pack a medicinal cream.

Bites and Stings

We once had to rush a fellow paddler to an emergency room because he calmly paddled under an overhanging cabbage palm—and face first into a huge wasp nest.

I carry over-the-counter antihistamines, which are designed to block general allergic reactions, including reactions to most stings. Look for the word "allergy" or "antihistamine" on the label.

Jellyfish stings can be very painful. A home cure is to soak the affected body part in hot water, as hot as you can stand. This "cooks" the toxins and lessens the reaction time. Remember that man-o'-war jellyfish, which look like pale blue bubbles, can have stinging tentacles ten feet long. Even dead-looking jellyfish on the beach can be surrounded by tentacles with active stinging cells.

The last health hint is . . . relax. You are in no more danger out paddling than you are doing yard work. Simply be aware of your health and be prudent. Even in the warm waters of Florida, the old Boy Scout motto Be Prepared is very apt.

4

Staying Safe

Capsizing

Beginners are always terrified that they might tip over. Why not prepare for the worst? This is also called *Capsizing Can Be Fun!*

Yup, that means capsizing on purpose. It's the first thing we have students do in any paddling class, and they find that, first, it's not so bad and, second, practicing a capsize takes all the terror out of anything else we do in class.

If you're learning how to paddle outside of a formal class, practice this on your own. You'll find that even a swamped boat full of water will float. Sit with your legs wide apart to help you keep balanced, and paddle with your arms.

If you do capsize during a trip, remember that the first rule of the sea is to save human life. Retrieve people *first*, then go after your gear. Forget the lunch box and hat floating off until you've made sure your partner or kids are okay.

Now relax. Capsizing just means getting wet. I tip over all the time to get cool, to wash out the boat, and to make a fun diving platform.

Storms

I personally think storms are exhilarating, and one of the finest shows Ma Nature can put on. The first ten to fifteen minutes of a storm are the worst, with hard rain, lightning, and sometimes even hail. I keep my rolled-up raincoat or poncho tied on close to my seat so it is easy to reach. A wide-brimmed hat that keeps water off my face and glasses is invaluable too.

Paddlers usually don't worry about lightning—after all, what could be lower than a riverbed? But it makes sense to stay away from open bays, or very tall trees.

If there are bits of debris caught in the treetops or over your head, that river is prone to flooding. If you're camping on a white sandbar, it's sure to be covered in high water—that's what has kept the sand white and plant-free.

What to do? Make yourself and any metal gear a low target until the lightning front passes. You might get off the river to huddle under a tarp. Tie your painters tightly so your canoe or kayak won't float away in rising water. In extreme situations, abandon your boat or campsite and get to higher ground.

Again, the best cure is heads-up awareness. Carry a radio and listen to weather reports. With the others in your group, discuss in advance what to do if a storm or flood happens. Look at the waterway itself to estimate what problems are likely to develop in a storm. Eyeball various routes of escape. Carry a raincoat.

Navigation

Along with your whistle, tie a little compass onto your PFD, and learn to find north. Collect whatever maps, charts, or drawings of the waterway you can find. If your trip is one-way downstream, watch the underwater grasses to find the main channel.

If you plan on coming back over the same route, look behind you often, especially at curves and forks. Waterways can look completely different seen from another direction. Try to pick out tall landmarks, such as power towers or trees, to keep your bearings.

If you're using the sun to navigate, remember that only at the equinoxes at March 20 and September 22 does the sun rise and set at true east and west. At the solstices, which are around June 20 and December 21, the sun can be 30° north or south of the equator. That means in midsummer the sun is slightly to the north, and at midwinter the sun is slightly to the south.

Avoiding Other Boats

Avoiding collisions seems self-evident, but I've seen three near crashes just in the Tampa Bay area. Florida does not require powerboaters to pass any kind of piloting test. Speedboats continually run into each other. Keeping them from running into you is the paddler's version of Defensive Driving. In most cases that means hugging the shore and staying alert.

Airboats have an interesting trick. They're just big metal trays, you know, with an airplane motor and propeller mounted at the back. If one is going full speed, then stops suddenly, its wake catches up with it, washes right over the low stern, and swamps the airboat.

We got to watch this in action on the Tamiami Trail west of Miami, not too far from the Miccosukee Indian Village. We were lily-dipping around in one of the little coves off the main canal, and the other canoe (not me this time!) was going along one of the airboat lanes that cut through the saw grass.

An airboat came roaring around a stand of willows and was about to hit the canoe, which had somehow turned sideways, completely blocking the lane. The airboater, cussing up a storm, quickly killed his engine and frantically swished his fan vanes from side to side to kill his speed. The airboat stopped within a foot of the canoe.

A second later we saw why the driver was cussing—his wake came rushing up, spilled over the back of his boat, and filled the sled. We were only in knee-deep water, so the airboat just settled down in the water. The prop stopped with a jerk.

All four of us in the canoes watched in utter, boggled silence. When the waves, curses, and general pandemonium died down, I timidly asked the man if we could help him some way. He gave me a sour look.

Then I asked him if he could just turn on his motor and let the propeller push the sunken hull along the bottom. He told me that (1) the bottom foot of the prop was in the water and couldn't possibly operate half submerged and (2) he'd have to cross the main canal to get back to his trailer and car, and as soon as he hit that he'd be six feet deep, instead of two feet. That meant my next offer—to tow him back—wouldn't work either, so I kept my mouth shut.

We slunk away. I never did figure out how he got his airboat afloat again.

If you see a tanker, cruise ship, or freighter approaching, get out of the way fast. These huge ships average twelve knots, which looks slow from a distance, but it is the speed of a freight train up close. They have deep drafts and must stay in the dredged channels. A large ship simply cannot stop dead. At full reverse, loaded tankers or container ships take two to three miles to come to a dead stop. When they do, the helmsmen have lost all steerage and control of the ship. With such high sides, the lightest wind will blow these ships out of the channel and the deep keels will dig into the bottom. Once aground, these monster ships have to be pulled off with monster tugboats. This costs a mint, takes up to a month, and blocks the shipping channel to other boats. The captains and pilots lose their jobs, the shipping company gets a big fine for blocking the channel, and some of the oil- and fertilizer-bearing ships have been known to break apart and dump their deadly cargo in the water, killing all the local sea life and birds. And your little canoe or kayak would have caused all that damage.

On the other hand, they might not even see you, and just run over you.

Don't get cocky and assume you can skim by a big ship or yacht, staying close to its side. Big ships put up a huge wake that will dump you over in a second. At the stern, their house-high propellers produce cavitation and crosscurrents that could pull you into the prop, which means you'll get chopped up like hamburger. Gruesome, huh? But I'm not making this up. Every one of these scenarios has actually happened. If you're in a shipping channel, rotate your head like an owl, and if there's a ship in sight in any direction, stay away.

As this book repeats over and over, to be safe in the water exercise reasonable prudence. Plan ahead, anticipate problems, calmly discuss emergency procedures with your companions, stay alert—and have fun.

5

Camping the Florida Way

Why stick to only day trips? Florida rivers and beaches are gorgeous at dusk and dawn, and you can enjoy the wilderness so much more by camping out.

Canoes and kayaks hold enormous amounts of gear. With a bit of experimentation, you can easily carry gear and food for a week or more on the water.

To get you started, John Phillips gives you camping pointers, then I'll add more ideas.

Basic Florida Camping

John Phillips

Equipment

Your first consideration is a tent and ground cloth. Make sure that whatever you plan to sleep under or in is waterproof, sturdy, and big enough for two. Good features to consider are zippered windows and a mesh ceiling panel for ventilation.

Before you head out, practice setting up or building your over-night home a couple of times. You will feel more confident in setting up your tent, and you'll know what tools you need to do it. Seal all of the seams in the tent prior to packing out.

The more efficient sleeping bags are the mummy types. Before you buy one, get inside and zip it up to make sure you fit. For hot nights bring along a twin-sized sheet. Make it a dark color, as it will get a little dirty on the trip.

Clothing

Weather will ruin a trip if you don't have the right clothing. I've been many places in Florida where you see all four seasons in one day.

The bottom line with clothing is layering. Your base layer should be something other than cotton. Cotton tends to absorb moisture, dries slowly, and doesn't insulate well, especially when wet. Look for T-shirts that wick away moisture from your body.

More Florida camping tips:

- An unscented clothes-dryer sheet pinned to the front of your shirt will ward off mosquitoes.
- Lots of morning dew or frost on the grass normally means the day will be fair. Little or no dew or frost means the air has been moving and wet weather is on the way.
- When smoke from the campfire hangs low, a storm is moving in. Smoke rising straight up means clear weather.
- Wind blowing from the south, east, or northwest usually means there's a storm a-comin'.
- A styptic pencil will relieve the irritation of an insect bite. Put a tiny dab of water on the bite and then apply the styptic pencil.
- A quick way to freshen up when there's no hope of a shower or dip in a lake is to use baby wipes. I have gone an entire month without taking a shower and these things work great. They clean, deodorize, and are available in travel packs.
- Carry a stick of hot glue (used in hot glue guns) for a variety of minor repairs. Simply melt the glue with a match, lighter, or candle and use it to repair air mattresses, cracked water bottles, boots, and the like.
- Use Eveready lithium AA batteries instead of alkaline or carbon-zinc batteries in your AA flashlight. Lithium batteries have a ten-year shelf life, are one-third lighter than carbon or alkaline AAs, have a slightly higher power output, and will power your equipment about three times as long as alkalines in continuous use. Your cost per hour of use will be about the same as with alkalines.

- Cotton balls smeared with petroleum jelly make great long-burning fire starters, and you'd be surprised at how many you can get into a tiny film can or pill bottle.
- In the event of an injury, a good item to have is a 10cc irrigation syringe with an 18-gauge catheter tip. It is the best wound-cleansing tool because of the high-pressure jet action (seven pounds to the square inch).
- One-gallon zip-shut bags and heavy-duty trash bags make great waterproof bags for all of your clothes and sleeping bag.
- If you want to waterproof your boots, I recommend Kiwi Camp Dry Heavy Duty Water Repellent Spray. It is a silicone-based spray and dries in about four hours. For your equipment and clothes, use Kiwi Performance Fabric Protection. I waterproof my tent and clothes with this before the trip.

Recommended Packing List (coordinate this with team members)

Clothes: boots (waterproofed), tennis shoes, sandals, socks, underwear, pants, T-shirts, rain jacket or poncho, bandannas, shorts, sweatshirt, wide-brimmed hat, gloves

Gear: flashlight, batteries, candle lantern, candles; water bottles, filter, iodine tablets; compass, rope (para cord, 100 feet), knife (sharpened), hatchet, folding saw, folding shovel, whisk broom (for sand); fishing pole, tackle, license; folding chair or stool; sleeping bag, sleeping pad (self-inflating), ground cover, sheet; stove, fuel, lighter, matches (waterproof), cooking set, cutlery, plate, bowl, cup; trash bags (for trash), scrub sponge, biodegradable soap, towel(s), moist wipes, toilet paper (your friend!); sunscreen, insect repellent, snakebite kit, first-aid kit, pain relievers, antacids, antidiarrhea tablets, styptic pencil, lip balm, gum, toothbrush, toothpaste, mouthwash; sewing kit, clothespins; camera, film; notepad, pencil/pen

Extra paddle (a must)

Map (a good map with a real grid and latitude, longitude, and GPS numbers, not just the map you get from the outfitter)

Radio (for weather reports, not music)

Cell phone (you never know when you'll need it)

The Lazy Woman's Guide to Camping

Sandy Huff

It was a lovely spot on the Suwannee for a campout. The sand was clean, the rising moon promised to shine through a break in the tree canopy, a brisk breeze wafted the smell of pine and bay across our noses, and a million tiny frogs were warming up for a serenade in F-flat.

I laid out my two-man North Face tent on the bright blue ground cloth, inserted the shock-corded poles, and had the little igloo-shaped contraption up in minutes. The sand was too loose to hold ground pegs, so I skipped them. I set my pickle barrel of clothing and the sleeping bag beside the tent, then dashed away to help with supper.

A shout from another camper made me turn around to see a gust of wind pick up the tent, tumble it end over end, and blow it into the river. It floated like a giant bubble—heading downwind at breakneck speed.

The next ten minutes turned into a mad scramble to launch a canoe, paddle after the retreating tent, and get a towline around it. Do you have any idea how hard it is to tow a big bubble against the wind? By the time I got back to that dream of a sandbar, I was hot, sweaty, and exasperated, and the tent was sinking.

Another paddler helped me unzip the flap, turn the tent upside down, pour out the water, shake off a couple pounds of sand, and set it back onto the ground cloth—which the wind had now blown into a tangled mess. This time I anchored the tent with ground pegs, weighed it down with all the extra paddles from all the boats, and stowed my pickle barrels and sleeping bag inside. I even considered pulling my whole canoe inside the tent, until a calmer head suggested I put my overturned canoe beside the tent and tie the two together. I also ran a rope some forty feet to the nearest tree for extra insurance.

Even with all that, my tent bounced all night in the wind. I ended up sleeping pressed against the windward side, using my weight to keep the fool thing from blowing back into the water and taking me with it.

Another paddler told me he'd pitched his tent on one of those platform chickees on the Everglades Wilderness Waterway and it blew away. So the moral of this story is: Make your camp as windproof, rainproof, and animalproof as you can. Tie down your tent, and all your gear. Stow your extra items underneath an overturned canoe or kayak.

Look around your campsite and say to yourself, "What's the worst thing that could happen here?" Could your boat sink if it filled with rain? Could a rising tide unhook your painter and carry your kayak away? Could a falling tide leave your canoe a city block from the water?

An ounce of prevention is worth a metric ton of cure. Fix problems before they happen.

Finding a Camping Spot

Pure white sandbars, neat little islands, that level spot on the bank—no matter where you want to camp, somebody has probably been there ahead of you. Old campfire rings are a sure sign that somebody used that spot for camping before.

Be careful of private property. An unfenced area isn't necessarily public land. By Florida law, riverfront owners need to fence only the land sides of their property. Check with the local livery, FWC (Florida Fish and Wildlife Conservation Commission) office, or even the local police department about where to camp before you go. Many times private owners don't mind your camping on their land if you ask in advance. Just the fact that you asked usually means that you're also considerate enough to not leave a mess behind.

If your group has several tents, pitch them around the outside of the area. Leave a "living room" in the center of the enclave. Also beware of pitching your tent right in the middle of the path to the "latrine area," or you'll be awake all night as other campers stumble past, over, or through you to get to the designated woods.

Eyeball the ground under your tent. If there's a shallow vale there, it means that rainwater will run through your site to get downhill. Either move your tent or dig a moat around it to divert the runoff. Relocating is the better option. Earthmoving is hard work, and it messes up the ecosystem.

Camp Cleanliness

If the campers just ahead of you were messy with their food scraps, you're going to find zillions of bugs waiting for you. A ground cloth under your tent keeps the little nasties away—or at least slows them down.

Be considerate of the people coming after you. Burn your food scraps. For liquids, such as bacon fat, sardine drippings, and the extra liquids from cans of food, use your folding shovel or trowel to make a deep hole as far away from your tent as you can manage. Raccoons will smell the bacon fat and arrive to dig it up. When their digging produces only damp sand, they'll keep looking for something edible.

If you have tall trees around, suspend your food in a "bear bag" a good six to eight feet off the ground. That extra hundred-foot coil of rope comes in handy here. Tie a rock at one end to pitch the rope over a branch.

Metal cans will actually burn in a very hot fire. Don't leave them behind—whatever you packed in, pack it out. Leave your campsite cleaner than you found it. Many access points do not have trash pickup, so at the end of the trip, don't just leave your bags of garbage beside the ramp. As much as you want to get rid of it, load that trash into the car until you can find a real garbage can to put it in. Don't bury it—wind and raccoons will have it dug up in an hour, making an unsightly mess. And never, never bring glass. If you see any broken glass, take a few minutes to walk around and pick it up, and get it off the waterway completely.

Toilet Facilities

Hmm . . . how can we discuss this delicately? When you head to the woods for a pit stop, get at least fifty feet from the water to avoid polluting the water. Take along a shovel or trowel and dig a "cat hole" before you urinate or defecate.

First-timers have a real problem with hitting the hole they just dug. Here in America, we're so used to using sit-down toilets that we simply don't know how to gauge where our "droppings" go. So pay attention the first time you squat. The bull's-eye spot is usually a few inches behind your heels.

If you have trouble keeping your balance when you squat, find a tree trunk to grab. Remember to keep your feet uphill of your cat hole. Have your toilet paper ready before you start. And bury that very deeply too.

Keeping Warm

The men always laugh at this, but I've packed a hot water bottle from Greenland to the Amazon, and wouldn't think of going camping without one. On cold nights, it's a lifesaver. On hot, steamy nights, fill it with river water for a nice cool spot.

Mattresses

Sleeping on the ground is overrated. That's what happens when you buy a cheap inflatable mattress and it goes flat in the middle of the night. Camping stores sell little self-inflating pads in two sizes—full length, and those that reach from your shoulders to your hips. I usually carry one of each, and then spend the rest of the night making sure I don't roll off the stack.

An old Amerindian trick is to dig a hole for your shoulders and your hips. If it's a gorgeous night *and* you're sleeping out under the stars *and* you're not lying in a bed of rare and endangered posies, scoop out two shallow holes and see how much more comfortable you are.

Campfires

Having a campfire while camping is traditional. Toasting marshmallows over a Bic lighter just doesn't have the same effect. But most campsites have already been scoured for dead wood. Never cut down living plants to burn.

Instead, plan ahead for the evening's campfire. After lunch, start gathering bits of burnable wood you pass on the river. If you've gathered too much, leave a stack for the next camper. And remember that the Amerindians had a word for a huge, roaring bonfire. It was a "white man's fire." Try making a tiny little fire. It will still put out enough smoke so you can shine your flashlight up into the billows and tell ghost stories.

Use a fire pan instead of putting your fire on the bare ground. This can be an old cookie sheet or metal trash can lid. You'll still need to rake dead leaves away from the fire, keep a bucket of water nearby, and be on the lookout for loose embers. Starting a forest fire is not a river-friendly thing to do.

Half-burned wood and ashes can be dumped into the ocean, or buried in wet sand near the water. Use common sense.

Bugs

If you're near the ocean, camp on the upwind side of the beach to keep away the mosquitoes and no-see-ums. However, remember that the wind shifts during the day, and usually dies at dawn. Keep the repellent close by.

Appreciation Breaks

Take time to stop and look to appreciate what's around you. That's what paddling and being outdoors is all about. It also helps you spot your missing tent before it gets too far downstream.

6

Food and Cooking

This chapter is in two parts. First, John Phillips gives you some tips on camp cooking. Next, I've stuck in a few of my own ideas on expedition food. You'll see that our two approaches to wilderness cooking differ wildly.

The chief rule is to pack out *whatever you packed* in. *Leave no trace of your picnic or campfire. That means you don't even attract bugs.*

Camp Cooking

John Phillips

There are a million varieties of camp stoves out there ranging from the elaborate let's-go-on-an-expedition type to multifuel to white gas. My friend Jerry and I use a plain old canister-type stove, and I bring along an MSR Dragon. You simply screw the fuel canister into the burner, then light it. The main advantage of canister-type is that we also have a lantern that will screw into the same canister, and then we have light!

For cooking utensils, I would recommend a Teflon-coated set (and all the side items). A frying pan plus a 1-, 2-, or 3-liter pot should do the trick.

I also bring along my Outback baking system. It works great and I always have fresh-baked bread with dinner. I freeze my dough prior to the trip and it works out quite nicely.

Finally, depending on the length of trip you are planning, I would recommend a reliable, top-of-the-line water purifier, plus an extra filter.

Menu Planning

You can find everything you need for delicious, healthy meals at your local supermarket.

Breakfast can be as easy as instant oatmeal and coffee, or a full-up eggs, bacon, toast, and more. Either one will stick with you and give the energy you need to paddle until lunch. Canned bacon is very good and really makes the difference if you want a full breakfast before you shove off in the morning.

I recommend a simple lunch, and a more elaborate evening meal. For during the day, stow snacks where you can get at them, so you won't have to pull over and unpack to find your munchies.

Dinner should be the best meal your group can whip up together. You can enjoy fresh fish, corn bread, veggies, potatoes, the works. For larger groups, it will take some coordination on who brings what. I pack MREs (Meals Ready to Eat) for lunch and for when I don't feel like cooking. They are self-heating, and the packets they come in burn like crazy. You can get these at your local army-navy store.

Those little coffee bags work great and don't take up much room. Ever had *hobo* coffee? The water-to-coffee ratio is one generous tablespoon of ground coffee per eight-ounce cup of water, plus a little more to grow hair. To settle the grounds, tap the sides of the pot or drop a cold pebble or a teaspoon of cold water into your cup.

Two basic approaches to making this stuff:

1. Start with a measured amount of cold water in any pot. Bring it a hard boil. Take the pot off the heat. Stir in your coffee and let it steep, tightly covered, for about ten minutes.

2. Put the measured cold water and grounds together in a pot. Bring the mixture to a beginning boil and immediately take the pot off the heat. Cover tightly and let steep for five minutes.

Packing

Besides the equipment listed in the previous chapter, you'll likely need a cooler, and block or dry ice for it.

I recommend you purchase what you want to eat on the trip, go home, and repackage it for waterproofing and in one-time amounts. Consider one-pot meals.

I am generous with the spices, such as onion, garlic powder, salt, pepper, curry. They give a pleasant zip to an otherwise bland meal.

Breakfast

Oatmeal, coffee (eggs, bacon, and such are in the nice-to-have category, but you need to plan for and coordinate these).

Munchies

Jerky, trail mix, dried fruits, energy bars, granola bars, instant tea mix or Gatorade, nuts, chips.

Dinner

Water-packed tuna, noodles (ramen; Lipton's with sauce), instant rice, instant soup mix, Stove Top Stuffing, water-packed chicken, fresh-caught fish.

The Lazy Woman's Guide to Camp Cooking

Sandy Huff

Been there, done that. When I first started canoe and kayak camping, I planned and produced some elaborate meals: eggs coddled in paper bags, Dutch oven cakes with hard sauce, fresh salmon steaks grilled with lemon grass. Now I'm happy to just open a can of beans. After years of cooking for an active family, the last thing I want to do after a hard day's paddling is to set up a camp kitchen, cook for an hour, and then clean up for another hour.

Zip-shut bags are a godsend to paddlers. Just remember that they are waterproof only against splashes. Holding them underwater will pop them open.

I've become the master of plastic-bag cooking, which uses a zip-shut bag (freezer types are sturdier) half filled with dried food that's ready to reconstitute with water. Roll the bag before sealing it to get out extra air. Sometimes I even stick a plastic spoon into the bag, so the whole thing is a self-contained meal, bowl, and utensil. Add hot water, and I have a meal that needs no cleanup. I can mix the whole mess by squishing it with my hands. In cold weather, this feels great on chilly fingers. I usually don't even bother heating my own water, but mooch a cupful off another camper. Here are some ideas for meals-in-a-bag:

- One package of instant mashed potatoes, three tablespoons of bouillon powder, and a packet of onion soup mix. Slice in a stick of beef jerky if you want to get fancy.
- Two packets of instant oatmeal with a quarter cup of raisins.
- Two packets of instant grits with cubes of Colby or American cheese. Cheese will keep without refrigeration for about three days, so eat this meal early on.
- One box of dried scalloped potatoes with a handful of sliced almonds or sunflower seeds.

You get the idea. I think all the ready-to-eat items that go into children's lunch boxes make fine wilderness food. Even oft-maligned Vienna sausages taste good if you're really, really hungry.

If you must cook, make yourself a camp kitchen. Turn your canoe or kayak over, and prop it up with logs or extra pickle barrels. Now you have a table, which saves you a tremendous amount of stooping and bending.

If you're planning on cooking over an open fire, don't depend on finding wood. That sandbar or riverbank that you're camping on may be so busy that every piece of dead wood was burned years ago. Either carry charcoal and lighter fluid or gather wood as you paddle. Branches about the thickness of your arm are easier to carry and to light than giant logs.

Wash your dishes and pots by scrubbing them in sand from the riverbank first. Then sluice them with a bit of bleach in a squirt bottle, and let them air-dry in your mesh bag.

In a canoe, you've got room for a standard Coleman stove. If you're in a kayak, look for the little Primus Spiders and fuel canisters that will fit through your portholes. Carry extra canisters, since all fuels run out at the strangest possible moments.

You don't necessarily have to carry a cooler full of ice. While they make good camp chairs, coolers are bulky, and even the hardest block of ice or even dry ice lasts only about three days. If you'll be stopping in at campgrounds with stores or at big marinas, or crossing a highway near a grocery store, plan to stock up daily. Freeze all your food before you launch, so it will contribute to the cold instead of melting your meager stock of ice. Freeze drinking water in zip-shut bags, so it stays clean as it melts.

But you sure can't restock ice while you're doing the Wilderness Waterway in the Everglades, or when you're halfway across the Okeefenokee Swamp. So just do without. If you want to cool off a paper lunch-box carton of apple juice, drag it over the side in a mesh bag for ten minutes.

Raw eggs will keep for up to two weeks if they have never been refrigerated. I've found flats of uncooled eggs at a local produce stand.

An old prospector's trick is to boil eggs while you make your coffee. The trick to not having boiling eggs split open is to make a tiny pinprick hole in the big end of the egg, and heat the water gradually, so the whole egg warms up slowly. The recipe is simple: into a tin coffeepot or saucepan, put in cold water, coffee grounds, and two eggs. Set the pot over coals or on a cooler section of your campfire. Let it come to a slow boil, and boil for a couple of minutes. Fish the eggs out with a spoon, and toss the eggshells back in the coffee to settle the grounds. Pour the coffee into your cup slowly so you don't disturb the grounds. Voilà—coffee and eggs. They'll need salt, so remember to stick a little Tupperware salt shaker into your pickle barrel of supplies.

Bring along a metal pan on which to make your campfire. In the morning, when you're ready to break camp, it's easy to flood the pan with water, then carry the ashes away and bury them. The ground below the fire will be hot, so remember to flood that too, and mark the spot so no one will step on it with bare feet.

Never short yourself on drinking water. Plan to use one gallon of water per person per day.

A drawstring mesh bag makes a good creel when you're fishing. I always bring along a hand line with several hooks. Some of my best catches have been during lunch hour, when it's never convenient to stop to clean and cook fish. That's where the mesh bag comes in—just hang it over the side, and the fish will stay alive until you get to your camping spot. To keep it from sinking and snagging on bump-overs, I tie floats to the back corners. Key chains with little foam floats are ideal for this. I've also thrown my bailing sponge into the mesh bag, which keeps it afloat while it trails behind the kayak.

In case I do catch fish, I usually carry a little Teflon pan, a small bottle of vegetable oil, and a gallon-sized zip-shut bag with cornbread mix in it. Just fillet or clean the fish, shake the meat in the cornmeal, and fry. If a frying pan is too much trouble, roll the fillets in aluminum foil and bake them in the coals of your campfire. If even that is too much trouble, fillet the fish the minute you catch them, and stick the meat in a zip-shut bag with a generous squirt of lemon juice. Turn it a few times so the lemon juice coats all the meat. By supper time, the lemon juice has cooked the fish while you've been paddling. This is how the airlines cook fish without heat.

Want a versatile plate? Try a frisbee. It will hold soup, cereal, sandwiches, and a whole mound of supper. Scrub it a bit with sand in between courses and games, and sterilize it with bleach. It floats too.

When the trip is over, load up your car, change into some dry clothes, and go out to a restaurant.

The heck with camp cooking. I can survive a week of Beanie Weanies.

I've even been known to eat Vienna sausages.

7

Group Activities, Games, and Sharks' Teeth

Got to your campsite too soon? You paddled a bit too fast, and now you have a half hour to kill before the livery pickup arrives? You're waiting on that always-late slowpoke to arrive? Here are some ideas to fill that empty hour:

- Swamped boat races. Unload your gear onto the beach, including your paddle, but keeping your PFD. Swamp the boat. Now hop in and paddle with your hands. Make the course short, say twenty to thirty feet.
- Backwards races. Line up the boats with the sterns facing the finish line. Say, "One-two-three, go!" and let the contestants paddle backwards as fast as they can.
- Stick races. Again, unload your boat. Instead of paddles, use sticks. To be fair, make sure all the sticks are the same diameter and length. If you have enough of them, brooms make good substitute paddles too, as do pickle barrel tops.
- Logrolling on a capsized boat. This takes partners, or even teams. Turn two boats upside down, and have a race to see how fast one person from each team can climb up and straddle a hull. If that's too easy, have the contestants stand up on their overturned hulls. The other members of each team can steady the boats, preferably while treading water.
- Team towing races. For each team, have one person in the canoe or kayak, and the rest of the team holds on to a rope attached to the stern. People in the water may kick, but must keep both hands on the rope while the person in the boat paddles. To make it harder, don't let either boat person

have a paddle. This works best in deeper water where the water people can't touch bottom.

- Canoe and kayak square dancing. You'll need sets of four boats, and a designated caller. If you don't have music, the caller can clap hands to make a beat. Most common square dance steps are: circle left, circle right, spin in place, come together in the center, back up to the circle. This works much better if there's no current. In fact, it works *only* if there's no current.
- Water fights. Equip everyone with pump-up water rifles, water pistols, water cannons—whatever the local toy store is selling. I don't think there are any rules for this. If you don't want to spend the money, try splashing each other with your hands or paddles. The boat loaded with the most water loses.

Practical Jokes

You didn't think that paddlers are serious and straitlaced while they paddle, did you? Here's a couple of underhanded, sneaky pranks you can try. If you have any different ones up your sleeve, send them to me quickly, please.

- Bug alert. Paddle up beside your friends and shout, "Good grief, what's that huge black bug crawling up the left side of your canoe?" They'll lean over to look, and fall in.
- Lead the calisthenics. When the others are all in their boats and you're still on the dock, organize a warm-up session. It goes like this. "All right, everyone, line up and face me, and we'll do a few little warm-up exercises. Put both hands straight up. Now both hands straight out to the side. Now hands on hips, and swivel those upper bodies. Hands overhead again. Now lean as far as you can to the left. . . ."
- Steal paddles. Dave and Carol Grantges of the Florida Sport Paddling Club taught me this one. Quietly paddle up beside another kayaker. Say, "You know, I've been admiring that paddle of yours. Could I see it for a minute?" When they hand it over, paddle away from them, keeping their paddle. Return it when they plead, or maybe before the next waterfall.
- Attach a sea anchor. Paddle up beside another boat. Quietly attach a bungee cord to the stern. On the other end of the bungee have an old sock

filled with gravel or sand. Keep attaching more and more drogues until the paddlers notice.

Collecting

During the trip, have a contest to see who can collect a set of something. The winner(s) get a free dessert from the rest of the group when you all go out to supper after the trip. Here are some ideas on what to collect:

- Trash. Flotsam and jetsam littering the waterway.
- Strangely shaped pieces of wood. Give 'em names and make up stories about each one.
- Fish. The most fish. The biggest fish. The biggest bass. The most species. The smallest fish. . . .

Campfire Stories and Entertainment

- Poetry. The Florida Sport Paddling Club has a Robert Service poetry reading every winter.
- Skits. Divide the group into teams. Give each team items from the camp kitchen. They have five minutes to come up with a skit using those items.
- Silly hat contest. If nobody brought really dumb hats along, give everyone a paper plate and some string, and give them fifteen minutes to decorate their hat with whatever they can find around camp. Be kind enough to announce to newcomers that Spanish moss contains chiggers.
- Sandcastle building.

Fossils and Sharks' Teeth

At various epochs in its history, Florida has ducked underwater. Now you can find sharks' teeth far inland, and collecting them is interesting. Fifteen or so different types of sharks have been identified from the teeth they left lying around. Some of these old teeth are indistinguishable from those of today's great white sharks.

Gravel banks in our rivers and springs are easy to get to. I've scrabbled for sharks' teeth in a foot-wide stream high atop the Devil's Millhopper outside Gainesville, found fossilized palm fragments in Rock Springs near Apopka, discovered a tooth that could very well have been from a giant sloth or wild-cat in the Peace River, and scraped a perfect shell out of a high limestone bank on the Alabama state line.

The technique is simple. Find a nice bank of gravel. Scoop up a handful. Poke through it until you spot something. My favorite position is sitting waist deep in the water. Since I automatically sit with the sun over my shoulder, I've come home with some mighty peculiar sunburns too.

Some of my cave-diving friends have found impressive sets of bones, skulls, and teeth. I'm satisfied with sharks' teeth. My kids love to hunt for them too. We've often stopped during a canoe or snorkeling trip, miles from civilization, to dig through a promising-looking gravel bed.

It's amazing that so many teeth have survived, especially when you consider that sharks don't have a single bone in their bodies.

Sharks are bona fide tooth factories. Scientists estimate that a modern shark keeps each tooth from two to seven weeks, when it is pushed out by a replacement tooth growing behind it. Many sharks have multiple rows of developing teeth that flip down into cutting position when they get to the front of the line.

The biggest tooth I've seen was eight inches long. An adult human would have stood up inside that shark's jaw. Check out the fossil museum in the town of Mulberry for some very impressive things that have been pulled out of the phosphate pits.

Most of the teeth you'll find in Florida gravel beds are the size of a thumb-tack head. Always triangular and always black, they range from thin and needle-pointed to fat and saw-toothed. Occasionally you find little pill-shaped lozenges, which are skate and stingray grinding plates—their equivalent of teeth.

A good container for your loot is a film canister, sandwich bag, or a plastic baby-food jar. Some people hold their finds in their cheeks, like a hamster. That works fine, if you remember to spit the teeth out frequently, and never swallow without thinking. You could chew your own head off!

8

Biters and Stingers

Florida does *not* have the highest concentration of biting insects in the country. That distinction goes to Alaska, the Canadian boundary waters, and a certain campground in Alabama.

However, that thought is no consolation when you've got a persistent mosquito buzzing in your right ear, or an invisible gnat just pricked your shin, or you stepped in a bed of fire ants.

Most bites and stings are just annoying, and the little bump or itch will fade within minutes.

Tuck a pump can of insect repellent in your day bag and use it freely. When you're walking, be alert to where insects and snakes might hide. Run your fingers through your hair often, and check your buddy for ticks. Ask everyone in your group if they're allergic to anything at all.

Stock your first-aid kit with tiny bottles of vinegar and rubbing alcohol to disinfect jellyfish stings and coral cuts. Stick in a half dozen packets of sting and itch soothers. If you want to get fancy, add a tick puller, a tiny suction pipe for pulling out injected venom, and whatever gizmos you see at the drugstore.

The most important rule is to be aware. Your most valuable first-aid item is your mind.

Insect Repellents That Work

The first defense against stings and bites is prevention.

Commercial bug repellents work well. I've been using Sawyer products for years, such as DEET Plus and Sawyer Gold. These have a combination of chemicals to work on mosquitoes, flies, and gnats. Try to get pump dispensers that spray the liquid onto your skin. Spreading repellent with your hands always leaves residue on your fingers, which invariably ends up in your eyes, mouth, camera lens, or paddle handle.

Long-term use of repellents irritates my skin. Using a combination of repellent and sunblock raises welts and rashes. My solution is to cover up with long sleeves and pants, and spray the repellent on the fabric instead of my skin.

You can buy 100 percent deet, but never put it on your skin. It goes on your clothing and tent. There's also a very strong chemical called permethrin which goes on your tent and sleeping bag, and is supposed to be waterproof and repel ticks up to two weeks.

Most repellents work only for an hour or two, and need to be replenished often.

Avon Skin So Soft has been touted as a good repellent, but I find it is effective for only about twenty minutes. Besides, the oily residue clogs my pores, and in hot weather that's intolerable.

Fishing guide Captain Ed Bigelow makes his own repellent. In a spray bottle he mixes two parts Skin So Soft, one part water, and one part alcohol, plus four drops of oil of citronella.

Do your own testing. Spray one product on your left side, another on your right side. See what works for your unique body chemistry.

Bug Suits

Several outdoor clothing manufacturers make terrific bug suits. These are the same size and shape as raincoats, but made of extremely lightweight netting lined with a tall mesh, so fly and mosquito mouth tubes can't reach your skin. Make sure yours is loose enough that the folds under the arms and inside the elbows don't chafe your skin.

DK Flatwoods Company, 12901 SR 54, Odessa FL 33556, phone (813) 926-8802, makes bug suits and camo clothing designed specifically for Florida.

Insects

Mosquitoes

On or off the water, mosquitoes will be present in any state you visit, but Florida has its share of the miserable little beasts.

Nicky Makruski, park ranger at Collier-Seminole State Park (destination 85), says, "We probably do have the highest concentration of mosquitoes in Collier County, primarily because we don't aerial spray.

"The brand of mosquito repellent we recommend is Deep Woods Off. The makers of DWO are Johnson and Johnson, who do their testing for mosquito sprays in our park. I also use Repel with good results, and I like the smell better than Off. Anything that has a high concentration of deet works well. We also wear bug jackets when we are out in the back forty, because they are worse there and we get tired of breathing deet. You should visit us in the winter because during January and February you rarely have to use repellent."

No-See-Ums

These nasty little flies are also called flying jaws, or mobbies. Each one is the size of a grain of pepper, so tiny that you never see it until it bites you. It's not a serious bite, just a tiny irritating prick. But get enough no-see-ums around you, and you'll be so distracted that the prettiest scenery goes unnoticed.

Ticks

Before a tick can give you Lyme disease, Rocky Mountain spotted fever, or ehrlichiosis, it has to drill into your skin right up to its snout. This takes four to six hours. So every few hours, run your fingers through your hair, especially the area right behind your ears. Also check your armpits, and anywhere your skin is folded—at your hips, toes, and knees.

Ticks hang out in moist, leafy habitats, ready to crawl onto your skin when you brush against the grass, bushes, and leaf mold where they hide. They are most prevalent in the central ridge that runs down the middle of the state. Florida has deer ticks, Lone Star ticks, and dog ticks. Wear light-colored clothing, and tuck your pant bottoms into your socks. There is a tick repellent for your tent and clothes that you must *not* get on your skin.

Don't just yank off a tick that's sucking your blood. Get a split twig, tweezers, slotted leaf, or some other lever. Insert this between your skin and the body of the tick, and lift gently. The tick will usually let go. If you pull too hard and fast, you leave the head of the tick in your skin, which festers. Wash the tiny wound with soap and water, plus alcohol.

If the tick was thoroughly embedded in your skin, keep track of any flulike symptoms you develop after two weeks, which is the incubation period for Lyme disease. For more information, you can contact the Florida Lyme Alliance at (352) 360-2301 or try www.lymealliance.org.

Horse and Deer Flies

Use repellent.

Spiders

Black widow spiders have a tiny red hourglass figure on their undersides. Brown recluse spiders have a violin shape on their backs.

You often don't realize you've been bitten by a spider. You might wake up in the morning with a small red bump that's already sealed over. There might be two tiny fang marks, but they're almost invisible.

Brown recluse bites look harmless at first, then fester, and may take months to heal. If you find a bull's-eye-shaped sore on your body, it might be a week-old spider bite. Call your doctor.

Scorpions

All those giant scorpions you see in movies are from Arizona. Florida scorpions are much smaller. A Florida scorpion sting is not lethal, but it can ache for a full day. Cold water and ice packs usually help numb the initial pain. Monitor the stung person closely for allergic reactions.

Other Stingers

Jellyfish

Portuguese men-of-war are beautiful, with iridescent blue-tinged bubbles about the size of your fist. But the ten-foot-long strings hanging down into the salt water below them are lined with poison pods, tiny sacs that each hold a coiled harpoon tipped with concentrated venom. A fish that blunders into the forest of tentacles is quickly paralyzed. A human feels intense pain.

Salt water holds several other types of stinging creatures, some of them so small that you know you've swum through a school only when your skin begins to itch. The easiest prevention is to cover up with a wet suit, thick clothes, or even a T-shirt. Vinegar and alcohol are the best first-aid treatments.

Stingrays

Learn the Florida "stingray shuffle." Drag your feet while you're walking in salt water. This scares away stingrays buried in the sand. If you're hit, get the afflicted area as hot as you can stand with a hot pack or very hot water to "cook" the venom. Get to a doctor. Stingray spines are pencil-long darts of brittle materials, and often bits break off between the many bones in the foot.

If you suspect a real emergency, call the U.S. Poison Control Center at 1-800-282-3171.

9

Raiders

Deer, boar, raccoons, and squirrels are grouped together because they like to visit campgrounds and raid picnic sites. Scrub jays should be in this category too. If you're picnicking or camping at a popular spot and are approached by wild animals, it means somebody ahead of you has already fed them. These animals now can't understand why you are being so mean and not sharing your food. The ants, cockroaches, and rats feel the same way. And an alligator fed marshmallows sure can't tell the difference between a handout and a hand.

City people raised on a diet of *Bambi, Song of the South,* and *Pocahontas* have a world picture in which deer are noble, raccoons are cute little masked bandits, and mice are rescuers. But every year, dozens of "nuisance" animals have to be killed by park rangers and campground managers. Feeding a wild animal may be signing its death warrant.

If you find an otherwise lovely site crawling with critter tracks and feces, you can be certain that the people there ahead of you left food scraps. Don't be one of them.

Around your tent, sprinkle mothballs or moth flakes. Once you make your sandwiches or cook supper, lock your food back up in your ice chest, pickle barrel, kayak port, or whatever. Dig a hole far away from your picnic site for bacon grease and any aromatic liquids.

Deer

White-tailed deer are a conservation success story. Back in 1900 there were only 500,000 of them across the whole nation. Now the numbers are in the neighborhood of 16 million.

I've been to two private campgrounds where the owners put out bread, scraps, and dried corn for the deer and turkeys, and then complained that they couldn't get rid of those *&^% raccoons and rats. Deer have even been known to attack humans, and those sharp hooves and antlers are lethal.

You've probably paddled past hundreds of hidden deer. Their tan coats blend into the background perfectly. They are very wary, and their wide-set eyes give them a wide range of vision.

Train your eye to spot deer. Look closely at the next one you see, and memorize the straight line of its back, its tan color, and that bright white "flag" tail that appears when it bounds away.

I like to watch them walk. White-tailed deer stay at the edge of cover, high-stepping over grass and effortlessly leaping pasture fences.

Fawns keep their spots for three to four months. They grow fast. A doe's milk contains three times as much fat and protein as the milk of a Jersey cow.

Down in the Keys, pay a visit to the Key Deer sanctuary around the "back country" of Big Pine Key (see destination 84). These stunted deer are the size of collies, and they're used to people, so you're very likely to see them as you kayak from island to island. Just ignore their begging and don't feed them.

Wild Pigs

Pigs are not native to Florida. When Hernando DeSoto landed in Tampa Bay on May 25, 1539, he had a herd of three hundred pigs with him. The idea was to have the pigs supply meat for his army of six hundred soldiers, twelve priests, and two women. He also added some hundred Indian slaves he "borrowed" from the cacique or chief near present-day St. Petersburg.

However, driving a herd of pigs through palmetto thickets and pine forests was downright impractical. Most of the pigs vanished in a wink. By the time the Spaniards got to the Indian village of Ocale, they were famished for meat and fought over the villagers' dogs. DeSoto's group spent Christmas in Apalachee, where archeologists have found one pig mandible.

Those Spanish pigs turned wild in just a few generations. As more settlers arrived, more porkers escaped and bred with their wilder cousins.

Feral pigs undergo a physical change. Little pink piglets have great-grand-children that are big black hogs. Up by the Alabama border there's a strain of wild ridgeback boar reputed to be the size of black bear, only meaner. Florida recently acquired its own strain of striped brown Mexican javelinas too.

Boar tusks can be deadly, and I've seen old logs shredded and the ground rooted up. The manager of River Ranch Resort hates wild pigs because a couple of pigs can dig up an acre of ground per night. They don't care whether it's a pasture, an airplane runway, or a beautifully groomed golf course green.

Wild pigs are normally shy. Just don't get between a mother pig and her babies, or make a big male think that he's cornered. And *please* don't feed them.

Raccoons

Across the river from the Wekiva Marina there's a feeding station for rac-coons. The patrons at Alexander's Restaurant can watch the cute little masked creatures while they eat. When I paddle past that spot, I carefully hug the right bank. Sorry, but I don't like raccoons.

Along the Archie Carr Sea Turtle Refuge south of Melbourne, the rangers tried an experiment. On one stretch they trapped and relocated all the rac-coons they could catch. On the next five-mile stretch, they left the raccoons alone. On the beaches where raccoons were gone, the success rate for sea turtle nests was astonishing. Wading bird rookeries flourished, and colonies of shorebirds that nest on the sand tripled in size in one season.

On the west side of the state, the Tampa Bay Sanctuary is a major bird rookery of ten islands off the mouth of the Alafia River, administered and protected by the National Audubon Society. One spring there was a drastic drop in the number of nests made by wading birds. Upon investigation, the naturalists found that a mother raccoon had somehow gotten onto the big-gest island, and had produced two babies. Together, the three raccoons were eating every egg and young bird they could reach. The Audubon people trapped the raccoons, but many of the birds had given up nesting that season.

On a canoe camping trip around Titusville, we carefully stored all our food inside the flap of the trip leader's tent. But she was a sound sleeper. Raccoons cut through the net door and pulled out every scrap of grub. Fortunately, they missed a sack of oranges inside my pickle barrel, so the next day all fourteen of us breakfasted and lunched on oranges and water.

On the Wilderness Waterway in the Everglades I was warned that the local coons have learned how to open the T-clamps on kayak ports.

A grad student doing a study on freshwater turtles reported that 100 percent of the nests she found had been dug up by raccoons.

Do you notice a theme here? Without natural predators, there is no curb on raccoon populations. They're too smart to get hit by cars, they can climb most fences and trees, and their sharp claws and teeth can open almost anything. They're dangerous too—in a fight between a dog and a coon, the coon always wins. Never, never back a coon into a corner, especially a big male coon. Those fangs are sharp. Also remember that there has been a rabies alert for the past six or eight years around the north part of the state.

If any coons venture into your camp or picnic site, shoo them away quickly. Never, never feed one, no matter how cute it looks. The next person to use that site may get bitten or robbed. Raccoons are dangerous.

Squirrels

It's amazing how fast a squirrel can pounce up on a picnic table, open a plastic bag of bread, and take a bite out of every slice. I call them rats with fluffy tails.

Like raccoons, squirrels will raid your stores of food. They're not as dangerous, but they sure can move faster. Don't try to grab one—those teeth can bite through your hand.

In conclusion, wildlife is fun to watch, and a major part of why we all like to go paddling. Just emphasize the word "wild." Do your part to keep the critters on their side of the woods.

10

Scales, Fangs, and Shells

Alligators

Newcomers to Florida paddling seem to arrive with a preset notion about alligators.

Half of the people view alligators as harmless little creatures whose sole function is to entertain humans. I've watched paddlers poke floating alligators with their paddles, toss them food, and even try to tiptoe up to a "sleeping" alligator on a bank.

Other people have seen too many horror flicks, and imagine an alligator the size of a Buick hiding under every lily pad. These folks will turn their boats around and flee at the sight of a newly hatched baby gator, *if* they even venture onto the water in the first place.

The truth, of course, is somewhere in the middle.

Alligators are mostly harmless to humans, but they *are* carnivores. They tend to avoid people, but nesting females and territorial bulls will stand their ground. Those that have been taught to expect food from humans will even approach a boat.

These holdovers from the Age of the Dinosaurs are actually Florida's oldest inhabitants. The Florida Museum in Gainesville has an exhibit of two gator skulls. One is a modern-day alligator. The other is 7.5 million years old. The two skulls are identical.

Back in 1771, an explorer named William Bartram reported that alligators were so thick in the rivers that it looked as if he could walk across on their backs and never wet his feet. Big gators too, up to twenty-three feet long, he said (the current state record is just under twenty). For fascinating reading, get his book *The Travels of William Bartram* and check out chapter 5.

In the last century, gator leather was in such demand that alligators seemed to be heading for extinction. Only strict laws protected the few animals the experts thought were left. However, gator numbers snapped back so quickly that other experts now wonder if thousands of the animals were simply hiding in the back swamps when they were supposed to be an endangered species. FWC biologists estimate there are well over a million alligators in Florida, which comes to one alligator for every fourteen humans. Nuisance animal removal, gathering eggs for commercial farms, and licensed hunts take only some 100,000 alligators a year.

In 1999 I won a gator hunting license in the state lottery, and in my first experience with crossbow hunting I took five bull gators that together measured more than forty-seven feet long. This was on Lake Trafford in Immokalee, a small lake that holds an estimated four thousand gators. It is *not* one of the paddling destinations in this book.

The size of the gator counts too. A baby alligator is not dangerous, except that even a scrape from its dirty teeth will need vigorous cleaning. Three-to-four-footers might give you a painful bite, though they probably couldn't hold an adult human underwater.

Big females will defend their nests and babies, and bull gators over nine feet can be aggressive, but they also have very good hearing. Sound travels much faster underwater than it does in air. Unless you have mastered the art of silent paddling, most gators know far in advance that you are arriving, and quietly hide. You'll see only 10 percent of all the gators you actually pass.

With a few simple precautions, you won't have any trouble with even the biggest animals. Freak attacks by alligators upon humans are extremely rare, and nine out of ten times are caused by a human putting himself in harm's way.

Of course, right now you're asking, "How do I stay out of harm's way?"

Here are some basic alligator avoidance techniques.

Paddlers, fishermen, and native Floridians have two sayings about alligators. One is "Alligators won't harm you if you leave them alone." The other is "Alligators never attack a boat, so stay inside your boat."

Watch for gators floating ahead of your boat. As you near, they'll sink lower and lower and finally disappear without the slightest ripple. Without dipping your paddle, glide across the spot where you saw a gator. If you touch the side of a submerged gator, reflex action will snap its powerful tail and toothy jaws into a circle. That might capsize you, and being in the water with an annoyed alligator is not where you want to be.

If you do capsize near an alligator, quickly get back inside your boat. Even sitting inside a swamped canoe will give you a different outline as seen from underwater.

Don't swim at night in big lakes and ponds. Gators feed at night.

Keep your dogs out of the water. Furred animals are natural prey for alligators.

In isolated stretches of water, make noise. Talking, singing, or thumping your feet against the inside of your hull will warn gators you are arriving. Startled alligators always head for deep water. On several solo trips I've had my canoe rocked when I came around a bend too quietly and surprised a gator dozing on a bank. The unexpected giant splash will certainly wake you up.

Learn to spot alligators. Study the next one you come across. Floating alligators usually have their eyes, nose, and back above water. They are a dull gray-black color, and the rippled line of bumps on their backs is distinctive. Alligator tracks on the banks show wide-set footprints, with a drag mark in the center made by the tail.

Never feed a gator. That gets them used to humans, so they'll come surging up whenever they see anybody. And today's harmless little three-footer will become a big adult by growing at the rate of a foot a year.

If you're fishing in a gator area, keep your catch in a bucket. Gators used to fishing boats soon learn they can sneak up and steal fish on stringers. It's like dangling candy in front of a baby.

Remember, Florida has plenty of alligators. They were here first, and they're here to stay. Keep alert, use common sense, don't tease or feed them, and enjoy watching the ones you come across.

Alligator Trivia

- An alligator cannot stick out its tongue.
- If you see a gator more than nine feet long, it's a male.
- The biggest gator ever captured in this century was twenty feet long. Anything longer is a submarine.
- Alligators are found in only two places in the world: the southeastern U.S. and the upper Yangtze River in China. Chinese gators are smaller than U.S. gators, probably because they hibernate without eating for five months of the year.
- The price of alligator skin varies wildly, according to supply. Prices for raw hides have gone from $65 to $9 a foot (measured across the belly) in the last decade.
- Only licensed hunters and trappers may hunt alligators. They have tags, permits, forms in quadruplicate, and other red tape. If you are interested, you can download a hunting license application from the FWC homepage, www.state.fl.us/fwc/.
- Gator leather was in such demand that between 1880 and 1894 more than 2.25 million gator skins were exported through the port of Jacksonville.
- Cooked alligator meat tastes like whatever the gator fed on—usually fish—and tail meat has the stringy consistency of chicken breast. It's delicious.
- Alligator jowl meat is the most tender. Next is the "tenderloin," two strips down the side of the tail bone. Leg meat can be as tough as old leather.
- Customs inspectors have a trick for telling alligator hides from other crocodilians. Belly scales of alligators are smooth, crocodile scales have a tiny pit or dimple, and caiman scales show five indentations.
- The name "alligator" comes from the Spanish *el lagarto,* meaning "the lizard."
- Because of their jaw hinge arrangement, you can hold a gator's mouth shut with only two fingers, but you will probably lose fingers if you try to hold it open. The reverse is true for crocodiles.
- Gators live up to seventy-five years.
- The bumps on a gator's back are called scutes.
- Gator eggs take nine to ten weeks to hatch.
- The temperature of the nest determines the sex of the baby gators. Warm

= males, cool = females. More males hatch from eggs near the top of a sun-warmed nest, with females at the bottom of the nest.

- For some reason unknown to medical science, a gator will never go into shock, no matter how badly it is wounded.
- A gator's snout is blunt, while a croc's snout is pointed.
- Alligators have eighty teeth. Crocodiles have only sixty.
- Gators crunch down at 1,350 pounds per square inch.
- Gators continually grow new teeth, which push out old ones and grow in the same spots.
- Alligators need braces. They have a terrific overbite. Their top teeth show when their mouth is shut. Crocs show their bottom teeth.
- Alligators grin. Crocodiles leer.
- Gators cannot chew their food. Small rocks in their bellies masticate the food.
- Alligators store large prey underwater until it softens up, or grab a mouthful and twirl their whole bodies until the piece twists off. Smaller animals are chomped until all their bones are pulverized, then swallowed whole.
- Gators eat about once a month in winter, once a week in summer.
- Gators swim with their legs flat against their body, swinging their tail from side to side.
- Gators can run as fast as a human sprinter or a slow horse. However, they are short-winded, and usually run less than thirty feet.
- A gator rises up on its toes to run, and then trots as lightly as a horse.
- A gator has ten front toes, but only eight back toes.
- The outside toe of each alligator foot has no claw.
- A female gator can lay more than a hundred eggs at a time. The older the lady, the larger her clutch.
- A baby gator starts with black and yellow stripes on its tail, which fade to black and cream as it ages. Crocodiles are yellow-gray.
- To estimate the size of an alligator in the water, figure the inches between its nose and eyes, and change that to feet.
- In nature's scheme of things, gators do perform useful functions. They eat "trash" fish and dead animals, and their deeply dug holes hold water for fish and animals in times of drought.

- Female gators can predict the coming rainy season: they build their nests exactly high enough to stay above the natural water level for a month. (However, they can't allow for humans closing dams and "managing" the water table.)
- Alligators love marshmallows.

Snakes

How to Spot the Poisonous Snakes

Something was splashing against the bank. We were on one of the red-water rivers in northern Florida. It was a beautiful spot, with sheer rock walls scalloped with tiny caves and fist-sized hollows. We paddled closer, and discovered a five-foot-long brown water snake fighting a big crappie. The snake's jaws were clamped across the fish's back, and the fish was flinging itself around, trying to get away.

The dark eye band and thick black body identify a cottonmouth moccasin, one of Florida's four poisonous snakes. Courtesy of Florida Fish and Wildlife Conservation Commission.

One of Florida's poisonous snakes, the pygmy rattler sports no rattles but has a recognizable checkerboard pattern. Courtesy of Florida Fish and Wildlife Conservation Commission.

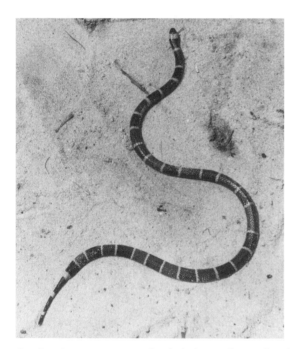

Coral snakes are gorgeous, but lethal. To tell a coral snake from a king snake, look for the black nose, and red and yellow bands touching. Remember the old pioneer poem: "Red touch yellow, kill a fellow." Courtesy of Jim Reed, Florida Fish and Wildlife Conservation Commission.

Rattlesnakes sport a distinctive diamond pattern, and sometimes a rattle buzzing at the end of the tail. Sandy Huff.

The snake glared at us, released the fish, and dove underwater. Mortally wounded, the crappie wobbled away, probably to be caught again later.

The next day, we pulled our canoes up on a sandbar to set up camp, and had to actually use a paddle to push away a smaller brown water snake in the shallows.

Brown water snakes live all over Florida. They're not the least bit dangerous to humans, but their fat bodies and pugnacious personalities look intimidating. On the other hand, the docile coral snake is a living gem—and its bite is deadly.

Florida has sixty-seven different kinds of snakes, but only four of them are dangerous: the eastern diamondback rattler, the Florida cottonmouth, the dusky pygmy rattler, and the eastern coral snake. Copperheads, as well as canebrake and other rattlers, are rare, and live at the extreme northwest end of the panhandle.

As a paddler, you're going to be out in critter country. Learn to tell snakes apart. Don't automatically kill or panic at every snake you run across out of ignorance and fear.

If you're uncertain as to what type of snake you've encountered, leave it alone. Look it over from a distance and try to answer the following questions:

- *What shape is it?* A rattler or cottonmouth generally has a fat, chunky shape. A long, finger-thin snake woven among tree branches is certainly not in that category. (Shape is not an infallible indicator, however. The benign brown water snake, which frequents fresh water, is chunky and broad-headed. And the deadly coral snake is decidedly svelte.)
- *What about the eyes?* Does the snake have cat eyes with vertical slitlike pupils? That means the rattlers and the cottonmouth. Most nonpoisonous snakes have round eyes, with solid black pupils. (But then, so has the coral snake.)
- *Is there a small pit on its face?* So-called pit vipers (which include all the bad snakes except, as you've guessed, the coral snake) have a small indentation on their faces, halfway between the nose and eyes. You have to be pretty up close and personal to spot this small dent, so don't look too closely.
- *Does it make noise?* Everyone knows a rattler rattles, but don't depend on the sound. Only the big diamondback and canebrake rattlers have rattles; the pygmy does not. Of course, if it's curled into a tight defensive coil, tail sticking up and buzzing like a demented alarm clock, it's a rattler. If it has its neck puffed up like a cobra, and hisses, you're looking at a harmless hognose snake trying to look tough. A hognose's next step is to roll over, stick out its tongue, and play dead.
- *What color is it?* Rattlers can come in shades of tan as well as the familiar gray-brown. Check for the distinctive diamond pattern on its back.

A cottonmouth or water moccasin is a dull black-brown, with a lighter belly. It's called cottonmouth because the inside of its mouth is snowy white (but if you're close enough to see that, you had better take a giant step backwards fast). Water moccasins have a dark line down each side of the head. It's the snake version of a raccoon mask. Their blotches or bands are hourglass-shaped, and light in the center.

Copperheads are very pretty snakes, with distinctive hourglass bands on a light tan background.

The eastern coral snake and the similarly-colored king snake are easiest to spot. Simply look for gorgeous snakes banded in bright red-orange, black, and yellow. But a deadly coral snake has a *black nose,* whereas the harmless king snake has a pure orange head. Right this minute, learn the old poem about telling a friendly king snake from a dangerous coral snake:

Red touch yellow, kill a fellow.
Red touch black, friend of Jack.

It's hard for a coral snake to bite a human. They're slow-moving and unlikely to execute one of those so-fast-you-never-see-it strikes. Their mouths are tiny, so small they can only grab thin pieces of skin, such as an earlobe, the webbing between your fingers and toes, or a lip. You're certainly not going to get your face that close to a coral snake. They also have teeth like dogs, and have to gnaw to grind the poison into the wound.

However, if you get bitten by a coral snake, no medicine will help you. A coral snake antivenin has yet to be developed.

Even nonpoisonous snakes will bite if provoked, and while they are rarely deeper than scratches, the cuts could get infected. If you do get bitten by a snake, and you think it's a poisonous snake, get to medical care fast. Don't trust the old apply-tourniquet-then-cut-an-X-and-suck-out-the-venom theory.

Again, the best rule of thumb is to leave all snakes alone. Watch them as you would any fascinating animals.

Turtles

Probably the most common animals you'll see while paddling are turtles. Florida's fresh water is home to sliders and river cooters, to red-bellied, red-eared, yellow-bellied, mud, stinkpot, and Cumberland slider turtles. In salt water, Florida has 90 percent of the world's sea-turtle nesting areas.

Freshwater swimming turtles have webbed feet and sharp claws. Saltwater turtles have flippers instead of feet. If you find a turtle with elephant-looking back feet stomping around on dry land, don't toss it in the water. It's a gopher

Keep a running count of the turtles you pass as you paddle. On most trips, you can see over 200. Sandy Huff.

tortoise, and can't swim. There's also a brackish-water turtle called a terrapin. If you find one caught in a crab trap, rescue it quickly—it has a fifty-fifty chance of reviving in about half an hour in the air.

Only two types of freshwater turtles bite. One is the softshell turtle, which has a leathery carapace that looks like a big brown pancake. If you pick one up, hold it by the extreme back of its shell, and beware of its extendable neck and sharp claws.

The other biting turtle is the snapping turtle. This animal is distinguished by high knobs on its back and sawtoothy spines on its tail and the back of its neck. If you corner one on land, it will lunge at you (but you can surely outrun it).

The snapping turtle's macho big brother, the alligator snapping turtle, lives on the panhandle. The biggest on record weighed 219 pounds and was twenty-six inches long, with a head the size of a grapefruit. Each one has a little "worm" on its tongue, and fishes by lying on the bottom with its mouth open and its tongue wriggling away.

If you're on a wave-stroked beach, watch for tracks in the sand leading to signs of digging. Mark the nest with two sticks stuck at least five feet to each side, and notify any ranger, park attendant, or even a sheriff's office. Don't try taking just a few eggs to watch them hatch. As a park ranger at Fort Matanzas near St. Augustine explained, "Turtle nests are exactly shaped so that the baby turtles can push through the sand to escape. If you change the shape of the nest by removing even the top layer of eggs, the hatchlings at the bottom can't get out and will die."

Sea turtles have swum under my kayak, and I've snorkeled beside both fresh- and saltwater species. In their natural element, turtles fly and glide and swoop. They're the birds of the underwater world.

When I paddle past a log full of turtles, and they all dive off, I often drift a bit downstream, grab a tree root for anchorage, sit perfectly still, and watch. Turtles can evidently only see movement, and will one by one climb back up, jostling for position with slow deliberation.

Watching a turtle traffic jam puts the world into an entirely different perspective.

Birds

Baby limpkins are my favorites. They look like caricatures of birds: grape-fruit-sized balls of gray-brown fuzz that have sprouted long legs and a tiny head. Every year three sets of these little guys appear around Alligator Lake here in Safety Harbor.

It's hard to sneak up on birds, since the bow of my canoe or kayak pokes around a corner before the rest of me can get there. And the animals I'm trying to watch have, literally, a bird's-eye view of me. But when possible, I become a bird voyeur, and stop often to watch our feathered friends.

Florida is a Mecca for bird-watchers, and viewing them from water level is the very best way to go. Not only do we have many resident birds but, every May and October, thousands of migrating birds travel between the U.S. mainland and South America.

I've been fortunate to be on trips with some real bird experts. On one of my first group trips, a tiny brown blur went by at the speed of *zip*. The birder with us calmly said, "Oh, that was an immature male orchard oriole, in its first spring plumage." Now, where else could I have gotten that information?

I now carry a birding book, or at least keep one in the car so I can look up that mystery bird we passed along the waterway.

Here are a few hints on how to identify the more common birds:

Anhingas and Cormorants

These skillful birds dive underwater to fish, and swim with their heads and necks out of the water, so pioneers called them water turkeys, and snake birds.

Anhingas, like this male, have no oil in their feathers, which helps them swim underwater but also means they are often seen drying out. Females have a tan neck and head. Courtesy of Lee Island Coast Convention and Visitor Bureau.

Here's an easy way to tell them apart. Anhingas, whose name starts with the letter A, have a sharp beak like the point on the letter A. Cormorants have a little curve at the end of their beak, like the letter C.

Eagles

Adult bald eagles are solid brown with a white head. Youngsters under four years old are harder to spot, being solid brown, but then go through a speckled stage as their white head feathers grow in.

I once watched an eagle steal a fish from an osprey down in the Ten Thousand Islands. The osprey was flying around with its catch, and the eagle dive-bombed it from above. I don't know if they actually hit, but the osprey lurched and dropped its fish. The eagle caught it in midair, and the two birds flapped away in opposite directions. The osprey landed quickly on a pine stub, ruffled its feathers several times, then started yelling in indignant protest. The eagle flew off to enjoy its ill-gotten gains.

Golden eagles live in the northern part of the state. They're also huge birds, but a solid dull brown instead of the chocolate and white of the bald eagle.

Great Blue Herons

Great blue herons are wonderful fishermen, and I've seen them spear and then swallow tilapia (Nile perch) as wide as their own shoulders. They'll also eat frogs, snakes, and baby gators (thank heavens something eats baby gators).

Great Egrets

Florida's other big wading bird is the great egret. Its beautiful long back plumes made it the hardest hit by the plume hunters at the turn of the century.

I once witnessed two great egrets doing a courtship dance in Flamingo. They pointed their heads up in unison and snapped their bills like castanets.

Owls

You may never see the owls you pass in the woods, but you'll hear them. The deepest tones are probably great horned owls. Even the babies sing bass. If you see a flock of jays and mockingbirds scolding something, they're probably after an owl.

Scan the sandbars for owl pellets, which are finger-long capsules of bones and hair that the birds spit up. I think that mice are attracted to places where humans have dropped food, and against the light sand they make easy pickings for owls.

The second most common owl is the screech owl, which has a piercing soprano whistle or whinny. These adorable little birds are smaller than doves, but act like they're the size of elephants.

You'll rarely see barred owls. With their mottled brown and gray streaking, they blend in superbly. Listen for their *hoo-hoo-hoohoo*, which birders say sounds like "Who cooks for you?" They carry on long conversations with their fellows, even in the daytime.

Green-Backed Herons

A bird whose name has been "officially" changed, the green-backed heron used to be plain "green heron" and, before that, "little green heron." Its neck can stretch out to ten inches, or retract so far that the bird looks like it has no neck at all.

Baby green herons have an endearing trait. When disturbed, they freeze, beaks pointing straight up. Each one thinks it's completely invisible. However, their eyes are set completely on the sides of their heads, so they can see what's under their chins.

Ibis

Adult ibis are pure white, with black "fingers" visible when they fly. A baby ibis with its first feathers is dark gray-brown. Any "pinto" ibis that you see are half-grown white ibis. What we call wood storks are actually in the ibis family. Their scaly black necks and heads are sure proof that God has a sense of humor.

Limpkins

Disturb a female limpkin on her nest, and she'll flap away, limping piteously, luring you away from her precious eggs. Thus her name. Early settlers also called these birds curlews, after the cry of a similar bird that lives out west.

Florida is the only U.S. habitat for these busy birds. They dig along shallow muddy stream bottoms for crawfish, snails, and mussels, and usually retire to a favorite stump to eat. If you spot a pile of empty shells under a perch, you're probably beside a limpkin sidewalk café.

Ducks

Florida has twenty-two species of ducks that either live here or visit as tourists. Male wood ducks are probably the prettiest birds in the whole state.

I've seen canoers deliberately run over tiny swimming ducklings. True, ducklings can dive, but it uses up a great amount of energy, and an exhausted duckling will probably die.

Ospreys

During breeding season, a male osprey has a surefire way to court his lady love. He'll catch a fish, fly around with it in his talons for about half an hour, eat the head off, and then present the headless fish to his mate.

This either means that (1) he's made sure the fish is dead and won't flop around or (2) she won't have to bother getting rid of the head and is getting only the body meat or (3) the head is the best part and he got to it first.

You can tell an osprey from a bald eagle because the osprey has a white belly. Females have a "necklace" of dark feathers across their chest.

Pelicans

Ogden Nash wrote, "Pity the poor pelican / His beak can hold more than his belly can."

Every paddler has seen pelicans dive. When one has gotten a fish, it will keep its head underwater, angling the fish around until it is securely in its pouch. This is to protect its catch from raiding gulls, which will often land on a pelican's back and try to snatch the fish out of the bigger bird's mouth.

Ospreys are talented fishermen. This male will eat the head off the fish before presenting it to his mate. Is that to make sure it is dead, or is the head the best part? Courtesy of Joanne Williams.

Roseate Spoonbills

Like wood storks, spoonbills have beautiful bodies and homely heads. Scarlet ibis, flamingos, and roseate spoonbills get their pink colors from an ingredient in shellfish.

Spoonbills feed like wood storks, swinging their spatulate bills from side to side in shallow water.

Terns

Birders come from around the world to admire Florida's bridal, least, royal, and sandwich terns. If you see a white bird about the size of a pigeon, with pointed wing tips, a V-shaped tail, and a pointed beak, it's probably a tern. Act all excited. The tourists will think they're having a great time.

Snowy Egrets

The snowy egret is one of the easiest wading birds to identify. Simply look for the yellow feet, and imagine the bird is wearing snow boots.

Birding can become a lifelong passion, and serious birders keep "life lists" of all the birds they see, stored on computer with programs that list the dates, sites, and what each bird was doing when it was spotted. Birding is probably the perfect companion hobby to paddling.

12

Florida's *Real* Mermaids

Manatees

A northern friend of ours was eager to see a manatee, so we took him to Homosassa Springs, Crystal River, and Manatee State Park.

At the first river, we paddled to a good spot and hopped overboard to snorkel around. Suddenly our friend scrambled up onto his kayak in a panic.

"What is that?" he exclaimed, pointing to the giant gray shape drifting under our moored kayaks.

Our friend, it seems, had assumed that a manatee was about the size of a cat.

Manatees are huge animals, with full-grown males getting up to thirteen feet long. Also known as sea cows, these completely harmless animals feed exclusively on vegetation. In clear water, they look like gray-green sweet potatoes about as long as a sports car. In dark water, they blend in so well that the only part of them you'll see is a broad snout coming up for air about every three minutes.

At Homosassa River a curious baby manatee came up to several of us wading in waist-deep water. When it got to me, it sank down and, before I knew it, started suckling on my big toe that was sticking out of my water shoe. Surprised, I jerked, and my knee brushed the animal. It evidently had perfect neutral buoyancy, and bobbed to the surface. Indignant that I'd taken away my toe, the calf swam off.

My friend SarahBeth says she once had a mother manatee push her away from a calf at the same spot. "I was standing there, just watching the calf, and

Ancient sailors thought these cow-sized animals looked like beautiful women, and called them Sirens. The old salts obviously needed glasses. Sandy Huff.

the mom came up, wrapped her flippers around my hips, and pushed me away," she said. "And when a full-grown manatee pushes, you know you've been pushed."

Manatees in the wild are in trouble. They are protected by law, but every year an estimated 10 percent are killed or maimed by motorboats. Almost every manatee I've seen has diagonal slash marks across its back, caused by the knife-blade action of boat props.

It's against the law to contact a manatee, but if one comes up to you, it is okay to pet it.

So watch for a big black muzzle to come poking above the surface, snort, and sink back down. The animal below that snout is a lot bigger than a cat.

Dolphins

I was noodling around on Tampa Bay one summer day and drifted close to the peninsula formed by the Clearwater airport runway.

Suddenly I heard a deep hiss, and a sleek gray snout popped out of the water beside me. We both jumped back in surprise, then peered at each other in mutual fascination. There were four other dolphins in the "pod" swimming in this lagoon—a mother with a tiny baby and two adults with deep scratches on their sides—besides this one, who seemed to be at the "teenage" stage.

For half an hour we all watched each other. The curious baby was firmly kept away from me by its mother.

I talked to them, slapped the water, sang, and spun in a circle. Then I remembered that dolphins communicate with whistles. So I puckered up

You can talk to dolphins, swim with dolphins, and even feed them fish. But never ever whistle at a dolphin. Sandy Huff.

and whistled a cheerful "Anchors Aweigh." In a flash, all five dolphins swam away at top speed, and I never saw them again. Evidently I'd said something really bad in dolphin language.

Anytime you're paddling in salt water, you have a good chance of seeing these wonderful animals.

"Flipper" and his relatives are members of the cetacean family, in the group of short-toothed whales. They get up to twelve feet long and can weigh four hundred pounds. A female carries a baby for twelve months, and gives birth every other year to a twenty-five-pound, 3.5-foot baby.

They're also extremely playful. If you're lucky enough to find a pod of dolphins that are used to humans, they'll soar and splash and dip right under your hull. They love to dive in and out of the wake of powerboats, and can keep up with the fastest cruise ships with ease.

Grin at them, talk to them, even sing to them. But never, ever whistle to a dolphin.

13

Plants along the Waterway

Florida has some unique plants that exist nowhere else in our nation. Many of the species were here when the first Calusas poled their dugout canoes down the rivers.

Mangroves grow in the saltwater shallows in the south half of the state. *Red mangroves* have arching roots, like bridges. *Black mangroves* have pencil-thick rootlets sticking up from the soft mud. Two tiny white bumps grow at the base of each leaf of *white mangroves. Buttonwoods* grow completely out of the wave line and have little buttony knobs along each branch.

In fresh water, you'll pass the knobby roots growing out of the water beside *cypress* trees. Botanists tell us that these aerial roots help the plant breathe while the rest of the root system is underwater.

Up near the Georgia border, you'll find *tupelo* trees, which look like big sweet potatoes growing upside down.

Around Kissimmee watch for *American lotus,* used in dried flower arrangements.

Another water lily is the *spatterdock.* These bright yellow golf-ball-sized flowers love clear, flowing water.

Cattails grow in marshes, and are indicators of pollution. The early settlers found they could make flour from cattail roots, eat the young catkins like corn on the cob, and make mattress stuffing out of the "cotton" from the mature catkins.

In the Everglades, examine a stem of *saw grass.* Its three edges are tipped with tiny spikes made of a silicate. As these stems die and drop into the muck, the tiny bits of silicate remain, which is why Everglades muck is so itchy.

Unfortunately, Florida has some imported plants that are causing tremendous problems.

Water hyacinths were brought to this country as a World's Fair exhibit more than a century ago. A few got dumped into a Florida canal, and they now cover south and central Florida. The plants grow incredibly fast, and can completely choke a waterway. They were the biggest factor in the demise of Florida's system of steamboats. I've been stuck in hyacinth jams that stretched for city blocks.

Hydrilla is an underwater aquarium plant that has also taken over Florida's freshwater lakes and streams.

So far the state botanists don't have good control of these invasive water plants. Do your part to keep them from spreading by making sure that not a single tiny piece of greenery is stuck to your gear as you visit different waterways.

Just like our towns and roads, Florida's greenery shows our history of exploration and colonization. Whatever the origin of the green mansions that you paddle past, they are still hauntingly beautiful.

Fishing from Your Boat

That shady nook behind a cypress stump looked promising. I glided my canoe out of the current, picked up my short rod, and flipped a worm into a likely-looking hole right behind the stump.

Blam! The worm didn't have time to sink before it was snapped up by a feisty bluegill. There was even some worm left. I quickly added the sunfish to the half dozen other panfish in my aerated bucket and cast again. By the time

Fishing from a canoe or kayak lets you get into hidden honey holes that power boaters never see. Courtesy of Rodney Smith.

Tom Brocato shows off a redfish he caught while fishing from his kayak. Courtesy of Broke-a-Toe's Outdoors.

I got to the takeout spot both pickle barrels were brimful of panfish. All of them were from spots most motorboaters never even see. And for a bonus, I'd floated down some of the prettiest waters in the whole state.

Fishing from a canoe or kayak is easy and fun. You need minimal gear too.

First, buy a Florida fishing license, for fresh or salt water, or both. These are sold in all bait and tackle shops, the sporting goods section of Kmart, and many marinas. You can even get an instant license over the phone from Bass Pro Shop at 1-888-347-4356. For additional information, check the FWC website at www.state.fl.us/fwc/fishing.

Next, research the specific rules where you're going fishing. A local bait shop is your best source for water conditions, laws, the best baits (it will be what the shopkeeper has the most of, but ask anyway), and other advice.

Look for tackle that fits your boat and will tie in place when you're not using it. That two-foot-long, kid-sized rod and reel you gave little Samantha last Christmas makes a great canoe or kayak accessory—steal it back for a day.

Hand lines work well too. With a bit of practice, you can toss a weight and baited hook right off the spool. A wide rubber band around the unused line keeps the rest of the spool from unwinding.

A tackle box the size of an old-fashioned cigar box will hold plenty of gear. Stuff in some extra monofilament, a couple of red and white bobbers, a few split-shot weights, and hooks in various sizes.

A short paddle comes in handy. You can move your hull sideways, forward, or backward by sculling one-handed in a figure-eight pattern.

Instead of a stringer, try a drawstring-top mesh bag, and dangle it overboard. Cleaned paint barrels make great fish wells for an open canoe. Toss in a couple of oxygenating tablets, or change the water frequently.

Bait can be anything edible. Tiny chunks of liver, hot dog slices, small cubes of cheese, and bits of your Whopper Burger work fine. Tear the center out of a slice of fresh white bread and mash it into a tiny ball around your hook. Earthworms sit quietly in their little plastic cup and don't bark, whine, or scare the fish.

For real fishing excitement, present each of your fishing partners with his own personal carton of crickets. Make sure these fishermen are not in *your* boat. Out of the dozens of crickets inside each carton, one or two might actually get onto a hook and get used for fishing. The rest will spring out of the carton onto your friend's hair or clothes, and spend the rest of the day merrily hopping all over the boat. Bring *lots* of film for the spectacle, and send me your best shot.

What will you catch? Try for a sixteen-pound bass, of course. Settle for a mess of panfish. Whether you call them bluegills, stumpknockers, sunfish, bream, crappie, red-ears, or just "them there littleuns," Florida's many species of smaller fish are all edible. The baby ones are more trouble to clean and scale, so keep only the bigger ones.

Catfish make delicious eating. There are channel cats, white, blue, yellow "butter" cats, brown bullheads, and a tiny species called madtoms. In salt water, you can get sea cats, and gafftopsail catfish. All of them except the madtoms are edible, but you must know one safety tip about "Mr. Whiskers." Each catfish has three sharp, slimy spines—one at the front of his top or dorsal fin, and one in front of each side or pectoral fin. Use a rag to grab a catfish, avoiding the spines. Snip or break these off with pliers as fast as possible for safety.

In salt water, fish around the base of pilings, sea walls, and other structures. There's usually a sheepshead or two hanging around in these spots.

There's nothing better than a meal of fresh-caught fish after a wonderful day on the water. My favorite outdoor cooking method is to bring along a big zippered plastic bag of cornmeal, flour, salt, and pepper. Shake the cleaned fish or fillets in this, fry in oil or bacon grease, and serve on a clean Frisbee. Add an egg and a bit of water to the rest of the cornmeal mix to make hush puppies. Yum!

Shellfish are easy to gather too. In fresh water, little nickel-sized clams live under the sand and boil up with salt and butter for a fine broth. In months with "r" in them, stick clumps of oysters over your campfire coals for easy opening and a wonderful smoky taste. Use a "claw" gardening tool to gather black mussels around mangrove roots. Scrub them lightly and steam them with wine for a gourmet meal.

For more ideas on living off the land, read *Stalking the Blue-Eyed Scallop* by Euell Gibbons. This is a fun book to read to others in your paddling group when you're not quoting Robert Service's outdoor poems to each other.

In my canoe, a bait bucket for shiners and a coffee can of worms go under and behind my seat. The pickle-barrel live wells are lashed ahead of the center thwart. Paddles go to port, and my two rigged rods live on the starboard side. I'd draw a sketch of all this, but it isn't necessary. By the time you've landed your first stumpknocker, the gear you're actually using will be jammed up under your knees, with all the unnecessary junk tossed into the bow.

Whether or not you actually fish from your canoe or kayak, learn to watch the water. Darting mullet, lurking lunker bass, or tiny killifish minnows are all part of the ecosystem. Healthy fish not only taste better, they indicate clean water, a balanced food chain, and, incidentally for you, a lively, bright environment for your paddling.

And remember—time spent fishing is never subtracted from your time on earth.

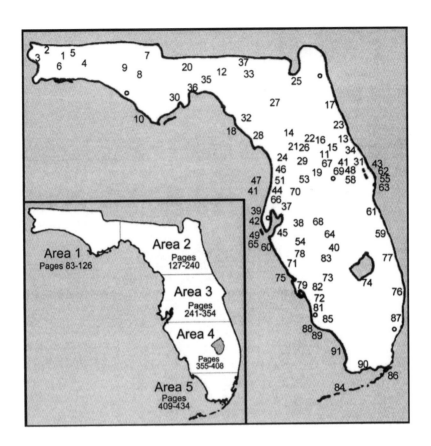

Area 1
Pages 83-126

Area 2
Pages
127-240

Area 3
Pages
241-354

Area 4
Pages
355-408

Area 5
Pages
409-434

Area 1. The Panhandle

Destination 1: Chipola River

> Miles or average time: 53 miles, in six segments of 10, 10, 2, 10, 8, and 13 miles; optional 1 mile above, 15 miles below
>
> Skill level: advanced beginner
>
> Current: averages 2–3 mph
>
> Wind problems: little
>
> Emergency numbers: 911; Jackson County sheriff, (850) 482-9624; Calhoun County sheriff, (850) 674-5049; Gulf County sheriff, (850) 227-1115
>
> Rentals: Bear Paw Canoe Trails, 2100 Bear Paw Lane, Marianna FL 32448, phone (850) 482-4948, e-mail canoeit@digitalexpress.com, website www.bearpawcanoe.com; Florida Caverns State Park, 3345 Caverns Road, Marianna FL 32446, phone (850) 482-9598
>
> DeLorme page 32, section B-1
>
> Official Florida canoe trail? yes

The Chipola River has two tricky parts that should not be attempted by be-ginners without an experienced paddler in the stern. These are the very first mile and the optional last fifteen miles to Dead Lake. For less-experienced paddlers, each of the middle six sections makes a nice one-day trip.

The Chipola is famous for its Look and Tremble Rapids. However, water level determines whether this section is a small rocky ripple or a gushing stream. Scope out the rapids before you tackle them.

Watch for sections of gravel on the Chipola. Scoop up a handful and paw through it looking for dull black triangles. These are fossilized sharks' teeth, circa the Cambrian period. Most of the teeth are tiny, but now and then

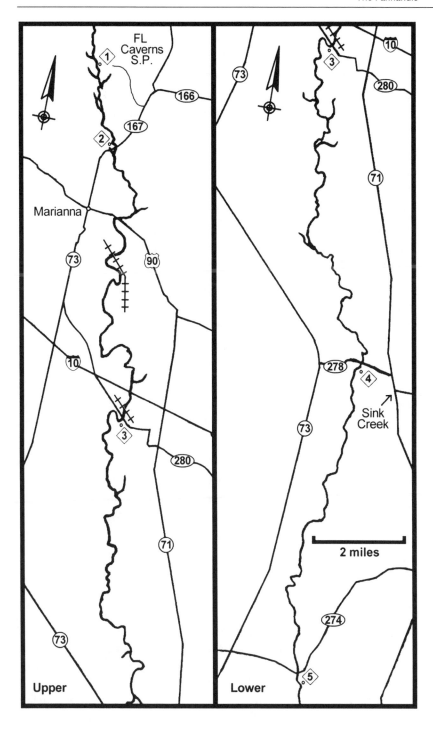

Upper

Lower

Sink Creek

2 miles

Marianna

FL Caverns S.P.

you'll find bigger ones. Finding one the size of your hand makes you very thankful that elephant-sized sharks had the courtesy to die out.

The Chipola is home to rare Barbour's map turtles. These little guys have dark green carapaces with a pattern of yellow lines that look like streams on a map. They're timid, and you may only get a glimpse of one sliding off a log.

Also, if you try fishing on the river, keep an eye out for a bass newly discovered by biologists. It's called a shoal bass. It has a smaller mouth than a large-mouth bass, and has no black markings but instead is bright bronze. *Micropterus cataractae* occurs only from here to southwest Georgia and southeast Alabama. On the Chipola, it has been found only from Marianna to Clarksville. Mike Allen of the University of Florida is doing a study on it. "They're not especially rare on this river, but they do have a limited distribution," he told me. "Right now we're trying to study their reproductive cycle, to find out where and when they spawn, and where the young grow up." So if you catch one, practice catch and release.

Marianna is on an old stagecoach road that you can still follow. It's called the Old Spanish Trail and is overhung with massive oaks festooned with Spanish moss.

The official canoe trail begins three miles north of Marianna, at Florida Caverns State Park, which is interesting to visit. The calcite caverns are unique. Florida has many caves, true, but most of the others are under water. Wear a sweater—it's a constant 61° in the caves. The caves were described by Spanish conquistadors in 1693. There is one little brown bat that I swear has been hanging in the same crevice for years. I suspect it is stuffed, and left behind by the CCC workers who put in the passageways in the cave.

Check out the wide, swirling pond (no swimming or boating!) where the Chipola River goes underground, then pops back up a quarter mile south— too far for me to portage.

1) This first one-mile section of the river is one that most paddlers avoid, and it is really not worth the effort during low water. It is an old logger's chute cut across the top of the natural bridge about a century ago. In periods of heavy rain, this is actually the above-ground overflow of the underground Chipola. The many windfall trees and bump-overs can make it a hassle.

2) SR167 to SR280, 10 miles. The "real" paddling starts at the SR167 bridge, a mile north of Marianna. The paved boat ramp is on the northwest

side, and looks like it was another CCC project. This stretch meanders through a hardwood forest, circles east of Marianna, and generally heads south. If you have a keen eye, you can spot the huge old stumps left from the logging that went on here around the turn of the century. They make you wonder how the loggers ever got in and out of this isolated area.

About a mile above the I-10 bridge, Spring Creek comes in from the left. This is the runoff from Merritt's Mill Pond and a series of scenic springs: Shangri-La, Twin Caves, Gator, Indian Washtub, and Blue Springs. You can paddle up Spring Creek to the dam at US90. From I-10 to the next ramp is .6 miles. It is on the left just past the bridge.

Bear Paw Outfitters offer tubing trips down Spring Creek, and trips to explore the caves.

3) SR280 to SR278, 10 miles. Now you're in some of the most isolated country in Florida. The access is at the Magnolia Road/SR280 bridge. To get there from I-10, exit at SR71, go south a half mile, and turn right/west at the little hamlet of Oakdale. The access is on the southeast side of the bridge. Unless it's been improved, the launch site is rutted and overgrown.

This is a low, swampy section, with many cypress trees. Two miles downstream a spring run comes in from the left. It is often choked with weeds, but might be open when you arrive. Watch for snakes—we saw two really big brown water snakes here, which are not dangerous but might give you a start.

Little Rocky Creek comes in from the left .8 miles further down. Then there's an unbroken stretch of the river west of Simsville until Dry Creek comes in from the right, then 1.6 miles further Rocky Creek enters from the left. From there it's about two miles to SR278. The access is on the left, a city block past the bridge.

4) SR278 to Altha, 2 miles. The SR278 ramp is southeast of the Peacock Road/SR278 bridge, off a little road. To get there from I-10, head south on SR71 about six miles, then west on Peacock Road/SR278. Or from Clarksville, head north on SR73. Exactly four miles after you cross into Jackson County, turn right on SR278, go over the bridge, and turn right at the next road. It's a paved ramp.

There is also a GFC ramp where Hollis Branch comes in from the left. Using my personal navigation system, after SR278 I'd count five creeks that enter from the left, then the fourth left turn, which is Hollis Branch. Or keep paddling for another two miles to the CR274 bridge.

5) Altha to SR 520, 10 miles. From I-10, go south on SR71 for eleven miles. Turn west on SR274 at the little town of Altha, and follow that three

miles to the bridge. Or, from Clarksville, head north on SR73 to the town of Chason, turn east/right on SR274, and go two miles to the bridge. The paved ramp itself is on the southeast side, down a graded dirt road that might be a problem in rainy weather.

The first four miles have the Look and Tremble Rapids, which are not at all scary. Wear boat shoes during low water, since you might have to portage or scrape across the rocks. During high water the rapids completely vanish.

6) SR20 to Clarksville, 8 miles. I remember this as the "ditch" part of the river, where the sides rose in steep honey-colored cliffs and I felt like we were paddling through a tunnel. I was in the lead canoe, and we drifted round a bend to surprise an entire herd of wild pigs. From the churned-up mud, they'd evidently been drinking or wallowing at a low spot where another rivulet entered on the left. I never heard such squealing and porcine cussing. Up the bank and into the trees they stampeded. It was hilarious, and I'm sure the pigs came right back to finish their bath as soon as our flotilla of four boats was out of sight.

7) SR20 to SR71 at Scott's Ferry, 13 miles. Launch at the SR20 bridge east of Clarksville. This is a small park, with a paved road and rest rooms.

If this section is too long for you, there are two unofficial ramps. The first is about six miles downriver, west of the tiny town of Abe Springs. From Clarksville, go east on SR20 to SR275, then south on SR275 about four and a half miles. You'll pass the weathered sign that says you're in Abe Springs. About half a mile south of this hamlet, turn right on a dirt road that leads to the river. It might be a tricky road to follow. If you can't find the river, ask a local person for directions.

The next ramp is about nine miles downriver from Abe Springs. To get there from Clarksville, head south on SR73 for eleven miles. Turn east/left on CR392 and go just a hair over five miles. Where 392 bends to go southeast, turn north on River Road, then northeast on Maulden Road.

8) There is another stretch, down the huge shallow Dead Lake to Dead Lakes State Recreation Area. We can't blame the Army Corps of Engineers for this backed-up water. Geologists say a natural dam was formed from sand dumped by the Apalachicola River during floods. Many trees were left standing, along with logs, huge branches, and other jumbles. It's terrific bassin' country, but wide open, and tough going during winds or droughts.

For more information, try www8.myflorida.com/communities/learn/trails/canoe.

Destination 2: Coldwater Creek

Miles or average time: 22+ miles, in six segments of 2, 4, 7, 4, 3, and 4 miles

Skill level: beginner, except at flood stage

Current: moderate, and faster during the rainy season

Wind problems: few

Emergency numbers: 911; Santa Rosa County sheriff, (850) 623-3691

Rentals: Adventures Unlimited Outdoor Center, 8974 Tomahawk Landing Road, Milton FL 32570, phone (850) 623-6197 or 1-800-239-6864, e-mail aunlimited@aol.com, website www.adventuresunlimited.com

DeLorme page 27, section A-2

Official Florida canoe trail? yes

Coldwater Creek is spring fed, and near its headwaters the water is a constant 76°F. The current is slightly faster than most rivers, mainly because of the drop in elevation—three feet per mile—which starts at about three hundred feet at the Florida-Alabama line, making it a veritable mountain for Florida. In the upper sections the current is quite fast, with many sharp turns.

The river drains Conecuh National Forest in Georgia and Blackwater River State Forest in Florida, so there is strong runoff during heavy rains, which also means high, fast current. During the dry season, exposed logs and sandbars mean more pull-overs.

Nearby Blackwater River gets more publicity, but Coldwater Creek is called the prettiest river in the state. The sandbars are made of "sugar sand"

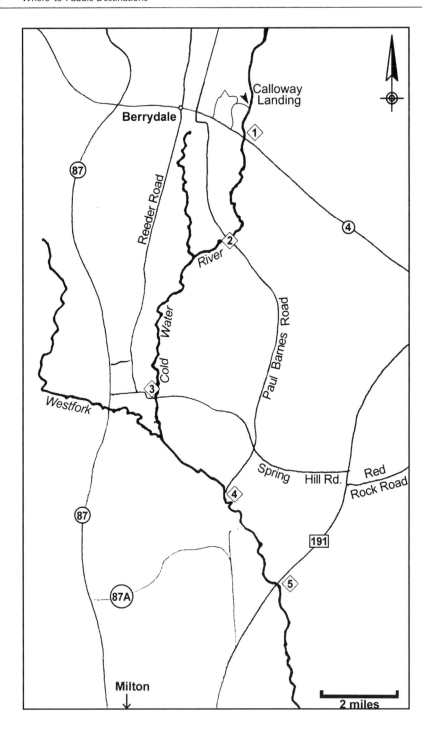

that's so fine it resembles honey-colored powdered sugar. Of course, that means it gets into all your camping gear, and your food will taste a bit crunchy, but it's worth it.

The upper nine miles are too shallow for motorboats, but perfect for tubes, skinny rafts, canoes, and kayaks.

The river guides take pride in keeping the river as clean as possible. In fact, when I paddled here, our guide was highly indignant to come across a picnic site where someone had left three pieces of debris.

The most popular part of the river has five access points, with a total mileage of twenty-two miles. You can also do the two miles upriver from SR4, from Calloway Landing to SR4.

1) SR4 to Coldwater Recreation Area, 4 miles. Start at the SR4 bridge over Big Coldwater Creek. The access is a sandy sloping bank on the northeast side. To get there from SR87, go east five miles on SR4. From SR191, go west five miles on SR4.

2) Coldwater Recreation Area to Springhill Road, 7 miles. From Munson, take SR191 southwest for two and three-quarters miles until you see a dirt road on the right. This is the west side of Juniper Creek. Turn right/west and travel five miles to Jernigan Bridge. If you're coming from Berrydale, go east on SR4 for two miles to the paved road. Turn right/south and go four miles to the bridge. It's a very low bridge, but you can duck under easily except during extreme high water.

This is the State Forest Campground and Stable, and at 183,153 acres the state forest here is the largest in the state. This park was developed for horseback riding and hunting-dog field trials, though they don't shoot live birds.

We got "bayed" at by an overenthusiastic puppy standing in the safety of a trail high atop a bank. She'd obviously never seen a canoe before, but she was enthusiastically letting her owner know she'd found a strange "critter."

3) Springhill Road to Adventures Unlimited Outdoor Center, 4 miles. This section is my favorite. To reach the bridge from SR87, take Springhill Road east to the bridge. Access is on the northwest side of the bridge.

4) Adventures Unlimited to Old Steel Bridge, 3 miles. To get to the canoe livery from SR87, go east on Springhill Road for three and a half miles until you see their sign, then turn right/south to the river.

5) Old Steel Bridge to the SR191 bridge, 4 miles. Access at SR191 is downstream from the bridge, on the southeast side of the river. The stream speeds up a bit here, so hug the bank. It's hard to see the ramp until you get almost on top of it.

For more information, try www8.myflorida.com/communities/learn/trails/coldwater.

Destination 3: Econfina Creek

Miles or average time: 22 miles, in four segments of 10, 5, 1, and 6 miles

Skill level: advanced for upper river, strong beginner on lower river

Current: fast

Wind problems: few

Emergency numbers: 911; Washington County sheriff, (850) 638-6111; Bay County sheriff, (850) 747-4700

Rentals: Econfina Creek Canoe Livery, 5641A Porter Road, Youngstown FL 32466, phone (850) 722-9032, website www.canoeeconfina.com; Creek Cruisers, SR20 at bridge, phone (850) 722-8001; Cabin Fever Outfitters, phone (850) 914-2364, e-mail dbarfield@bellsouth.net

DeLorme page 31, section D-2, to page 47, section A-1

Official Florida canoe trail? yes

The scenery all along the Econfina is superb. Tiny rivulets pop out of the high rocky walls, and lush green ferns cling to tiny cracks. Giant cypresses arch overhead. Then another creek will come sweeping in. The main channel twists and turns and periodically opens up into beautiful vistas that should be in a Tarzan movie.

The upper Econfina is considered the roughest water in Florida, and is not for beginners or children. Don't go if the water-level gauge at Scott's Bridge reads more than six feet—the current is too strong. Two-and-a-half to four feet is the best level for paddling. The six-mile stretch downstream from SR20 is a better choice for beginners or casual paddlers.

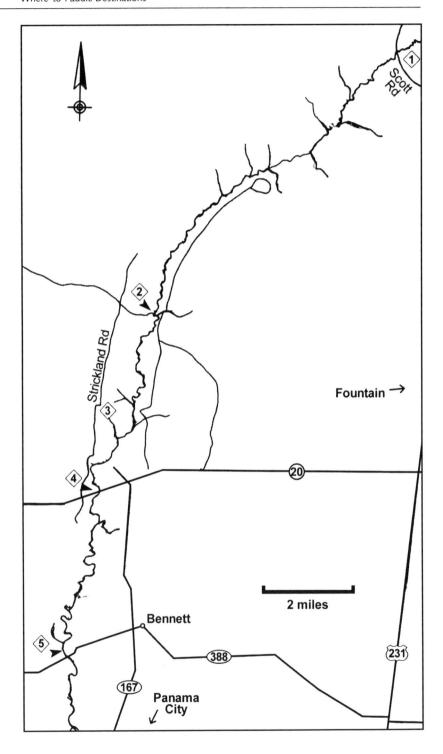

This part of the state is interesting. You'll drive through vast forests of pine and hardwoods. To the northwest by the town of Chipley is Falling Waters State Park, which is a good place to camp. The waterfall there is sixty-seven feet high and is Florida's answer to Niagara Falls—when there's been some rain and there is water around. The lake water eventually ends up in a sink-hole.

Bring along your snorkel. Several springs run into the river, and in warm weather the cool, clear spring water feels wonderful. The lower part of the river is refreshed by three first-magnitude springs: Williford and Pitts Springs on your right north of SR20, and Gainer Springs on the left about a mile south of SR20. Some of the smaller springs are posted, and the owners are serious about keeping out trespassers.

1) Scott's Bridge to Walsingham Bridge, 10 miles. Experts can begin here. To get there, start at the town of Fountain (DeLorme page 47, section A-2). Head north on US231 for four miles, then turn left/west on Scott's Road. It's another four miles to the bridge.

2) Walsingham Bridge to Econfina Creek Canoe Livery, 5 miles. This section starts only six miles due west of the town of Fountain. However, the sayings "You can't get there from here" and "Going around your elbow to get to your thumb" were never truer. Frankly, this route is hard to manage in good weather, and the road can be a sand or mud trap.

The directions again start at Fountain. Head south on US231 to SR20. Turn right/west and drive four miles to the creek. After you cross the Econfina, turn right/north on Strickland Road, a dirt road that's graded and usually passable. (You'll pass Econfina Canoe Livery—stop and ask if the rest of the route is open.) Strickland becomes Porter Pond Road. Now watch for either Hampshire Road or a fence on the right. Follow the fence, making two right turns, and you should end up on Walsingham Bridge Road.

3) Econfina Creek Canoe Livery to SR20, 1 mile. To get there from SR20, on the west side of the creek, head north on Strickland Road. Watch for the signs. Close by are Williford Spring and Pitts Spring, which are open to paddling.

4) SR20 to CR388 bridge, 6 miles. On the left/east, after the bridge, is Gainer Springs, which is a major gusher. This is a great place to hop over-board and take a swim, or at least splash in the cool (72°) water.

5) CR388 bridge. This is the end of the official canoe trail. To get there, go east from the creek on SR20 for half a mile, turn south on CR167. At the hamlet of Bennett, turn right/west on CR388, and go a mile and a half to the bridge. The takeout is at the end of a dirt road on the west side of the bridge.

Continuing downstream, the river loops and twists for two miles, then opens up into Deer Point Lake. A ramp is two miles further south, on the left/east bank. To drive to McAllister Landing, start on SR20 east of the creek. Head south on CR167 for seven miles. The ramp is on the northwest side of the bridge over Bear Creek.

For more information, try www8.myflorida.com/communities/learn/trails/canoe or www.srwmd.state.fl.us/rec_guide/locator.html or www.wildflorida.tlh.fl.us/canoeing/econcrk2.html or www.paddlefl.com/Destination/Descriptions/econfina.htm.

Destination 4: Escambia River

Miles or average time: 2 hours for each of two sections

Skill level: beginner

Current: averages 2–3 mph

Wind problems: mixed

Emergency numbers: 911; Escambia County sheriff, (850) 436-9630

DeLorme page 26, section A-2

Official Florida canoe trail? no

A favorite fishing river of mine is the Escambia. It's the boundary between Santa Rosa County and Escambia County. It begins up in Alabama and runs down into Pensacola Bay. I like to drift down the river, dropping a baited hook in likely spots.

This is a brown-water river, looping back and forth between lush greenery and red clay banks. Dozens of smaller streams and tiny rivulets join the main channel. Canoe Creek actually cuts into the Escambia in three places. And in times of high water the old gravel pits around McDavid community flow into the river.

The section of the Escambia I usually fish starts between the tiny towns of Jay and Century, near the Alabama border. The advantage of this stretch is that the launch and takeout ramps are only ten minutes apart by car, but a good two hours away via canoe or kayak.

You can launch at the public ramp at Bluff Springs, about two and a half miles south of Century. Turn east off 29/95 at the intersection of Burneville Road and Bluff Springs Road. Cross the railroad tracks, then turn right to get

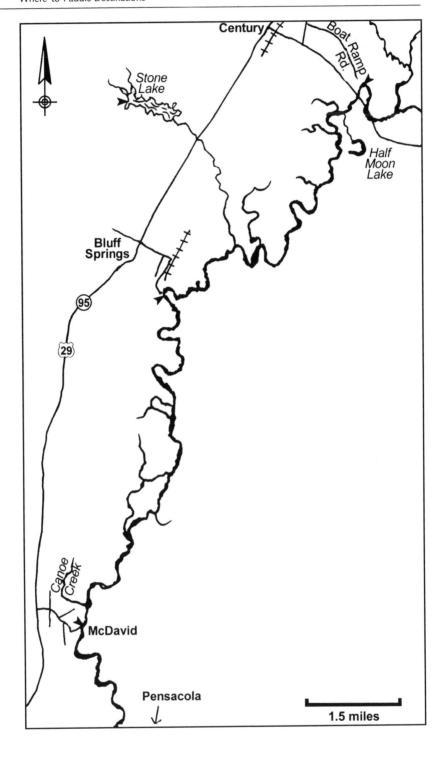

to the ramp. There is a fish camp there, but it's not always open and doesn't seem to have a telephone.

You can deadhead a car downstream at the public ramp at McDavid, five and a half miles south of the Blue Springs 29/95 intersection. To find the ramp, turn east on Mystic Springs Road, about three-quarters of a mile south of the SR164 intersection in McDavid, and watch for the ramp sign.

If you want a longer trip, again leave a car at McDavid, near the old B&L catfish pond, and launch your boat further upstream at Happy Valley ramp. This ramp lies north of SR4, a couple of miles south of Tarzan, Florida. From the intersection of US29 and SR4, go east on SR4 for a quarter mile, then turn left/north on Campbell Road. Follow this as it arches south. On the left Old Ferry Road and Boat Ramp Road merge. Take Boat Ramp Road to Oyster Lodge at the end.

If you do this longer section from Happy Valley to McDavid, plan on three to five hours of float time, plus fishing time.

Try to leave the Happy Valley ramp early, so you can visit Half Moon Lake. This old oxbow lake was once the main channel of the Escambia. The outlet canal is the first stream to the left after you pass under the SR4 bridge. The canal is sometimes narrowed by weed growth in late summer, but it's usually open in the spring. The lake is shaped like a horseshoe, with the open end facing due west. The outlet canal is at the north tip.

About halfway down between Bluff Springs and McDavid, the surrounding land lowers, and you're in a marshy area that extends all the way down to Escambia Bay. The banks are deceptively overgrown, and from the water you'll think you're in a full-growth forest. While it is possible to run the entire river, none of the fisherfolk I talked to knew of any camping areas.

Destination 5: Holmes Creek

Miles or average time: 19 miles, in four stages of 3, 9, 1, and 6 miles

Skill level: advanced beginner

Current: slow

Wind problems: mixed, mostly sheltered waters

Emergency numbers: 911; Washington County sheriff, (850) 638-6111

Rentals: Cypress Springs Canoe Trail, PO Box 726, Vernon FL 32462, phone (850) 535-2960, website www.cypressspringsfla.com

DeLorme page 30, section C-3

Official Florida canoe trail? yes

Many springs flow into this waterway. The largest is Cypress Springs, which the U.S. Geological Survey measured at 89 million gallons per day. The next largest is Becton Springs (recently renamed Magnolia Springs), with 40 million gallons a day. The whole area is riddled with deep springs that open far underground into vast, dark, silty caves. Scuba divers come from around the world to dive these truly hidden realms.

While the springs contribute some of the water in Holmes Creek, rainwater adds a huge volume. At low water, stumps and fallen trees are visible, while at high water you'll be weaving your way through tree branches.

You can add an extra three miles by putting in at Cypress Springs, which has rental canoes for the three-mile section of the run. The spring itself gushes from a pool 150 feet wide and 30 feet deep. Divers can go down 65 feet, and the snorkeling is good. The spring pool is surrounded by thick over-

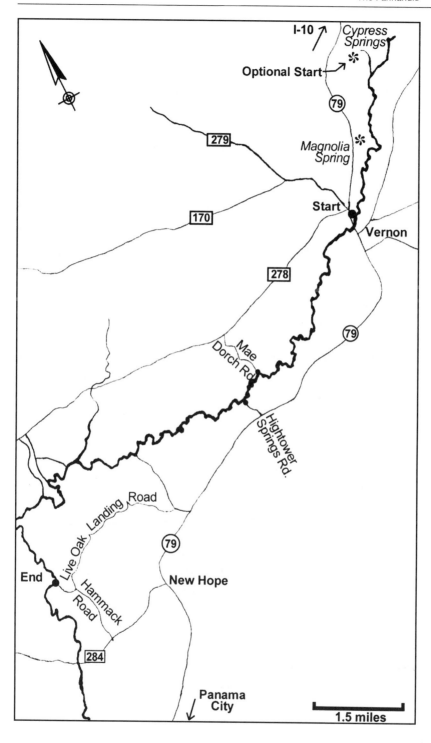

I-10 ↗ Cypress
Springs

Optional Start ↗ ✻

(79)

(279)

Magnolia ✻
Spring

(170)

Start

Vernon

(278)

(79)

Mae
Dorch Rd.

Hightower
Springs Rd.

Live Oak Landing Road

(79)

Hammack
Road

End

New Hope

(284)

Panama
City

1.5 miles

hanging trees, and in the dry season the outflow canal from the spring is bigger than the main river.

There is a small concession stand at the spring. The spring operators ask that all boaters check their gear to make sure no water weeds are brought into the basin.

To get to Cypress Springs, take exit 17 from I-10 and go south on SR79 for seven miles. The spring entrance will be on your left—watch for the red canoe sign. To get to the springs from the south, drive north from the Vernon Bridge for two and a half miles. The spring is on your right.

About halfway between Cypress Springs and the tiny town of Vernon, Magnolia/Becton Springs comes in from the west. This small spring is on private property. Plans are reputed to be in the works to improve this area for scuba diving, camping, and swimming.

1) Vernon Wayside Park to Brunson landing, 9 miles. From Vernon, head north on SR79. Cross the bridge, and turn right/east to the little park.

2) Brunson landing to Hightower Springs landing, 1 mile. By car, take CR278 from Vernon. Watch for a dirt road named Mae Dorch Road going off to the south. Keep to the left/south when it splits. Follow that for a mile to Brunson landing.

3) Hightower Springs landing to Live Oak landing, 6 miles. From Vernon, take SR79 south for 4 miles. Turn north onto Hightower Springs Road and go half a mile to the river.

4) The last landing is at Live Oak, six miles downstream. From the tiny town of New Hope, go west on CR284 for a mile and a half to a second dirt road called Hammack Road. Take Hammack north just under a mile until it gets to a T-intersection. Turn left on Live Oak Landing Road and go to the water.

From here the river continues south and goes under CR284. There is access there, for a small fee, which gives you a bit more river to explore.

The river has been described as "primitive wilderness swampy Florida." If the ground is really soggy, be careful where you drive. Locals claim that in the rainy season, the dirt roads have potholes big enough to hide a Buick.

Also try www8.myflorida.com/communities/learn/trails/canoe or www.panamacity.com/recreation/springs/cypress/.

Destination 6: Perdido River

> Miles or average time: 9 miles
>
> Skill level: beginner
>
> Current: slow, except for heavy rains
>
> Wind problems: few
>
> Emergency numbers: 911; Escambia County sheriff, (850) 436-9630
>
> Rentals: Adventures Unlimited Outdoor Center, 160 River Annex Road, Cantonment FL 32533, phone (850) 968-5529 or 1-888-863-1364
>
> DeLorme page 26, section C-1
>
> Official Florida canoe trail? yes

I saw a whole family of wild hogs here. Mom and her eight or nine Chihuahua-sized piglets were milling around on a sandy beach when I rounded a curve. The mom grunted and took off, with the piglets squealing behind her. Every single black back disappeared within four seconds.

This north-south-running river is the border between Florida and Alabama. It is lovely, full of shady bends and nooks, lined with towering cypress trees. If you paddle early in the morning, either try to get way out ahead of the other canoes or remind the other paddlers of the tradition that no one talks during a dawn paddle. You'll hear an amazing array of birdcalls, the plop of turtles diving into the river, the *kee-row* of hawks, and maybe the full gallop of piglets that I heard.

Like the Blackwater and the Coldwater Rivers, the Perdido has a white sand bottom, with numerous sandbars and sandbanks. The water itself is honey-colored, shading to darkest red in the deep spots. Unlike the Escambia

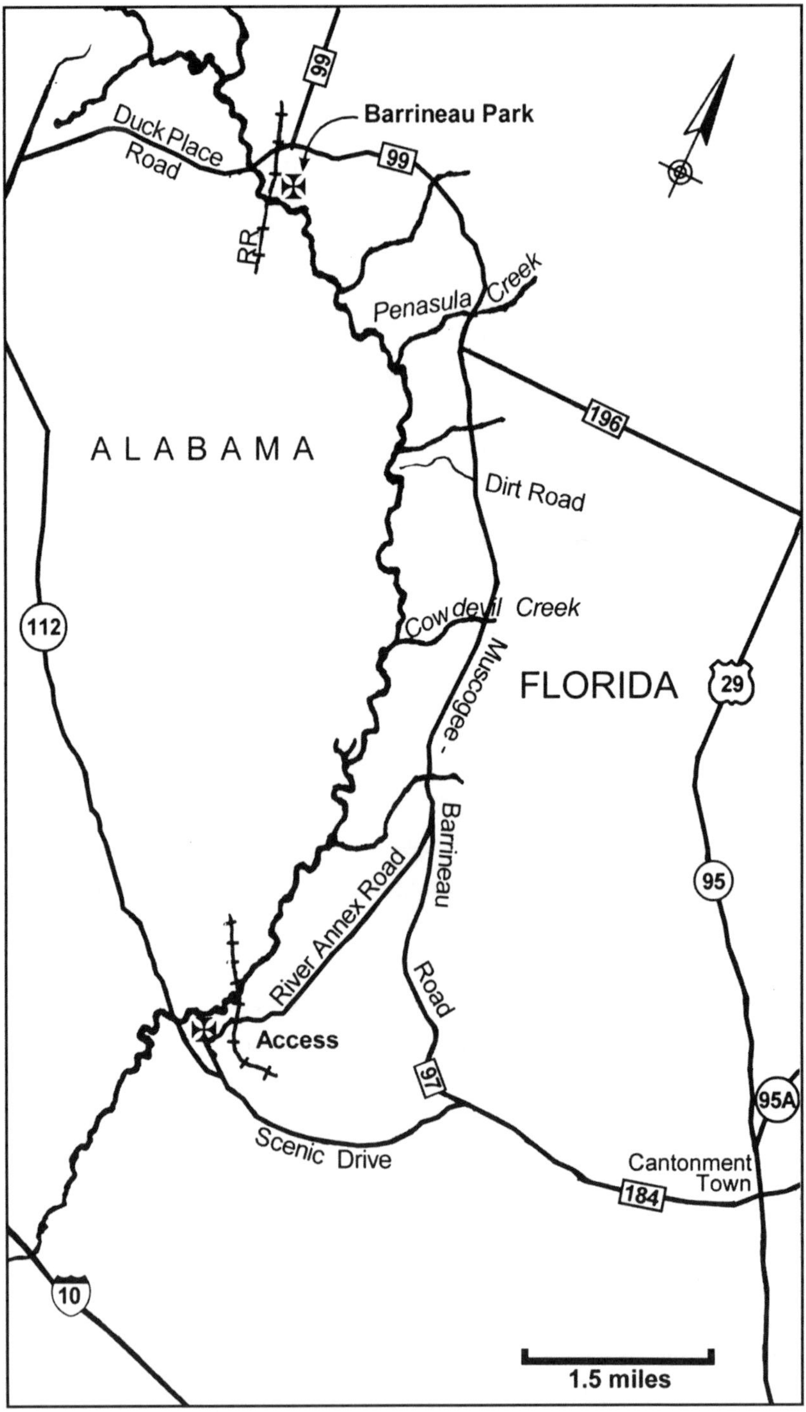

Barrineau Park
Duck Place Road
99
99
RR
Penasula Creek
196
ALABAMA
Dirt Road
Cowdevil Creek
112
Muscogee - Barrineau Road
FLORIDA
29
River Annex Road
95
Access
97
95A
Scenic Drive
Cantonment Town
184
10
1.5 miles

River, which parallels it about ten miles to the east, this is not a swamp-bordered river. For the most part, the Perdido runs between high, dry banks.

The fishing is good, and you'll find both largemouth and smallmouth bass, plus a half dozen kinds of panfish. I was told that my Florida fishing license was okay and I didn't need to buy an Alabama license to fish this river. No guns or dogs are allowed on the Alabama side.

The official canoe trail is nine miles long, and begins at Barrineau Park, which is beside the railroad tracks on the east side of the river, where CR99 turns north from CR196. The river access is at the end of the dirt road that heads west.

Both locals and the Department of Environmental Protection warn that this is an iffy place to leave a car. If you are deadheading cars, leave the oldest one here, with all valuables tucked out of sight.

The river makes a long arc, heading southeast for the first three miles, then slowly turning to head due south. By my rough way of estimating distance, I count fourteen left turns.

There are many places to picnic, but watch for No Trespassing signs on either side. These are probably landowners that had their riverbanks trashed by boaters in the past and now won't allow anyone to set foot on their land.

About two-thirds of the way down, the river narrows and bumps over shoals. There are a few deadfalls and stumps that you can squeeze past, but the river is mainly clear.

The official trail ends at Adventures Unlimited. To get there from Cantonment, head west on CR184 until you reach a fork. The pavement changes here, and CR184 becomes a narrower "scenic drive" with overhanging branches and a tunnel effect. This same road becomes Alabama 112 on the west side of the river. This hamlet is called Muscogee. After a mile and a half, turn right/north on River Annex Road. Watch for the signs for the livery about a mile up the road, on the left. There is an access fee to launch your own canoe or kayak.

Other paddle-able parts of the river start at Jackson Springs Road and go all the way to US90. The upper part is narrower and faster, with more logjams. The folks at Adventures Unlimited can tell you what sections are doable on the days you plan to paddle.

For more information, try the Escambia County Tourist Bureau, phone 1-800-874-1234, or www8.myflorida.com/communities/learn/trails/canoe or www.floridaparks.com/canoeflorida or www.abfla.com/1tocf/natf/canoe or www.visitpensacola.com/nature.html.

Destination 7: Shoal River

Miles or average time: 27 miles, in three segments of 10, 8, and 9 miles

Skill level: beginner to intermediate

Current: easy, but fluctuates at high water

Wind problems: few, almost all sheltered waters

Emergency numbers: 911; Okaloosa County sheriff, (850) 651-7400

DeLorme page 29, section B-1

Official Florida canoe trail? yes

In this area of the Florida panhandle, most people head to Milton and the Blackwater River or Sweetwater Creek when they want to go paddling. But there is another beautiful river that is about thirty miles east of the Blackwater, even more secluded, and practically nontraveled—the Shoal River.

It's a narrow, twisty river. I've paddled it during the rainy season, and the water was waist deep. Its average depth the rest of the year is about to your knee, with occasional deep spots.

There are plenty of sandbars for camping. The river has uncountable little coves and niches, and further downstream are spatterdock-covered ponds to explore. This is a good river to angle for bass, panfish, and catfish.

We had catfish for breakfast one morning. We were doing the first two sections for a total of eighteen miles. We'd done the longest portion the first day, and found a sandbar on the left downriver from SR393. After supper I baited a #4 hook with a chunk of Vienna sausage, slid a big sinker onto some 50-pound-test line, tossed it into a deeper hole under an overhanging tree,

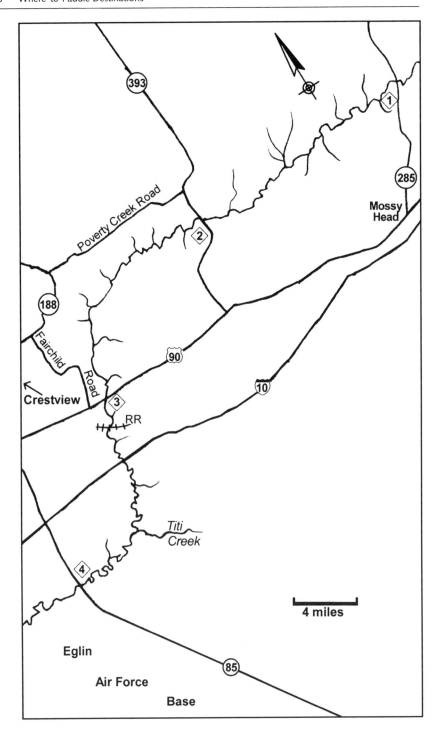

and tied the line to a root. I checked it several times during the evening, and had to replace the bait once. Then I forgot it and went to bed.

The next morning, the line was taut. I pulled in a huge catfish, as long as my arm. Everyone scrapped other plans for breakfast while a buddy skinned and cleaned the cat. Rolled in cornmeal, flour, and a pinch of salt, it was wonderful—fresh, steaming, and delicious, positively the best breakfast I've ever had on the water.

This is a dark-water river, shading from the lightest honey color at the edges to darkest wine-black in the deep holes. Trees overhang the water, and there are the usual number of spiderwebs. The bow person on the first canoe to head downstream each morning gets to find all these with her face.

Some thirty-three creeks empty into the Shoal River, at regular intervals about a mile apart. That means that during the rainy season, a huge volume of water is dumped into this river. I've wriggled past head-high piles of debris snagged on fallen trees. If you're heading out during extremely high water, be prepared to stop often to watch for strainers (fallen trees that the current will trap you against).

1) SR285 to SR393, 10 miles. The official trail starts in Walton County, at the SR285 bridge. (On some maps, SR285 is marked as SR2A or CR1087). From I-10, take the SR285/Mossy Head exit. Turn north, and SR285 joins US90 for about two miles, then splits off and heads north. The river is just short of three miles northeast of Mossy Head. The main access on the southwest side of the bridge has some potholes and loose sand, so check out all four sides of the bridge to see what is drivable the day you arrive.

During flood stages, dangerous debris can pile up in the first ten-mile section of the river at the base of two small wooden bridges, the Hinote Road bridge and the Richardson-DeShaoz Road bridge.

In this section, I counted nine creeks coming in from the South, and six from the north, and thirty-four left turns.

2) SR393 to US90, 8 miles. The river arcs to the west, then slowly bends south until it hits the Old Spanish Trail/US90. This part is a bit wider, and truly wilderness, with no roads getting too close. I counted only eight clear left turns, but another way to tell when you're close to the end is with your compass. You'll run at a compass reading of 200° for about a mile, hit a

small arc to the west, then south for a mile, then run 200° for a half mile before you come to US90. Of course, you'll hear the cars on US90 for the last half hour, which is another way of telling where you are.

3) US90 to SR85, 9 miles. The last official section makes a nice day's paddle. You'll start about four miles due east of the town of Crestview, at the bridge over US90. The ramp is on the southeast side of the bridge.

About a quarter of the way, you'll pass an old railroad trestle. At half-way, which is usually two miles or two hours, you'll pass under I-10 (no access). This is a wide part of the river, with turpentine pines on the sandy high banks. There's one creek coming in from the right and two from the left.

After you pass under I-10 the river becomes more twisty. I counted twenty-one left turns, with four rivers coming in from the right/north and seven from the south/left. About an hour and a quarter after you go under I-10, you'll see a big creek entering from the south. This is Titi Creek, and the edge of Eglin Air Force Base. The Shoal River now dips in and out of the north boundary of the base. If you want to paddle through Air Force prop-erty, you'll need a permit. It's easiest to do it by mail a couple of weeks before the trip. Send $5 and a photocopy of your driver's license to Eglin AFB, Natural Resources Branch, 107 Highway 85 North, Niceville FL 32578, phone (850) 882-4164.

4) The official trail ends at the SR85 wayside park five miles south of Crestview. About fifty yards on the north side of the bridge is a little road going off on the right/east, which leads down the river and the picnic tables and ramp.

You can continue downstream with a bit more paperwork. The Shoal River enters the Yellow River (see destination 11) about six miles down-stream, and the Yellow continues into Blackwater Bay northeast of Pensacola.

For more information, try the Walton County Chamber of Commerce at (851) 682-3212, or www8.myflorida.com/communities/learn/trails/canoe.

Destination 8: St. Joe Bay

Miles or average time: no limit, explore at your own pace

Skill level: beginner near shore, strong paddler in wind

Current: steady tidal flows, especially near mouth of bay

Wind problems: yes, in open waters

Emergency numbers: 911; Gulf County sheriff, (850) 227-1115

Rentals: Broke-A-Toe's, PO Box 486, Port St. Joe FL 32457, phone (850) 229-WAVE, e-mail mmc1@gtcom.net, website www.capesanblas.com/broke-a-toes/

DeLorme page 59, section B-3

Official Florida canoe trail? no

Years ago, I met an old fisherman who lived in Port St. Joe, and told him I was looking for a place to go canoeing in the bay. This was long before modern materials made kayaks popular, and canoes were all we had. Was there a good launching spot, and a pretty place to go paddle, I asked? He grinned, waved his hand toward the sparkling waters and said:

"This here's the perfect place. Really. There's room for fishermen and oyster tongers and even women that want to waste time paddling when they could be using a motor. If you're determined, go ahead. Inside the bay you can always find a place to take that canoe of your'n, if you really want to paddle. There's creeks and sandbars and bayous. Jist watch out for the wild hogs—they'll get into your gear and tear it up, jist for meanness."

I haven't seen a wild hog here yet, but I've visited the bay in both summer and winter, and it does indeed have room for everyone.

St. Joseph Bay is a huge, shallow bay snuggled inside the long crooked

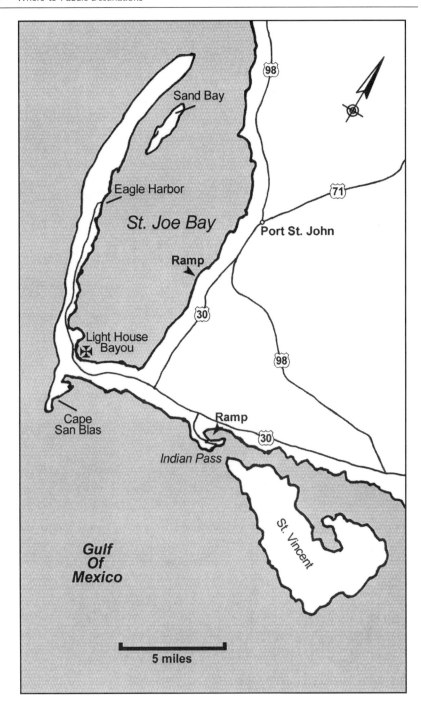

For 10,000 years the clean waters around St. Joe Bay have produced luscious oysters. The scenery is good too. Courtesy of Tom Brocato.

finger of St. Joseph Peninsula and Cape San Blas. Fortunately, a third of the peninsula has been made into a 2,516-acre state park and wildlife refuge. The land area boasts dense pine and cabbage palm forests, a long stretch of white beach on the Gulf side, and some remarkable sand dunes.

Just to the east of St. Joseph Bay is Apalachicola Bay, but the two don't connect. St. Joe Bay extends north and south in almost a perfect rectangle. Apalachicola Bay is a long minnow shape that stops with its nose up against the base of Cape San Blas. The two bays are quite different, even though they're within ten miles of each other.

In the fall, both monarch butterflies and several species of hawks make this part of their migratory flyway. More than 216 species of birds have been seen here, including bald eagles that nest and stay year-round.

Canoe rentals are available from Broke-A-Toe's canoe liveries. There are two walk-in shops, one at Turtle Beach Inn B&B, phone (850) 229-9366, in the Camp Palm area where CR30A makes an abrupt east turn to head toward

Indian Pass, and the other at Indian Pass Campground. Tom recommends that you call in advance to (850) 229-WAVE to reserve boats, get weather reports, or get help finding a place to stay.

There are no motels on the peninsula. You can stay in the campground at the state park, or if you make reservations far in advance at (850) 227-1327, you might get one of their cabins.

Because the bay is almost landlocked, with only a relatively small opening at the top end, you'd think the waters would be stagnant. Not so. The opening at the north end of the bay is five miles across. The level of pollution in the bay is supposed to be the lowest in the entire Gulf area. True, there are stretches of pebbly sand, but no mud banks. The miles and miles of sea grasses grow in firm sand.

The nearby waters are ideal for shellfish. Scallops thrive in the grassy flats. Apalachicola Bay oysters are world famous. Large stretches of spoil banks and oyster beds are leased to commercial oyster fishermen, such as the Cat Point, Dry Bar, Ward, and McNeill beds.

Eating shellfish here is a tradition that stretches back at least ten thousand years, to when the earliest Indians arrived. Archeologists have identified seven different cultures or waves of immigration in this area. These old Indians ate so many oysters that they left behind huge mounds of the empty shells. One is visible in Indian Pass, between St. Vincent Island and the mainland.

I thought the mounds in Indian Lagoon, which marks the western end of Apalachicola Bay, were middens or kitchen mounds, but Tom Brocato, the original livery operator, says they are believed to have been made as deliberate fishing stations for the Indians. Shell middens, he says, are present on St. Vincent Island and Indian Pass.

St. Vincent Island was a hunting preserve years ago, and some of the original sambar deer have stayed. They seem to like the coastal areas, while the native white-tailed deer stay more inland. The wild hogs may be descendants of the three hundred pigs Hernando DeSoto brought over from Spain in 1513.

The Cape San Blas Lighthouse is one of the most photographed structures along this coast. Painters love to portray the two old wooden houses of the light keepers. One is decaying picturesquely beside the Gulf of Mexico, while the other is undergoing careful restoration. Further south is the St. George Lighthouse, which used to lean at a 30°-plus tilt. Every time a storm brewed, pundits predicted with absolute authority that *this* time the lighthouse would go over, but it obstinately refused to topple, and has recently been righted.

The Intracoastal Waterway comes into the north end of the bay, so watch for motorboat traffic there and in the open waters in the center of the sound. But there are many miles of shallows that are perfect for kayaking. You might even have an entire beach to yourself.

Most people take I-10 to zoom east and west along the Florida panhandle. But if you have time, opt for US98, the coastal highway. On the way to St. Joseph Bay, stop off at the tiny town of Carabelle, at the "tail" of Apalachicola Bay. A phone booth there is marked "the world's smallest police station, established 1963." The Carabelle Chamber of Commerce is at (850) 697-2585. The pies at Julie Mae's restaurant, located at the west end of Tillie Miller Bridge, were written up in *Southern Living* magazine. Ask about their parrot in the kitchen. Tom also recommends the Beachcombers Restaurant, "located on the Cape road, within a mile of the C30 turnoff. They're known for their veggie and seafood pizzas, subs, and prime rib dinner specials."

For more information, contact St. Joseph Peninsula State Park, 8899 Cape San Blas Road, Port St. Joe FL 32456, phone (850) 227-1327.

Destination 9: Sweetwater and Juniper Creeks

Miles or average time: 11 miles, in 5- and 6-mile sections

Skill level: intermediate in upper part, beginner downstream

Current: swift, especially after heavy rains

Wind problems: few open areas

Emergency numbers: 911; Santa Rosa County sheriff, (850) 983-1100

Rentals: Adventures Unlimited, Route 6, Box 283, Tomahawk Road, Milton FL 32570, phone (850) 623-6197 or 1-800-239-6864, e-mail aunlimited@aol.com

DeLorme page 27, section B-3

Official Florida canoe trail? yes

These are beautiful rivers. The water is clear reddish brown, and the white sandy bottom almost glows through the shallower parts. There are usually plenty of white sandbars for picnics and camping.

You're inside the Blackwater River State Forest, with almost no access points except at the three bridges, which means you're out in the boonies with no civilization. Because the water is too shallow and logjammed for motorboats, the only people you will meet will be other canoers. It makes good sense, then, to make sure you have a first-aid kit and lots of water, snacks, and other common-sense supplies.

The canoe trail runs for eleven miles. The upper part, on the Sweetwater, is tunnel-like, with overarching trees and cool shadows. It's intermediate in skill level, as it is narrower and more tortuous and has more logjams, pull-

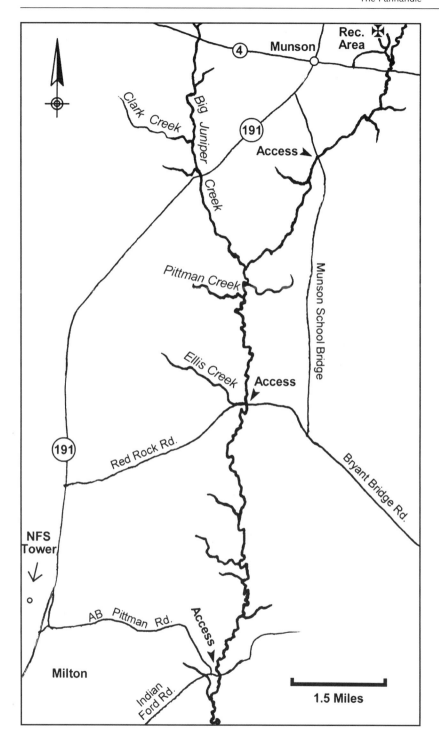

overs, and bump-overs. The current is also faster, and after heavy rains it can be tricky.

Big Juniper Creek comes into the Sweetwater about halfway down the first run. It adds much more water, and the river now widens and slows down. It's deeper too. Check with Adventures Unlimited for their advice on running the river at both high and low water levels.

You can try a couple of older runs. Several old canoe guidebooks show a run starting at the SR4 bridge, but the access is weedy and overgrown, plus this is a very narrow part of the river, with many obstructions.

There is also access at Munson Recreation Area. From Munson, head east on SR4, and turn left/north on Krul Recreation Road. You'll find a horseshoe-shaped lake with an outfall canal that runs into Bear Creek and from there to Sweetwater Creek.

A third old run is Big Juniper Creek, putting in both at SR4 west of Munson and where the Juniper crosses under SR191 south of Munson. Just keep in mind that these runs are not kept open, and are probably more work than they are worth.

From the end of the official canoe trail, Sweetwater-Juniper Creeks run almost three miles to join the Blackwater River. If you're a strong paddler, you can paddle to the Blackwater, then turn left/east and paddle upstream for two miles to Blackwater River State Park.

1) Munson School bridge to Red Rock bridge, 5 miles. From the town of Munson, head south on SR191 for about half a mile. Turn left/southwest on Munson School Bridge. This road is also called Sandy Landing Road, and leads to the river. The access is on the northwest side of the river.

2) Red Rock bridge to Indian Ford bridge, 6 miles. From Munson, head south on SR191 for eight miles. Turn left/east at Spring Hill on Red Rock Road, and go three miles to the bridge. The access is on the northeast side of the road, at a picnic area that is popular in the summer.

The name comes from a forty-foot sandstone cliff on the east side of the creek. The clay on the bank has been worn into a short water slide by countless bathing-suit bottoms. According to historians, Andrew Jackson crossed the river here during the Seminole Wars.

3) End your trip at Indian Ford Road. To get there from Milton, head north on SR191 for eight miles. Turn right/east on Indian Ford Road and

drive six miles to the bridge. Access is on the northwest side of the bridge. You can also go east on Ab Pittman Road, across the road from the Forestry Service lookout tower.

For more information, try www8.myflorida.com/communities/learn/trails/canoe or www.gorp.com or www.paddlefl.com.

Destination 10: Wakulla River

> Miles or average time: 3.5 miles or 4 hours round-trip
>
> Skill level: beginner
>
> Current: almost imperceptible
>
> Wind problems: mostly sheltered
>
> Emergency numbers: 911; Wakulla County sheriff, (850) 926-7171
>
> Rentals: TNT Hideaway, 6527 Coastal Highway, Crawfordville FL 32327, phone (850) 925-6412
>
> DeLorme page 50, section C-3
>
> Official Florida canoe trail? yes

There are two access points on the official canoe trail. First is SR365, with a sandy boat ramp beside the bridge. Next is US98, where TNT livery is located. The current is slow enough that you can do a round-trip between these two points in about four hours.

From the starting point at the SR365 bridge, you can paddle upstream only a bit to the fenced edge of Edward Ball Wakulla Springs State Park. Private boats are not allowed inside the park, and it's a good thing. The place is overrun with alligators. There's a swimming area beside the spring that I wouldn't enter on a bet. Alligators may be fine for the tourists who pay to take the guided tour boats, but they're a little stressful for canoers and kayakers. Stay in the main river and you'll be all right.

The spring itself is advertised as "one of the largest and deepest freshwater springs in the world." Over two thousand ducks, coots, herons, and other birds winter and breed near this short stretch.

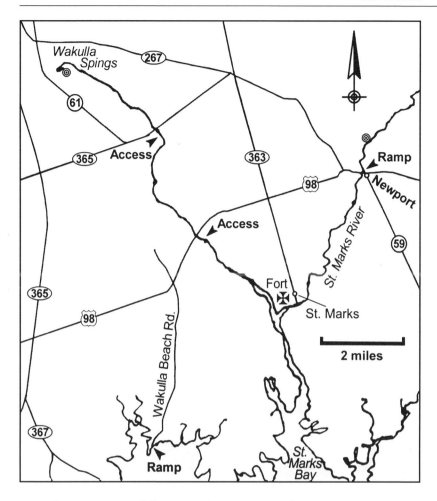

In the upper part of the river where motor craft are more sparse, you'll find a delightful realm of ancient cypress trees bedecked with Spanish moss. Watch for wood duck nest boxes—they are mounted on sturdy tree trunks as high as the box builder could reach while standing in a boat. If you're lucky, you'll see a female duck fly in at full throttle. It always looks like she's going to kill herself, but at the last possible moment she pulls up and zips inside the hole without mussing a feather.

Because of the volume of water coming out of the spring, the river stays quite clear down to the US98/SR30 bridge, which is the end of the official trail.

It is also possible to continue downstream. The river widens and there is more boat traffic and wind, so be careful. You can deadhead a car at Shell Island—drive down SR363 to the end, turn right, and watch for St. Marks City Park. You can keep paddling to the conjunction of the St. Marks and Wakulla Rivers. Turn left/east, and hug the left bank until you get to the Wakulla County ramp.

From this point the river slowly expands into a wide tidal marsh. Watch for mud flats and exposed sandbars at low tide. The fishing is pretty good along here. Treble hooks are illegal.

San Marcos de Apalache State Historic Site is an interesting place to visit. It was first visited by Pánfilo de Narváez in 1528. The fort was started in 1679. I spent an hour talking to the ranger whose grandfather collected the artifacts that are in the small interpretive museum. He has a dozen stories, and makes the site come alive.

For more information, contact Wakulla Springs State Park, 1 Spring Drive, Wakulla Springs FL 32305, phone (850) 224-5950.

San Marcos de Apalache State Historic Site is on Old Fort Road. Information is available from San Marcos de Apalache State Historic Site, c/o Tallahassee–St. Marks Historic Railroad State Trail, 1022 Desoto Park Drive, Tallahassee FL 32301, phone (850) 922-6007, www.abfla.com/parks/SanMarco.

Also try www8.myflorida.com/communities/learn/trails/canoe or www.paddlefl.com/destinations/Wakulla.

Destination 11: Yellow River

Miles or average time: 56 miles, in four segments

Skill level: intermediate

Current: fast upstream, slower past Route 90

Wind problems: lower river is open and wide

Emergency numbers: 911; Santa Rosa County sheriff, (850) 983-1100; Okaloosa County sheriff, (850) 651-7400

DeLorme page 28, section A-2

Official Florida canoe trail? yes

The Yellow River is an official canoe trail. However, it has a few problems. Tiffany Hardy, at Blackwater Canoe Rental in Milton, won't go near it.

"The Yellow River is infested with alligators," she said. "When I go horseback riding along there, I won't even let my horse dip her nose in it. It's always muddy, treacherous, and not friendly at all. It's only good for bass fishing." Her favorite place to paddle is the Sweetwater-Juniper run (destination 9).

On the other hand, the shortest part of this trail, from Crestview to Gin Hole, is the favorite river of a friend of mine. He says, "Hey, it's not for sissies. This is a man's river. You gotta go under a few logs now and then. Make lots of noise and the gators won't bother you. I grab one of my buddies and we do it every spring. It's real pretty."

If you want to extend your paddling, it is possible to paddle the river both north and south of the official trail. You can start in Alabama, cross the Florida line, and end at the SR2 bridge. From the downstream end of the official canoe trail, you can also keep going past SR87 all the way to Blackwater Bay.

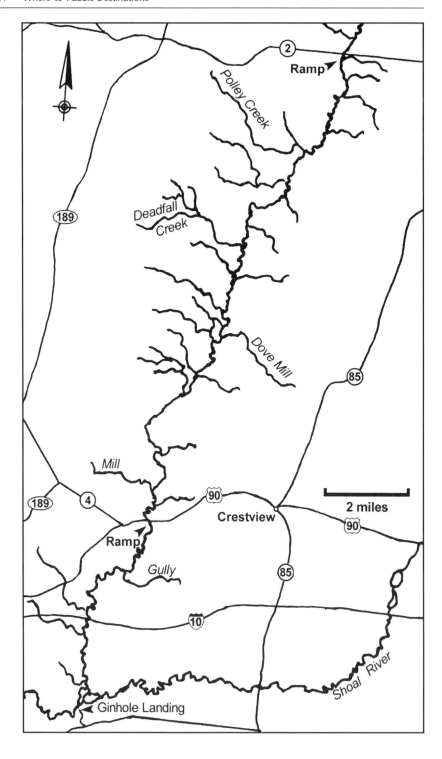

This lower section, however, is through the wide, windy delta of the river, and the boat ramp at Pine Bluff can be hard to find from the water.

The banks are steep at the upper part of the trail, with high bluffs that can reach thirty feet. These alternate with low swamps and small creeks that come in from both sides. Sandbars are few except at low water, so use the ones you do find to stretch your legs. Watch for rocky shoals, which can be completely out of sight in high water, or can form formidable dams in really low water.

To do the ten-mile stretch that starts in Alabama, head north from Crestview on SR85 until you reach Laurel Hill. Go west on 85A. At the Alabama line this becomes CR20. At Alabama SR4, turn west for two miles to the river.

1) SR2 to US90, 17 miles. The official canoe trail begins five miles due south of the Georgia border. Plan on seven to nine hours. The current is a bit fast, but there are enough twists, turns, and tree jams that you won't build up much speed.

From I-10, take the Crestview/SR85 exit. Head north through Crestview (the county seat of Okaloosa County, and also the last place to stock up on supplies) and go thirteen miles. Turn left/west on SR2, which goes straight to the river. The access is on the northeast side of the bridge.

There's a monitoring station on the river at this point. You can check the water level for the day you want to paddle by going to http://waterdata.usgs.gov/nwis-w/FL/?statnum=02368000.

2) US90 to Gin Hole landing, 10 miles. The access is down a dirt road on the southwest side of the river. I count sixteen very short left turns on this section. About halfway down you'll go under I-10 (no access). About a mile above the next stop the Shoal River comes in from the left/east. The river splits up here into two big creeks and a couple of rivulets.

Now the river turns southwest to Gin Hole, then west to its end. All the property on your left belongs to Eglin Air Force Base.

After the Shoal River comes in from the east, it's only about three-quarters of a mile to the next access point, which is Gin Hole landing. It's not an official trail launch area but is popular with Air Force fishermen. Watch for a medium bluff on your left. This is called Rattlesnake Bluff. Gin Hole landing is past this on the left.

3) Gin Hole landing to SR189, 8 miles. To get to Gin Hole by car, go south on SR85 from Crestview. One mile south of the Shoal River, turn right/west onto a military road. Just over a mile after this road turns to the southwest, watch for another dirt road going north to the river.

4) SR189 access, 14 miles. From I-10, take the Holt/SR189 exit. Turn south on Log Lake Road. Just under two miles south, watch for the access by the old fish camp on the left/south. This part of the river is full of shellcracker and bluegill.

5) The end of the official trail is at the SR87 bridge. From the tiny town of Harold, head west for six miles on US87, then left/south on SR87. The bridge is three miles past I-10.

For a permit to enter the military reservation, send $5 and a photocopy of your driver's license to Eglin AFB, Natural Resources Branch, 107 Highway 85 North, Niceville FL 32578, phone (850) 882-4164.

For more information on the little-known Yellow River, try the Okaloosa Convention and Visitors Bureau at 1540 Miracle Strip Parkway SE, Fort Walton Beach FL 32549, phone (850) 651-7131. The official Department of Environmental Protection directions are at www8.myflorida.com/communities/learn/trails/canoe. Also try www.paddlefl.com.

Area 2. Northeast Florida

Destination 12: Alexander Springs

Miles or average time: 7.5 miles

Skill level: beginner

Current: moderate and steady

Wind problems: some open areas

Emergency numbers: 911; Lake County sheriff, (352) 343-2101

Rentals: Alexander Springs Recreation Area, 49525 County Road 445, Altoona FL 32702, phone (352) 669-3522

DeLorme page 73, section D-3

Official Florida canoe trail: no

Alexander Creek starts off in a narrow channel bottomed with brilliant white sand. It widens out to a broad river for about the first five miles, narrows for two miles, and then widens again when it gets to the first ramp seven miles to the southeast. It meanders past some beautiful piney woods, with a selection of water meadows and marshes along the way.

Alexander Springs Recreation Area is a popular park, with a campground, a tiny food concession, and white sandy beaches. The local scuba diving schools bring their students here for their final checkout dives. They always head for hidden holes, so watch for diver's flags and/or bubbles coming up from below.

The park concession owns fifty-eight two- and four-person canoes, and arranges pickup downstream. As with any state park, bring food only in nondisposable containers, such as Tupperware.

If you have your own canoe, there is an extra three-and-a-half-mile section beyond the park shuttle pickup site. You have to follow the forest roads

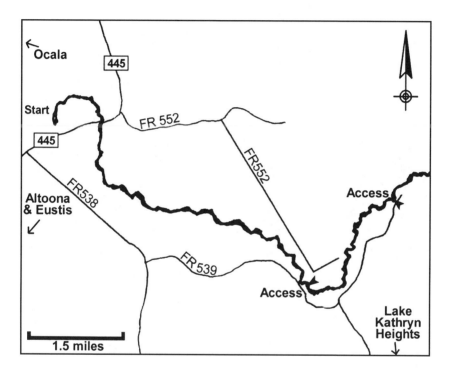

White sand bottoms and clear water mark central Florida's springs. Courtesy of Gloria Kuchinskas.

south of the streambed to deadhead your car. However, it's tricky getting there by car. The narrow forest roads all look alike, don't seem to have numbers, and have dead ends heading off at odd angles. So if you're interested in this stretch, ask the ranger at the park for one of her free, informal maps—or find a bass fisherman going in that direction and tag along behind.

Carol Beal, who helps run the concession, had just gone down the seven-and-a-half-mile run from the park two weeks before I called to check out the shuttle service. "We'd had complaints that people couldn't find the main channel, so one of our workers went down and marked trees with bright orange paint," she said. "But when we paddled it, we came to an unmarked fork, and went to the right. Evidently the main channel went to the left, because we came to a very narrow section, and had to go under tree limbs, and push our way along with our hands. Still, it was exciting, and fun, and we got to the end of the run just fine. And our worker is going back to remark the route."

You can reach the park by taking SR445 from US19. There is a usage fee.

Destination 13: Ashby Lake and Cassadaga Town

Miles or average time: no limit, paddle at your own speed

Skill level: beginner

Current: no

Wind problems: some, in open part of lake

Emergency numbers: 911; Volusia County sheriff, (904) 736-5961

Rentals: Beachside Bike & Kayak, 533 Third Avenue, New Symrna Beach FL 32169, phone (904) 426-8684

DeLorme page 81, section A-1

Official Florida canoe trail: no

The town of Cassadaga is due north of Deltona, north of exit 54 on I-4. And it's actually not that close to Lake Ashby.

Cassadaga is special because it is a village (once called a camp) just for spiritualists. Back in 1894 an Indian ghost named Seneca led two "seekers" to this precise spot. Now the Southern Cassadaga Spiritualist Camp Meeting Association owns thirty-five acres of the town, with headquarters right in the town center. In this community of small streets and Depression-era wooden homes, the locals are quite happy about being undiscovered. You can have your palm read, the bumps on your head read, your horoscope read, and your runes cast. Just drive up and down the four north-south streets that comprise the village, and watch for signs in the oak-shaded cottages. Be sure to check the bulletin board at the meeting hall downtown to see who is giving readings, or which big-name mediums are in town to lead the Sunday church

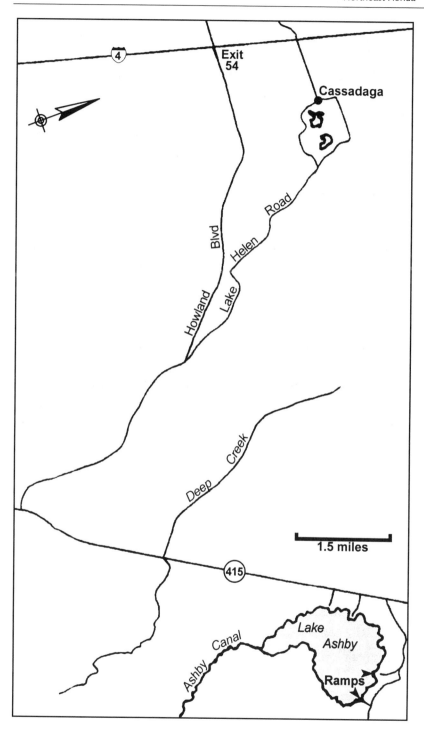

services and the Tuesday and Thursday night sessions. Of course there are always the weekly bingo games.

To get to Lake Ashby from Cassadaga, head southeast on Lake Helen Road/Howland Boulevard to where it intersects with SR415. Turn north on 415 and go about five miles to Lake Ashby Road.

Here are the directions put out by the Florida Wildlife Commission to the ramp they maintain: "From the intersection of SR415 and Enterprise Osteen Road in the town of Osteen, go north on SR415 for 8.0 miles to Lake Ashby Road. Turn right onto the unpaved road, and follow it to the ramp at the dead end of the road. The ramp is single lane, with an unimproved parking lot that can hold six vehicles."

The lake itself is notable in that it is only eight miles (as the crow flies) west of I-95, yet few tourists know about its secret location so close to the ultrabusy Space Coast. This is one lake that is so far out in the sticks that it's hard to even describe where it is.

Lake Ashby Canal wanders south to join the old Deep Creek riverbed, and eventually connects with the St. Johns River just above Lake Harney.

The lake is reputed to hold some of the biggest bass in the state. But if you don't catch a lunker during your own visit, it might be because some of the Cassadaga psychics knew just exactly where to fish, and got there ahead of you.

Destination 14: Aucilla River

Miles or average time: 19 miles, in 6- and 13-mile sections

Skill level: intermediate to advanced

Current: strong

Wind problems: some open stretches

Emergency numbers: 911; Jefferson County sheriff, (850) 997-2523; Madison County sheriff, (850) 973-4151; Taylor County sheriff, (850) 584-4225

Rentals: The Canoe Shop, 1115 West Orange Avenue #B, Tallahassee FL 32310, phone/fax (850) 576-5335, www.paddlenorthflorida.com

DeLorme page 51, section B-3

Official Florida canoe trail: yes

Two of my friends had a big argument about the Aucilla. One said it was so easy that he went through both dams without touching his paddle, and he pronounced it doable for everyone and his ninety-year-old grandmother. The other friend insisted that the river was just a series of little ponds connected by an almost dry river channel, and said she had never worked so hard in her life.

These folks went paddling at completely different times of the year. Try to go at medium to high water. In times of drought, or of very high water, use caution. The current on the Aucilla is usually swift, and there are a goodly number of curves, rapids, deadfalls, and rocks to navigate.

This is a wilderness trip. You'll see very little evidence of mankind for most of the route. The Aucilla starts in Georgia and crosses into Florida almost directly between Tallahassee and Perry. It travels through forest for

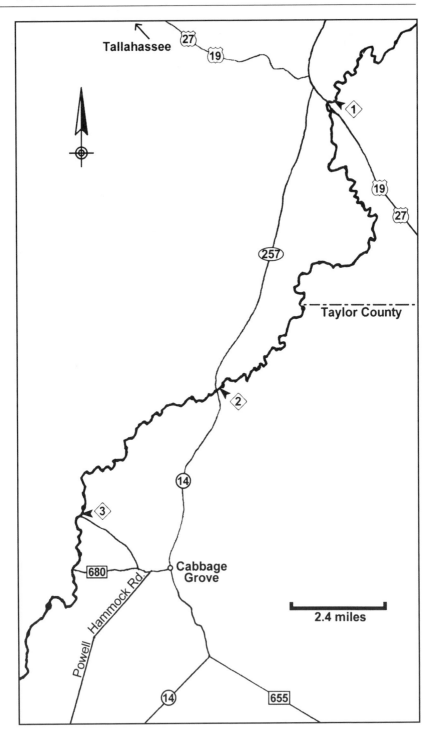

most of its length. It parallels the Wacissa, which lies to the west, and they open into the Gulf of Mexico only two miles apart. The old Slave Canal dug in the 1800s connects these two rivers close to US98.

Because of overhanging trees and logjams, you'll need to bend down or step out of your boat now and then, so open canoes or sit-on-top kayaks are the recommended boats for the Aucilla.

The two ruined man-made dams might have to be portaged. Check these out first, and don't try to "run the vee" if there is a "hole in the water" right below the outfall. A hole in the water is a permanent backwards roll of water, and can suck you or your canoe under and keep it there.

1) US27 to CR257/SR14, 13 miles. Start just south of the town of Lamont, where the river crosses under US19/27.

Just over a mile downriver you'll see the first old stone dam. Approach it slowly and look it over. If need be, portage around it.

You'll see several camping areas on the sections of high ground. In late summer the thick undergrowth makes them hard to see. There is a large one on the left about halfway down this run.

2) CR257/SR14 to the Logging Road, 6 miles. From US27/19, head south on CR257/SR14 to the bridge. The access is a dirt landing that is often rutted. The other side of the river is Taylor County, and the road name changes to CR14.

About two-thirds of the way down the river you'll hear Big Rapids. There are few shoals big enough to be considered real rapids in Florida, and this is one of them. The shape and difficulty of the rapids is very dependent upon water levels.

There is a flat rocky spot on the east side that is often used for picnics and rest (one wag said it's a good place for beginners to work up their courage), and this is the side you'll portage your gear along if you decide to walk instead of ride. Make sure your boat has both bow and stern lines to warp your empty canoe or kayak over the rocks.

3) Logging Road access. The end of the official canoe trail is a bit tricky to find. Here's the description from the Department of Environmental Protection: "To find the finish, take SR257 south from Lamont, over the Aucilla, until the pavement ends. Continue south on the graded road about ¾ of a mile to a tee-intersection at the fire tower. Turn right, go another

¾ mile, and turn right again on a narrow dirt road. Follow this 3.5 miles to the bridge. The takeout is about 300' [a football field length] upstream."

The river goes underground about three miles downstream from here, so you'll need to get out at this point. It comes back up at Nutall Rise, just north of US98.

It is possible to do this section of the Aucilla, then drive to Goose Pasture landing and continue south on the Wacissa. To do this from the last Aucilla takeout, go back to SR14 and head south on Power Hammock Road for two miles, then turn right/west on Goose Pasture Road to the east channel of the Wacissa. From here follow the directions in the chapter on the Wacissa River (see destination 39).

For more information, try www8.myflorida.com/communities/learn/trails/canoe.

Destination 15: Bulow Creek

Miles or average time: 13 miles, in three segments

Skill level: easy, with many gentle bends

Current: little upriver, some tidal flow near mouth

Wind problems: moderate

Emergency numbers: 911; Flagler County sheriff, (904) 437-4116; Volusia County sheriff, (904) 736-5961

Rentals: Bulow Plantation Ruins State Historic Site, PO Box 655, Bunnell FL 32110, phone (904) 517-2084

DeLorme page 74, section A-3

Official Florida canoe trail: yes

In 1823 John Bulow inherited a 4,675-acre plantation from his father. He was only seventeen. His father's two hundred slaves had cleared 2,200 acres and built a sugar mill from huge blocks of coquina rock.

John was friendly with the local Indians and traded with them. But other settlers were having trouble with the Indians. General Hernandez sent Major Benjamin Putnam to set up a command at Bulow's plantation to protect the area's plantations. To show his disapproval, John ordered a three-pound cannon to be fired at the troops when they came up the creek.

His show of protest didn't work. Bulow's slaves were confiscated and he was put under house arrest. The Indians who evaded being moved snuck back at night and burned down the plantation. Disheartened, Bulow finally moved to France, where he died, unmarried, before his thirtieth birthday.

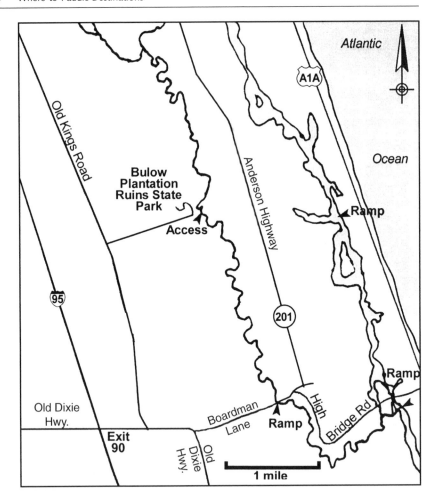

The long graded dirt driveway from Old Kings Road to the ruins is now almost a tunnel. Gnarled junipers and palmetto thickets border the drive where once fields of rice, sugar cane, indigo, and cotton grew.

About a city block from the canoe launch area are the ruins of the old molasses plant and sugar mill. A nicely done display beside the old gray stones shows you what the mill looked like when it was in operation.

Just south of the ramp, notice the four or five boat slips cut into the bank. They're silted in now, but in young Bulow's day, these housed pleasure boats, cargo barges, and even Indian dugouts.

The upstream part of this Florida Primitive Trail runs three and a half miles from the State Historic Site ramp, making a seven-mile round trip. It is a tangled but scenic area, purposely left rough, and you'll appreciate how hard those slaves had to work to clear the land. The ranger said that he often sees wild hogs and a bobcat, but I can only vouch for several ospreys and a giant spiderweb that stretched completely over the creek.

To get to Bulow Plantation Ruins State Historic Site from I-95, take exit 90 and head east on Old Dixie Highway. Turn left/north on Old Kings Road, also called CR2001. Go seven miles to the park. If you bring your own boat, there is a fee for the ramp, plus an entry fee of $2 per car, with up to eight people.

If you go downstream, it is six miles to the Intracoastal Waterway. You can deadhead a car at the ramp that lies just north of the mouth of the creek, on the east side of the Intracoastal Waterway. Maps are available from the ranger.

To drive there from the ruins, head south to Old Dixie Highway. Turn left/east, and go half a mile to Walter Boardman Lane. The bridge of the same name is a mile further east. The parking area has room for only four cars.

There is an additional three-mile section from Walter Boardman Bridge to Highbridge Park. To get there, travel east on Walter Boardman Lane over Bulow Creek to Highbridge Road. Turn right/south to Highbridge Park. Ten to twelve cars can park here.

By canoe or kayak, the round-trip from the ruins to Highbridge Park is nine miles. I recommend checking the tides and wind before you decide which direction to paddle, since it is always easier to paddle with them at your back instead of heading against you. Powerboats share the creek, but there is a posted speed limit and you can always hear them coming. Be alert for big yachts on the Intracoastal, as well as heavy wind and crosscurrents.

For more information, try www.funandsun.com/parks/BulowPlantation/bulowplantation.html or www8.myflorida.com/communities/learn/trails/canoe.

Destination 16: Cross Creek

Miles or average time: no limit, paddle at your own pace

Skill level: beginner

Current: slight

Wind problems: some on the open waters

Emergency numbers: 911; Alachua County sheriff, (352) 955-2500

Rentals: Twin Lakes Fish Camp, 17105 South County Road 325, Hawthorne FL 32640, phone (352) 466-3194

DeLorme page 72, section A-1

Official Florida canoe trail: no

Before you hit the water, read any of Marjorie Kinnan Rawlings's books. Start with *Cross Creek,* then go to *The Yearling* or *South Moon Under.* Or you can rent the tearjerker movie *The Yearling.* Also, J. T. Glisson has written *The Creek.* Any of them will give you a glimpse into backwoods Florida.

Cross Creek is a one-mile channel that runs north-south between Orange and Lochloosa Lakes. It is a dark, slightly curving waterway lined with tall trees that drip with Spanish moss and air plants. You'll meet bass boats and airboats here, but the creek is wide enough that you're not crowded.

The open lakes have recently been rid of acres of floating tussocks of grass, giving boaters more room to roam. Peggy Goldberg, a nature and underwater photographer who explores this creek often, cautions, "The lakes are quite large, and weather can change quickly, making the lakes like an ocean with large waves. Canoeists should exercise caution and stay near the shoreline, where all the wildlife is anyway."

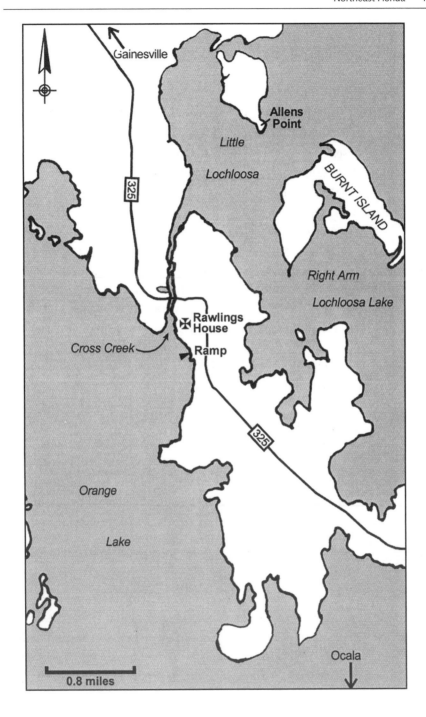

Gainesville

325

Allens
Point

Little

Lochloosa

BURNT ISLAND

Right Arm

Lochloosa Lake

Rawlings
House

Cross Creek

Ramp

325

Orange

Lake

Ocala

0.8 miles

The two lakes are about halfway between Ocala and Gainesville. To get there from Gainesville, take SR20 east toward Hawthorne, then turn right/ south on CR325.

You'll first come to the Marjorie Kinnan Rawlings State Historic Site (Route 3, Box 92, Hawthorne FL 32540, phone (352) 466-3672). Lady guides in high-top shoes and flour-sack dresses take small groups through Marjorie's house. The tours are limited to ten people and fill up fast, and the rangers close for lunch and all possible holidays, so make a reservation early. If you plan your paddling right, you can fit in either an early-morning or a late-afternoon tour.

Rawlings was a journalist from "up north" who bought a small Florida orange grove in the middle of nowhere after a divorce. She brought her city-slicker insights and newspaper writing skills to this rural area, and wrote about the lives and farms of the Florida crackers around her.

Marjorie was a water lover. She certainly paddled Orange and Lochloosa Lakes. This was back when women hadn't been emancipated long, and the farm ladies around Cross Creek didn't go on adventures. Marjorie wrote about a week-long trip she and another woman made on the St. Johns. They sailed off and had a fine time exploring the river. Upon their return they were met by a search party of men, who had assumed that two women alone couldn't possibly cope with a boat and must need rescuing.

The boat ramp shares the same parking lot with the Rawlings house. After you launch, turn right/north and follow the shoreline into Cross Creek. Peggy says, "If the water is real low, you may want to go straight out into Orange Lake, then turn right, hugging the water lilies to avoid the wind and chop of the lake, then turn into Cross Creek."

Unfortunately, the old Yearling Restaurant closed down, as well as a couple of the old fish camps. Instead of orange groves, today you'll pass a mix of cracker dwellings and some nicer homes with docks or grassy lawns going into the creek. A fancy housing development is being advertised too.

Peggy says, "Some of the old wooden cracker houses are still at the end of long weedy driveways, and you can explore the small coves and marshy swamps of these two old lakes. Among the marshy cypress hammocks watch for bald eagles, ospreys, herons, gallinules, and red-winged blackbirds."

This is also big bass country, so if you're looking for a lunker, bring along your tackle box and freshwater license.

There are gators. Peggy saw "numerous huge gators, some of the biggest in the state," but I saw only a couple of babies. When Rawlings lived here, it was the height of the alligator poaching and export business, so you'll probably see more gators than she did.

Cross Creek is an interesting place to paddle. With a bit of imagination, you can easily imagine this area back when it was the rustic home of deep-woods farmers and fishermen. Come to think of it, much of it still is.

For more information, try the Alachua County Visitors Bureau at 30 East University Avenue, Gainesville FL 32601, phone (352) 374-5231. Also try www.theozone.com/history/rawlings526.html or www8.myflorida.com/communities/learn/stateparks/district2 or www.floridainfo.com.

Destination 17: DeLeon Springs

Miles or average time: no limit, paddle at your own pace

Skill level: beginner

Current: slight current in Spring Garden Creek

Wind problems: yes, open marsh areas

Emergency Numbers: 911; Volusia County sheriff, (904) 736-5961

Rentals: DeLeon Springs State Recreation Area, PO Box 1338, DeLeon Springs FL 32130, phone (904) 985-5644

DeLorme page 74, section D-2

Official Florida canoe trail: no

Be sure to have breakfast at the Old Spanish Sugar Mill. Each table has its own built-in grill, where you pour your own pancakes with batter made from flour ground on the old French millstones. You can also order a full picnic at their takeout window.

This area has been occupied by humans for at least eight millennia. A six-thousand-year-old dugout canoe was found here.

The springs are named after Juan Ponce de León, who supposedly stopped here on his journey to find the Fountain of Youth in the late 1500s. There's a road still in Port Orange called Old Sugar Mill Road, and it is probably the original rutted track that led to this plantation. When Audubon visited in 1831, he spoke of the tedium of a full day's journey in a carriage drawn by Indian horses as he came from the Bulow Plantation (see destination 15).

When England took over Florida from 1763 to 1783, a fur-trading company set up shop here to trade with the Indians.

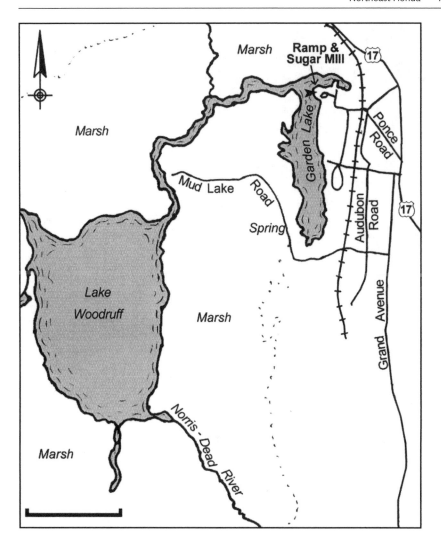

Colonel Orlando Rees originally put in the famous waterwheel to grind sugar cane. The plantation was sacked by Indians during the Second Seminole War (1835 to 1842). The old mill ground away again during the Civil War, producing corn meal and sugar for the Rebels. When Union troops took it over, they demolished more of the facilities to make sure Johnny Reb didn't get to use it again. The restaurant is inside/beside the old mill.

In the 1880s the spring became a resort. Going on the theory that anything that smelled bad had to be good for you, the stinky water was billed as

Some 215 species of birds have been spotted at DeLeon Springs, including great blue herons like this one. Courtesy of Joanne Williams.

a "deliciously healthy combination of soda and sulphur." It's still a pretty spring, surrounded by old oak and cypress trees. You can swim in the 72° spring pool, but not in the outfall channel.

Start your paddle at the boat ramp below the spring basin. You can launch your own craft, or rent a canoe, kayak, or paddleboat. You can stay around the recreation area and explore Spring Garden Lake, or head west on Spring Garden Creek, which leads into the 21,500-acre Lake Woodruff National Wildlife Refuge.

There are no other access points into Lake Woodruff, so you'll paddle back to your car at the original launch spot. The marshes and watery forests of Lake Woodruff are separated here and there with low earthen dikes, but you'll easily spot the open creeks.

Some 215 species of birds have been spotted here, including all of Florida's wading and diving birds. The refuge headquarters on Grand Avenue will have more information and birding lists.

Bring your fishing pole and your freshwater license, since the fishing is good.

For information, contact DeLeon Springs State Recreation Area, PO Box 1338, DeLeon Springs FL 32130, phone (904) 985-4212. The Old Spanish Sugar Mill Grill and Griddle House handles the boat rentals at (904) 985-5644. Also try www.wvolusia.com/deleon or www.abfla.com/parks/DeLeon-Springs/deleon.

Destination 18: Drayton Island

Miles or average time: no limit for exploring NE shoreline; 5–7 hours to circle the island

Skill level: intermediate

Current: yes

Wind problems: yes, and watch for chop

Emergency Numbers: 911; Putnam County sheriff, (904) 329-0800

Rentals: Harley Paiute's Camping Village & Marina, 1269 County Road 309, Crescent City FL 32112, phone (904) 467-7050

DeLorme page 73, section A-2

Official Florida canoe trail: no

I hesitated about including this destination in the book. Lake George currently has the highest concentration of alligators in the state. Botanist William Bartram stopped in this area on his solo trip down the St. Johns in 1772, and this could be the spot where he was attacked by a squadron of huge gators.

But Drayton Island is a lush, deserted place. Centuries ago, the Timucuan Indians lived here and left pottery and shaped shell tools. Just a few miles away (one mile north of the intersection of CR309 and CR308) is Mount Royal, the largest sand mound in Florida. In Florida's pioneer days the island held a strategic place on the St. Johns River, and sprouted piers, docks, warehouses, and cottage farms.

This three-and-a-half-mile-wide island now slumbers quietly. From the waterside you can see almost every house there is on the island. Most of these belong to winter visitors. One old fisherman told me that exactly twelve

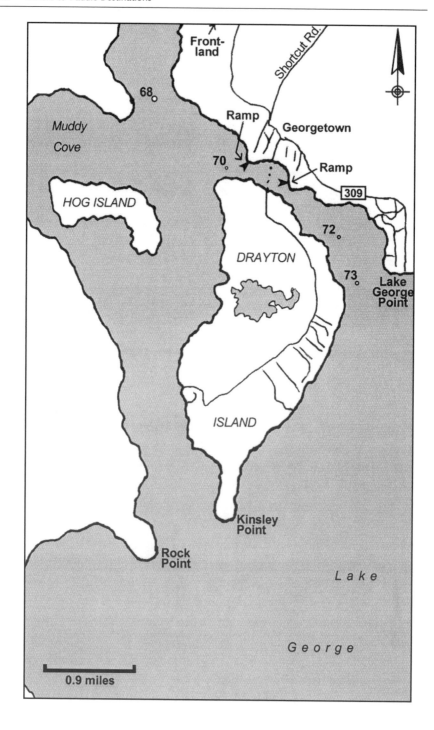

people lived on the island during summer, "but we get lots and lots of people down here in the winter, close on to a hundred!"

A ferry crosses the quarter mile of water separating the island and the mainland. I heard you could bring your canoe or kayak on the ferry, depending on which person is operating the ferry that day. The ferry departure times also differ according to which sign you read, so check first if you're interested. On the island a graded road curves south from the ferry dock to the old abandoned airport with its grassy runway. Short dirt roads head off this main road, going to the eastern shoreline like the spokes on a bicycle.

There are many little nooks and crannies to explore as you paddle around the island. You'll pass whole fields of marsh grasses that sway in the least breeze, duck into tiny coves green with spatterdock lilies, and pull up under the shade of ancient oaks and cabbage palms.

Watch where you get out of your boat. Even if a dock doesn't have a "Private" sign on it, it's privately owned and off limits.

Some huge bass are said to hide under the rickety little docks that front the closed-up cottages. Like my fisherman said, "They stay there all winter, and they's so smart, the minute somebody gets back and opens up one of them houses, the bass feel the vibrations and move away. We got some smart bass 'round here."

Bass fishermen have caught some spectacular lunkers here. A fourteen-pounder had been pulled out of the water just a week before our last visit. The crappies, specks, and bream are also full-sized.

Putnam County calls itself the Bass Capital of the World. The east side of the St. Johns River has some forty fish camps in this county alone, listed at www.lakegeorge.com/marina. Georgetown restaurants specialize in pre-dawn breakfasts for fishermen. You can even paddle up to several for lunch or dinner.

The west bank of the island and the facing side of the St. Johns River is undeveloped. Watch for wild hogs, deer, and possibly a panther. You also have a good chance of seeing sandhill cranes, kites, and all the egrets.

Use normal caution when crossing the main shipping channel on the St. Johns—some big yachts and freighters churn between Georgetown and Drayton Island, plus there's the usual complement of speed-crazy fishermen in overpowered bass boats.

One of the closer ramps is just north of the ferry dock, at the west end of Drayton Island Road. This is at Lunker Lodge Resort (PO Box 659, George-town FL 32139, phone (904) 467-2240), sited directly east of channel marker #70.

South of the ferry dock there are ramps near River Bass Realty and at Riverwood RV Village (PO Box 365, Georgetown FL 32139, phone (904) 467-7144 or 1-888-467-7144), located off CR309 about a mile and a half south of the ferry. Georgetown Marina & Lodge (1533 County Road 309, Georgetown FL 32139, e-mail georgetownmarina@gbso.net) is just a half mile west of the intersection of CR309 and Georgetown Denver Road, across from marker #72.

While you're on CR309, stop at the Welaka National Fish Hatchery, phone (904) 467-2374, just north of Fruitland. It's free, and during the spring and summer up to five million fish are reared in the two sections behind the office building. There's an observation tower at Beecher Spring, and a small aquarium at Welaka, where you can get eyeball to eyeball with critters that normally swim silently under your craft. Largemouth bass, striped bass, and bluegills have been raised here since 1926. I was especially fascinated by the five-foot-long river sturgeon that are being bred here and at Mote Marine in Sarasota. These prehistoric-looking bottom feeders once thrived in Florida waters, and the state is working on regenerating their population.

For more information, contact the Putnam County Chamber of Com-merce, PO Box 550, Palatka FL 32178, phone (904) 328-1503.

Destination 19: Guana River

Miles or average time: no limit, paddle at your own pace

Skill level: beginner in low wind, intermediate with wind

Current: weak, with tidal influence in river, little current in Guana Lake

Wind problems: yes—very open area

Emergency numbers: 911; St. Johns County sheriff, (904) 824-8304

DeLorme page 58, section D2

Official Florida canoe trail: no

All the high spots you see against the horizon here are historic. The Indian mound beside the Tolomato River has been dated between 3000 B.C. and 1300 A.D., meaning Indians were here in the Middle Archaic, Deptford, and St. Johns periods. It's a shell midden, extending 450 meters north-south along the bluff. Another mound, called the Sanchez Mound, is at Wrights Landing.

A forty-foot-high sand dune fronts the ocean. From the observation platform atop the dune you have a spectacular view, both of the beach to the north and south and of the marshes and Lake Guana to the west.

The presence of the giant landmark dune might have played a part in European history too. Local historians cite a 1592 letter to Spain as proof that this was where Ponce de León first set foot in the New World. A mission named the Nativity of Our Lady of Tolomato was erected somewhere near here, but the exact site has been lost. A new visitor and education center near the dam explains the legend.

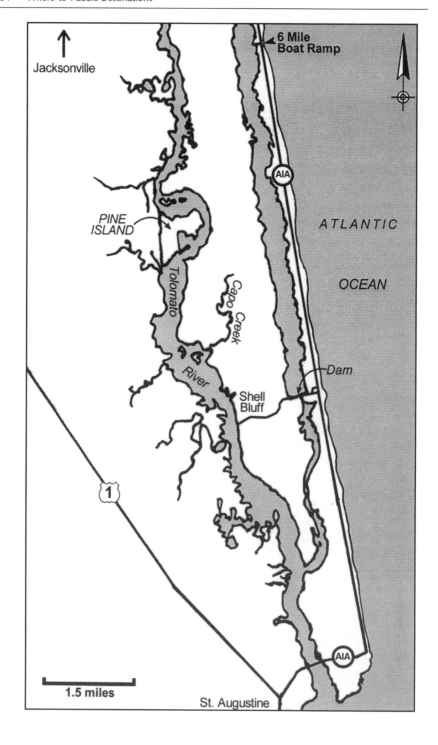

The 2,400-acre Guana River State Park is actually on a long barrier island that extends from Jacksonville to St. Augustine. There's a $2 entrance fee.

Some 226 species of birds have been observed here. White pelicans float in the lake in January and February, along with thousands of ducks. Peregrine falcons usually come through here in early October, and a smaller number in early April. The Christmas Bird Count always lists close to a hundred species.

Long stretches of the beach are not readily accessible by car. These are purposely left as refuges for least terns and loggerhead turtles.

Guana River is one of the sites for the "special opportunity" alligator hunts for people with disabilities. Big gators can stand salt water, but baby gators need fresh water, so you're more liable to see female gators at the top end of Guana Lake, and even more on the Tolomato River.

You can paddle three distinct waterways—Guana River, Guana Lake, and the Tolomato River.

- Guana River: On the south side of the dam, a ramp leads to the original Guana River, which is an estuary between the barrier islands of the Atlantic and the salt marshes to the west. This is what the whole area looked like before the dam was put in. The banks, especially the west bank, are full of niches and coves and crannies. Here you'll see the broad silver backs of tarpon rolling on the surface.
- Guana Lake: Long and skinny Guana Lake, also inside the park, was formed by a 1957 dam that blocks off the upper part of the river. There are two places to launch. First is the ramp on the north side of the dam. The other spot, called the Six Mile Boat Ramp, is indeed six miles to the north on A1A.

  The lake is open and unsheltered, with salt marshes and dunes on the east, piney woods on the west. Only boats under ten horsepower are allowed on the lake. It is brackish near the dam, and fresh as it gets further north. Both fresh- and saltwater species live here, so you can go crabbing and shrimping near the dam, then bream fishing upstream.
- Tolomato River: The Tolomato River runs parallel to Lake Guana, and is part of the Intracoastal Waterway. This is actually a more interesting (read winding and twisting) waterway than long, skinny Lake Guana. It is bordered by swamp, with few access points.

Head due west from the dam on Shell Bluff Road to reach the launch site. You can go either north or south. We paddled north to explore Capo Creek, then let the wind blow us back to Shell Bluff Landing.

You can get to the park by following A1A ten and a half miles north from St. Augustine. This is a pretty drive, but not very fast, since you have to go through St. Augustine to get to this section of A1A. Or you can take the SR210 exit off I-95, then head east on SR210 to Mickler Landing on the coast, and from there drive south on A1A.

For more information, contact Guana River State Park, 2690-E South Ponte Vedra Boulevard, Ponte Vedra Beach FL 32082, phone (904) 825-5071, or call the St. Johns Visitors Bureau at 1-800-OLDCITY.

Also try www.funandsun.com/parks/guanariver/guanariver.html or fcn. state.fl.us/gfc.viewing/sites/site26.html or www.nettally.com/fltws/tourof. htm.

Destination 20: Historic Big Bend Saltwater Paddling Trail

Miles or average time: 91.5 miles, in eleven segments ranging from 1.5 to 19 miles

Skill level: little skill, lots of brute force

Current: tides and river channels to cross

Wind problems: extremely important

Emergency numbers: 911; also (by county, given for individual trip segments): Dixie County sheriff, (352) 498-1220; Jefferson County sheriff, (850) 997-2523; Taylor County sheriff, (850) 584-4225; Wakulla County sheriff, (850) 926-7171

Rentals: Canoe Rentals, Highway 98, St. Marks FL 32355, phone (850) 925-6412; Dragonfly Watersports, 20336 East Pennsylvania Avenue, Dunnellon FL 34432, phone (352) 489-3046 or 1-800-919-9579; Riverside Recreational Rentals, 69 Riverside Drive, St. Marks FL 32355, phone (850) 925-5668; Silent Waters, 15 NE Second Avenue, High Springs FL 32643, phone (904) 454-1991; TNT Hideaway, Highway 98, St. Marks FL 32355, phone (850) 925-6412

DeLorme page 50, section D-3, to page 69, section B-2

Official Florida canoe trail: yes

This was the first canoe trail laid out by the State of Florida. It stretches from Fort San Marco de Apalache in St. Marks to the mouth of the Suwannee River, passing seven river mouths and innumerable creeks, bayous, bays, and nooks.

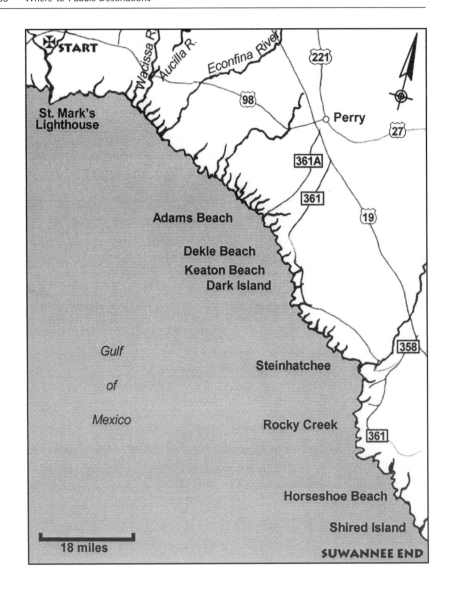

You can do the whole trip, or just a section here and there. I met a couple who paddled the whole length in ocean kayaks—with lots of advance planning, freeze-dried foods, and all-weather tents—and they said it was wonderful. At times, they were the only humans in sight, and from the water the shoreline stretched with few signs of habitation. They were on no schedule, and often camped for a couple of days if they found a great campsite.

You'll need permits to camp on property managed by the Florida Wildlife Commission. Apply at least two weeks in advance to Big Bend Wildlife Management Area, 663 Plantation Road, Perry FL 32347, phone (904) 838-1306.

You won't get lost. The Florida Department of Transportation is in the process of putting up paddling trail signs at "major access points," such as the seven big rivers and a few boat channels. The numbered buoys of the Intracoastal Waterway will also be in sight. The Department of Environmental Protection recommends two sets of maps. First is the bulky but detailed NOAA 1:80,000 nautical charts 11405 (Apalachee Bay), 11407 (Horseshoe Point to Rock Islands), and 11408 (Crystal River to Horseshoe Point). They also recommend the set of thirteen 1:24,000 USGS topographical maps that cover the area. Local maps are also available from marinas and fish camps. Tide charts, cell phone, and a handheld GPS would also come in handy.

Before you launch, drive up the coast to check out your stopping points. Ask at parks, marinas, and fish camps about how to spot their channels from the water, whether they are open on weekdays, and such.

If you are planning on sleeping ashore, remember that on this coastline the scallop season runs from July 1 to September 10, making it the busiest season for the motels and campgrounds.

Some of the offshore islands have resident raccoons and rats who have learned that boats carry delectable food. Red pepper or pepper spray on straps and soft gear will cut down the gnawing.

Because of winds in these open waters, a big ocean kayak is the craft of choice for ease of paddling and lower wind resistance. Also, a polyethylene hull will survive oyster beds best.

The legs are:

1) Fort San Marco to St. Marks Lighthouse, 5 miles. Wakulla County. The trail begins inland, at the junction of the Wakulla and St. Marks Rivers.

Take route 363 south from US98 to get to Shell Island. You'll paddle south into Apalachee Bay. The lighthouse is southeast, and you will see it from several miles away.

2) St. Marks Lighthouse to the Aucilla River, 12 miles. Wakulla and Jefferson Counties. The road to the lighthouse is CR59, which heads south from US98 just east of the Newport bridge over the St. Marks River. Paddling from the lighthouse, follow the shoreline east to the mouth of the Aucilla. Be prepared to camp, since there are no roads or facilities here.

3) Aucilla River to the Econfina River, 8 miles. Taylor County. Econfina Resort (phone (850) 584-2135) has motel rooms.

4) Econfina River to Hickory Mound Impoundment, 7 miles. Taylor County. Econfina River State Park (Route 1, Box 255, Lamont FL 32336, phone (904) 584-2135) is two and a half miles upstream from the mouth of the river. It has a campground and a full-time ranger/manager. To reach it from US19 in Lamont, take CR14 south to the end of the road.

5) Hickory Mound to Keaton Beach, 8 miles. Taylor County. From Perry, take US98 north for four miles, then turn left/south on SR356. Go approximately eight miles, then turn right on CR651 to Hickory Mound ramp.

6) Keaton Beach to Dark Island, 1.5 miles. Taylor County. To drive to Keaton Beach from US19 in Pineland, head south/west on SR356, then south on SR361.

7) Dark Island to Hagans Cove, 3 miles. Taylor County. From Keaton Beach, head south on SR361 to Dark Island Road, to Gulfview Road.

8) Hagans Cove to Steinhatchee, 15 miles. Taylor County. Hagans Cove is off SR361 also, tucked in between Sponge Point and Piney Point.

9) Steinhatchee to Horseshoe Beach, 19 miles. Dixie County. This is a long stretch, but there is a halfway ramp on Lucy Lane, off SR361 about five and a half road miles south of the Steinhatchee bridge.

10) Horseshoe Beach to Shired Island, 6 miles. Dixie County. From US19 at Cross City, drive south to the end of SR351.

11) Shired Island to Suwannee, 7 miles. Dixie County. From Cross City, drive south on SR351, then turn left/south on SR357 to the end.

12) Suwannee River Delta. See destination 31.

Also try www.florida-outdoors.com/bigbend.

Destination 21: Homosassa River

Miles or average time: no limit, paddle at your own pace

Skill level: intermediate in current, beginner in side canals

Current: strong, affected by tides in main channel, little in side creeks

Wind problems: yes, many open areas

Emergency numbers: 911; Citrus County sheriff, (352) 726-1121

Rentals: Homosassa Kayak, 5300 South Cherokee Way, Homosassa FL 34448, phone (352) 628-3183, e-mail CEDAV53@xtalwind.net; MacRae's, 5290 South Cherokee Way, Homosassa FL 34448, phone (352) 628-2922; Nature's Resort, 10359 West Halls River Road, Homosassa FL 34448, phone (352) 628-9544 or 1-800-301-7880

DeLorme page 77, section B-1

Official Florida canoe trail: no

The Homosassa River is famous for its manatees. During the winter, these huge sweet-potato-shaped animals come up the river to keep warm.

If you don't see one while paddling you can visit the captive herd at Homosassa Springs State Wildlife Park (admission fee). Four times a day a manatee expert wades into the manatee enclosure to hand out lettuce and grass sprouts while tourists watch from bleachers.

The park also has an underwater viewing room, where you can watch schools of salt- and freshwater fish circling the manatees, plus a bird area, reptile lectures, and a big pen of alligators. When the state took over the attraction, it got rid of all nonnative animals except for Lucifer, the Happy Hippo of Homosassa. If you call "Looooo" in your deepest voice, he'll surface and grunt "ho ho ho."

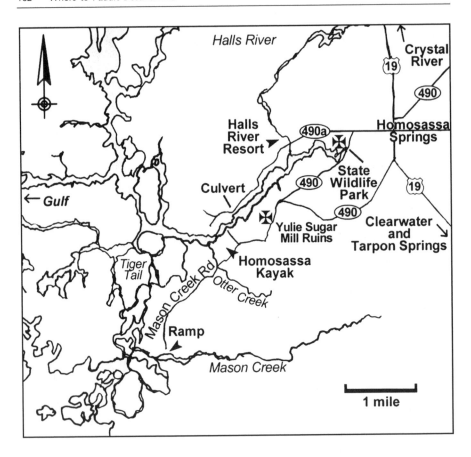

Outside the park, you can paddle almost up to the viewing bridge where the main spring flow enters the river—but do observe the posted signs. I almost got arrested when I snorkeled too close to the fence. Wild manatees hang around this area, and often come up to humans to be scratched. They have to initiate contact. Be careful not to "mug a manatee" by chasing or interfering with one in any way.

There is also a thriving otter population, five kinds of sea turtles, and two hundred kinds of birds, hundreds of powerboats, a big commercial fishing fleet, and some interesting waterfront houses.

On the main river, you can paddle the five miles all the way to the Gulf of Mexico. However, the current rips through Hell's Gate, a narrow slot between two fingers of tough coral rock. So many powerboats have smashed their lower units that a nearby marina has created fake palm trees out of broken props.

Tour boats leave hourly from K. C. Crumps restaurant (11210 West Halls River Road, phone (352) 628-1500) on the north side of the Homosassa, and can sometimes be persuaded to tow you back upstream, for a fee. But if possible, plan your trip to take advantage of the tide. And don't forget you can stay out in the middle of the channel to take advantage of the current or stick close to shore where the eddy currents go upstream. You shouldn't have any problem getting anywhere in the whole river system.

Site of Civil War skirmishes, the Homosassa is braided with hidden trails among the marshes. Watch for manatees. Courtesy of Joanne Williams.

Getting away from the main river, there are miles of back-country creeks, rivulets, canals, and river edges to explore. Hall's River extends almost up to US19, and most of it is uninhabited. Idle speed is strictly enforced in the entire river system in the winter manatee season, which makes paddling easier. However, remember that in the main channels the current can be fierce during wintertime dead low tide. Tides extend far up the river, and wind is a factor in the open marshes.

Also on the main channel, you can circle Tiger Tail Island, 1.7 miles south of Old Homosassa. Before the Civil War, pioneer and later state senator David Levi Yulee settled here, but his mansion was burned by northern troops during the Civil War. The remains of his old sugar mill are on SR490 southwest of the state park on Fish Bowl Road. After the Civil War a thriving fishing, lumbering, and tourist village sprang up, on islands since all travel was by boat. There was even an island school.

You can take a guided tour through the juniper and marsh grass trails with Susan at Homosassa Kayak. She has her own private island, complete with composting toilet. She is also active in creating a new thirteen-mile canoe and kayak trail, involving the Little Homosassa and Salt Rivers.

In Old Homosassa, access to the river is beside Homosassa Kayak and MacRae's marina, and at Mason Creek Park, 6891 South Mason Creek Road. On the north side, you can launch at Nature's Resort.

There is a hidden route to the marshes north of the river. From MacRae's ramp, paddle about ten minutes east/upstream, hugging the north shore. You'll see a giant concrete culvert pipe, just wide enough for a canoe. Paddle through this, under Halls River Road, and you'll be in a huge area of canals. Remember how you got in, since it is easy to get turned around.

For more information, contact the Homosassa Springs Chamber of Commerce, PO Box 709, Homosassa Springs FL, 34447-0709, phone (352) 628-2666, www.homosassachamber.com/areainfo.html.

Destination 22: Juniper Springs

Miles or average time: 7 miles or 4–5 hours

Skill level: beginner

Current: mild and steady

Wind problems: few—the run is mostly protected by trees

Emergency numbers: 911; Marion County sheriff, (352) 732-8181

Rentals: Juniper Springs Recreation Area (only before high noon), 17147 East Highway 42, Silver Springs FL 34488, phone (352) 625-2808

DeLorme page 73, section C-2

Official Florida canoe trail: no

This is the spring of the "sand boils." Watch for white circles on the bottom, especially where the Fern Hammock run joins the Juniper Springs run. Pure white sand churns and rumbles and writhes as cool water pushes its way up from the aquifer.

The boils look scary but are actually great fun—or used to be, before the Forest Service said nobody could play in them. I remember stepping into each boil up to my waist, and feeling the sand massage my legs. It helps to have lots of natural buoyancy (also called "fat") so you don't sink.

The spring starts at a swimming area in the Juniper Springs Recreation Area, twenty-two miles east of Silver Springs. Only swimmers are allowed in the pool area—the canoe launch is below the Mill House. No canoes are rented after noon, and on weekends they sell out fast, so plan to arrive early if you are renting. If you're toting your own craft, the walk from the parking lot to the put-in is about a city block.

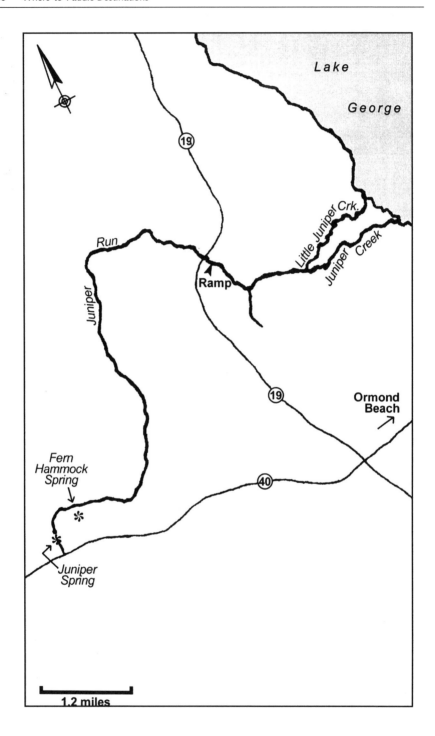

1.2 miles

The pool was developed in the 1930s as a Civilian Conservation Corps project. The mossy stone and concrete walls that enclose the 135-by-80-foot swimming area would never be allowed today, but they are picturesque. The old Mill House actually produced DC electricity when it was new.

Juniper Springs and Fern Hammock Springs together produce about 20 million gallons of water a day. The stream starts as a six-foot-wide meandering path paved with pure white sand. After the first two miles, it widens and slows as it enters broad stretches of grassy marsh called the Juniper Prairie Wilderness. A picnic spot called Half-Way Landing is 3.6 miles from the start. The takeout spot is on SR19, on the southwest side of the bridge.

This is a delightful run, cool and shady, with enough twists and turns to keep the paddlers happy, and few obstacles. Canoes and kayaks only are allowed on the run—no waders, swimmers, snorkelers, or tubers.

You'll see black gum, red maple, rare needle palm, bay trees, and two distinct pines: the tall, straight loblolly pine and the sand pine with bent, crooked trunks.

It is possible to paddle from SR19 to Lake George, but I don't recommend it. The last section, at the delta where the creek enters the lake, is not readily accessible for boats since it is very wide and only about eighteen inches deep. This part of the river is not as pretty as the winding section upriver, you have to buck the current coming back, there are more alligators, there is no pickup point, and you have little protection from the wind. The best trip is the seven-mile stretch from the spring to SR19, which is also the shuttle stop.

Juniper Run has one scary story.

Lake George is said to have the highest concentration of alligators in the state, and there's nothing to keep them from coming up the stream. That was evidently the case in October 1997, when a canoer hopped out of his boat into waist-deep water to cool off. He was about a mile upstream from the pickup point at SR19R. Jim Morrow put on a mask and snorkel and was happily swimming when he saw something move in front of him. It was an eleven-foot bull alligator. Here's his account as it was reported in the *Miami Herald*:

"I saw the head coming toward me, then I saw its mouth open. Next thing I knew my head was inside the gator's mouth. He started shaking me like a rag doll. He just kept shaking me from side to side, shaking and shaking." The man tried punching the gator, but said his blows were "ineffectual." The reptile released him after about thirty seconds. Morrow says, "I think my head was so far down in his mouth that I touched his taste buds. When he tasted me, I think that's why he let me go."

Fortunately, Morrow was with five friends, who quickly paddled him the last mile to their car. "I think my mask saved me," he said. "If I hadn't had it on, he could have put one of my eyes out or punctured my jugular."

The guilty gator was quickly killed by trappers, and was estimated to be between thirty-five and forty years old. Rangers now recommend that you swim only in the pool at Juniper Springs.

For more information, contact Juniper Springs Recreation Area, 17147 East Highway 42, Silver Springs FL 34488, phone (352) 625-2520.

Destination 23: Lake Panasoffkee

Miles or average time: 5 hours round-trip

Skill level: intermediate

Current: little in the open lake, moderate in the outflow canal, and strong in Little Jones Creek

Wind problems: open, unsheltered lake, sheltered creeks

Emergency numbers: 911; Sumter County sheriff, (352) 793-0222

Rentals: Pana Vista Lodge, 3417 County Road 421, Lake Panasoffkee FL 33538-4437, phone (352) 793-2061

DeLorme page 78, section B-2

Official Florida canoe trail: no

I heard about this trip from Chris Linhart, a resource protection specialist for Swiftmud—formally, the Southwest Florida Water Management District—who lives at the Lake Panasoffkee project. "You can paddle up Big Jones Creek," he said, "but the really pretty place is Little Jones Creek. It's a beautiful spring, very narrow and winding. Not too many people know about it, but it is one of the prettiest runs around." So I tried it.

Little Jones Spring actually emerges inside an impenetrable jungle just west of I-75, about a thousand feet behind the Days Inn. The easiest access to Little Jones Creek is from the top end of Lake Panasoffkee. It's a twisty, turning run, and you'll have to duck overhanging branches of oak, cypress, and bay trees. The creek narrows in places so you feel the force of the current, but it spreads out again and you can usually hug either of the banks to take advantage of any eddy currents.

The water is crystal clear, with long strands of eel grass rippling in the cur-

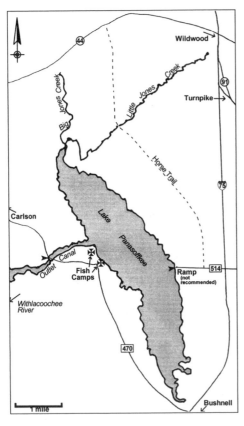

rent. I only went up halfway before the stream narrowed. You could probably push your way up higher, but I was too lazy. It was a pretty paddle, and the ride back downstream was like riding a log chute.

You can launch at the fish camps or use the public ramps. The rustic Pana Vista Lodge, just south of the entrance to the outflow canal, has rental canoes. Tracey's Fish Camp is on the southwest side of the lake, where CR470 makes a right-angle turn.

A Sumter County ramp is located just west of the CR470 bridge over the Outlet River that leads to the Withlacoochee River and Lake Tsala Apopka.

Another public ramp is at Coleman Landing, on the east side of Lake Panasoffkee, at the western end of CR514/Warm Springs Road. However, Chris cautions, it is so overgrown that you probably can't find it, and there is a danger of vandalism to your car.

Interestingly, this six-mile-long, one-mile-wide lake is one of the few spots in the whole Southeast where the Florida aquifer is exposed to the surface. The water quality is good. Some 70 percent of the bottom is covered with a healthy growth of eel grass. A program by the Florida Wildlife Commission to remove floating tussocks of grass has resulted in more open areas.

If you're interested in fishing, Lake Panasoffkee has produced some real lunkers. The lake averages only six feet, going down to about ten feet in the center. So ignore the weed lines and put your bait right into the middle of the lake. One guide I know actually trolls for bass, using wild shiners with twenty-five-pound-test line.

The biggest bass ever caught here was a huge sow bass weighing in at fifteen pounds. For years the lake also held the state records for the biggest shellcracker ever caught, at three pounds four ounces, and the biggest garfish, at forty-one pounds. Some of the dusty stuffed carcasses are on display at Pana Vista Fish Camp.

The town of Lake Panasoffkee has a mottled history. Around 1880 Bachelor's Lumber Mill hired hundreds of workers to haul cypress logs out of the woods. By 1887 this was the largest settlement in the state, and a major depot for the Central Florida Railroad. This led to miles of orange groves that produced trainloads of citrus for northern markets.

The town fathers were determined to make this the fanciest resort town in Florida. In the winter of 1883 they invited a bunch of rich northern investors to visit. However, nature didn't cooperate. The bigwigs stepped off the train into the worst freeze in the town's history. Instead of oranges, icicles dripped from the dying citrus trees. The investors climbed right back into their heated train car and left.

Eventually the town dwindled to the sleepy, oak-shaded community you see now.

In the 1950s a tourist attraction called Rain Forest was built on the west side of US301, just below Warm Spring creek. The attraction offered exotic birds and animals, a swamp walk to a small lake with a mill dam, beautiful stained glass windows, a museum—and my grandfather Jim Miller's snake show.

Grandpop also made up ten wood-and-plaster dinosaurs, a couple of them twenty feet high, and put them on tracks beside the nature trail. When visitors walked up, a roaring dinosaur came rushing at them through the bushes. It was great fun—at least for the employees—until one of the dinosaurs scared a tourist so much that she had a heart attack. The dinosaurs got turned off, to Grandsire's utter disgust. Then the owner of the site had a vision that the world was going to end, so he dismantled the whole place. The old Rain Forest is now a golf course. Granddad and I have always wondered if his bright green and black dinosaurs are still lurking in some hidden nook.

For more information, contact the Lake Panasoffkee Project via the Southwest Florida Water Management District, 2379 Broad Street, Brooksville FL 34609-6899, phone (352) 796-7211 or 1-800-832-8435. You can read about the history of Lake Panasoffkee at www.qsy.com, or stop in at the new library in town. Chris recommends the Wild Bill airboat tours, and a local restaurant called Catfish Johnny's.

Destination 24: Ochlockonee River (Upper)

Miles or average time: 26 miles, in three segments of 14, 6, and 6 miles

Skill level: intermediate on upper section, beginner on lower two

Current: varies according to rain

Wind problems: little

Emergency numbers: 911; Leon County sheriff, (850) 922-3300; Gadsden County sheriff, (850) 627-9233

DeLorme page 34, section C-2

Official Florida canoe trail: yes

The Upper Ochlockonee is probably the twistiest river in all of Florida. The first section is only 6.6 miles as the crow flies, but fourteen miles for the paddler. The goosenecks and hairpin turns are stacked so close together that you can hear conversations from other boats that are ten minutes behind you.

This river is also one of the longest in this neck of the woods, extending some seventy-plus miles from its beginning near Moultrie, Georgia.

So you'd assume that a river that drains that big a watershed would always have water, wouldn't you? Nope. During dry spells this first section of the river, from SR12 to SR157, becomes so low that from the air it looks like a string of pearls—deepish holes connected by strands of tan sand.

I think that the reason the official canoe trail ends at the US90 bridge instead of going on to Lake Talquin is not because it's easy to get to that

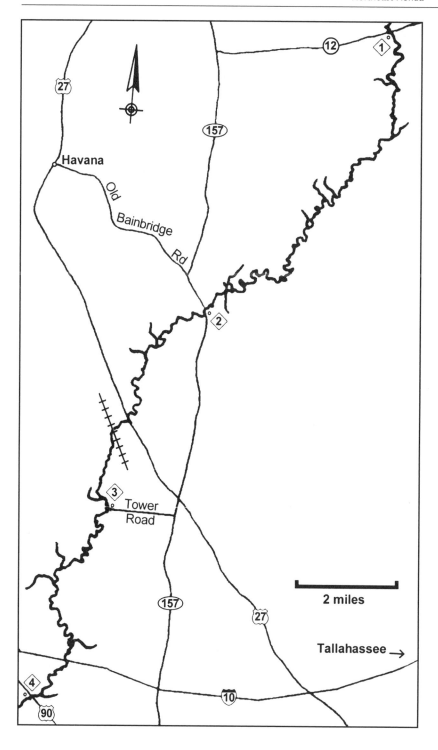

bridge, it's because the people who explored the trail got tired of pushing alligators and bass boats out of their way.

A couple of years ago I was in a bass fishing tournament on Lake Talquin. A fellow in another bass boat was upset because a gator grabbed his brand-new five-dollar Twelve-Fathom tiger-striped floating jig. The water is also cloudy. I've never had an urge to hop overboard and swim here.

The Ochlockonee (pronounced Oak-LOCK-nee) is a favorite weekend paddle for many of the students at Florida State and Florida A&M Universities. Add to that the excellent bass fishing and easy access for bass boats at SR157 and US90, and you'll find that parts of the river can get downright crowded on holidays.

Still, it's a great place to paddle. My favorite memory is of the six-mile section from Tower Road to the US90 bridge. It was a sparkling clear, cool day in October, and the water level was perfect. We had three husky college men with us, who not only insisted on doing all the heavy lifting but competed to see who could tell the corniest jokes. I tried to adopt all three.

Of course, with all the chattering going on, we didn't see much wildlife. But if you paddle early in the morning—and keep your mouth shut—you should see deer, bear, huge turtles, and wild hogs.

I found the scenery soothing—banks lush with trees and high grasses. Low grassy banks make great picnic spots with convenient tree roots at just the right height for seats and back rests. We had to push through overhanging willows, magnolias, and oaks a few times, but it wasn't backbreaking. The current was moderate, probably 1–2 miles per hour.

1) SR12 to Bainbridge Road/SR157 bridge, 14 miles. From I-10 northwest of Tallahassee, get off at US310/Thomasville Road. Head north for about a mile, and turn left/west onto Maclay Road. Pass Maclay State Gardens and turn right/north onto SR155. Follow this up to SR12. Turn left/west on SR12 and follow this two and a half miles to the river. The access can be overgrown.

This section is best done at medium to high water. The first half is narrow, with many pull-overs at low water. The second half is wider and easier. Two miles from the put-in, Shaw Creek comes in from the right, and a mile further on, another unnamed river comes in again from the right, and you'll make almost a ninety-degree turn to the left.

2) Old Bainbridge Road to Tower Road, 6 miles. The access at the Old Bainbridge Road/SR157 bridge is on the northwest side. About two-thirds of the way down you'll pass the US27 bridge, which has no access. The railroad bridge is about a third of a mile downstream from that. From there you have maybe an hour to go, depending on the speed of the current.

3) Tower Road to US90/New Quincy Highway, 6 miles. Access is at the west end of Tower Road. To get to it, head west on Tower Road from either SR263 or US27.

4) The bridge at US90/New Quincy Highway. The ramp is on the northwest side of the river.

You can continue paddling downstream through the nineteen-mile-long Lake Talquin area (DeLorme page 49, section A-3). I found the scenery low and the wind high, but you can hug the banks until you get to the C. H. Corn earthen dam. There are four big coves where feeder rivers and creeks come in from the north, plus a series of boat ramps about every mile, and several fish camps and marinas.

The lower Ochlockonee canoe trail starts at the dam at SR20 and extends south for fifty-four miles to Sopchoppy, Ochlockonee Bay, and the St. Marks Wildlife Refuge.

The Barry Laffan Apalachee Archaeological Boat Trail is a new fifteen-mile canoe and kayak trail that leads past Indian middens. Access points are at Ochlockonee River State Park, the ramp on the southwest end of the US98 bridge over Ochlockonee Bay, and at Mash Island Park at the edge of the Gulf. Interpretive signs are near the ramps, and brochures on the history of the Indians are available at local restaurants.

For more information, try www8.myflorida.com/communities/learn/trails/canoe or www.state.fl.us/gfc/hunting.

Destination 25: Ocklawaha River (Lower)

Miles or average time: 8.5 miles to St. Johns

Skill level: strong beginner

Current: slow, with some dead ends

Wind problems: yes, some wide parts

Emergency numbers: 911; Marion County sheriff, (352) 732-8181; Putnam County sheriff, (904) 329-0800

Rentals: Ocklawaha Outpost, 15260 NE 152 Place, Fort McCoy FL 32134, phone (352) 236-4606; Florida Pack & Paddle, PO Box 879, Altoona FL 32702, phone (352) 669-0008, 1-800-297-8811, www.floridapackandpaddle.com

DeLorme page 72, section A-2, to page 67, section D-1

Official Florida canoe trail: no

The Lower Ocklawaha (you will also see it spelled Oklawaha) starts at the Rodman Dam and ends at the St. Johns River. The seven-channel area is so wide that at times you'll feel like you're in a swamp or forest-marsh. A few high white banks make fine spots for camping or picnics.

Start at the ramp on the east side of Rodman Dam. To drive there from Palatka, head south on SR19. Cross the ruler-straight Cross Florida Barge Canal and turn right onto Rodman Dam Road.

It's about five paddling miles between the dam and SR19. The main channel is marked, or you can explore the little braided rills that run in and out of the main channel. After you pass under the SR19 bridge, turn right/south

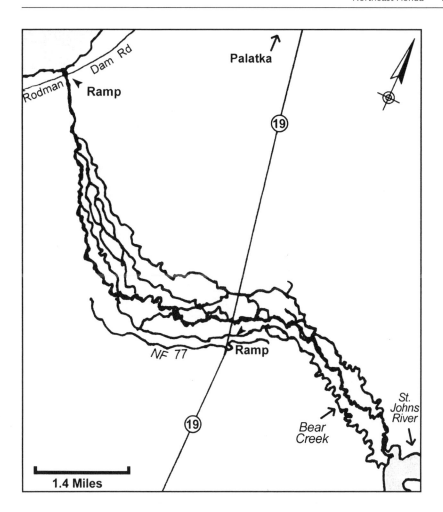

down a narrow canal to get to the parking area beside National Forest road 77.

You can also paddle from SR19 to the St. Johns River, about four river miles. It's a round-trip, unless you cross to one of the many ramps on the east side of the St. Johns, but driving there to leave a car takes almost as long as the paddling.

If you'd like to explore a different route back to SR19, paddle upstream/south from the mouth of the Ocklawaha to Bear Creek, and take Bear Creek west back to SR19.

Photographed in 1905, the William Howard was one of many steamboats that made regular trips from Jacksonville to Silver Springs. The fare was $1.25. Poet Sidney Lanier described the Ocklawaha as "the sweetest water-lane in the world." University of South Florida archives.

I was nervous about doing this the first time, especially after I talked to another paddler who was the size and shape of Grizzly Adams. He thought nothing of carrying his old-fashioned, heavy wood canoe around on his shoulder. He mumbled something about how getting from one channel to the other was "no problem a-tall."

With trepidation, we made the turn into Bear Creek. It turned out to be no problem a-tall. The current on any of the channels is slow, so paddling upriver was comfortable. In spots the Ocklawaha and Bear Creek channels run close together and even mingle, so getting back to SR19 was easy.

While you're on the river, imagine yourself on an old stern-wheeler paddleboat back in 1870. You've boarded the boat at the landing just a block from your fancy gingerbread hotel in Palatka, and you're heading to Silver Springs. The fare is a whopping $1.25, with meals an extra 25 cents each, but you've splurged on top-deck tickets to enjoy the gentle breeze and fine view, much nicer than the heat and noise of the lower decks. You spot two black bear and a deer swimming across the channel. So many flocks of egrets and ibis are startled up by the churning, noisy wheel that they darken the sky.

You see a couple of baby alligators, but no big ones. After all, this is the height of the alligator skin export business, as attested by the boasting of the two rough and rude gator trappers swilling rotgut liquor at the bar on the main deck. The dusty hide of an eighteen-footer is tacked to the wall by the gangplank, and you hear that more than a million alligator skins have gone out of the port of Jacksonville, so you know you'll see a big 'un sooner or later.

In a few years, poet Sidney Lanier would follow on this same trip, and write his impressions of the Ocklawaha: "the sweetest water-lane in the world, a lane which runs for more than a hundred miles of pure delight betwixt hedgerows of oaks and cypresses and palms and bays and magnolias and mosses and manifold vine-growths, a land clean to travel along."

It's still that good today.

Destination 26: Ocklawaha River (Upper)

Miles or average time: 47 miles, in six segments of 10, 3, 10, 8, 6, and 10 miles

Skill level: beginner

Current: slow until Silver River joins at SR40

Wind problems: narrow river widens after SR316 to become Rodman Reservoir

Emergency numbers: 911; Marion County sheriff, (352) 732-8181

Rentals: Ocklawaha Canoe Outpost, Route 1, Box 1462, Fort McCoy FL 32134, phone (352) 236-4606; Florida Pack & Paddle, PO Box 879, Altoona FL 32702, phone (352) 669-0008 or 1-800-297-8811, website www.floridapackandpaddle.com

DeLorme page 72, section B-3 to C-3

Official Florida canoe trail: no

Back in the 1800s, the Ocklawaha was the superhighway of Florida, with some seventy-five landings along its hundred-mile length. River steamboats ran from Jacksonville down the St. Johns, turned into the Ocklawaha near Palatka, and delivered tourists to Silver Springs. The oak, cypress, and magnolia trees lining it were the image of Florida every visitor took home.

It's still a gorgeous river, sedate and winding, with few signs of civilization. More than two hundred species of birds, including several huge colonies of ibis, and some three hundred different mammals still live there.

Rodman Dam now divides the river into the Upper and Lower Ocklawaha.

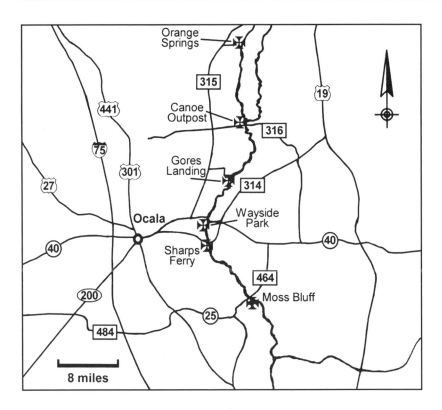

There are two portages: downstream from Moss Bluff and at the old Eureka dam at SR316. Like the St. Johns, this river flows north.

1) Moss Bluff/SR464 to Sharps Ferry, 10 miles. The river is narrow, brown, and slow moving here. Watch for hawks, both red-shouldered and red-tailed, and wood storks nesting or hanging out in the taller trees on the east bank. From the west fence of Silver Springs, drive south on CR35/Baseline, left/southeast on Maricamp, left/east on SR464 to bridge.

2) Sharps Ferry to Ray Wayside Park, 3 miles. From the west edge of Silver Springs attraction, turn south on CR35/Northeast 58 Avenue, then east on CR314 to the river. There is little shoulder near this bridge, so if you plan to leave a car, check out the parking situation first.

3) Ray Wayside Park to Gores Landing, 10 miles. (See the trip description for Silver River.) This is my favorite section, as the clear water from Silver Springs now boosts you along with less paddling. Driving directions:

Just west of the SR40 bridge, turn south into Silver River/Ray Wayside park. There is a $2 usage fee. To paddle to the park from the Ocklawaha River, turn west or upstream into the Silver River. The canal to the park is on the right/north side.

4) Gores Landing to Eureka, 8 miles. Driving directions: From SR40 east of Ocala, head north on SR315 approximately six miles. Turn right/east onto Northeast 105 Street, then right/south onto Gores Landing Park Road. The park has rest rooms, a small camping area, and two splashable springs. From here you can also take side trips south on Dead River and north on Cedar Creek.

5) Eureka to Cypress Bayou, 6 miles. Driving directions: From Ocala, take SR40 east, then drive north on SR315 ten-odd miles to Fort McCoy. Turn right/east on SR316 and go about four and a half miles to the river. The Ocklawaha Canoe Outpost is on the northwest side of the river.

6) Cypress Bayou to Orange Springs, 10 miles. Though Cypress Bayou is listed as six miles downstream/north from Canoe Outpost, I somehow missed it as we paddled past. Get a map and directions from them.

7) Orange Springs, 16 miles from Canoe Outpost. Driving directions: From Ocala, follow SR315 north to Orange Springs. The ramp is at the east end of NE 245 Road.

Destination 27: Pellicer Creek

Miles or average time: 4 miles

Skill level: beginner

Current: tidal

Wind problems: many in the bay, but protected inland

Emergency numbers: 911; Flagler County sheriff, (904) 437-4116; St. Johns County sheriff, (904) 824-8304

Rentals: Faver-Dykes State Park, 1000 Faver Dykes Road, St. Augustine FL 32086, phone (904) 794-0997

DeLorme page 68, section C-2

Official Florida canoe trail: yes

The official Florida canoe trail begins at US1 and ends four miles east at the boat ramp at Faver-Dykes State Park. But you can paddle a lot further, both inland and out to the marshes of the Matanzas River.

When there's wind, head for the protected creeks. The tributaries start on the west side of US1: Huelett Branch heads south to parallel US1, while Cracker Branch goes north. About a mile further west, Stevens Branch breaks off to head northwest to drain Fish Swamp, while Pringle Branch heads southwest to Pringle Swamp. Accessibility depends on tides, windfalls, and the current stage of regrowth after a hurricane, but you can always find some nook to explore.

Head east when the wind is calm, into the salt marshes. Directly east is Marineland of Florida (9507 Oceanshore Boulevard/A1A, phone (904) 471-1111), the very first marine life attraction in the state. It was started in 1938

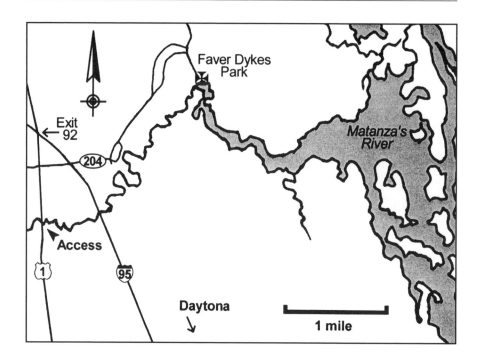

as a movie site by the simple process of throwing a bunch of fish together and keeping the ones that survived. There is an active marine research lab associated with Marineland, and you'll often see their research boats out in the marshes.

The Intracoastal Waterway is narrow here, but you won't be in danger of being run over, since the channel is beyond a marsh/sand spit. There are extensive oyster beds, so wear tough-bottomed boating shoes.

The fishing is good. Check at the park office for slot and creel limits, and don't forget your saltwater fishing license.

Canoe rental is $3.17 per hour, but the park has a limited number of canoes, so reserve yours in advance. Their gear is pretty basic, so if you have a favorite PFD (that's a *life vest* for any landlubbers) or smooth-shafted paddle, bring them along.

To get into the park: From Exit 92 of I-95, turn north on US1 and go under the overpass. Entrance to the park is between two gas stations on the

At Pellicer Creek you can head inland to the jungles or paddle out to the endless salt marshes. Courtesy of St. Johns County Convention and Visitor Bureau.

east side of the road. For more information, contact Faver-Dykes State Park, 1000 Faver Dykes Road, St. Augustine FL 32086, phone (904) 794-0997.

Also try www8.myflorida.com/communities/learn/trails/canoe or www. dep.state.fl.us/parks/FaverDykes/faverdykes.html.

Destination 28: Rainbow River

Nancy Scharmach

Miles or average time: 5.8 miles in two sections

Skill level: beginner

Current: 3–4 mph and steady

Wind problems: few, mostly sheltered

Emergency numbers: 911; Marion County sheriff, (352) 732-8181

Rentals: Dragonfly Watersports, 20336 East Pennsylvania Avenue, Dunnellon FL 34432, phone (352) 489-3046 or 1-800-919-9579; Anglers Resort, 12189 South William Drive, Dunnellon FL 34432, phone (352) 489-2397; Rainbow Springs Campground, 18185 SW 94 Street, Dunnellon FL 34432, phone (352) 489-5201

DeLorme page 71, section D-2

Official Florida canoe trail: no

The Rainbow is one of the prettiest runs in all of Florida. You can tube, paddle, or snorkel down this crystal-clear run. The white sand bottom is dotted with gushing springs, and schools of mullet, bass, and various panfish dart over the waving beds of turtle grass. From the head of the river at the state park, the Rainbow River runs for only 5.8 miles before it meets the larger Withlacoochee River. The main spring is a mile and a half upriver from the KP Hole (no, I don't know why it's called KP).

This might be Florida's first health resort, and the place where the entire Florida phosphate industry began.

Back in 1837 this was known as Amanina Springs, which was another name for the Withlacoochee River. In 1921 a newspaper account called it

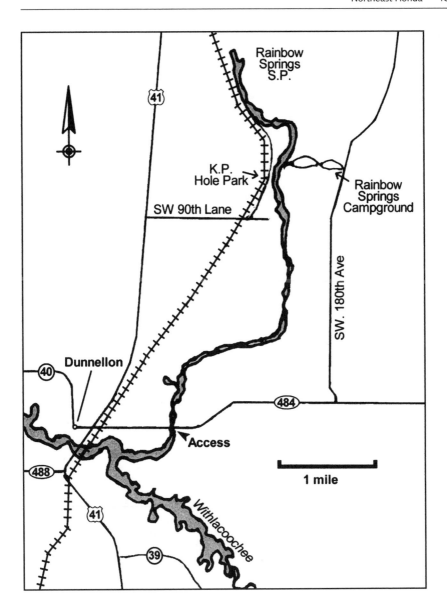

Blue Springs, and the five-mile river that flowed to join the Withlacoochee was called the Wekiwa River. But don't confuse it with the Wekiva River north of Orlando (see destination 67). The word *wekiwa* seems to be an Indian name for flowing spring.

John F. Dunn, a prominent Ocala attorney, ran a health resort here. He was so active in promoting this area as beautiful, healthful, and generally wonderful that the town of Dunnellon was named for him. When phosphate was found here, he organized the first exporting plant.

A series of more than twenty photos of the river and spring were circulated up north to lure tourists to Dunn's resort. Dunns Bluff, shown in the old photo, was close to the junction of the Withlacoochee with the Rainbow. See if you can spot the same place.

In the 1950s and 1960s the springs were a private tourist concession, with a fleet of glass-bottomed boats. Sunlight dancing off the bottom made beautiful rainbows in the glass windows. The spring was named Rainbow Springs, and the name has stuck. A giant walk-in aviary was added, with pretty waterfalls and paths through the lush gardens.

But that was B.D.—before Disney. With the advent of interstate highways, all leading to Mickey Mouse, many of the smaller tourist destinations around the state faltered. After sitting idle for years, the spring and the surrounding thousand acres were taken over by the State of Florida and made into a state park.

The spring offers a protected swimming and snorkeling area in the clear 72–74° water.

Although you can canoe and kayak right up into the state park boundaries, you are only allowed to dock your boat at the designated landing. But you can paddle up to the roped-off swimming area, swim on the downstream side, and paddle back down to KP Hole.

There are two main places to get onto the upper river. Marion County's KP Hole Park, located off SR41 north of Dunnellon, offers a sandy beach, a protected swimming area, and picnic tables, as well as canoe and inner tube rentals. A public boat ramp is immediately to the north of the KP Hole parking lot. You must have a wristband (price $2) from the park concession stand for use and parking.

The other access point is the Rainbow Springs Campground, on the east side of the river. Access is usually restricted to patrons of the campground.

Around 1900 this photo of "Dunns Bluff" was taken near the end of the Rainbow River. See if you can find the same spot today. University of South Florida archives.

Most people tube the river, renting tubes at KP Hole and taking out at the southeast side of the SR484 bridge.

Paddling up to the head of the spring from KP Hole takes about an hour and a half, with another forty-minute paddle back to your launch spot. From KP Hole to the SR484 bridge takes about two hours of paddling, or four and a half if you're merely drifting in a tube. From SR484 you can also continue downstream another mile and a half to the junction of the Withlacoochee River. At the Withlacoochee, turn right/downstream and go under the bridge to the ramp on river right.

Bring water and snacks in Tupperware. No alcohol or animals are allowed in the park, and it is unlawful to possess any food or beverage in a disposable container on the Rainbow River.

The Rainbow River is great for canoeing and kayaking, and its crystal clearness makes snorkeling and scuba diving a delight. Bring your underwater camera and your dive flag.

For more information, contact Rainbow Springs State Park, 19158 SW 81 Place, Dunnellon FL 34432, phone (352) 489-8503.

Destination 29: Salt Springs Run

Miles or average time: 10 miles round-trip, 3–4 hours

Skill level: beginner, except in high winds

Current: steady and mild

Wind problems: yes, open areas

Emergency numbers: 911; Marion County sheriff (352) 732-8181

Rentals: Salt Springs Run Marina & Landing, 25711 NE 134th Place, Salt Springs FL 32134, phone (352) 685-2255

DeLorme page 73, section B-2

Official Florida canoe trail: no

In the novel *Alas, Babylon* the time is after "the Bomb" and the characters have retreated to their old Florida homestead, which is near a salt spring. I've always wondered if this was the salt spring of the book. The refugees also discover that fried armadillo tastes pretty good, but I haven't had the urge to try that yet.

This is a pretty little run. It's crystal clear, fairly wide, and on the north side you can picnic or camp on top of three old Indian mounds, about a mile from the end of the run. On a calm day you can even venture out into Lake George. About the only problems are (1) fishermen in powerboats and (2) alligators.

The first third of the run goes through marshy lands. It's wide until the second turn, when the run narrows down a bit. In the middle of the run is a one-mile section of higher ground before the banks lower again. Duke Rountree, who works at the Salt Springs Marina, estimates you could fit about three tents atop each Indian mound.

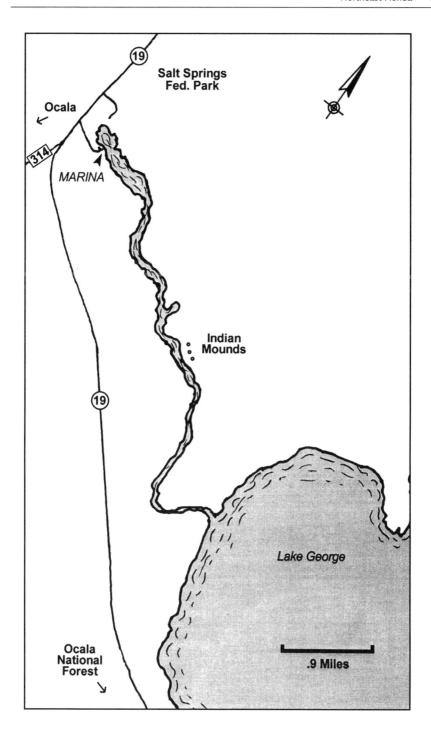

In 1908 President Teddy Roosevelt declared Salt Springs a national forest because of this beautiful spring basin. Sandy Huff.

At the mouth of the river is the wide sandbar called the Salt Springs Bar. There you can either turn around and paddle back upstream to the marina, which makes a ten-mile round-trip, or go over the bar into Lake George.

If you continue into Lake George, you could paddle up the west bank of the lake to Rocky Point, and then cross to Drayton Island (see destination 18), and thence to one of the fish camps at Georgetown. However, the lake is open to the wind, so pick your weather and crossing time carefully. I spotted six big alligators near the bar, and had no trouble deciding to turn around and paddle back to the marina.

The springs themselves rise up inside Salt Springs Federal Park (phone (352) 685-2048), which is inside Ocala National Forest. Teddy Roosevelt declared this a national forest in 1908, in part because of the wonderful waters of this spring. It's a first-magnitude spring, gushing some 64 million gallons a day out of five deep cuts in the rocky bottom. The spring area is dotted with shady oaks, and the swimming area is a nice place to snorkel.

In 1979 the springs became a federal park, and a new campground was installed in 1999. The only ramp in the park is for the use of campers only.

The last time I was there, a big bull alligator was sunning himself at the edge of the water.

It costs $3 for a day-use permit to swim in the springs. You can either drive in from SR19 or anchor your boat outside the floating ropes and swim in.

Wonderful schools of catfish hang around the spring. Since this run flows into Lake George, which is part of the St. Johns River, fish can easily get up into all the little nooks and crannies. There are even blue crabs, and this is a loooong way from salt water. The lady at the concession stand told me that a big flock of wild turkeys hangs around the lawn surrounding the springhead, and you're most likely to see them early in the morning. That's the best time to spot deer and other wildlife too.

In the winter, watch for swallow-tailed kites, which spend the rest of the year in Argentina. There are eagles and ospreys, and both red-shouldered and red-tailed hawks. Remember how to tell these apart—a red-*tailed* hawk wears a dark cummerbund, as if he's in formal tails. A red-shouldered hawk has a dappled honey-colored chest. This lake also has plenty of turtles.

Salt Springs Marina, located just a quarter mile south of the entrance to the federal park, is a good place to launch your own boat. You can see the docks from the swimming area inside the park. Coming out of the park, turn left/south on SR19 and watch for a dirt road and their sign on the left/east side.

The marina has six canoes for rent, at $10 for a half day and $20 for a full day. They also rent rowboats, a small power skiff, and a pontoon boat. Their paddles looked a bit short, so if you have your own, bring it along. They sell snacks and fishing supplies, but fishing advice and fishing tall tales are free.

Destination 30: Santa Fe and Ichetucknee Rivers

Miles or average time: 26 miles, in three sections of 3, 10, and 13 miles

Skill level: beginner

Current: steady and moderate

Wind problems: few

Emergency numbers: 911; Alachua County sheriff, (352) 955-2500; Columbia County sheriff, (904) 752-9212; Suwannee County sheriff, (904) 362-2222

Rentals: Silent Waters/Brasington's, 310 North Main Street, High Springs FL 32543, phone (904) 454-1991 or 1-888-454-1991, e-mail silentwaters@homepage.com; Santa Fe Canoe Outpost, PO Box 592, High Springs FL 32643, phone (904) 454-2050, website http://riverise.com/canoe.htm; Ichetucknee Family Grocery and Campground, Route 1, Box 1756, O'Brien FL 32701, phone (904) 497-2150; Suwannee Expeditions, 614 Ivey Memorial Park Drive SW, Branford FL 32008, phone (904) 935-9299, www.canoeflorida.com; O'Leno State Park, Route 2, Box 1010, High Springs FL 32643, phone (904) 454-1853; Treefrog Adventures, 145 DeBary Drive, DeBary FL 32713, phone (407) 668-1222; Ginnie Springs Resort, 7300 NE Ginnie Springs Road, High Springs FL 32643, phone (904) 454-2202, website http://ginniesprings.com; Poe Springs County Park, Poe Springs Road/SR340, High Springs FL 32643; Ichetucknee Springs State Park, Route 2, Box 108, Fort White FL 32038, phone (904) 497-2511

DeLorme page 65, section B-1

Official Florida canoe trail: yes

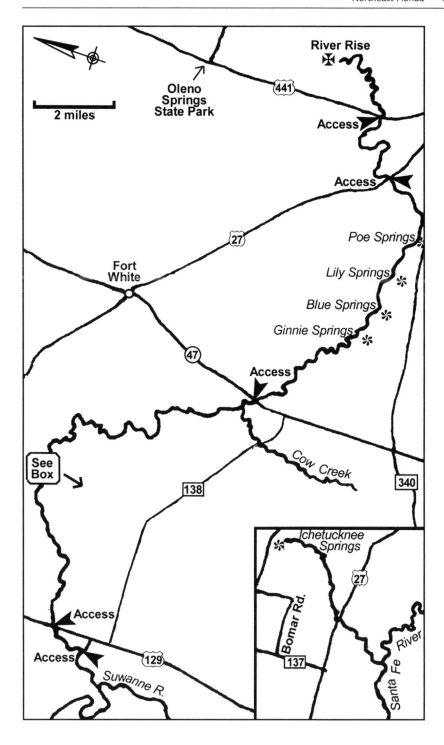

Up to my neck in the cool, clear water, I was happily enjoying the day when something tickled my foot. I looked down to see a tiny black turtle calmly walk across both my feet, then continue on its way across the white sand bottom.

I took a breath, went underwater, and grabbed it. The creature barely filled my palm. It had a high domed carapace, and a slight smile on its perpetually wizened face. By the flat shape of its small yellowish lower shell or plastron I guessed that it was a female. Then another miniature turtle popped up on the surface just a yard away. I scooped that one up too. Its plastron had more of an indentation, so it was probably a male. I took both turtles over to where my friends were wading beside a bed of elephant ears.

"Musk turtle," our amateur naturalist instantly said. "Out west they call them stinkpots. Look at the male—he's got a little thorny tip to his tail. These turtles have tiny sharp claws and are quite good climbers." He demonstrated by letting the female climb up his palm. After everyone had a chance to thoroughly inspect the turtles, I carefully put them back in their patch of turtle grass.

The turtles have a great place to live. We were on the Santa Fe River, right where the Itchetucknee Spring run joins in. Next to Rock Springs Run (destination 67), the Santa Fe is my favorite river.

The Santa Fe River begins miles away, on the other side of Gainesville. It flows from Lake Santa Fe (DeLorme page 66, section B-2), southeast of Waldo in Alachua County.

There's a paddling spot here too. Waldo was the first English-speaking town in this area, and its big railroad depot was the center of commerce for local farmers. To help get the harvests to the railroad, a canal was dredged between Lake Santa Fe and Lake Alto. This canal is still open. You can launch at the public ramp off SR325 in Shenks, paddle the two-mile canal, and take out at the ramp on the east side of Little Lake Santa Fe on CR21B. The first section of the river itself, from the top of Little Lake Santa Fe to O'Leno, is generally impassable.

The river goes underground at O'Leno State Park. You aren't allowed to swim or paddle close to the point where it disappears, of course, and the warning signs are highly necessary. The river doesn't look dangerous as it rolls into a wide, circular basin in the middle of the woods. There's a bit of

A 1910 photo of the Santa Fe river sink, now part of O'Leno State Park. Watch for the "hump" in the water after the "disappearing" river rises to the surface again. University of South Florida archives.

swirling motion in the middle, shown by the slow drifting of bits of wood and a few streamers of river foam, but no dramatic plunge. The river just quietly stops.

The river pops up again at River Rise State Preserve, three miles across land and three miles upstream from the US441 bridge. Dye and ping pong balls released in O'Leno State Park clearly prove that this is the same river that disappears underground there. However, it has now grown in size and speed, having somehow gained water during its underground sojourn.

You can put in at US441 and paddle upstream to River Rise. It's just under six miles for the round-trip. Give yourself three hours unless you're a very strong paddler. Just east of the US441 bridge, watch for Darby Spring coming in from the south bank.

There are a number of canoe and kayak outfitters in this area, and they offer a good selection of trips, ranging from a one-hour paddle to three-day camping adventures. If you're there during a full-moon weekend, check with Canoe Outpost about their nighttime paddling trips.

1) US441 to US27, 3 miles or 1.5 hours. The official canoe trail for the Santa Fe begins at the US41/441 bridge about two miles northwest of the town of High Springs. To get to High Springs, take exit 78 off I-75 and go west on US441 through the town of High Springs. The ramp is on the northwest side of the bridge, and Canoe Outpost on the southeast side.

Watch for a slightly unnerving sight about halfway down this run. A hump in the water will seem to rush at you. It's a bottom current that has been diverted about a city block upstream, and comes gushing up here. The boil is actually stationary, and you're the one who is rushing toward it. It's completely harmless, and our group promptly named it the Loch Ness Monster of the Santa Fe.

2) US27 to SR47, 10 miles or 5 hours. From High Springs, go three miles northwest on US27 to the bridge. The public boat ramp is off a short road on the southwest side of the bridge.

You'll pass a bunch of springs on this section: Poe Springs, Ginnie Springs, Blue Springs, Lily Springs, and more. In high water the river backs up into the springs, effectively hiding them.

The Florida Sport Paddling Club has an annual Robert Service Poetry Trip, and they sometimes meet at Ginnie Springs campground. The idea is to give dramatic readings of great outdoor poetry during a potluck supper. True, Robert Service wrote about Yukon scenery, but this is usually a January trip and this is north Florida, so with a bit of imagination it all fits together.

I once made up about six songs about the river, and presented them to my hapless friends (you have a lot of thinking time while paddling). Fortunately, my scribbled notes have disappeared, and the only one I remember started off (to the tune of "O Christmas Tree") "O Santa Fe, dear Santa Fe, we love thy pristine waters." It went rapidly downhill from there.

3) SR47 to US129, 13 miles or 6 hours. From the town of Fort White, go southwest four and a half miles to the bridge.

4) The end of the official trail is at the US129 bridge, three miles upstream from the confluence of the Santa Fe and Suwannee Rivers.

You can paddle upstream to Ichetucknee Springs State Park (Route 2, Box 108, Fort White FL 32038, phone (904) 497-2511) on the Ichetucknee River, which is world famous as a tubing and floating river.

From the confluence of the Santa Fe and the Itchetucknee, you can paddle down to the Suwannee. The closest ramp is just over a mile upstream from the Suwannee, so once you take a look at the Suwannee, allow an hour to paddle back to the ramp. To drive to this access, go about a mile south of the US129 bridge and turn right/west to the river. Or you can paddle all the way back to the US129 bridge.

Both rivers, especially the Santa Fe, do flood during heavy rainfall, so during the rainy season call either a livery or one of the parks to check on the water level.

Also try www8.myflorida.com/communities/learn/trails/canoe or http://ginniesprings.com.

Destination 31: Shingle Creek and the Suwannee Delta

Miles or average time: no limit, go at your own speed

Skill level: beginner

Current: strong in the main channel of the Suwannee

Wind problems: mostly sheltered, but some straight open stretches on the Suwannee

Emergency numbers: 911; Dixie County sheriff, (352) 498-1220

Rentals: Miller's Marine Campground, Highway 349, Suwannee FL 32692, phone (352) 542-7349

DeLorme page 69, section B-2

Official Florida canoe trail: no

The three canoe trails at the end of the Suwannee River feature history and maybe prehistoric fish. This is also the southern end of the Historic Big Bend Saltwater Paddling Trail (see destination 20).

The town of Suwannee was founded back when water was the only means of transportation. Now you can drive to it from US19/27/55, turning south at Old Town. I suspect the first buildings were put on the only patch of high ground the builders could find. All the roads in the town dead-end in a creek or canal. You can launch at several places, including Angler's Resort (phone (352) 542-7077), Bill's Fish Camp (phone (352) 542-7086), and Munden Camp (phone (352) 542-7480).

You'll see civilization only while you're close to town. Paddle around a bend, and you're in wilderness.

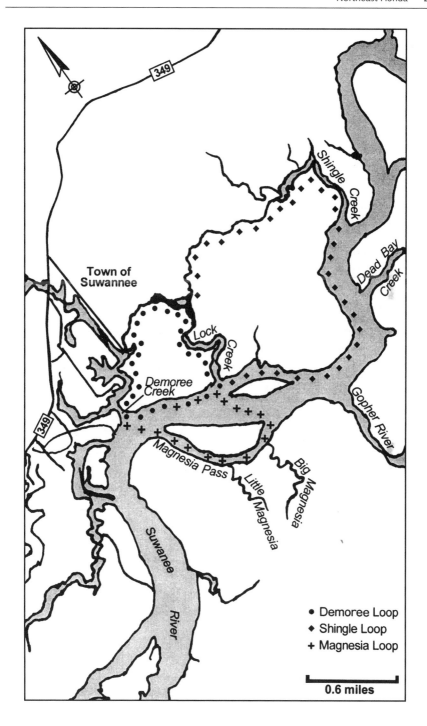

Town of
Suwannee

Shingle Creek

Dead Bay Creek

Lock Creek

Demoree
Creek

Gopher River

Magnesia Pass

Little Magnesia

Big Magnesia

Suwanee River

349

• Demoree Loop
♦ Shingle Loop
+ Magnesia Loop

0.6 miles

The forest is almost virgin. I saw the remains of an old logging road, and mossy stumps that looked like they'd been cut a century ago. With good management, the old-growth forest is coming back, thanks to the 52,110-acre Lower Suwannee National Wildlife Refuge established in 1979.

The three canoe trails listed here are southeast of town. However, my friend Dick Bowles says that the Salt Creek area, north of town, is another great paddling adventure.

Demoree Creek is the first loop trail. It takes about an hour and a half. From town, head left/north up Demoree Creek. Once you pass Bay Street, you'll enter the narrow shaft of the creek. It makes a gentle arch to the north, and at the east end you'll come to Maple Island and the junction with Lock Creek. Turn right/south and follow Lock Creek to the Suwannee. Turn right/west and follow the current back to Demoree Creek. (Do this clockwise so you go with the current on both the Suwannee and Lock Creek.)

The next loop trail, Shingle Creek, is simply a larger loop that extends east beyond Lock Creek. The average time is three and a quarter hours. Again, head up Demoree Creek, but when you get to Maple Island, turn left and go up Lock Creek. After you pass the mouth of Lock Creek on the left (yes, this sounds confusing—look at the map), keep heading east to Shingle Creek. Watch for the sign, and you'll make an acute right turn into Shingle. This runs for only half a mile before emptying into the Suwannee. From there, you'd again head west or downstream to get back to town.

The third canoe trail, which is actually in Levy County, is Magnesia Pass, a two-hour loop. This is easier to do on a rising tide, since you're heading parallel to the main channel of the Suwannee.

To get to Magnesia Pass, launch and head right/south out of Demoree Creek. When you get to the Suwannee, look across the river and slightly to your left. You'll see the mouth of Magnesia Pass. If you have a compass, the opening will be at 170° from true north.

In the pass, you'll pass two estuarine rivers coming in from your right, Little Magnesia Creek, then Big Magnesia Creek. Stay to the left, and you'll hit the Suwannee again. Cross the channel to the north bank, and follow it back to town.

Keep an eye out for strange shapes underwater. The big rivers in this part of the Gulf are the home of the endangered river sturgeon. These hard-shelled, sloop-nosed fish grow to be five or six feet long. Fish biologists are researching how to rebuild their stocks. The sturgeon come up the river to spawn in the spring, spend the summer in the rivers, then head back out to the Gulf in the fall.

I've seen sturgeon twice. Once, a huge black shape slowly undulated under my canoe. This was far upstream on the Suwannee, and the bottom was white sand. At first I thought it was a gator, then a big garfish, but finally I decided it had to be a sturgeon. Or a prehistoric monster—I'd just seen a scary movie and having this "thing" pass under my keel gave me goosebumps.

The other time all I saw was a black, scaly back roll on the surface, about ten feet from my bow. Again I thought it was a gator, until the flukes of its tail appeared. I quickly paddled the other way.

Dick Bowles says, "Especially in early spring, when mature sturgeon return from their offshore migration, they leap clear of the water, landing with a monumental splash, scaring the wits out of innocent anglers."

Despite their prehistoric appearance, these are completely harmless fish. They're bottom feeders, using their whiskerlike barbels to smell out snails, mollusks, and other treats. Someday while I'm out bottom fishing for catfish I hope to hook one of these giants, and take lots of pictures before I release it.

For more information, contact the Suwannee River Chamber of Commerce, PO Box 373, Suwannee FL 32692, phone (352) 542-7845. Also try the Lower Suwannee National Wildlife Refuge, 16450 NW 31 Place, Chiefland FL 32626, phone (352) 493-0238 or 1-800-344-WILD, on the web at www.fws.gov/~r4eao.

Destination 32: Silver River

Miles or average time: 8 miles or 4 hours round-trip

Skill level: beginner to intermediate

Current: moderate and steady

Wind problems: moderate, in straight runs

Emergency Numbers: 911; Marion County sheriff, (352) 732-8181

Rentals: Colby Woods, 10313 East Highway 40, Silver Springs FL 34488, phone (352) 625-1122; Lake Waldena Resort, 13582 East State Road 40, Silver Springs FL 34488, phone (352) 625-2851; Ocklawaha Outpost, 15260 NE 152 Place, Fort McCoy FL 32134, phone (352) 236-4606; Florida Pack & Paddle, PO Box 879, Altoona FL 32702, phone (352) 669-0008 or 1-800-297-8811, website www.floridapackandpaddle.com

DeLorme page 72, section C-2

Official Florida canoe trail: no

Silver Springs has been famous since 1878 for its crystal clear water, glass-bottomed boats, and reptile institute. It's a first-magnitude spring, billed as the world's largest artesian spring. The 500 million gallons of 71° water that flow out of its huge caldron every day feed the wide and rushing Silver River.

Johnny Weismuller filmed some of his Tarzan movies here. The glass-bottomed boat operators point out the site, as well as the petrified trees on the bottom.

The Ross Allen Reptile Institute once had Florida's largest alligator and largest crocodile, until one day the gator stuck his nose through the wire into

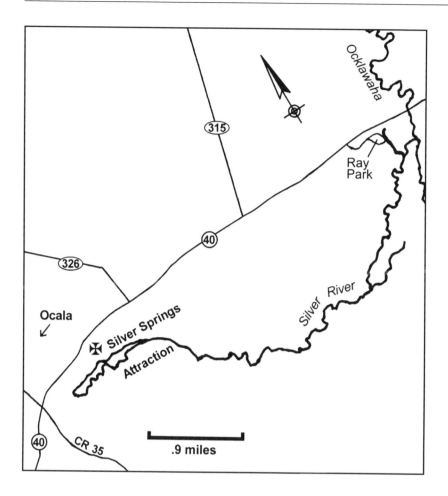

the croc's pen. The croc grabbed it, and held on tight until Big Henry drowned. Now Big Henry is stuffed and mounted on the wall of the gift shop.

I've heard three stories about how all the rhesus monkeys came to live on the south bank of the river. One says they are escapees from a medical research lab, the next that they were put there as a tourist attraction for the glass-bottomed boat customers, and the third that they were low-paid extras for the Tarzan movies. Whichever is true, be careful around them. These lightning-fast extortionists are accustomed to humans, are very pushy in pursuit of handouts, and have a nasty bite. They can also jump into your canoe from a good six feet away, and aren't the least bit worried about tipping over your canoe. The good news is that the main tribe (horde? flock?) stay close to the glass-bottom boat route.

In 1768 the native Indians, including the Seminoles, were given the "useless" interior of the state. A big contingent of them settled around Silver Springs, and a few still live there.

The Silver River flows into the Ocklawaha River, which is covered in destinations 25 and 26. From 1963 to 1971 there were plans to dredge a Cross Florida Barge Canal. It was defeated, but not before Rodman Dam was built further downstream on the Ocklawaha. Before the dam, hundreds of catfish as long as your leg congregated in the main spring. The glass boat operators would toss them a ball of white bread so the tourists could watch the resulting game of "catfish football." Now you see very few catfish, since there's no way for them to travel upstream from the St. Johns River.

Launch off SR40 east of the Silver Springs attraction. The turnoff to Ray Wayside County Park, also called Ocklawaha River Park, is southeast of the bridge over the Ocklawaha. There is a $2 usage fee.

Paddle south from the ramp. The channel dead-ends into the Silver River. Go right to do the round-trip paddle up the Silver River, or left to paddle the Ocklawaha River.

There is a steady current going up to the spring, so the paddling is a bit easier if you hug the sides of the river. The current makes coming back a breeze. There is a sand beach for the Silver River Museum about halfway up the Silver River, and on the right is a place to get out and have lunch. Look for old campfires and pipes from artesian wells along the banks. Beyond this point you are inside the Silver Springs attraction property, and are not allowed to get out of your boat. Also, you may not fish, swim, feed animals, or remove plants on their property.

This is a beautiful river, with deep jungle on each side, forests of grass beds waving underwater, and an interesting tourist attraction at the end.

Destination 33: Sopchoppy River

Miles or average time: 15 miles, in three segments

Skill level: beginner to strong intermediate

Current: average, 2–3 mph

Wind problems: few in upper section, some in wider lower part

Emergency Numbers: 911; Wakulla County sheriff, (850) 926-7171

Rentals: Ochlockonee State Park, PO Box 5, Sopchoppy FL 32358, phone (850) 962-2771

DeLorme page 50, section D-1

Official Florida canoe trail: yes

Not only is this a fun river, I like the sound of its name. There's a little mom-and-pop catfish restaurant in the town of Sopchoppy that we visit every time we pass through this area. About the only place to get supplies is the Sopchoppy Grocery, phone (850) 962-2231.

The name means "long, twisting river" in Creek Indian, and those Indians knew what they were talking about. The water is clear red, and usually very low. During droughts it can be a mere trickle, especially upriver where it comes up out of a deep swamp. In several places you'll have to portage, with many bump-overs. You can call the U.S. Forest Service for water level information at (850) 926-3561.

The Sopchoppy is almost two different rivers. Upstream you'll be working your way down a limestone ditch with windfall trees, cypress knees, and tight corners.

About 1.8 miles north of the town of Sopchoppy the river suddenly widens, slows, and deepens. From here on you'll paddle through flatlands, shar-

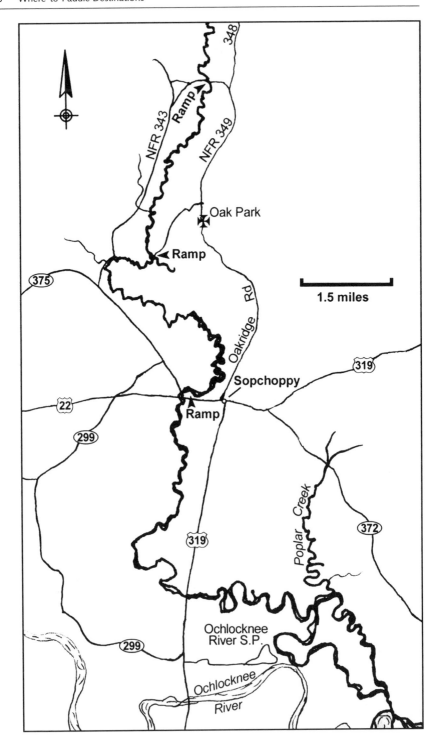

ing the water with fishermen and powerboats. After US375, the river makes some huge oxbow loops through marshland.

1) Oak Park Cemetery Bridge to Mount Beeser Church Bridge, 5 miles. From the town of Sopchoppy, head northwest on SR375. About three and a half miles past the intersection of SR375 and SR22, turn right/north on Forestry Road 343. This will bend to the east and join NFR346. Go east to the bridge.

2) Mount Beeser Church Bridge to SR375, 5 miles. Again from the town of Sopchoppy, head northwest on SR375, right/north on NFR343, cross a tiny bridge, and take the next right/east turn. This leads to the landing just a short distance to the east.

The middle part of this run is uninhabited, but you'll see homes and a couple of old abandoned cars at the beginning of the trip. About two-thirds of the way down, the river widens out.

3) SR375 bridge to US319, 5 miles. Access is in a city park on the northeast side of the bridge, right in the middle of the town of Sopchoppy.

4) The official canoe trail ends at the US319 bridge. If you wish, you can add another three-mile leg by continuing on to Ochlockonee River State Park. For about two miles after the US319 bridge, the old oxbow loops braid together, but you won't have any problem following the current downstream. Finding the canal that leads to the park is the trickiest part. Take the first big right turn, which is the main channel, to paddle to Ochlockonee State Park (it's pronounced Oak-LOCK-nee). You'll see the high bluff at the park.

For more information, try www8.myflorida.com/communities/learn/trails/canoe.

Destination 34: Spruce Creek

> Miles or average time: 16 miles round-trip
>
> Skill level: beginner
>
> Current: tidal
>
> Wind problems: yes, in open marsh
>
> Emergency numbers: 911; Volusia County sheriff, (904) 736-5961; Port Orange Police, (904) 756-5333
>
> Rentals: Avalon Historical Canoe Tours (guided), PO Box 23831, Allandale FL 32123, phone 1-800-929-9854
>
> DeLorme page 75, section D-1
>
> Official Florida canoe trail: yes

Doris Leeper, president of the Friends of Spruce Creek Preserve, raves about this waterway. "You can spend a lifetime exploring all the little creeks and back bays and backwaters here in the preserve," she says. "It's a fabulous opportunity."

To the east you're paddling through wind-rippled grass flats. The salt marshes and mangrove forests are good places to watch for mangrove crabs, both yellow and black night-crowned herons, and red-billed oyster catchers.

To the west you're inside a dark-water Florida river that originates in a freshwater cypress swamp. Watch for red-cockaded woodpeckers, wood storks, and Florida's ever present alligators. Sandhill cranes have been spotted here too.

Timucua Indians had large towns here when the area was first explored by Europeans in the late 1500s. A French artist named Jacques LeMoyne made a sketch of the area back in 1564.

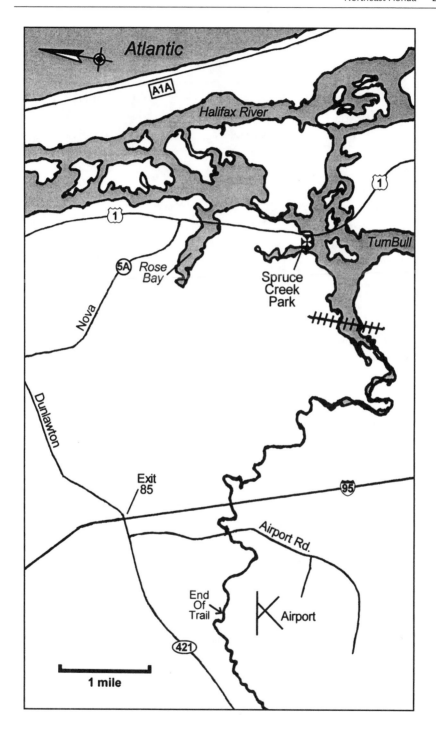

When artist Jacques LeMoyne visited in 1564, Timucua Indians traveled up and down the coast in long dugout canoes. University of South Florida archives.

Archeologists tell us that the Timucuans had sophisticated astronomy, toolmaking, a trading and tribute system that reached for hundreds of miles, and elaborate tattoo and hair arranging practices. Nowadays the only traces left by these tall, powerful people are the few shell mounds that dot the coast. One of the largest is the enormous ceremonial Spruce Creek Mound, located in another park upstream from Spruce Creek via Martin Dairy Road.

The two-thousand-plus acres of the Spruce Creek Preserve were established in 1997, thanks to Leeper and her band of determined folks. Some of the land is still in private hands, but monies from the state, the county, cities, and other organizations have been earmarked to buy up these parcels, so the area will someday be restored to its pre-European state.

In addition to being an official Florida canoe trail, Spruce Creek has been dubbed an Outstanding Florida Waters designation, and has class III (darned good) water quality.

At the present time there are only two places to access the creek.

1) Spruce Creek Park. By car, take I-95 and get off north of New Smyrna

Beach at exit 85, Dunlawton Avenue/SR421. Go east on Dunlawton, then turn right/south on Nova Road/SR5A. Turn right/south again on US1. Pass Rose Bay Bridge. Go about a mile and a half, and watch for the brown and white Volusia County Parks and Recreation sign on the right. If you pass the three bridges (under construction until the year 2002) at the head of Strickland Bay, you're too far south. The twenty-four-acre Spruce Creek Park has a ranger on duty, and a new ramp was recently installed.

From the park, head east to enter the wide saltwater estuary system, with rivers, creeks, and tiny rivulets that braid the marshes all the way out to the Intracoastal Waterway. If you're feeling really strong, you could paddle past the barrier island and out Ponce de Leon Inlet to the Atlantic Ocean. There's a boat ramp at the extreme south tip of A1A, on the north side of the inlet. This opening to the sea drains a huge body of water, and the current and wind are usually rough.

2) The next access is a wide spot in the road used by local boaters. It is the southeast side of US1, the northbound lane, south of the three bridges of Spruce Creek.

If you've paddled this river before: the rickety old ramp on the southwest side of the Airport Road bridge is now fenced off. You could probably squeeze a canoe or kayak into the water from the northeast side of the bridge, but parking would be a problem.

For more information, contact Spruce Creek Park, 6250 South Ridgewood Avenue, Port Orange FL 32127, phone (904) 736-5953. You can contact the Friends of Spruce Creek Preserve at (904) 428-6578. Spruce Creek Park office is at (904) 322-5133, and the Volusia County Parks and Recreation Department at (904) 736-5953.

Also try www8.myflorida.com/communities/learn/trails/canoe.

Destination 35: Steinhatchee River

Miles or average time: 14 miles, in three segments of 2, 7, and 5 miles

Skill level: beginner

Current: mild upstream, tidal near mouth

Wind problems: open water in second half of trip

Emergency Numbers: 911; Taylor County sheriff, (850) 584-4225

Rentals: Steinhatchee Landing Resort, PO Box 789, Highway 51 N, Steinhatchee FL 32359, phone (352) 498-3513, website www.steinhatcheelanding.com

DeLorme page 63, section C-1

Official Florida canoe trail: no

First of all, it's pronounced STEEN-hatchee. Every local person you meet will gleefully jump on the least mispronunciation.

The river drains Mallory Swamp to the northeast. The water is dark reddish brown, stained by the marshes it has passed on its way to the Gulf of Mexico. It goes underground for three-quarters of a mile, and emerges near Tennille RV Park.

In high water Steinhatchee Falls can provide a short bit of white-water experience, depending on the amount of recent rainfall. If the water is too low over the falls for paddling, it is easy to portage around them.

At the falls the river heads southwest. It starts shallow, narrow, and slow. You'll pass water oaks with tangled roots crocheted down into the water, big cypress trees draped with Spanish moss, and willow thickets. Some of these trees predate the Civil War.

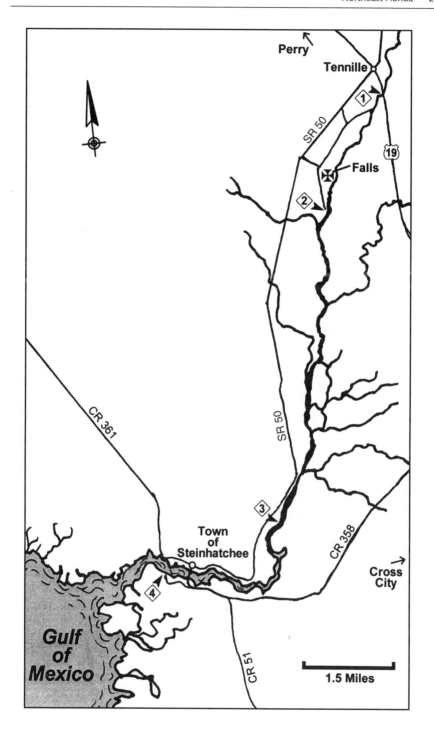

The Gulf end of the river is lined with fish houses, fish camps, marinas, waterside restaurants, and boaters heading offshore for trout, redfish, and other game fish. The Historic Big Bend Canoe Trail runs down the coast here (see destination 20).

For a fee, all the marinas in Steinhatchee have launching facilities. At Ideal Marina and Motel (phone (352) 498-3877), for example, the launch fee for canoes and kayaks is about $5.

Be warned that from July 1 to September 10 is scallop season, and the motels and campgrounds are booked up solid until about mid-August. If you're camping, try Wood's Gulf Breeze Campgrounds at (352) 498-3948.

1) US19 to Steinhatchee Falls, 2.2 miles. Start from Tennille Convenience Store and RV Park at US19 and SR51.

2) The falls to Steinhatchee Landing Resort, 7 miles. This is the most popular canoe and kayak run. To get to Steinhatchee Landing Resort from US19 at Tennille, head south on SR51 for one mile and watch for the Water Management District signs on the left that mark the entrance to the small public park beside the falls.

This tiny park has some interesting history. The ancient West Coast Indian Trail crossed the river here. The crossing was heavily used during the nineteenth century by the U.S. military and by settlers. Wagon ruts are still visible immediately above the falls, on both sides of the river.

3) Steinhatchee Landing Resort to the mouth of the river, 5.5 miles. The resort has two free canoe launch sites but no powerboat ramp. This is an upscale resort, with cottages built to look like old-timey cracker houses. President Jimmy Carter once stayed here, and you can even rent the same two-story house his family used.

4) The mouth of the Steinhatchee River. To get to this ramp, go south over the river bridge in the town of Steinhatchee, from Taylor County to Dixie County. Turn right/west on Ed James Road. The ramp is at the end of this road. The river is very wide at this point, with strong tides, but on a calm day you can explore the tangled channels that meander through the saltwater marshes south of the river.

If you're into catfish, this is a great fishing river. Since the river runs into the Gulf of Mexico, you can often catch saltwater catfish, such as sea catfish and gafftopsail catfish, close to the mouth of the river. I watched a couple of kids fishing off the Route 358 bridge who quickly pulled in two "hardhead" sea cats.

Though it wouldn't take my bait, I watched a foot-long plecostomus catfish wiggle underneath my canoe far upriver. South Florida canals are full of these aquarium escapees, but I was surprised to see one this far north.

Dean Fowler, who runs Steinhatchee Landing Resort, tells me that the Suwannee River Water Management District has employed an engineer to design a trail that will eventually go from Steinhatchee to US19 on both sides of the river for a twenty-three-mile round-trip. It will be available for bicycling and hiking. He says, "A paddler will be able to ride a bicycle from the village to Tennille, rent a canoe, and return by river to the landing." The trail is expected to be open in the year 2002.

I like the Steinhatchee. It has good fishing, changing scenery, and a pleasing air of tranquillity. Sometimes I even pronounce it correctly.

Destination 36: St. Marys River

> Miles or average time: 51 miles, in five sections of 9, 12, 17, 7, and 6 miles
>
> Skill level: beginner
>
> Current: easy, steady flow
>
> Wind problems: few until you get past Trader's Hill
>
> Emergency numbers: 911; Nassau County sheriff, (904) 225-5174
>
> Rentals: Hidden River Ranch, 885 Reynolds Bridge Road, St. George GA 31646, phone (912) 843-2603, e-mail hiddenriver@planttel.net; Canoeport, Route 1, Box 152, St. George GA 31646, phone (912) 843-2688
>
> DeLorme page 56, section B-1
>
> Official Florida canoe trail: yes

It was on a deserted stretch of the St. Marys River that I stopped my boat for half an hour and watched a baby osprey and its parents.

The youngster was easy to spot. It was sitting in a tall pine on the north side of the creek, shrieking at the top of its lungs. Both parents flew nearby, briefly landing in the same tree, then flying off for short distances. They were clearly trying to coax it to fly, but the youngster wasn't having any of it.

It was fully fledged—with feathers—with just a hint of downy baby fluff on its back and the top of its head. It looked bigger than both parents.

It clearly wanted both parents to bring it nice, deheaded fish at regular intervals, just as they had for the past two months. When a parent would land near the huge baby, it would crouch down, bob its head, and do its best to look hungry and downright pitiful.

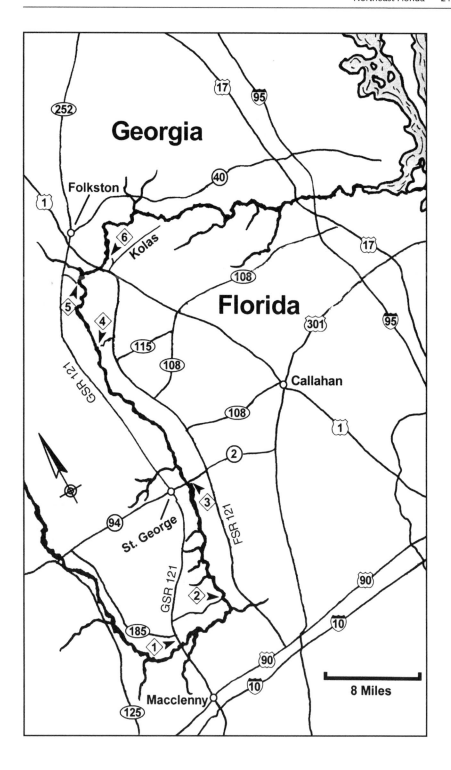

It finally decided to fly to another tree, with about six dozen aborted starts—*I think I can . . . here I go . . . spread those wings . . .* NOW *I'm gonna let go of this branch . . . nope.*

At long last the bird launched itself out of sight. It obviously made it to the next tree, as revealed by another set of panicked calls to Mom and Pop.

In another day or two the youngster would fly with more confidence, and eventually learn to swoop down and grab a fish right out of the water, flying far better than anything Jonathan Livingston Seagull could ever achieve. But that day it was an endearing sight.

The St. Marys River is slightly disorienting. Here in Florida we're accustomed to seeing all our waterways heading south or west. But the St. Marys is like the St. Johns—it flows north before it heads for the Atlantic. It is the dividing line between Georgia and Florida, and its meandering is what gives Florida that little "tab" in the upper right corner.

One simple ridge of Georgia real estate is responsible for that "tab." It's a strip of high ground called the Trail Ridge, and it runs north-south just about seven miles west of Folkston, Georgia. Everything east of the Trail Ridge flows to the Atlantic Ocean. Everything west of the ridge is the vast Okeefenokee Swamp, which drains either to the Suwannee or the St. Marys. The Suwannee drains the western edge, and the St. Marys drains the southern edge of the Okeefenokee. These two mighty rivers originate at points in the swamp only about seventeen miles from each other.

Some paddlers have done the entire 125 miles of the St. Marys. If you like more challenging paddling—in low water, that can mean logjams, strainers, bump-overs, and portages—try the North and Middle Prongs of the river. They can be daunting in both low and flood stages, so pick your section of river carefully. Hidden River Ranch is a good place to start for this upper section.

The fifty-one miles of the official Florida canoe trail are well below where the North and Middle Prongs of the river come together. This part of the river is narrow enough to be interesting, yet wide enough to be fairly easy to paddle. While it will seem that you are out in the wilderness, two highways parallel the river, so you could always hike out.

This is a good camping river, with plenty of sandbars and high banks. Note that during the rainy season these sandbars vanish.

At some points you'll feel like you're down inside a hole. High above you will be dry lands, growing nothing but longleaf pine and palmetto scrub. In other areas you'll think you're in a swamp, with wide marshy areas extending on either side.

There are six access points on the official Florida canoe trail.

1) CR121 to Stokes Bridge, 9 miles. From the town of Macclenny (DeLorme page 56, section B-1), head north on SR121 for 5½ miles. The access to the river is on the northwest side of the bridge.

You are starting off at a fairly wide section of the river. The dark reddish tan water makes a startling contrast to the white sandbars and dark green foliage of the tupelo trees, which don't grow much further south.

2) Stokes Bridge to SR2, 12 miles. From Macclenny, take US90 east about six miles to SR121. Turn left/north and go about six and a half miles, crossing Brandy Branch. Turn left/west on Stokes/CR3 and go to the bridge.

Canoeport livery is on the left in the town of St. George, just a couple of city blocks before you get to the SR2 bridge.

3) SR2 to Tompkin's Landing, 17 miles. The river crosses the road about two miles west of the intersection of SR2 and SR121. Access is on the northwest side of the bridge.

4) Tompkin's Landing to Trader's Hill, 7 miles. From the little town of Hilliard, head west on CR115 for 5.5 miles, then north on SR121 for 2.3 miles. You'll pass over Dunn's Creek. Turn left on Tompkin's Landing Road and follow it to the river.

5) Trader's Hill to Scots Landing, 6 miles. You'll get to the Trader's Hill Recreational Area from the Georgia side, off SR121. From Folkston, head south on Georgia SR121 for five miles. The sign for the recreation area will be on your left/east.

Trader's Hill is on a bluff, and was once a bustling trading post. For a short time it was the county seat for Charlton County, Georgia. That was back in the time when rivers were the superhighways of the nation. When roads were put in, the county seat moved to Folkston. There are still a couple of old wooden stumps on the left/west bank that were pilings for the trading post.

The river winds back and forth for the first half, and then straightens out to head southeast. Just a quarter mile after you pass under the railroad trestle, the river suddenly widens out, and you'll see more motorboat traffic.

The takeout is about a mile past US1/301. Pigeon Creek will come in from your right/east, and the Scots Landing ramp is shortly after that on your right/east.

6) Scots Landing is the end of the official trail. To get there from Hilliard, take US1/301 north about eight miles. You'll pass a Florida Information station on your left. In the tiny settlement of Boulogne, turn right/east on Kolas/Colas Ferry Road. If you cross the river on US1, you've gone a quarter mile too far. Head down Kolas Road for three-quarters of a mile and turn left/north on the next road after St. Marys Circle Road to the ramp.

While you're paddling, watch for ospreys. One of the birds you spot may be that baby, all grown up and flying high.

Also try www8.my florida.com/communities/learn/trails/canoe or www. paddlefl.com/Destinations/StMarys/StMarys.htm. You can check water levels on the river at http://websflals.er.usgs.gov/rt-cgi.

Destination 37: Suwannee River

Miles or average time: 141 miles, in eleven sections ranging from .5 to 22 miles

Skill Level: intermediate

Current: variable, averaging 2–3 mph

Wind problems: wildly variable

Emergency Numbers: 911; Columbia County sheriff, (904) 752-9212; Hamilton County sheriff, (904) 792-2004; Madison County sheriff, (850) 973-4151; Suwannee County sheriff, (904) 362-2222

Rentals: Suwannee Canoe Outpost, 2461 95th Drive, Live Oak FL 32060, phone (904) 364-4991 or 1-800-428-4147, website www.canoeoutpost.com; American Canoe Adventures, 10315 SE 141st Boulevard, White Springs FL 32096, phone (904) 397-1309 or 1-800-624-8081; Santa Fe Canoe Outpost, PO Box 592, High Springs FL 32655, phone (904) 454-2050, website www.riverise.com/canoe.htm; Ichetucknee Family Grocery & Campground, Route 1, Box 1756, O'Brien FL 32071, phone (904) 497-2150; Manatee Springs State Park, 11650 NW 115 Street, Chiefland FL 32626, phone (352) 493-6072; North American Canoe Tours, 107 Camellia Street, Everglades City FL 34139, phone (941) 695-4666, website www.evergladesadventures.com; Outdoor Adventures, 1626 Emerson Street, Jacksonville FL 32207, phone (904) 393-9030, e-mail outdoorfl@aol.com, website www.OutdoorAdventures.FLA.com; River Rendezvous, Convict Spring Road, Mayo FL 32066, phone (904) 294-2510 or 1-800-533-5276; Suwannee Expeditions Canoe & Kayak, 614 Ivey Memorial Park Drive SW, Branford FL 32008, phone (904) 935-9299; Treefrog Adventures, 145 DeBary Drive, DeBary FL 32713, phone (407) 668-1222; Twin Rivers Outfitters, PO Box 62, Pinetta FL 32350, phone (850) 929-2200

DeLorme: page 39, section B-2, to page 54, section B-2

Official Florida canoe trail: yes, for the river inside Florida

Ever since Stephen Foster wrote the song about the Suwannee River, it's been the signature waterway for Florida. Historians say he was only looking for a river with two syllables, never saw it, and even misspelled its name. Who cares? The wide brown Suwannee is long, interesting, and worth a visit.

The river starts in the Okeefenokee Swamp in Georgia and goes some 62 miles before it gets to the Florida border. Officially, 141 miles of the Florida part of the river are in the canoe trail, but I can find only 120.3 miles of it. Downstream from that is another long stretch to the river's end past the town of Suwannee at the Gulf of Mexico (see destination 31).

The Suwannee River officially begins in Georgia at the Sill, a manmade earthen dam that runs for a dozen miles across what used to be the low western edge of the swamp. It was put in to keep the water level constant to reduce fires in the swamp, and separates the Okeefenokee Swamp from the Suwannee River. I spent a week in the Okeefenokee, putting in near Folkston and getting out at Fargo, and have vivid memories of the swamp. I was intrigued by the tupelo trees that dot the upper river. These look exactly like the sweet potato plants you stuck with toothpicks and rooted in a jar of water when you were a kid.

If you want to paddle the Georgia portion of the Suwannee, there are a couple of places to enter the Okeefenokee. One is the Suwannee Canal, on the east side of the swamp off SR121 south of Folkston. The other is Stephen C. Foster State Park, located at the north end of SR177 in the middle of the swamp.

The official Florida canoe trail consists of seven sections for the Upper Suwannee. The river is narrow, winding, and brown here.

Upper Suwannee

1) SR6 to Cone Bridge Road, 8.9 miles, Hamilton and Columbia Counties. From the town of White Springs, drive seven miles north on SR135, turn right/east on SR6, and go less than a mile to the bridge.

2) Cone Bridge Road to Big Shoals, 9.7 miles. From I-10, go north on SR441 for 14.7 miles. Turn west on Cone Bridge Road.

3) Big Shoals Recreation Area to US41, 6 miles. From the town of White Springs, go north on SR135 for 3.5 miles. Turn right to the recreation area.

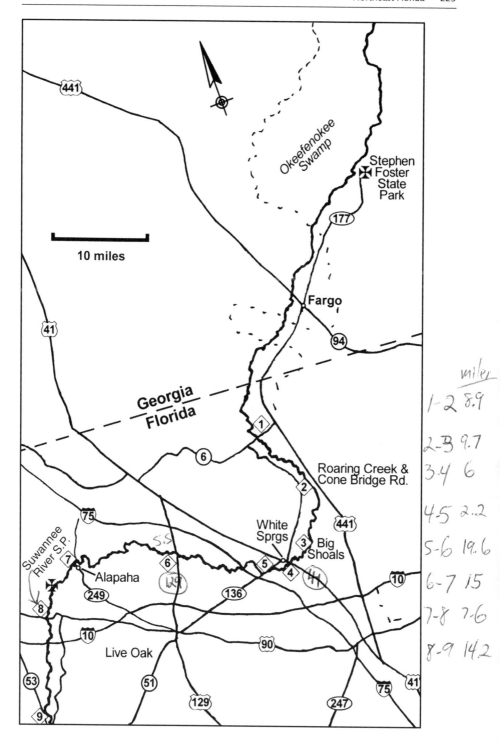

miles

1-2	8.9
2-3	9.7
3-4	6
4-5	2.2
5-6	19.6
6-7	15
7-8	7.6
8-9	14.2

4) US41 to SR136, 2.2 miles. From the town of White Springs, go south-east for one mile on US41 to the river. The ramp is on the southwest side of the bridge.

5) SR136 to US129, 19.6 miles, Hamilton and Suwannee Counties. Put in at White Springs.

6) US129 to SR249, 15 miles. From I-10, head north on CR129. Just south of the bridge, turn right/east to Suwannee Springs.

7) SR249 to Suwannee River State Park, 7.6 miles, Madison and Suwannee Counties. From Live Oak, head north on SR249 to the bridge.

Lower Suwannee

8) Suwannee River State Park to US90, .5 miles. The state park is off US90 near Live Oak. Now you're starting the 51 miles of the wider Lower Suwannee.

The Stephen Foster State Folk Culture Center features Florida pioneer exhibits, including the desk that Foster used when he composed "Old Folks at Home." The annual Folk Festival is great fun. You can contact the Stephen Foster Center at PO Drawer G, White Springs FL 32096, phone (904) 397-4331.

9) US90 to SR251, 14.2 miles. Start at the Ellaville bridge.

10) SR251 to SR51, 14.6 miles, Madison and Suwannee Counties. Start at the town of Dowling Park.

11) SR51 to Branford, 22 miles. Start at the ramp on the southwest side of the bridge, two miles north of Mayo. Telford Spring will be on your left about half a mile from the SR51 bridge. The runoff channels from Peacock and Bonnet Springs, in the Peacock Springs State Recreation Area, are about two miles down from that.

Another boat ramp is on the west side of the river, about ten miles downstream from SR51. From Mayo, drive east on US27 for about seven and a half miles, then east on CR251 for three miles. Follow the signs to Mearson and Owens Springs.

The next four miles to Troy Springs are almost straight. Watch for them on the right. On the sandy bottom are what's left of an old Confederate river runner, the *Madison*. After a century and a third in the water, the old logs are slowly petrifying. It's against the law to disturb them.

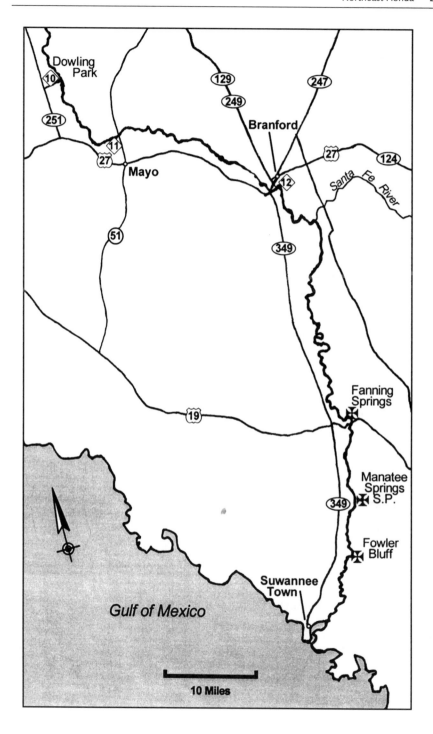

12) End the official state canoe trail at the town of Branford (DeLorme page 64, section A-1.)

Going On

With a bit more planning you can continue downriver to the town of Suwannee and the Gulf of Mexico.

Be sure to stop at Manatee Springs State Park, which is twenty-three miles upstream from the river's mouth. There's a nice boardwalk, campground, swimming area, boathouse, and canoe rental. In the winter you're sure to see the giant forms of manatees dozing underwater. They come in for the constant 72° water being gushed up at the rate of 117 million gallons per day. Watch for the school of panfish that hang out where the clear spring water enters the red-brown river.

Just as entertaining is snorkeling or watching the scuba divers in the big spring or Catfish Hotel Sink. You can contact Manatee Springs State Park at 11650 NW 115 Street, Chiefland FL 32626, phone (352) 493-6072.

Several detailed reference books on the Suwannee River are available. Clyde C. Council has written an excellent book called *Suwannee Country*. It covers the river all the way from the Okeefenokee to the Gulf of Mexico, mile by mile. Most camping stores and canoe liveries stock the book, or you can order it from Council Company, PO Box 5822, Sarasota FL 34277. At $6 a copy, it's a good resource.

Another good book, video, and home page is *Canoeing and Camping the 213 Miles of the Beautiful Suwannee River* by William A. Logan. Contact him at billlog@brevard.net or www.Canoe-Suwannee.com and he'll send you a periodic update on river conditions.

For cyberspace information, try www.dep.state.fl.us/parks/ManateeSprings/manateesprings. The official descriptions of the canoe trail are at www8.myflorida.com/communities/learn/trails/canoe.

Destination 38: Tomoka River

Miles or average time: 13 miles

Skill level: beginner on calm days, intermediate during wind and tide changes

Current: tidal

Wind problems: yes, in open bay—stay in creeks

Emergency numbers: 911; Volusia County sheriff, (904) 736-5961

Rentals: Tomoka State Park, 2099 North Beach Street, Ormond Beach FL 32174, phone (904) 676-4050

DeLorme page 74, section B-3

Official Florida canoe trail: yes

Tomoka was the thriving Timucuan Indian village of Nocoroco when it was discovered by Alvaro Mexía in 1605. The spot was perfect—right between the salty Halifax River and the fresh Tomoka River. The long barrier island to the east kept giant waves away, and the peninsula that is now Tomoka State Park had constant breezes to help control mosquitoes. A huge cement statue by Fred Dana Marsh shows an Indian with the trademark Timucuan hairdo and grass skirt.

You have four places to launch on Tomoka Creek, or you can launch at SR40 and deadhead a car at the state park. Parking where the river goes under US1 looked iffy—look it over and decide if you want to leave a car there. The end of the trip, at the northern end of the state park, is actually the open water of Tomoka Basin, and can be windy. On calm days when the bugs are biting inland, this is a nice paddle into the salt marshes to the north.

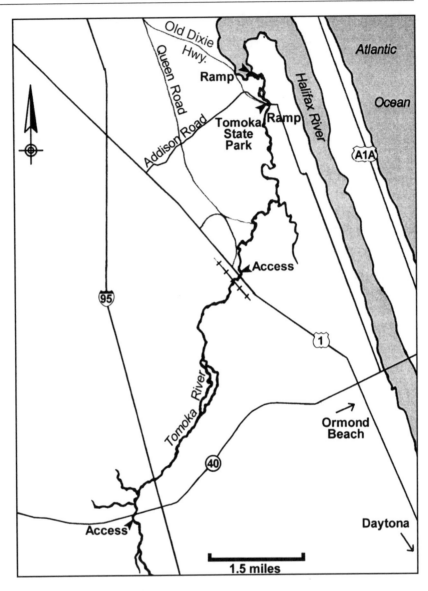

You'll find saltwater fish far up the river. The salt marshes extend from US1 to the mouth of the river, and the brackish water actually extends to I-95. Notice how the salt grasses gradually give way to freshwater plants, including cypress trees with their characteristic knobby knees.

Just north of SR40 Little Tomoka River heads west to peter out in Hull Swamp. The main river bends south, goes under SR40, and runs just west of

Tomoka was the thriving Timucuan Indian village of Nocoroco. A giant art-deco statue is artist Fred Dana Marsh's salute to these first Floridians. Sandy Huff.

I-95. There used to be access to the river at Eleventh Street, but that might have changed—check it out.

If you're there on a Saturday, ask if the free, ranger-led canoe tours are available. These visit some of the old Mount Oswald Plantation ruins, and follow a canoe trail that was used by the Indians for centuries before white men arrived.

The ranger also gives a fascinating talk on indigo. Production of colorfast dye from these spindly plants was a major cash crop for early plantation owners.

You can contact Tomoka State Park at 2099 North Beach Street, Ormond Beach FL 32174, phone (904) 676-4050, or www.dep.state.fl.us/parks/Tomoka/tomoka.html or www.dep.state.fl.us/gwt/canoeing/tomoka.htm.

Destination 39: Wacissa River

Miles or average time: 14 miles

Skill level: beginner

Current: easy

Wind problems: some in the wide spots about a third of the way down

Emergency numbers: 911; Jefferson County sheriff, (904) 977-2523

Rentals: Canoe Shop, 1115 West Orange Avenue #B, Tallahassee FL 32310, phone (850) 576-5335

DeLorme page 51, section B-2

Official Florida canoe trail: yes

My first visit to the Wacissa was when the willow trees were shedding their "cotton," and a million tiny bits of white fluff frosted the water. It was like being in a warm snowstorm.

There are only two hard parts to this trip. First, finding the main channel after Goose Pasture, since just upstream the river splits into three main streams plus a dozen little rivulets called Hell's Half Acre. Second, finding the takeout spot, which is actually a bit upstream (say, two football fields) on the Aucilla River.

Other than that, this gently curving river is a joy. There are so many vine-draped trees that you have to remind yourself not to think of any Jurassic Park movie. You're only sixteen miles from the Tallahassee city limits, but you'll think you've lost civilization completely. You'll hear dozens of birds that you can never spot, and the turtle population seems out of control.

Polaroid sunglasses come in handy in the upper part of the river, because

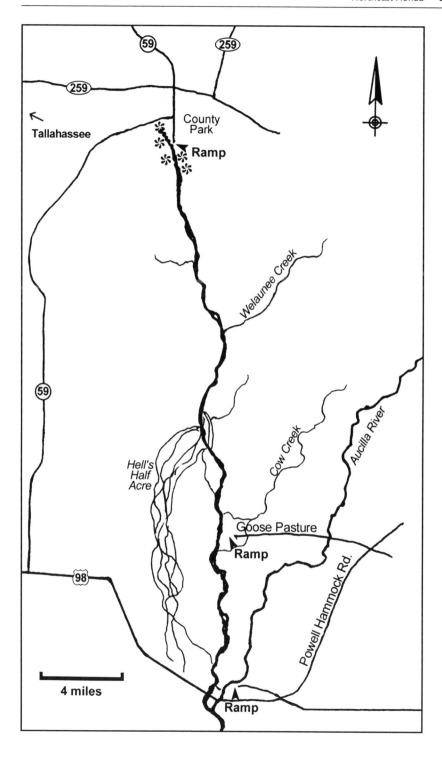

there's lots of action going on beneath you in the clear water. Watch for panfish and even a few mullet. Herons and egrets are common on the banks.

Start your paddle at Wacissa Springs. From the town of Wacissa, take SR59 south. The highway will bend to the southwest, but continue on straight to the public park at the end of the road.

There are actually twelve springs within the first mile and a half of the run. Big Spring is popular with scuba divers, plus there are Hot Spring, Aucilla Spring, Cassidy Spring, and Little Blue and Big Blue Springs.

You could probably swim in these springs, but right at the entrance to one of the smaller spring runs we spotted a big softshell turtle, and then, a dozen feet beyond it, a medium-sized alligator. So we kept our toes in our boats.

This first run is nine miles. There's flowering forest magnolia around you, amid what's known as "swamp forest."

About halfway down, Welaunee Creek comes in from your left. This water is tannish red, and more opaque than the clearer water you started with.

About three-fourths of the way down the run, you'll find a tangle of rivulets on both sides of the river. Some of them are out of sight in the undergrowth, especially in late summer. Keep paddling in the main channel. Goose Pasture is a landing on your left.

To get to Goose Pasture by car, head south from Wacissa on SR59. Go fourteen miles to US98. Turn left/east and go 8.5 miles. Turn left/north onto Powell Hammock Road. Go 4.3 miles and turn left/west on Goose Pasture road. The landing is at the end of the graded road.

For the next section of five miles, you might have trouble finding the main channel. The river braids as it travels south. Stick close to the right bank for the first mile. Watch for the canal mouth hidden in a grove of willow trees. This will lead you to Nutall Rise Landing, which is actually on the Aucilla River (see destination 14).

To get to Nutall Rise Landing by car, again head south from Wacissa on SR59, and turn left/east on US98. Cross the Aucilla River and go about a mile. Turn left/northwest onto CR685. This is a graded dirt road, and leads to the landing.

For more information, try www8.myflorida.com/communities/learn/trails/canoe.

Destination 40: Withlacoochee River (North)

Miles or average time: 27 miles, in three sections of 5, 10, and 12 miles

Skill level: beginner with moderate experience

Current: averages 2–3 mph

Wind problems: mostly sheltered

Emergency numbers: 911; Hamilton County sheriff, (904) 792-2004; Madison County sheriff, (850) 973-4151

Rentals: Twin Rivers Outfitters, PO Box 62, Pinetta FL 32350, phone (850) 929-2200, e-mail canoeguy@digitalexp.com

DeLorme page 37, section D-1, to page 53, section A-2

Official Florida canoe trail: no

There are *two* Withlacoochee Rivers. This is the one in northern Florida, thirteen miles due south of Valdosta, Georgia. The paddle-able Florida section begins just a hair over the Georgia line and ends at the Suwannee River State Park outside Ellaville.

Jim Wagner, who operates Twin Rivers Outfitters, calls this river "the gateway to North Florida spring country" and "the best kept secret in Florida."

The river begins in a system of creeks and springs in Georgia but, unlike the Suwannee, it doesn't come from the Okeefenokee Swamp. "People usually think the With's conditions are the same as the Suwannee," Jim says. "When the upper Suwannee is so low you have to drag boats, we have water here on the With. Last year when the Suwannee flooded for four months, we only flooded for three weeks. The Withlacoochee is a great alternative to the

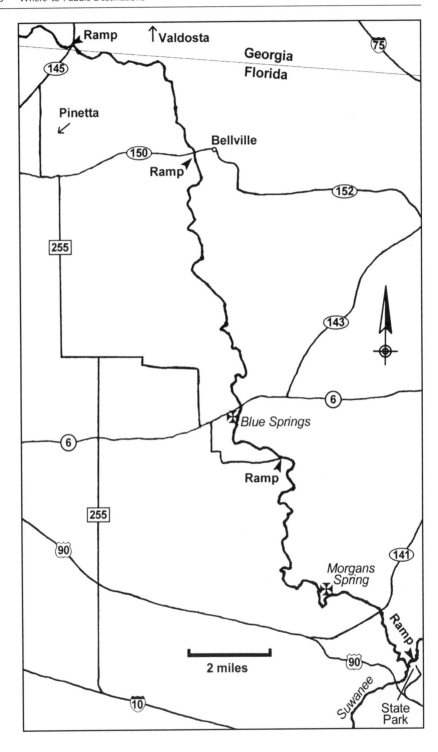

Suwannee when the conditions are less than favorable there." He goes on, "I also rent canoes and kayaks for people that want to paddle the Suwannee, so I am not totally prejudiced. But I think the Withlacoochee is just better for canoers and kayakers."

You might want to leave your own fragile boat at home and rent from Jim. "The Withlacoochee is very hard on fiberglass, and especially hard on aluminum canoes," he says. "I use Old Town, Cross Link 3 canoes, and kayaks made of polyethylene."

Most of the river runs through the Twin Rivers State Forest, a 14,713-acre woodland made up of old-cut longleaf pine, live oak, and turkey oak. Along the river you'll see tree species such as magnolia, red bay, red maple, and laurel oak. In the flood plain and bottomland hardwood swamps, you'll find black gum cypress, elm, ash, and Ogeechee tupelo, which look like above-ground tubers with a few leafy branches sprouting from the top. In the fall these sport purple berries. Autumn is a good time to paddle this river, for the colors.

Common animals include belted kingfishers, wood ducks, red-tailed hawks, wild turkeys, bobcats, and deer.

You'll feel like you're in a tunnel. "The river is better known for its high banks—ten to thirty or more feet—and the bottomland is less distinctive," Jim says. "The feeling is more of canoeing through high limestone banks."

Easy-to-run shoals occur about every mile, but there is one larger rapid. It lies about a mile upstream from the confluence with the Suwannee River. "During periods of low water, it is advisable to portage equipment around it and use a twelve-foot lead rope to guide the empty canoe across," says Jim Wagner. "If the water is extremely low, portage the canoe also." I recommend good water shoes that stay on your feet.

1) Georgia border to Bellville Road bridge, 5 miles. This first five-mile section starts just over the Georgia state line, some four miles north of Pinetta on SR145. The put-in is on the northwest side of the bridge. This section is uninhabited, so wildlife sightings are common, especially if you're the first paddler of the day. "This area is alive with kingfishers diving for small fish," says Wagner. "I watched an osprey launch itself off a tall cypress, swoop down to the water, and come up with a fish. The fishing was good that day for both the big birds and the little birds."

2) Bellville Road bridge to SR6, 10 miles. This middle section starts at the southwest side of the SR150/Bellville Road bridge, which Wagner asserts has the best launch and takeout spot on the north Withlacoochee. "Special use groups" can camp on the Twin Rivers State Forest sandbars and banks, with permission from the Division of Forestry, Live Oak Work Center, phone (904) 208-1462.

You'll now start to see a few houses and camps, with long stretches of natural river in between. About eight miles downstream is a sandbar frequently used by canoe campers and picnickers. Camping is allowed without a permit only if you are canoeing.

The shoals south of the Bellville bridge are all class one, and easily crossed. This includes the one right above the Suwannee, which keeps motorboats and jet skis from entering from the Suwannee.

3) SR6 to Suwannee River State Park, 12 miles. Start at SR6, nine miles east of the town of Madison. Across the road is Blue Springs, a privately owned park for swimming and diving, where you can pay to launch and leave a car. The rental canoes are only for the use of divers.

This last stretch has more houses. You'll pass several springs that are popular swimming holes for the local folks. The banks are higher here, and erosion has cut them into interesting shapes. See if you can spot the Elephant, the Two Fat Women, and the Waterfall.

Seven miles downstream is a primitive campsite on the left/east bank. The only access is by canoe, and you're unlikely to be bothered by any other humans, but there are raccoons, so secure your food. This is also a good spot for great horned owls, pileated woodpeckers, otters, and even beavers.

After you pass under SR141, listen for the gurgle of water. This is the large shoal already mentioned. Most of the year these shoals are fun and keep the trip interesting, but it's a good idea to reconnoiter first.

About two miles from the end, the Suwannee River State Park will begin on your left/east.

When you get to the Suwannee River, turn left/east and paddle upstream for a bit. The current is fairly placid here, but if you're having trouble, try hugging the eddy currents along either bank. The takeout is on the right/south side of the Suwannee, by the outflow of Lime Spring. The park offers camping with facilities and is a good place to leave a vehicle while paddling.

While you're at the park, check out the 1860s earthworks dug by Confederate troops during the Civil War. There's also an old pioneer cemetery, and a landing that was used by steamboats that plied the Suwannee before roads existed.

To drive to the takeout from Ellaville, go south from the Suwannee River on US90 for two miles and turn left/east onto the River Road extension. Watch for the sign for the Suwannee River State Park.

For more information, contact Suwannee River State Park, Route 8, Box 297, Live Oak FL 32060, phone (904) 362-2746.

Area 3. Central Florida

Destination 41: Alafia River

Miles or average time: 9 to 15 miles

Skill level: beginner except at flood levels

Current: moderate, but swift at flood levels

Wind problems: few, mostly narrow and sheltered

Emergency numbers: 911; Hillsborough County sheriff, (813) 247-8000

Rentals: Alafia River Canoe Rentals, 4419 River Drive, Valrico FL 33594 (about 5.5 miles south of Route 60 off Lithia Pinecrest Road), phone (813) 689-8645

DeLorme page 92, section A-1

Official Florida canoe trail: yes

Only a half-hour drive from downtown Tampa, this river used to be out in the sticks. Now housing developments line the roads.

There is little motorboat traffic in the upper Alafia, since old coral reefs break the surface in a dozen places, making this the central Florida "rapids." In low water, be prepared to either step out and pull your boat across the rocks or to find a shallow spot and "oooch" your way over by bouncing up and down in your seat. Be careful of your paint and gelcoat—despite centuries of water wear, these rocks are not smooth.

The river changes levels often, since it drains a big area. The river actually starts forty-five miles from its mouth, near the town of Mulberry. There is an upstream section from Keysville Bridge to Alderman's Ford that you can paddle, but it is not maintained by a canoe livery, and besides several shoals,

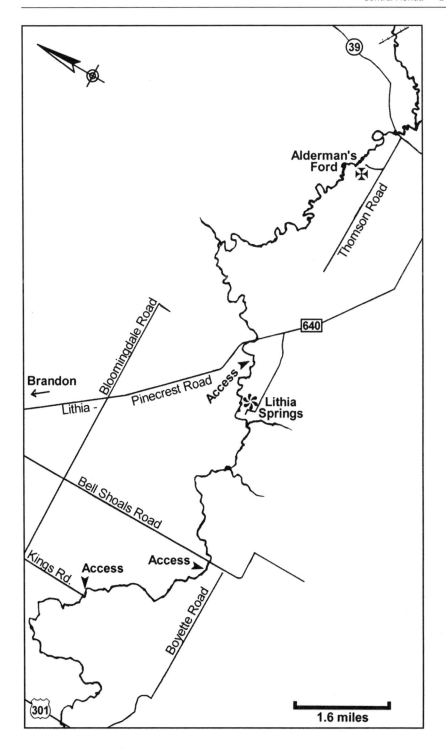

Alderman's Ford

Thomson Road

39

640

Bloomingdale Road

Brandon

Lithia -

Pinecrest Road

Access

Lithia Springs

Bell Shoals Road

Kings Rd.

Access

Access

Bovette Road

301

1.6 miles

there are often fallen trees and other obstructions. The more popular section of the river starts at Alderman's Ford.

It is possible to canoe all the way from Keysville Bridge out to the Gulf, but past Kings Avenue ramp the river opens up to a wide, windy bay.

1) Keysville to Alderman's Ford: 6 miles. This is a narrow, twisting path with many obstacles. *If* they have been recently cleaned out, launch north of Keysville on the Keysville/Henry George Road.

2) Alderman's Ford Park to CR640, 9 miles. The park is on Thompson Road, half a block west of CR39, one mile north of Lithia.

Sonny Norris, of the Central Florida Paddlemasters, says, "Before you put in, check out the watermark post at the docks. If the water is up to the red mark and the docks are underwater, *do not* make the run unless you are very, very good. The river itself will be up into the treetops and the whole trip will be mostly through treetops (called sweepers and strainers). The speed of the river gives you almost *no* time to react. Before you leave home, it's a good idea to call Alafia River Canoe Rentals for a water report. There are some picnic/camping sites, mostly after you pass the old stone railroad bridge supports."

3) CR640 to Alafia River Canoe Rental, .25 miles. At the bridge six miles southeast of Brandon there is no parking, but you can get a boat up or down the banks.

4) Alafia River Canoe Rental to Lithia Springs, 1 mile. The livery is on the southwest side of the CR640 bridge. They provide shuttle service to Alderman's Ford Park.

5) Lithia Springs County Park to Bell Shoals, 3 miles. The park is a mile east of Lithia Springs Road off CR640. On summer weekends the white-bottomed, shallow springs area can be crowded. Paddle and park further around the circular park road to avoid the jam. It is interesting to see how far the clear, bluish spring water pushes into the brown river water.

6) Bell Shoals Road to Kings Avenue, 3 miles. No parking at the Bell Shoals bridge.

Bell Shoals is the end of the official canoe trail, but you can keep paddling to the mouth of the Alafia. The river widens, with houses on each side. Here are several options:

7) Hidden River Travel Resort (12500 Mcmullen Loop, Riverview FL 33569, phone (813) 677-1515). From Bloomingdale Avenue, go south on John Moore Road.

8) Kings Avenue ramp. The ramp is four miles south of Brandon on Kings Avenue.

9) Lil Bullfrog Campground (14206 US301 S, Riverview FL 33569, phone (813) 634-2310).

10) Alafia River RV Resort (9812 Gibsonton Drive, Riverview FL 33569, phone (813) 677-1997) on the southeast side of the I-75 bridge.

11) Mouth of the Alafia. On a *calm* day, put in at Williams Park Pier in Gibsonton (DeLorme page 91, section B-2). This trip has been done by the Tampa Bay Sea Kayakers Club.

Just offshore are ten islands under the official wing of the Tampa Bay Audubon Society. Twenty species of waterbirds nest there. The closest islands are Bird and Sunken Islands. *Do not* set foot on the islands. They are hotbeds of avian activity for most of the year. October and November are about the only time some species of bird is not nesting, and even then the islands are used as daytime hangouts and nighttime roosts. Bring binoculars and ogle the birds from well offshore.

Also watch the weather. Because of the shape of Tampa Bay, this area can get very rough and wave-tossed.

For more information on the official Alafia canoe trail, try www8.myflorida.com/communities/learn/trails/canoe.

Destination 42: Anclote River

Bryce Huff

Miles or average time: no limit, go at your own pace

Skill level: beginner

Current: slow upriver, strong at mouth, with tidal rise

Wind problems: yes, this is mostly open water

Emergency numbers: 911; Pinellas County sheriff, (727) 582-6200

Rentals: Agua Azul Kayaks, 343 Causeway Boulevard, Dunedin FL 34698, phone (727) 738-4576; Anclote Boatworks, 1102 Island Avenue, Tarpon Springs FL 34689, phone (727) 942-1511; Florida Kayak & Canoe Centers, 3011 19A, Palm Harbor FL 34683, phone (727) 784-6357; Osprey Bay Kayaks, 17952 US19, Clearwater FL 33764, phone (727) 524-9670; Sail Honeymoon, 61 Causeway Boulevard, Dunedin FL 34698, phone (727) 734-0392

DeLorme page 82, section C-3

Official Florida canoe trail: no

Greek sponge fishermen moved to Tarpon Springs in 1876 because of the abundant sponge beds in the Gulf of Mexico. They also had a wonderful place to dock and shelter their boats in the Anclote River, and during the town's heyday in the 1930s more than two hundred sponge boats docked along Dodecanese Boulevard.

With the advent of artificial sponges, and a blight that killed most of the wild sponges, the industry collapsed. But several years ago a hurricane sat offshore for three days, and it revitalized the sponge beds by spreading sponge spores far and wide. A few boats have taken up sponging again, mostly shipping their harvest to European markets. The old Sponge Ex-

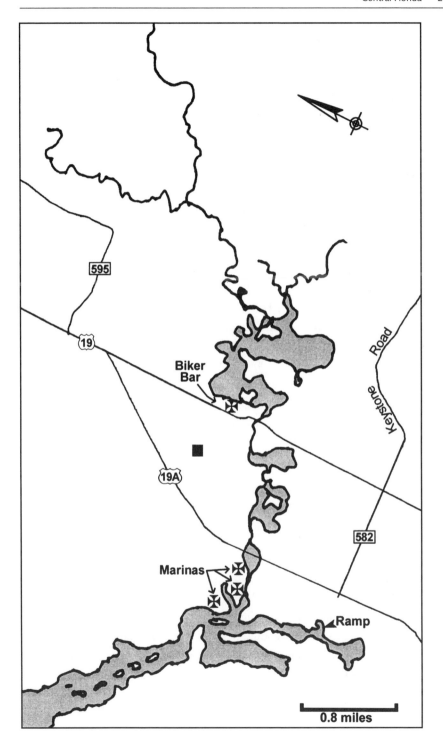

change building and the dozens of little gift shops around it are still a big tourist attraction, and you can stop for lunch right in the center of all the action. Ask permission before tying up to the seawall, since that space may be reserved for a fishing boat.

The river the tourists see from the seawall, however, is completely different from the wonderfully diverse river you'll see from the water.

The river starts five miles northeast as a weedy ditch, meanders past unkempt yards and old trailers, is strictly seawalled as it creeps past hundreds of white-painted retirement homes, spreads out into a marsh between US19 and 19A, then erupts with fishing boats and fancy yachts near the Sponge Docks. From there it dips south to form two huge bayous, then finally heads west to join the Gulf of Mexico.

To get to the sole public boat ramp from 19A, turn west onto SR582, which is also Tarpon Avenue/Main Street/Keystone Road. When you reach the water, turn left/south. Follow Spring Boulevard around the edge of Spring Bayou (site of the annual January 6 Epiphany Diving for the Cross), and turn right into Library Court. The ramp is to the left/west of the tennis courts.

There are a couple of unofficial access spots. One is on the north side of the US19 bridge, north of the St. Luke's Eye Clinic parking lot. A grassy sward leads to the water beside a biker's bar. Another access is a bit of beach beside a parking lot on the southeast side of the 19A bridge. I like to launch here, head upstream to regular US19, and circle back for a relaxing two-hour paddle.

From Spring Bayou to the Gulf the river widens and speeds up. Some very fancy mansions line the water. The north bank is a graveyard for old abandoned fishing boats.

The tide and current pick up strongly at the mouth of the river. Hug the north bank to find the public ramp beside Duke's Fish Camp (1029 Baillies Bluff Road, Tarpon Springs FL 34689, phone (727) 937-9737).

If you wish to paddle across the three miles of open water to Anclote Key, a safer way to start is to drive south to Fred Howard Park and launch from the north side of the causeway. Head for the lighthouse at the south end of Anclote Key. On weekends, a snackbar boat sells hot dogs, drinks, and chips. Check wind and tides before launching.

Destination 43: Arbuckle Creek

Miles or average time: 26 miles, in 15- and 11-mile sections

Skill level: beginner

Current: nonexistent to fast, depending on rainfall

Wind problems: can be, across open pastures

Emergency numbers: 911; Polk County sheriff, (941) 533-0344; Highlands County sheriff, (863) 465-4343

DeLorme page 94, section D-1

Official Florida canoe trail: no

Just because the river runs beside the Avon Park Bombing Range doesn't mean you'll be dive-bombed, strafed, or even crop dusted. I've seen military flights overhead on only two occasions, and they droned by peacefully. Vicki Bailey, who has led this trip for the Florida Sport Paddling Club and the West Palm Beach Pack and Paddle group, says it's electronic bombing, and you hear only the fighter planes.

Lake Arbuckle is about three and a half miles due south of Walk-in-the-Water, also known as Lake Weohyakapka (see destination 64). However, when I've visited there was no access between the two lakes. There is water flow, but it's through a swamp, with an irregular channel.

The Arbuckle Creek trip starts at Williams Fish Camp (phone (941) 453-6229) at the east end of SR64. To get there from the town of Avon Park, follow SR64/Main Street east for about thirteen miles to the creek.

The Highlands County boat ramp is about three miles south/downriver. Coming east from Avon Park on SR64, turn right on Earbuckle Road. It's a dirt road, beside a small convenience store. The ramp is about two and a half miles down the road, on the right.

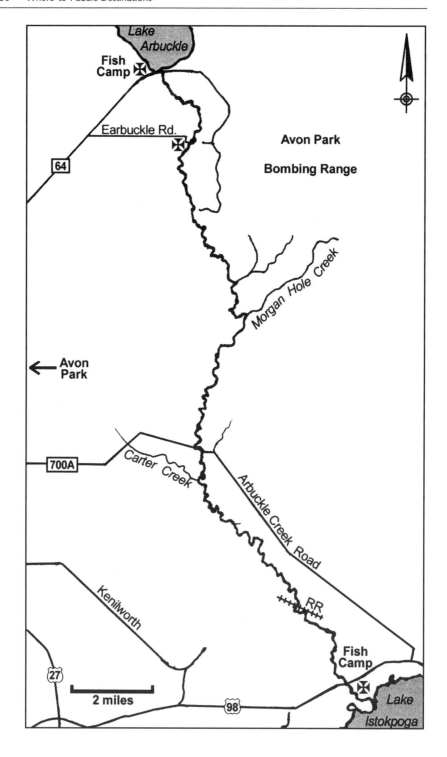

Vicki Bailey has organized several trips on Arbuckle Creek for the Florida Sport Paddling Club. Her pretrip announcements read:

Arbuckle is a black water creek, which is not rare in the state, but the pristine nature of the northern section is well worth the journey. The creek is home to many species of birds, among them the Crested Caracara. So be on the lookout for new birds to add to your list. This indeed is a beautiful paddle. Don't miss this chance.

We will put in at Williams Fish Camp at the eastern end of SR64, coming driving east from US27 in Avon Park. There's a charge for a launching and overnight parking—it was $1 at last visit—honor system in a metal box at the ramp.

Camping will be on the right bank below Arbuckle Creek Bridge Road. The following day, we will paddle to US98, to Cracker Trail Fishing Resort, (941) 655-1416, in Lorida [DeLorme page 100, section A-2]. We always seem to be able to arrange a shuttle for one-day trippers.

Arbuckle Creek flows 23 miles starting in Lake Arbuckle in Polk County. After exiting Lake Arbuckle, the creek's eastern border is the Avon Park bombing range. This section has a narrow, swift channel. About three miles from the lake, ranch land borders the western shoreline for several miles. Below this area both sides of the creek return to dense cypress and swamp. About eight miles from the lake, Morgan Hole Creek enters from the eastern side. Now you will begin to encounter high dike lines on the western bank. The creek widens out and has lake-like sections. The banks revert to ranch land, and your camping spot for the night will soon appear. On river right below the bridge, Carter Creek will join the flow. More ranch land and finally a dense oak forest lines the banks. You will encounter a few small rapids (Florida style) and enter a man-made canal. Your journey will end at Lake Istokpoga, which is Indian for "dangerous waters." The lake is one of the five largest lakes in the state.

After one trip, she wrote:

After weeks of rainy, unsettled weather, seven of us spent two beautiful Technicolor days on Arbuckle.

It was about a 5.5 hour paddle to the campsite just below Arbuckle Creek Road bridge. The current was not very swift, but the water was high. The four poles in the water that mark the camp site were clearly visible.

We had many laughs around the campfire under a full moon as some of the participants from the Green River trip recounted the "new piece of equipment" which became well used.

We were serenaded first by Mr. Hartt's dogs across the river. When they stopped the cows started up, and finally, the bombing began at 10 P.M.

Next day, it took us about three hours to the take out on SR98. One change along the way was the barbed wire fence that has been installed close to the water's edge on the east bank opposite the rapids at the Amtrak trestle. Due to the high water, there were no rapids, but in the past we sometimes camped or lunched there. For those who didn't want to run the shoals, the fence came in handy for lining the canoes downstream. There is a nice spot on the right bank, however, just before the shoals area. It's still a very worthwhile trip.

After her next trip here, Bailey wrote in the newsletter:

Originally this was planned as an overnight paddle with the option to day trip. At one point it swelled to 11 people, then dwindled down to three, who made it a day trip. With frost during the preceding week, and threats of heavy rainstorms for the over-nighter, it wasn't exactly ideal conditions. However, the threesome enjoyed a beautiful clear and mild day, making the 15 mile trip (on Howard's GPS) in five hours. We experienced some headwinds, but saw an abundance of wildlife which more than made up for the bare trees and frost damaged vines.

Destination 44: Caladesi and Honeymoon Islands

Miles or average time: no set mileage, explore at your own pace

Skill level: easy to challenging, depending on surf, tide, and wind

Current: strong current between islands, strong surf on Gulf side, more protected on St. Joseph Sound side

Wind problems: yes—plan to go on calm days

Emergency numbers: 911; Pinellas County sheriff, (727) 582-6200

Rentals: Sail Honeymoon, 61 Causeway Boulevard, Dunedin FL 34698, phone (727) 734-0392; Florida Kayak & Canoe Centers, 3011 19A, Palm Harbor FL 34683, phone (727) 784-6357

DeLorme page 82, section D-2

Official Florida canoe trail: no

The sun-speckled salt water looked irresistible. I hopped overboard into the waist-deep water and snugged my tiny mushroom anchor into the white sugar sand bottom. I was on the northwest side of Caladesi Island, on the big triangular sandbar that has developed south of the channel between Honeymoon and Caladesi Islands.

It was the type of day that the tourist bureaus promise and every tourist hopes to encounter. White puffy clouds scalloped the blue, blue horizon. A stream of sailboats, kayaks, and fishing boats plied the channel. Across the channel on "dog beach," a big shepherd lunged high into the air to catch the Frisbee her owner was tossing. The air had that fresh, tingling smell of salt and sand.

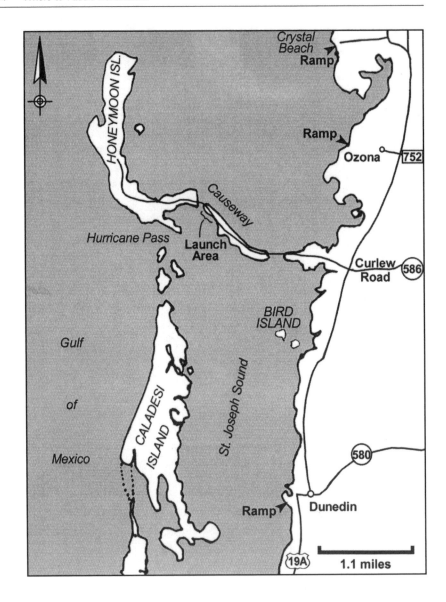

I dug my toes into the sand, idly feeling for sand dollars. The cool Gulf water felt wonderful.

But—what was that? There, about fifty feet away from me. What looked like dozens of brown leaves were slowly rippling across the bottom.

A closer look revealed it was a group of stingrays, the little Atlantic stingrays that rarely get above plate size. I started edging back toward my boat, careful to shuffle my feet to scare off any rays burrowed into the sand around me.

As soon as I moved, the whole school headed right toward me. I waded faster. Another school appeared beyond the first school, also headed my way. I dashed the last few feet, diving headlong into my kayak.

For the next few minutes I had a front-row view of the graceful little animals as more than a hundred rays surrounded my boat. Always on the lookout for anything edible, they'd sensed my digging and come over to see if I'd kicked up any mollusks, worms, and other delicious tidbits.

I sat quietly, watching as these little "birds of the sea" swirled around my kayak, then rippled away. These creatures weren't just swimming. They were waltzing. It was a magical moment.

I later heard that I hadn't been in much danger. In the warm summer months, schools of small stingrays drift off the sandbars of Pinellas County. They seldom touch a wader while they are free-swimming, and even the largest school will split to avoid contact with a human.

Honeymoon Island to the north is now a state park. It once had the very unromantic name of Hog Island. Nude sunbathers still stroll around the distant northern tip, and are regularly chased off by the beach patrol.

Caladesi Island is currently attached to Clearwater Beach. It once was separate. But barrier islands change, and the channel that previously separated Clearwater and Caladesi Island slowly filled in, then vanished. At the same time, a narrow gap opened at the top end of the island. When this gap first appeared, it was only the width of a car. Some of my friends and I had a great time playing in the "flume" one day, as the incoming tide rushed through the new narrow opening. We'd walk to the Gulf side, hop into the stream, and bob over to St. Joseph Sound.

Within months the tiny canal had widened, trees fell, and now three small islands lie where the north tip of Caladesi Island used to be.

You can easily launch a canoe or kayak off the south side of Dunedin Causeway. From there, you have the choice of circling Honeymoon Island or heading south across the channel to Caladesi Island.

Parking and rest rooms are beside Sail Honeymoon, the array of rental sailboats on the left/south before the last little bridge. The free parking area next to the road is mostly packed gravel, but watch out for tire-swallowing patches of loose sand. The entrance to Honeymoon Island State Park is at the end of Dunedin Causeway. There is an admission fee, but you don't need to enter the park to launch.

To the left of the state park entrance is a small ferry that takes tourists to the docks and concession stand at the "waist" of Caladesi Island. The ferry costs about $6 per person, but it's easy to paddle the distance yourself. Once you're past the "new" islands, stay close to the mangroves that line the eastern edge of Caladesi and you'll be in a protected zone where only nonmotorized craft are permitted to enter.

If you want to keep paddling south, you'll come to another west-heading channel that used to be the old pass. On your right/north is an inlet, and if you explore carefully you'll find the old dock pilings that led to the house in Myrtle Scharrer Betz's book *Yesteryear I Lived in Paradise: The Story of Caladesi Island.*

St. Joseph Sound is dotted with tiny islands, spoil banks left when the Intracoastal Waterway was dredged. The island just south of Dunedin Causeway is a bird sanctuary, and dotted with dozens of pelicans. You can't go ashore, but you can circle the island, and dip close to the mainland to admire the fancy waterfront houses.

This is a neat spot. If there's too much chop, stay in the protected inlets on the east side of Honeymoon Island. If the weather is nice, paddle across to Caladesi.

And watch for stingrays. If you're lucky, a school will come over and put on their ballet, just for you.

Destination 45: Canaveral National Seashore

Miles or average time: 2-, 4-, or 6-hour segments

Skill level: beginner

Current: small tidal flow

Wind problems: yes—open area

Emergency numbers: 911; Volusia County sheriff, (904) 736-5961

Rentals: Avalon Historical Canoe Trails, PO Box 238631, Allandale FL 32123, phone 1-800-929-9854; Beachside Bike & Kayak, 533 Third Avenue, New Smyrna Beach FL 32169, phone (904) 426-8684; A Day Away, Guided Kayak Eco-Tours, phone (321) 268-2655, website www.nbbd.com/kayaktours

DeLorme page 81, section A-3

Official Florida canoe trail: no, official trail of Canaveral National Seashore

I first paddled this area with two instructors from an Outward Bound program based in Scottsmoor, Florida. It was a marvelous trip, and a wonderful history lesson.

You have three directions to go in this area.

First is the Shipyard Island Canoe Trail. This series of lanes winds through a low, marshy island west of the A1A boat ramp at Bethune Beach. Watch for the first trail sign directly west of the ramp. The runs are evenly spaced, and the trail looks like a combination of natural creeks and old mosquito control ditches.

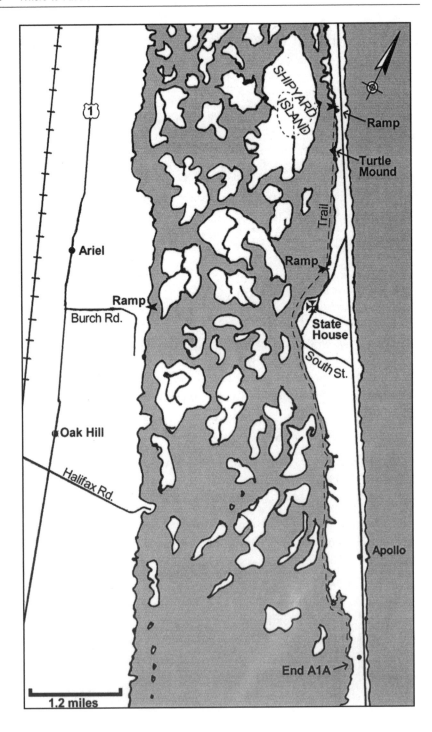

This is a typical salt marsh island, which means that if you paddle quickly through it you'll think you've wasted your time. But go slowly, letting your boat drift a bit, and you'll see fiddler crabs peeking out of their pencil-poke holes, tiny brown marsh wrens bobbing up and down on stems that look too fragile to hold them up, and perhaps the head of a baby green sea turtle as it comes up for a breath.

The next segment to paddle is south to Eldora. About a half mile south of your put-in is a tall lump on the left/east. That's Turtle Mound. This famous mound has been in place for centuries, and was put up by the Timucuan Indians. It's forty feet high and the size of a football field. There is evidence that it was seventy feet high at one time. From the 1500s to the 1800s it was used as a navigational aid by passing ships out in the Gulf Stream. Made entirely of shells, the mound has a boardwalk to its top. You access it from A1A, not the lagoon side.

Eldora is just over a mile south of the put-in. There's a boat ramp beside some retirement homes there, on the right/west side of A1A. We paddled about half a city block beyond that, and tied up our kayaks beside a low grassy bank. From there we walked another half block south to see the local sight.

Facing west over Mosquito Lagoon, a stately old wooden building called the State House is all that now remains of what was this once lively little pioneer town.

Back in 1877 George Pitzer bought land on the island, and named his new community after his daughters, Ellen and Dora.

There were no roads on the mainland, so steamboats traveled up and down the inland waterway. The Eldora citrus groves prospered, and lemons, grapefruit, oranges, and tangerines were shipped to Jacksonville and northern cities. Evaporation pens produced sea salt. Some fifty to seventy-five people lived here, complete with horse-drawn wagons, farms, and a school. There was even a saw palmetto berry picking operation that sold the dried palmetto berries up north as a miracle cure-all—Eldora's version of snake oil.

Remember, this was only a decade after the Civil War ended in 1864. Reconstruction was winding down, and settlers were discovering Florida.

Eldora might have been as famous as St. Augustine and Jacksonville, but two things happened. First, three killer freezes in five years destroyed the groves. Then a railroad was built on the mainland west of the lagoon, and prospective tourists bypassed Eldora as they headed for points south. Families moved away. The post office that had opened in 1882 closed again in 1899 for lack of business.

Today you can go inside the State House, an interesting old building with a widow's walk and a wide verandah facing the lagoon. It's been refurbished, with new wood and fresh plaster. A collection of old photos shows the town in its heyday. Call (904) 428-3384 for information and hours.

As you walk to it, you'll pass under ancient oaks and cedars hung with Spanish moss. Across the lagoon to the west are some random bumps that are Indian mounds, more indications that this spot has been occupied by humans for thousands of years. Lefils Fish Camp in Oak Hill sits where a huge Indian mound stood, before the shell was carted away to build roads.

You have a choice as to where to go next. You can paddle back to the ramp at Shipyard Island, take out at the Eldora ramp, or keep going south.

If you head back to the first launch site, you can choose a different path through the islands.

If you paddle south from Eldora, you'll have five miles of wilderness. A row of grass-covered sand dunes will be on your left/east. In an emergency, you could climb over these to A1A, but they're full of sand spurs and protected sea oats.

You'll paddle through shallow mud and grass flats, with tiny islands here and there rising out of the sun-heated water.

We paddled this section in the heat of the afternoon, and heat waves rising from the water produced genuine mirages. A flock of six white pelicans napping on a tiny island looked as large as houses, then cars, then shrank to mere bird size as we got near them. Giant mountains and glassy lakes appeared in the distance, then went away.

Closer to the end of the trail, where A1A used to go before Cape Canaveral was established, you'll spot a tiny black and white box on the southern horizon. This is really the huge Vehicular Assembly Building at the Kennedy Space Center (see destination 55).

The Vehicular Assembly Building at NASA is so big it can be seen for miles away.
Sandy Huff.

The takeout is at the very southern end of A1A, inside Apollo Beach Park.
From the water you'll see the roof of the rest rooms, with a wide pebbly beach
leading up to the parking lot.

From November 1 to April 1, camping is allowed on the beach with a
permit, then the beaches are closed for sea turtle nesting. We pitched our
tents on the narrow stretch of dry sand between the Atlantic Ocean and the
grassy dunes. Our leaders made a delicious open-fire supper, complete with
a Dutch oven cake. Waves crashed only fifteen feet from our tents. Stars
twinkled brightly, undimmed by the glow of city lights.

With dusk, our wonderful evening changed. The mosquitoes arrived, by
the millions. Despite liberal amounts of bug repellent, they whined and dive-
bombed, and a hundred or so got inside my tent. It was a loooong night.
Again, my thanks to our Outward Bound teachers for this demonstration
trip, but I recommend that you spend only daylight hours here. Mosquito
Lagoon is well named, and I don't see how the pioneers or Indians survived.

To get to the Shipyard Island ramp from I-95, take exit 84 and head east on
SR44 to New Smyrna Beach and A1A. Take A1A south for about seven miles
to where A1A splits and then comes back together. The ramp is on your right/

west. You'll be in the Canaveral National Seashore boundaries. Keep going south to reach Eldora and the south end of A1A.

Laurilee Thompson, who writes about Turnbull Creek (see destination 62), added a bit more information:

> You can access the west side of the maze of mangrove islands from the town of Oak Hill. North of Oak Hill is a gorgeous Volusia County park named River Breeze Park, where you can launch for free.
>
> Further south you can launch for a small fee from either Lopez Fish Camp on the north side of the Oak Hill waterfront or LeFil's Fish Camp on the south side of the waterfront.
>
> Even if you do not choose to launch from either fish camp, the drive along the waterfront in Oak Hill is worth the effort. Head east from the blinker light on US1 in the middle of Oak Hill. You will see a historic fishing village where generations of people have made their living from the waters of Mosquito Lagoon. You can paddle right up to Goodrich's seafood restaurant as it is right on the lagoon.

For more information, contact Canaveral National Seashore, 308 Julia Street, Titusville FL 32796, phone (321) 267-1110. There is a Visitors Center at 7611 South Atlantic Avenue, New Smyrna Beach Fl 32169, phone (904) 428-3384.

The Titusville Area Chamber of Commerce, 2000 South Washington Avenue, Titusville FL 32780, phone (321) 267-3036, website www.nbbd.com/ fly, hosts an annual Space Coast Flyway Festival in November with varied outdoor trips and seminars.

Also try www.nbbd.com/godo/cns.

Destination 46: Chassahowitzka River

Miles or average time: no limit, paddle at your own pace

Skill level: beginner upstream from launch, intermediate in main river, depending on tides and wind

Current: medium but constant

Wind problems: little, only at Gulf end

Emergency numbers: 911; Citrus County sheriff, (352) 726-1121

Rentals: Chassahowitzka River Campground, 8600 West Miss Maggie Drive, Homosassa FL 34448, phone (352) 382-2200, website www.cclib.org

DeLorme page 77, section C-1

Official Florida canoe trail: no

This river is pronounced chass-a-WIS-ka. It is about five and a half miles south of Homosassa Springs and about fourteen miles north of Weeki Wachee Springs.

The Chassahowitzka has four different faces.

First, you can turn right/east after you launch and head up into the canals beside little retirement homes.

The next face is all the springs. If you turn left/west from the ramp, you'll head downstream. The first big opening on your left leads to a rocky set of shoals. We usually leave our boats there and walk up to the deep, circular spring named the Crack.

The third face is the meandering course of the river through tall jungles and tiny hidden coves and niches. Four miles from the launch site is the Chassahowitzka National Wildlife Refuge. This thirty-thousand-acre refuge

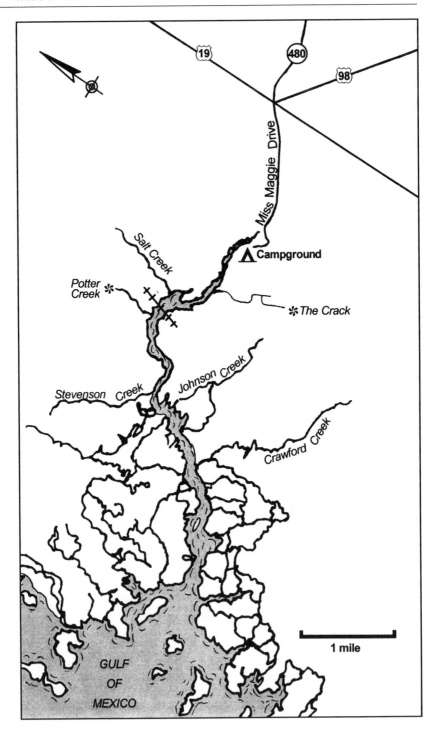

is not only a recharge area for the local freshwater wells but a major bird sanctuary. The inside areas are closed October 15 to February 15.

And finally, you emerge into the bewildering shoreline mazes that front the Gulf of Mexico. Dog Island has a little picnic shelter with a metal roof and tiny dock, and is a nice place for picnics. Tidal influence is strong here.

If you do head out into the islands, be aware that you're sitting below the tops of the marsh grass and won't be able to see where you're going. Bring a compass, and if you do get lost, head west out to open water in the Gulf and/ or watch for powerboats. There are a couple of small channel markers, but they're hard to spot.

Rentals and a ramp ($5 launch fee) are available at the campground, along with snacks, fishing tackle, and ice cream—always an important part of any trip. The Chassahowitzka River Campground is operated by the Citrus County Division of Parks and Recreation. Be sure to get one of their simplified maps showing the river.

My friend Gail Allen reported seeing a mother manatee with a radio collar around her tail during an April visit. I asked her if that might tangle with something. Gail said: "I assume the manatee stays in the general area. At least I hope so, because the water depth in general on the river is very shallow, and she would not be able to go deep enough to miss the boats. I guess that is the reason for the float. She has a harness around her tail with about six feet of line ending with a small yellow float. She can easily pull the float down under the surface to deeper water. You are probably right to be concerned about tangled line and drowning her, but the real danger is from boats. They far outweigh the danger from drowning."

So pack your bathing suit, snorkeling gear, and a dollar or two for ice cream. And keep your eye out for that mother manatee.

Destination 47: Cockroach Bay

Miles or average time: no limit, paddle at your own speed

Skill level: beginner

Current: irregular tides

Wind problems: yes, very open area

Emergency numbers: 911; Hillsborough County sheriff (813) 247-8000

Rentals: Little Manatee River Canoe Outpost, 18001 US 301 South, Wimauma FL 33598, phone (813) 634-2228 or 1-800-229-1371, e-mail canoeski@gte.net, website www.canoeoutpost.com

DeLorme page 91, section C-1

Official Florida canoe trail: no

Cockroach Bay is a saltwater tributary on the east side of Tampa Bay. The nearest towns are Ruskin and Sun City.

This is an easy paddle, through a maze of mangrove islands and grass flats. No powerboats are allowed in much of the area. The marked canoe trail begins at the ramp and ends in the bay.

There are several picnic/camp sites. Look for sand beaches on the bigger islands, or use the boat ramp. Any canoe or kayak is good, including long sea kayaks with retractable rudders. A compass and a map of the area are recommended, since you will be lower than the surrounding greenery.

When you get to the ramp, take the time to look around and get your bearings. Notice the high radio tower near the ramp, and the fact that the St. Pete Sundome stadium is directly across the bay from the ramp.

Most of the islands look exactly alike. If you get lost, paddle west until you

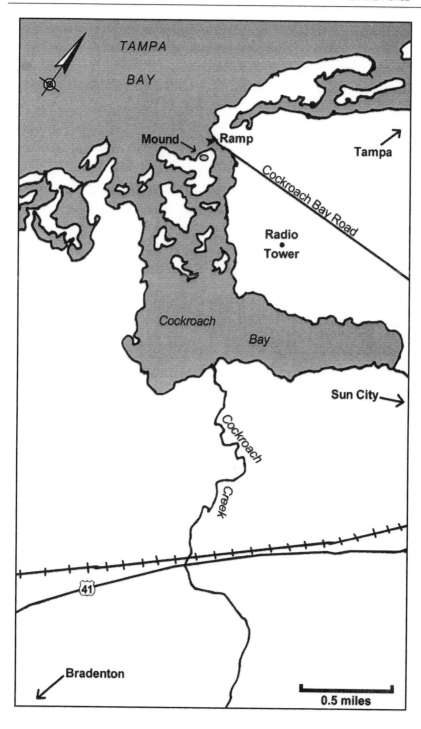

TAMPA

BAY

Mound → Ramp

Tampa

Cockroach Bay Road

Radio
● Tower

Cockroach

Bay

Sun City →

Cockroach

Creek

41

Bradenton

0.5 miles

break out into the bay, then look for the channel markers that the power-boats use to get out into the bay. Follow them east to the ramp.

This is a great place to fish, explore, beachcomb, and check out the marine life. Birds are everywhere for the watcher or photographer. And we didn't see one cockroach!

There's also an Indian mound on Big Mound Key, just southwest of the ramp. Big Cockroach Mound tops the southwest side of the peninsula closest to you.

From the intersection of I-4 and I-75 in Tampa, travel south on I-75. Get off at exit 674 for Sun City. Go west to US41, a four-lane highway. Turn left/south on US41. Cross the Manatee River Bridge. Look for a Circle K convenience store on the left, which has the only rest room in the area. Turn right/west on Cockroach Bay Road and continue to the boat ramp at the end. (If you see fish swim by your car windows, you drove too far.)

For more information on Cockroach Bay Aquatic Preserve, contact Hillsborough County Parks and Recreation Department at (813) 671-7754.

Destination 48: Crystal River

Miles or average time: no limit, paddle at your own pace

Skill level: beginner downstream, intermediate upstream

Current: strong in main river

Wind problems: yes, very wide, open waterway

Emergency numbers: 911; Citrus County sheriff, (352) 726-1121

Rentals: Indian River Tours and Water Sports, 2380 NW Highway 19, Crystal River FL 34428, phone (352) 564-0887; Kayak Shack, 300 NW US 19, Crystal River FL 34428, phone (352) 564-1334; Plantation Inn, 9301 West Fort Island Trail, Crystal River FL 34428, phone (352) 795-4211 or 1-800-632-6262, website www.plantationinn.com

DeLorme page 77, section A-1

Official Florida canoe trail: no

Crystal River is a great place to see two forms of aquatic life—manatees and scuba divers. This is a checkout dive site for many of the scuba schools in the area, and their dive flags look like a garden of bobbing red and white posies. On any given Saturday you'll spot a dozen pontoon boats anchored around King's Bay. In some places the water seethes from all the bubbles rising from the scuba divers exploring underwater caves, coves, and ledges.

In the winter you'll see the roughly two hundred West Indian manatees that come in to the constant 72° water. These animals are fairly accustomed to humans over, under, and beside them, so while you are not allowed to actually come up to them, they will probably swim close if you sit quietly.

All of the rental liveries have places to launch a boat, with a fee if you use your own boat. Pete's Pier Marina, phone (352) 795-3302, charges a parking fee, but usually allows paddlers to drop off their boats for free. To get to Pete's Pier from US19, turn west on SR44/King's Bay Drive at the light, then turn right into Pete's Pier. Plantation Inn is also off King's Bay Drive, and you ll see the signs for it at the intersection of US19 and SR44.

There are several ways to explore the river. First, you can paddle around the seawalls and canals that edge King's Bay. The southwest side is lined with tidy little retirement homes, and several canals meander through the developments. Next is the Crystal River State Archeological Site. You can deadhead cars beside the canal that cuts across Museum Road. The access beside the bridge is very rocky, so watch your step. You'll spot the little canal that leads to the archeology site on the right/north side of the main channel, about a mile past King's Bay. From the bridge over the canal, drive or walk about three city blocks south and check out the park. There's a big mound with steps leading up to the top. From there you can see the river. The mound was once much bigger, but was cut away around the 1930s so a trailer park could be put in beside it. The site is open seven days a week, from 9 A.M. to 5 P.M. Admission is $1 per car. A small museum on the grounds gives you a good idea of how the Indians lived there for the past two thousand years. (My grandfather made most of the reproduction pots in the display cases.) Park authorities tell us that this was a regional religious center. High-ranking Indians from surrounding villages were brought here for burial. Since this involved up to a week's travel by canoe, the bodies were first smoked to preserve them.

When I was a kid, there was a glass window set into the side of one of the smaller mounds, showing actual bones and broken pots in position. In the 1970s some of the North American tribes spoke up, saying they objected to having their ancestors on display like that, so the little window was first boarded up, then removed.

This site may also have the only solstice stone in the entire southeastern U.S. A carved limestone stele, now very eroded, shows the face and profile of a human. It looks like a simple smiley face now, but was more complex when it was first carved. Other steles, plus old postholes north of the mound, are in the right position to be solstice and equinox markers. This might be an American Stonehenge. Look around from the top of the mound. This was an ideal site for an Indian town. To the east was fresh water, with a plentiful supply of bass, bream, and game. Just a short distance to the west was the Gulf of Mexico, with marshes, mud flats, and open water where they could gather ducks, mussels, and saltwater fish.

The final option is to deadhead a car at the ramp at the very western tip of SR44 and paddle across King's Bay and down the length of the river. From the archeological park canal mouth, it is about four miles to the end of the river, or eleven miles from the head of King's Bay. This part of the river is entirely natural, and except for passing motorboats, you'll feel you're in a wilderness.

At the mouth of the river, watch for a channel heading off to the left to the boat ramp. The river current is strong, especially if it is aided by an outgoing tide, so don't plan on paddling back upriver. You'll also be at the mercy of any winds.

If worst comes to worst, you can usually flag down a passing fisherman in a powerboat, but no paddler worth her salt wants to be towed home. Besides, there's not a powerboater in the state that won't try to tow you at full speed, which will instantly pull your bow up, which pushes your stern underwater, and before you can holler "Whoa!" you'll be dumped into the water.

Inside King's Bay, watch for scuba divers. In the river, watch for manatees. At the mouth of the river, a large colony of otters lives in the marshes. Add to that the rippling grasses under the clear, cool water, the waterbirds that dot

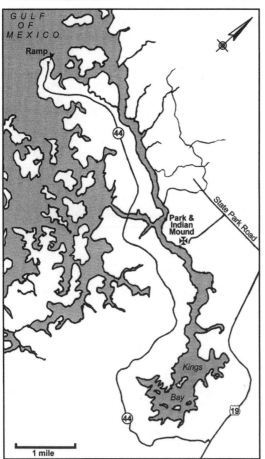

the shores, ospreys that soar overhead, and the hundred or so species of migratory birds that visit the area during the year. It's a fine place to visit.

For more information, contact the Nature Coast Chamber of Commerce, 28 NW Highway 19, Crystal River FL 34428, telephone (352) 795-3149.

Destination 49: Double Branch Creek

Miles or average time: 2 hours upstream, no limit in bay

Skill level: beginner

Current: little

Wind problems: little upstream, lots in open salt marshes

Emergency numbers: 911; Hillsborough County sheriff, (813) 247-8000

Rentals: Gulfcoast Kayak Center, 8802 Rocky Creek Drive, Tampa FL 33615, phone (727) 738-4576

DeLorme: page 83, section D-1

Official Florida canoe trail: no

Very few paddlers know about the little creek that leads north from Mobbly Bay. But if you're near the north end of Tampa Bay, just east of Oldsmar, Double Branch Creek makes a relaxing paddle.

In one trip, you can explore a freshwater creek, salt marshes, and an open saltwater bay, plus visit the small but interesting ecological exhibits at Upper Tampa Bay Park in Oldsmar (8001 Double Branch Road, Tampa FL 33635, phone (813) 855-1765).

There are two launch sites for Double Branch Creek. My favorite is about a block south of the SR580/Hillsborough Road bridge at the end of State Street. The other is the tiny beach and dock at the east side of the park building.

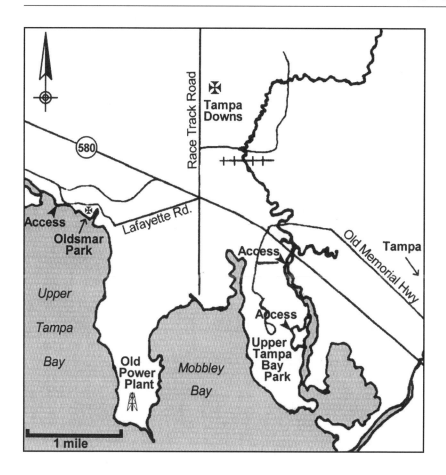

To paddle into fresh water, turn left/north and go under the SR580 bridge. The river splits immediately north of the bridge, but the entrance to the short right/east branch is usually too shallow to cross. The left/north branch changes to fresh water as it meanders past mobile home parks, wasteland, and a housing development behind Tampa Downs racetrack before it finally becomes too narrow to paddle.

To head to the salt marshes, turn right after you launch. The channels look alike, so pay attention to your route to find your way back to your car.

Try the fishing on both the fresh- and saltwater sections. At high tide, the shallow flats around the park building are great spots for redfish and sea trout. The old water discharge channel at the east side of the shut-down electric power plant on Mobbly Bay is a fishing hot spot. However, at really low tide Tampa Bay turns into acres of exposed mud, so plan this part of the trip by the tides. The creek channel usually has enough water to float a canoe, but wear water shoes in case you have to pull across oyster beds.

Another paddling area is around Upper Tampa Bay. You can launch at R. E. Oldsmar Park (named after the founder of the Oldsmobile cars). Old-timers claim that in the early 1900s you could stand on the Indian mound in Safety Harbor (now inside Phillippe Park) and see three smaller mounds on what is now fenced-in property at the power plant. If you paddle around the power plant peninsula, see if you can spot them.

Destination 50: Econlockhatchee River

Miles or average time: 19+ miles

Skill level: intermediate, plus some agility required

Current: changes according to water level

Wind problems: no, entirely sheltered

Emergency numbers: 911; Seminole County sheriff, (407) 330-6600

Rentals: Florida Outback, 1242 Majestic Palm Court, Apopka FL 32712, phone (407) 884-1802; Hidden River Park Canoe Rentals, 15295 East Colonial Drive, Orlando FL 32826, phone (407) 568-5346

DeLorme page 80, section C-3

Official Florida canoe trail: yes

While thousands of tourists are pretending to be pioneers at Disney World's Mike Fink keelboats thirty-four miles away, you can be in a true wilderness. This narrow, twisting river is only nine miles due east of the Orlando city limits, but you'll feel like you're a thousand miles from civilization.

Oaks, maples, cabbage palms, and bay trees top high white sand banks. The steep sides remain barren even at low water, the result of having all organic materials leached away over centuries, leaving only sterile sands.

The river can fluctuate twenty feet, from high flood to a trickle. If the water is low, you'll need agility to get in and out of your boat, strong shoulders to "oooch" your way over scrape-overs, and a nice long painter or end rope to help with portages. At high water you'll be dodging treetops as the current zips you along.

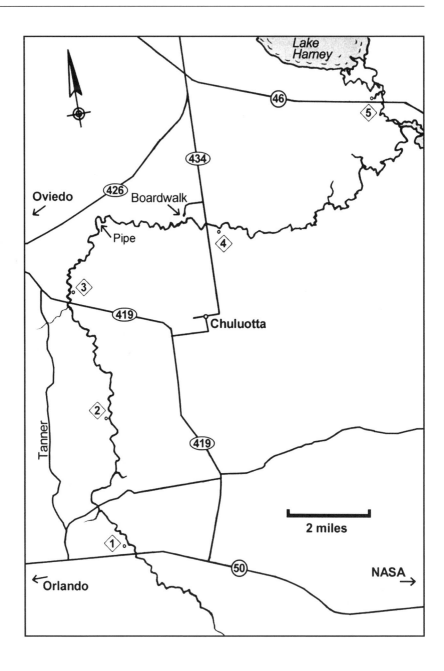

Still, to paraphrase the old fisherman's saying, even a bad day paddling is better than a good day working. It's a fascinating river, and I loved it.

The official canoe trail runs between CR419 and SR46 on the St. Johns River. However, if you're into real wilderness clambering and hard work, you can launch at SR50 and paddle south/upstream as far as you are able.

1) Hidden River RV Park to Hidden River Park #2, 9 miles. The canoe livery is on the northwest side of the SR50 bridge.

2) Hidden River Park #2 to SR419, 6 miles. This access is privately owned, so you'll need permission to launch and/or camp.

3) SR419 to Snowhill Bridge Road, 10 miles. Access is on the northeast side of the SR419 bridge. Camping is allowed on the banks in the state forest, but only upstream of the Snowhill Road bridge. We paddled this section one March, after a long dry spell. The ideal water level is between 1.5 and 3 feet. The river gauge at the Snowhill bridge read .8 feet that day. So we had lots of bump-overs and scrape-overs, and five portages. Fallen trees that would have made interesting shapes under the surface had to be carefully negotiated, and long stretches of white sand bottom were exposed. In higher water, the trip takes four to five hours. It took us seven.

A half-grown bald eagle flew along with us for half an hour. At first I thought it was a limpkin. It was clearly brown, with white speckles on its tail and back. A closer look revealed its huge size, white head, and strong hooked beak. Then I remembered that young eagles are pure chocolate brown and achieve their white head and tail only around age five or six. This was an eagle "teenager."

The river widens and deepens in just one stretch, about a third of the way down, and it's like entering a completely different river. You round a corner, and there is a wide, placid, stump-free river.

Around the next corner, we surprised a gator sunning on a beach. It slid slowly into the dark water, its pointed tail almost white with powdery sand. Was it truly fourteen feet long, or was the "good grief, look at that gator" factor working, making it a mere ten-footer? Two more turns, and a fat eight-footer slid off a sloping tree stump. For the rest of the trip, anytime we were in deep, dark water, I made it a point to talk, rub my feet along the inside of the kayak, and even thump the deck with both hands.

Around the halfway mark a mossy PVC pipe sticks out of a right-hand bend, gushing sulfur-scented water from an artesian well. A metal pipe used to bring water up for cattle before it rusted away and someone stuck in this plastic pipe.

At the wooden footbridge of the Florida Trail, you have one hour to go.

4) Snowhill Bridge Road to SR46, 18 miles. The access is down a dirt lane on the southeast side of the bridge. A new launch area is being installed on the northwest side as part of the Little Big Econ State Forest.

5) SR46 ramp. The last mile and a half will be on the St. Johns River. Pass under SR46, then take the first canal on the left to get to the public ramp.

To find out the state of the river, and the water levels, call Don Hastings at Hidden River Park.

Also try www8.myflorida.com/communities/learn/trails/canoe.

A Florida Trail footbridge spans the Econlockhatchee. Sandy Huff.

Destination 51: Fort DeSoto Park

Miles or average time: no set mileage

Skill level: beginner inshore, advanced in open water

Current: strong tidal flow, up to three knots

Wind problems: yes

Emergency numbers: 911; Pinellas County sheriff, (727) 582-6200

Rentals: Canoe Outpost, Fort DeSoto Park, St. Petersburg FL 33733, phone (727) 864-1991; Sweetwater Kayaks, 1136 Pinellas Bayway (next to JoJo's restaurant), Tierra Verde FL 33715, phone (727) 906-0708

DeLorme page 90, section D-3

Official Florida canoe trail: no

This is a favorite trip for several paddling clubs. Sonny Norris, with the Central Florida Paddlemasters, says, "There are many islands to visit as well as Egmont Key [about 1.5 miles offshore]. The paddling outside in the Gulf can be easy to challenging, depending on the surf, tide change, and wind. Inside the bay area it is easy to moderate."

Mullet Key is reputed to be the landing place where Hernando DeSoto stepped ashore in 1513. Directly south, in Bradenton, is the DeSoto National Memorial Park, where rangers and volunteers dress up like conquistadors and demonstrate how these old Spaniards cooked, slept, and generally hung out when they weren't harassing the Tocobaga Indians. Historians in my town of Safety Harbor, 'way up in the left-hand fork of upper Tampa Bay, claim that DeSoto made his main camp there. In any case, almost everyone

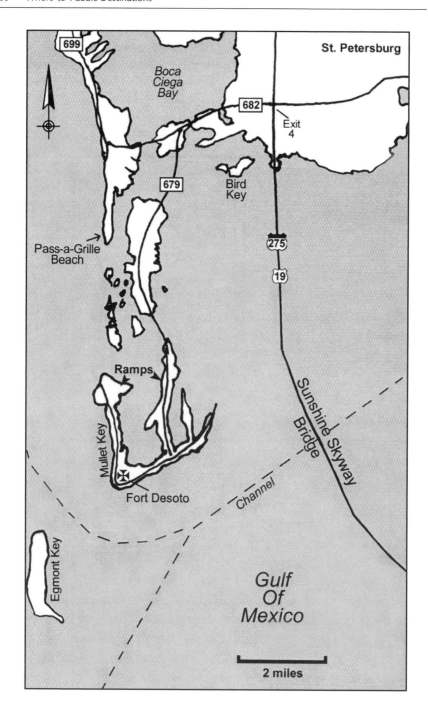

Fort DeSoto and Fort Dade still face each other. But these Fort Dade ruins on Egmont Key are slowly sinking into the Gulf of Mexico. Sandy Huff.

agrees that DeSoto did land somewhere in Tampa Bay in 1513, and named the place Espiritu Sanctu.

Old Fort DeSoto (phone (727) 866-2484) at the southwest tip of Mullet Key was built during the Spanish-American War as a sister fort to the one on Egmont Key, visible to the southwest. It never fired a shot in anger. The sand-banked walls and twelve-inch mortar cannons are worth a tour, if only as a reminder of how war was fought before rifled barrels and guided missiles came along.

Across the channel, Egmont Key has an equally long history. It began as Castor Key, home of pirate Henry Castor in the 1700s. The 1848 lighthouse was the only lighthouse between Key West and the St. Marks delta. A hurricane wiped it out a year after it was built. The lighthouse keeper and his family survived the storm by huddling in a tiny dory roped to a cabbage palm. He quit as soon as they got to dry land.

The old 1898 Fort Dade is now sinking into the water as the beach erodes. One ranger told me it was because of the channel dredged for the supertankers. Sand that should be washing down onto the Egmont Key beaches is going into the dredged channel instead. The dredged sand is claimed by the beachfront motel owners to nourish their beaches. This is the original sand wars—and Egmont is losing.

You can walk the old concrete walls and explore the tiny inside rooms, or volunteer to help keep the rampant vegetation in check. Weeds are fast covering the old building foundations of the tiny settlement.

Egmont Key is also famous for its gopher tortoises, periodically decimated when storms flood their tunnels.

If you do paddle to Egmont Key, remember that you're crossing Egmont Pass, which means strong current, high winds, and big ships. Do not take a canoe or any swampable boat that a single wave could sink. A sit-on-top or sit-inside kayak with a spray skirt is necessary. Cross the dredged channel quickly to avoid bigger boats.

One good thing about heading for Egmont Key is that the afternoon sea breezes will usually blow you back to shore. Don't count on it, of course, but if they're going your way, you'll just zip back to your car.

Even without heading out to sea, or if you only have an open canoe, it's also fun to paddle around the inside of Mullet Key, which is shaped like a V and has plenty of protected waterways. It's a bit muddy inland, but the clearer water and sandy west beaches are easy to get to. Stay clear of the fishing piers, which are spider-webbed with monofilament fishing line and lost hooks.

There's a ramp at the north end of the parking lot, but most paddlers launch just past the boat ramp in the small lagoon on the north side of the road. Or put in anywhere you can get to the water.

During warm weather you'll want to hop out of your boat and take a dip. Just remember to do the "stingray shuffle," as this is a favorite area for small stingrays to dig into the sand.

Speaking of live creatures, the long beach that runs north-south on Mullet Key is a nursery for baby sand dollars. I've waded into waist-deep water and found there was literally no place to put down a foot without breaking five or six of the little guys, all about the size of a half dollar. There had to be thousands of them, piled up so thick they were layered on top of each other.

Some 150 species of birds have been spotted on Mullet Key, including the mangrove cockoo and the red-bellied woodpecker. Besides your birding book, bring along a shell guide, since many species of shells wash up on these beaches. After a storm the tiny outer islands and sand flats are good places to find exotic seashells. Just remember to put back any shells that have live inhabitants.

Lawson Mitchell, at Sweetwater Kayaks, also recommends Passage Key for kayakers. It's the island due south of the southern tip of Egmont Key. "Canoes wouldn't do this trip because it crosses the Southwest Passage, but for kayaks it's just a short paddle," he said. "It's a National Wildlife Refuge, and an Audubon Sanctuary, so you're not allowed to land on the island, but it makes a good circumnavigation."

Lawson also mentioned Shell Island, the long, skinny sandbar that has recently appeared and fills the void between Pass-a-Grille Beach to the north and Summer Resort Key to the south. "This is famous for shelling, and is protected in the spring and summer by the Audubon Society as a spring rookery," he said.

So there is lots to see and do around Fort DeSoto. Take a picnic lunch and lots of sunscreen, and plan to spend a long, lazy day.

Destination 52: Hillsborough River

Jean Faulk

Miles or average time: 42+ miles, in five segments, q.v.

Skill level: beginner to strenuous

Current: usually slow

Wind problems: almost all sections are sheltered

Emergency numbers: 911; Hillsborough County sheriff, (813) 247-8000

Rentals: Canoe Escape, 9335 East Fowler Avenue, Thonotosassa FL 33592, phone (813) 986-2067; Hillsborough River State Park, 15402 US 301 N, Thonotosassa FL 33592, phone (813) 987-6771

DeLorme page 83, section D-3

Official Florida canoe trail: yes

Shadowed, jungly, and mysterious in its upper reaches, the fifty-four-mile-long Hillsborough River starts in the Green Swamp northeast of Tampa.

Humans have lived here for ten thousand years. The Timucuans were the earliest to use the springs and the workable silica-based chert rock found along the river.

The name of the river has changed several times. The Seminoles called it Lockcha-popka-chiska, the river one crosses to eat acorns. The Spaniards called it the River of San Julián de Arriaga. The English next named the river after the earl of Hillsborough, Britain's colonial secretary, in an effort to get his sympathy for the colonists.

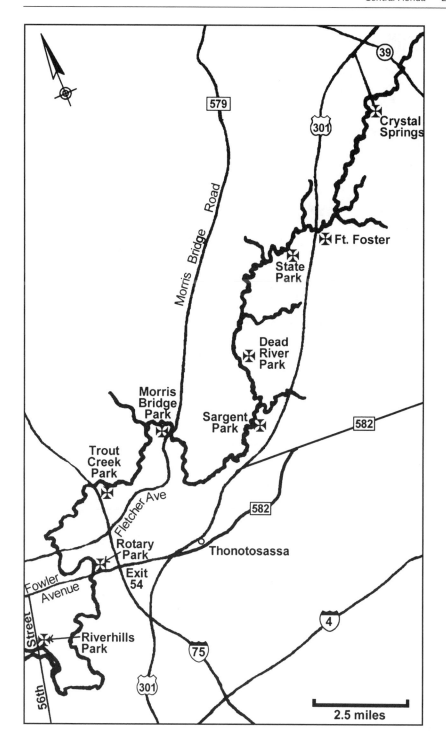

39

579

301

Crystal
Springs

Ft. Foster

State
Park

Dead
River
Park

Morris
Bridge
Park

Sargent
Park

582

Trout
Creek
Park

Morris Bridge Road

Fletcher Ave

582

Rotary
Park

Thonotosassa

Exit
54

Fowler
Avenue

4

Riverhills
Park

56th Street

75

301

2.5 miles

When the water levels are exactly right, you can begin your paddle of the Hillsborough at lovely Crystal Springs. Brian Faulk.

For the canoe or kayak enthusiast, the Hillsborough presents a multitude of faces—a crystal-clear spring run section; the rough and tumble Seventeen Runs section; outstanding bird and other wildlife observation in the Wilderness Park; and a wide, gentle, easy, part-natural-part-suburban section. Small parks located every two or three hours along the banks make access and rest stops easy.

There are alligators, so leave your pets at home and save the swimming for another day on a different river.

Canoe Escape offers three different two-hour trips beginning at various Wilderness Park sites, plus a two-and-a-half-hour trip from Crystal Springs. They rent canoes and kayaks, and also do shuttle service if you bring your own boat.

Canoe Escape is located on the south side of Fowler Avenue (SR582), half a mile east of I-75. If you're traveling on I-75, take exit 54, Fowler Avenue, and go east half a mile. If you're traveling on I-4, take exit 7 (I-75); go north on I-75 to exit 54, Fowler Avenue. Reservations are suggested.

Hillsborough River State Park rents canoes by the hour, and has a private canoe launch area and a nice campground. There's almost no overnight camping along the Hillsborough, so it's best to set up camp in the state park or another area campground or motel and experience the river in day-trip segments.

Hillsborough River State Park is located on US Highway 301. From I-75, if you're traveling northbound, take exit 54 (Fowler Avenue), go east one mile to US301, then north on 301 about nine miles; the park entrance is on your left. If you're traveling south on I-75, take exit 58 (SR54), go east on SR54 about fifteen miles to US301, then south on 301 about six miles; after you cross the Hillsborough River, the park entrance is a short way on your right.

The Hillsborough River canoe trail is divided into five segments:

1) Crystal Springs Recreational Preserve to Hillsborough River State Park, 6.5 miles or 3 hours. Skill level: intermediate, with a strenuous level portage at the state park rapids.

Crystal Springs is the northernmost point of the canoe trail. It is a second-magnitude spring with a constant flow of 40 million gallons a day. The crystalline spring water runs through a short slough that leads to the river. From this point downstream the river is natural for several miles.

At low water there are several rocky shoals, which might become rapids at some water levels. At high water, the rapid flow will sweep you into rocks, fallen trees, and strainers, and the run is not recommended. The Faulks of Canoe Escape warn, "Because this sector of the river has several areas with potentially exposed rock outcroppings, the use of fiberglass craft is strongly discouraged." Upriver of Dead River Park, where the riverbed is confined, the current becomes increasingly swift if the water level rises and may be unsafe even below flood stage.

Fort Foster is a re-created living history center. The original fort was built during the Second Seminole War in the early 1800s to protect the bridge over the Hillsborough River. At the time, it was on the Fort King Military Road, the only road that ran between Ocala and Tampa.

2) Hillsborough River State Park to Dead River Park, 2.6 miles or 1–1½ hours. Skill level: beginner.

This is the shortest part of the river and, at normal water levels, probably the easiest. Watch for river otters. As soon as you launch you'll be in a wilderness area. The river changes from a hardwood hammock to a cypress swamp, with high, overarching trees and a dense understory.

At very low or very high water you'll need more skill to navigate exposed rock shoals or sharp turns. Motors under five horsepower are permitted in this section, but I imagine most of them would quickly lose a prop on the underwater rocks and logs.

3) Dead River Park to Sargeant Park, 4.2 miles or 3–5 hours. Skill level: strenuous. This run is not advertised, and most people are discouraged from trying it. It's called the Seventeen Runs of the Hillsborough River. There are many logjams and several long portages. Add in a couple of dozen alligators, so you won't want to hop in and out of the water, and this is *not* a trip for the single paddler, youngsters, or nonlimber people.

A canoe with lots of leg room is the preferred mode of travel; river kayaks with spray skirts can be too hard to get in and out of for the numerous pull-overs. Make sure your boat has long bow and stern tow ropes. Shorter boats work best because of the acute turns and shallow water.

Sandy Huff says, "Does this sound challenging and a whole lot more effort than you care to expend? Good. The Seventeen Runs is a wild part of the river, purposely kept this way to keep casual paddlers out. The scenery is great, but if you can't hack it, you'll see about the same scenery at other sections of the river. I've done the Seventeen Runs twice, both times with a group of a dozen women, and we had a ball."

At the end of the run, you'll emerge into an open area created by the confluence with Flint Creek, with a dock straight ahead of you. If this is the only part of the river you'll be doing and you still have some energy, turn left and paddle about three hundred yards upstream into Flint Creek. This is the most dependable place to see alligators. Then make a U-turn, come back to the dock, and take the cut downstream of the dock to Sargeant Park.

4) Sargeant Park to Trout Creek Park, 8.5 miles or 4 hours. Skill level: beginner.

This is another section of the river where you can bring your out-of-town guests and beginning paddlers to see Florida wilderness and wildlife. Motorboats are fortunately rare. You'll pass an old wooden trestle from a 1930s logging operation about fifteen minutes before the midpoint, Morris Bridge Park. On the second half of this run you'll pass Nature's Classroom, an educational facility owned by the Hillsborough County School Board. Notice the vultures that hang out here.

5) Trout Creek Park to Riverhills Park, 10.5 miles or 4½ hours. Skill level: beginner.

The river widens now as houses, bridges, flood control dams, roads, and seawalls appear. Rotary Park is the midpoint. After you paddle under Fletcher Avenue you'll be in the more inhabited areas. Birding is good through the reservoir area downstream of Busch Boulevard. The trail terminus at Riverhills Park is not part of the Canoe Escape itinerary, but you can deadhead a car there. Riverhills Park is south of Fowler, on the northeast side of the 56 Street Bridge.

Tampa Parks and Recreation Department is planning four more canoe launch facilities, at Tampa Crest, Sulfur Springs, Rowlett, and River Crest Parks. These will continue the canoe trail to the mouth of the river.

Destination 53: Hontoon Island

> Miles or average time: no limit, paddle at your own speed
>
> Skill level: strong beginner
>
> Current: moderate and steady
>
> Wind problems: few open areas
>
> Emergency numbers: 911; Lake County sheriff, (352) 343-2101; Seminole County sheriff, (407) 330-6600
>
> Rentals: Hontoon Island State Park, 2309 River Ridge Road, Deland FL 32720, phone (904) 736-5309
>
> DeLorme page 80, section A-2
>
> Official Florida canoe trail: no

Hontoon Island State Park is indeed an island. The west side of the island forms the county line between Lake and Seminole Counties. The only way to get there is by private boat or the free hourly ferry. Rental canoes are available on the island.

The 1,650-acre island is six miles south of Deland, off SR44 and/or US17. It's a good place to see manatees on their way in and out of the warm waters of nearby Blue Springs. The whole area is thick with alligators, so plan on swimming only in the roped-off area at the top of Blue Springs.

Two-hour boat tours from Hontoon Landing Marina (2317 River Ridge Road, Deland FL 32720, phone (904) 734-2474) circle the island, stopping at the tiny dock at Blue Springs State Park.

The Timucuan Indians obviously liked Hontoon Island too, and left behind two big mounds made entirely of empty periwinkle snail shells. Nowadays snails are a vector for a nasty parasite, so one wonders if the Indians either cooked their snails until they were very well done, or had severe stomach problems. Maybe that's why the owl totem that was dredged up here in 1955 looks like it has a terrible bellyache.

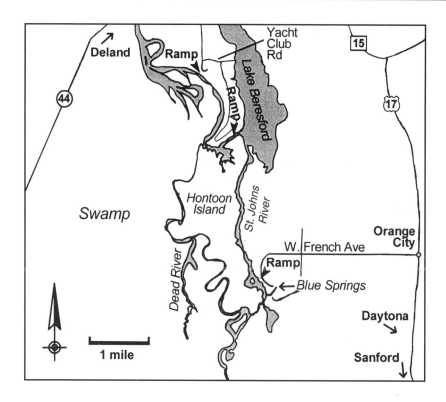

Over the years, the island has been a major Indian ceremonial ground, a boatyard, a fish-packing house, a pioneer homestead, and a cattle ranch. From the top of the eighty-foot observation tower you can see the St. Johns River twist and turn, and watch the antics of the resident grackles.

The six rental cabins have electric ceiling fans, screened porches, and bunkbeds. Showers and toilets are in a separate building. At $20 and $25 a night for the four- and six-person cabins, they are a good bargain, so make reservations well in advance. The island has rest rooms and a tiny store, but no food concessions.

There is a boat launch ramp beside Blue Springs State Park, or you can paddle south/upstream from the ramps at the Beresford peninsula on the west side of Lake Beresford. Other ramps are at the end of Yacht Club Road and at Hontoon Landing Marina on River Ridge Road.

For more information, contact Hontoon Island State Park at (904) 736-5309.

Destination 54: Little Manatee River

Miles or average time: 38 miles, in six sections

Skill level: beginner

Current: slow, except for flood stages

Wind problems: mostly sheltered

Emergency numbers: 911; Hillsborough County sheriff, (813) 247-8000

Rentals: Canoe Outpost, 18001 US 301 South, Wimauma FL 33598, phone (813) 634-2228 or 1-800-229-1371, e-mail canoeski@gte.net, website www.canoeoutpost.com

DeLorme page 91, section C-3

Official Florida canoe trail: yes, a 5-mile section

When I think of the Little Manatee, I think of baby flounder. These nickel-sized little fish hide in the river's white sand bottom. The baby flounder you buy at the pet shop might have hatched here. My friend Dick Bowles says these are probably "hog chokers," or right-eyed flatfish, and are different from the flounder you buy at the fish market.

Watch for flounder harvesters walking along in ankle-deep water, running wide-bottomed nets through the sand. The ones I talked to showed us the big fiberglass tank in the back of their pickup, complete with an electric bubbler for oxygen. I asked if they were breaking the law, and one said, "Nah, there are only about two places we can get to the river and net for flounder. We're leaving plenty of baby fish to grow up."

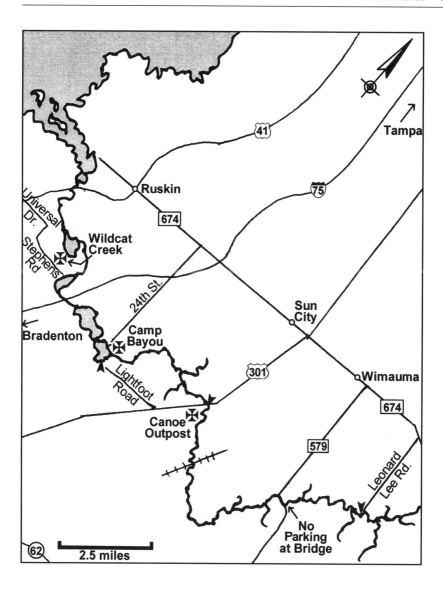

The Florida legislature designated this river an Outstanding Florida Water. The clear, tea-colored water is some of the cleanest and least polluted in the state.

It has a constant flow due to a fairly steep drop—a hundred feet in the first twenty-five miles. Like all rivers, it floods after heavy rains, and has bump-overs and pull-overs in the dry spells. One June we encountered extremely low water. The very next June the Canoe Outpost had to close because of flooding. It's a good idea to call Canoe Outpost at (813) 634-2228 or Little Manatee State Recreation Area at (813) 671-5005 to check the water level.

The official canoe trail is only five miles long, but the Canoe Outpost in Wimauma lists four other trips of varying lengths for a total of twenty-eight miles, plus you can paddle to a spot halfway between US41 and I-75 for another ten miles.

The upper part of the Little Manatee, east of US301, is considered more challenging than the five miles downstream that comprise the official State of Florida canoe trail. About a mile east of I-75 the river widens, and you'll see more motorboat traffic. The salt water and mangroves begin about here too, and the river changes from a sheltered, oak-canopied trail to open salt marshes and leaping mullet.

1) Leonard Lee Road to SR579, 7 miles or 2 hours. To start at the "top," launch at the Leonard Lee Road bridge south of SR674. This is a narrow and twisting run, as the river hasn't yet picked up much water. To get to it from Ruskin, head east on SR674 for nine miles. Pass Wimauma. A half mile after SR674 angles to the southeast, turn right/south onto Leonard Lee Road. Take this 2.3 miles to the river.

2) SR579 to US301, 9 miles or 3 hours. This section is where we saw the flounder fishermen, and if you look at the map, it's pretty far upstream from Tampa Bay—those mama flounders swam a long way in their search for the perfect nursery stream.

From Wimauma, turn south on SR579, and launch beside the bridge (no parking). You'll paddle past the intake/outflow from the Florida Power plant about halfway down the run. It's been reengineered so it's safer for humans and manatees alike, but give it a wide berth anyway. You'll pass under the Seaboard Coast Line railroad bridge about an hour after that.

3) US301 to Little Manatee River State Recreation Area, 5 miles or 2 hours. This is the official canoe trail. Canoe Outpost is on the south side of the US301 bridge. This is probably the prettiest part of the river—wide and deep enough for lazy paddling, and still sheltered by overhanging trees.

4) Little Manatee River State Recreation Area to Camp Bayou, 3 miles or 1½ hours. To get to the SRA, go south on US301 for 1.8 miles. Turn right/west on Lightfoot Road. The entrance to the SRA is .3 miles down Lightfoot. From the river, the ramp will be on river left.

5) Camp Bayou to Wildcat Creek, 10 miles or 4–5 hours. The bayou, and the river, are very wide and open here, so wind and waves and motorboats could be factors. Camp Bayou is at the end of East 24 Street south of Ruskin.

6) Take out at Wildcat Creek Park on Stephens Road east of US41. To get to it, head south on US41. About two miles south of the bridge, turn left/east onto Universal Drive, then right/south onto Stephens Road. Wildcat Creek comes into Hayes Bayou from the south.

Also try www8.myflorida.com/communities/learn/trails/canoe or www.canoe outpost.com.

Destination 55: Merritt Island

Miles or average time: no limit, paddle at your own pace

Skill level: advanced beginner

Current: tidal flow and strong current under bridge

Wind problems: yes, very open waters

Emergency numbers: 911; Brevard County sheriff, (321) 264-5100 or -5201

Rentals: Inlet Marina, 9502 South A1A, Melbourne Beach FL 32951, phone (321) 724-5424; A Day Away Kayak Tours, phone (321) 268-2655; Pedal Oar Paddle, 4300 South US1, Grant FL 32949, phone (321) 723-4486

DeLorme page 81, section D-3

Official Florida canoe trail: no

If there was ever a study in contrasts, Merritt Island National Wildlife Refuge is it. The island and surrounding waters teem with some of the rarest birds and animals in North America. The utterly flat islands and grassy marshes stretch to the horizon for miles, looking just as they must have looked when the first Ais Indians set foot on the land.

But looming in the distance is the black and white cube of the second largest building, containing the highest level of technology, in the U.S. It is the VAB—Vehicular Assembly Building—which is the giant garage where the space shuttles are erected.

Inside the 140,000-acre (220-square-mile) refuge is the John F. Kennedy Space Center and Spaceport USA. There you can touch actual early rockets,

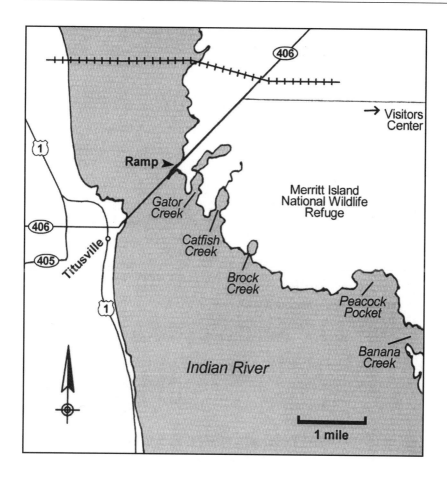

view movies of launches, watch demonstrations of shuttle tiles, peer through the visor of a space suit, taste freeze-dried ice cream, and talk to a robot.

But the 310 species of birds, 25 kinds of mammals, 117 brands of fish, and 65 types of amphibians and turtles that live in the refuge notice mankind only when there's a launch. Then, as the incredibly deep sound waves flatten grasses in concentric waves, flocks of hidden birds fly up, fish and turtles scoot to the bottom, and the fish definitely don't bite. That's okay, since humans are cleared out of Canaveral National Seashore for four days before each launch anyway. Call (321) 867-3217 for launch information. If you want a front seat for a launch, Merritt Island NWR is closed only one day before a launch, and you can still use the north end of the refuge on launch day. In fact, watching a launch from your canoe or kayak is the best seat in the house.

"Sea kayaks are best," says Sonny Norris of the Central Florida Paddle-masters Club. "The Indian River is wide and can get windy, so canoes are not recommended in the open river. Stay close to the shoreline or in protected inlets if you have a canoe. The difficulty is easy to moderate. Wind and tides can make the going a little harder, so keep an eye on the weather. A map and compass are recommended." Definitely wear water shoes—the rough sand beaches are interspersed with oyster beds and muddy lagoons.

From Titusville, cross the SR406 bridge to the island. About half a mile east is a small unmanned tourist kiosk with maps and information. The Merritt Island NWR Visitor Center is about four miles further east, and stocks more free maps and brochures.

Now backtrack to Parrish Park on the northeast side of the SR406 bridge. You can launch, picnic, and find rest rooms here.

The shoulders on both sides of the road east of Parrish Park are also good launch sites. If you do launch at the paved ramps, paddle under the bridge with caution—the riptides can be very strong here—and certainly stay out of the main span used by the yachts traveling the Intracoastal Waterway. Head south. Paddle to the small island, and then to the marshes on the east.

Some of the channels that lead to the inside of the island, like Banana Creek, are off limits as security areas—you'll see the signs. That still leaves miles of shoreline to explore.

This area is a great place to take a bird book and binoculars, since it's on the migratory route for some hundred thousand birds.

Watch for white pelicans. During breeding season, both males and females sport fleshy orange knobs on the top of their beaks, and black edges on the back of their wings. Naturalists have seen them fish cooperatively, swimming in a semicircle and beating the water with their wings. The gray-brown pelicans perched around them are the more common brown pelicans. White pelicans with a bit of gray on the wings are immature whites.

There are six thousand alligators around Merritt Island NWR. Laurilee Thompson, of Osprey Outfitters, says, "You could encounter one anywhere. I've seen them right next to the causeway."

The best seats in town for watching NASA's thundering launches, here the John Glenn shuttle, are in your kayak. Laurilee Thompson.

Also watch for manatees and turtles. Immature sea turtles use the Indian River and Mosquito Lagoon as a nursery area. The walnut-sized turtle heads that pop up are shy diamondback terrapins.

Maybe that's the origin of the name for Turtle Mound. It's exactly 20.5 miles north of your launch spot, but accessible only from New Smyrna Beach (see destination 45). Forty to fifty feet high and six hundred feet long, it holds 33,000 cubic yards of oyster shells gathered by the Timucuan Indians between A.D. 800 and 1400. Some sixty smaller mounds dot this coast, so any high spots of land you see were probably Indian sites.

More than a millenium ago Indians paddled their dugout canoes in these waters. Today you can explore these ancient waterways, side by side with the world's most advanced technology.

For more information, contact the Cocoa Beach Visitors Bureau, PO Box 320763, Cocoa Beach FL 32932-0763, phone (321) 459-2200, www.cocoabeach.com/nature.html.

The Department of Environmental Protection (DEP), 3900 Commonwealth Boulevard, MS 245, Tallahassee FL 32399-3000, puts out a *Boater's Guide to Brevard County* with close-up maps of the shorelines.

Destination 56: Mount Dora

Miles or average time: no limit, paddle at your own speed

Skill level: beginner

Current: none

Wind problems: some in open water

Emergency numbers: 911; Lake County sheriff, (352) 343-2101

Rentals: Fun Boats at Lakeside Inn, 100 North Alexander Street, Mount Dora FL 32757, phone (352) 735-2669, pager 326-7043; Triple Eagle Boats, Umatilla FL, phone (352) 669-0700

DeLorme page 79, section B-2

Official Florida canoe trail: no

The only lighthouse in Florida that's on an inland lake is in the town of Mount Dora. The bright red and white structure is at Gilbert Park, blocks from the downtown shops. It is a reminder of the time when Florida's waterways were the only mode of transportation, and steamboats would bring tourists all the way down the chain of lakes from Jacksonville.

If you like to paddle in perfect circles, Lakes Dora, Ola, Carlton, Beauclair, and Eustis are all part of the north-flowing ponds, canals, lakes, and rivers called the Harris chain of lakes. They form the headwaters of the Ocklawaha, which in turn feeds into the St. Johns River and out to the Atlantic. It's one of the few U.S. river systems that goes north.

You can even paddle the Beauclair canal, with its old dam, that feeds into Lake Apopka. The Mount Dora Chamber of Commerce bills the Dora Canal, which connects Lakes Dora and Eustis, as "the most beautiful mile of water in Florida."

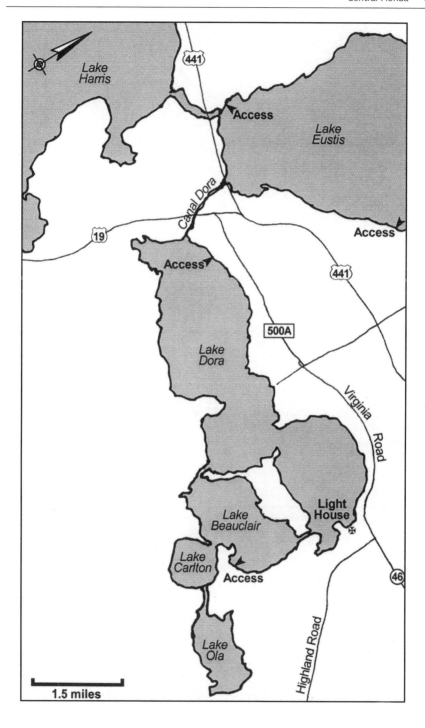

Lake Harris

441

Access

Lake Eustis

Canal Dora

19

Access

Access

441

500A

Lake Dora

Virginia Road

Lake Beauclair

Light House

Lake Carlton

Access

46

Lake Ola

Highland Road

1.5 miles

Mount Dora Lighthouse is the only lighthouse in Florida on an inland lake. C. J. Jean; Mount Dora Chamber of Commerce.

Or you can sedately paddle past the pretty houses above wide lawns, padlock your boat to a bench or post at the downtown ramp, and walk into town for a leisurely lunch and a ramble around the world famous antique shops. It's traditional to buy a bumper sticker that reads "I climbed Mount Dora." That's an inside joke, since the area is about as flat as a pancake. The city does lie at 184 feet above sea level, which is medium high for Florida.

Other odd facts: Back in 1934 a report said the area had "2293 lakes of which 1400 are named." Modern mapmakers can find only 642 named lakes and 310 unnamed lakes. The Indians came up with the term *ahapopka,* which means potato eating. Lake Dora was named for Mrs. Dora Ann Drawdy, who was hospitable to an 1846 surveying group, who were naming the various landmarks as they came across them. The quaint-on-purpose town is now known as "the New England of the South" and hosts a big antique boat show every March. The Lakeside Inn hotel is one of only five Florida "Historic Hotels of America" and has an interesting past.

Here are fish camps and other access points around the area:

Big Lake Harris: public ramp on US441 in Tavares
Dead River: Palm Gardens, 11801 Highway 441, Tavares FL 32778, phone (352) 343-2024
Lake Beauclair: Trimble County Park, off Highway 441 on SR448, phone (352) 383-1993
Lake Griffin: Al Jana Fish Camp, 2210 East Main Street (Highway 441), Leesburg FL 34748, phone (352) 787-2429; Lake Griffin Resort, 5620 Bertville Road, Lady Lake FL 32159, phone (352) 753-3241; Morgan's Fish Camp, 4056 Picciola Road, Fruitland Park FL 34731, phone (352) 787-4916; Twin Palms Resort, 35320 Cross Street, Fruitland Park FL 34731, phone (352) 787-4514

For more information, contact the Mount Dora Chamber of Commerce, PO Box 196, Mount Dora FL 32757-0196, e-mail chamber@mt-dora.com.

Destination 57: Pithlachascotee River

Miles or average time: 5 miles

Skill level: intermediate

Current: tidal downstream, slow upstream

Wind problems: yes, especially near mouth

Emergency numbers: 911; Pasco County sheriff, (352) 847-5878; New Port Richey Police, (352) 841-4550

DeLorme page 82, section C-3

Official Florida canoe trail: yes

Once you try to pronounce the name of this river, you'll call it what the locals do: "the Cotee." This is a beautiful river, meandering through the town of New Port Richey. Some fifty springs feed into the twenty-five-mile-long river, though the water is tea colored for most of its length. Boulevard Street follows several miles of the river on the east/north side, and is a scenic drive.

Back in 1879, archeologist S. T. Walker of the Smithsonian Institution found evidence that Indians had lived here since A.D. 1000 as part of the Weedon Island culture (see destination 65). The Olesner Mound is still visible near Sunset Boulevard.

Every year the town of New Port Richey puts on its Chasco Festival, celebrating a legend about an Indian maiden named Pithla who fell in love with a handsome Spaniard named Chasco. The story has two endings—either the girl's father got mad and sacrificed both of them, or they married and ruled the tribe with great success.

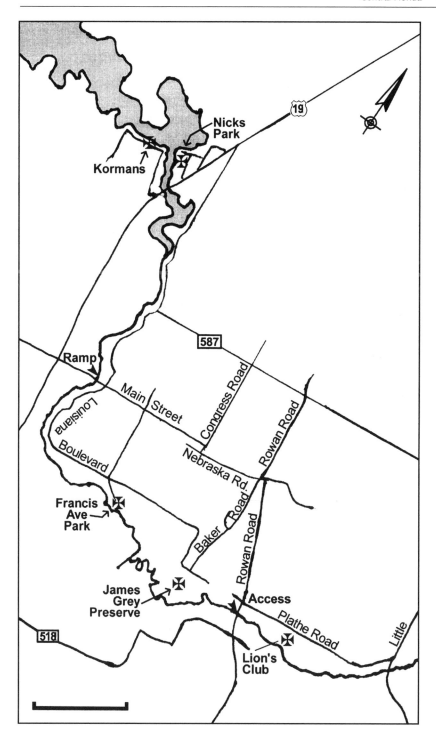

The word Cotee means "winding river" in Indian. The same people who tell you the Pithla-Chasco legend will give you their version of where the other syllables in the name originated.

The five-mile official canoe trail extends from Rowan Road Bridge to the Francis Avenue City Park. This upper part is a bit tricky, with twists and turns, and the official state guide cautions that it is not for first-time beginners. The current is usually slow, but the tide is evident far east of US19, so check the tide and wind conditions before deciding which part to paddle.

You can extend the official trail downstream. There is a ramp at Main Street, and another at Nicks Park on the west side of US19.

You can also head upriver a bit beyond Rowan Road. However, the mile-and-a-half stretch between Rowan and Little Roads has some fallen trees.

1) Lions Club to Rowan Road Bridge, .5 miles. This small ramp is on private property, so be polite. The Lions Club is on Plathe Road, which runs east-west just above the river.

2) Rowan Road Bridge to Francis Avenue City Park, 5 miles. From US19, head east on Main Street. Turn right/south on Congress, then left/east on Nebraska. This runs into CR518 or Rowan Road. Baker Street heads due south, but you want Rowan, which heads southwest. Access is on the southwest side of the new Rowan Road Bridge.

There are very shallow stretches on this section, so make sure you're wearing water shoes, and have a ten-to-fifteen-foot tow rope or end line so you don't break your back if you pull the boat over sandbars.

Pasco County recently acquired the James E. Grey Preserve. Driving access looks like it will be from either Baker-Rowan Street from the north or Louisiana/Plathe/Afghan from the east. For river access, two tiny canals on the north side of the Cotee River lead to two lakes in the Preserve.

3) Francis Avenue City Park to Main Street, 3 miles. From US19, head east on Main Street, then turn right/south on Madison. Turn left/east on Louisanna Avenue to the park. There's a path from the parking area to the canoe launch.

4) Main Street to Nicks Park, 6 miles. The Main Street ramp is tucked into the northwest side of the bridge behind the Chamber of Commerce. The river is wide, windy, and more populated on this stretch.

5) Nicks Park to Korman's Sunset Landing, .5 miles. After you paddle under US19, watch for Hooters on the right/north side of the river. Nicks

Park is beside it, at Bayview Street and Treadway Drive. The river is pure salt water now, and opens up to Millers Bayou.

6) If you'd like to explore the mouth of the river and out to the Gulf of Mexico, you can start at Korman's Sunset Landing. From here the river opens up again to a wide bay, dotted with shrimp boats and fishing shacks.

For more information, contact the West Pasco Chamber of Commerce at (727) 842-7651 or www.westpasco.com. Also try www8.myflorida.com/communities/learn/trails/canoe.

Destination 58: Reedy Creek

Larry Reed

Miles: 8 miles round-trip

Average time: 4–5 hours

Skill level: intermediate

Current: slight

Wind Problems: none

Emergency numbers: 911; Osceola County sheriff, (407) 348-2222

Rentals: Wilderness Adventures, Kissimmee, e-mail
mail@wildernessadventures.com

DeLorme page 85, section B-3

Official Florida canoe trail: no

Reedy Creek snakes some twenty miles across the southwest corner of Osceola County, originating in Disney World and emptying into Lake Russell and beyond. Who knows—you might be paddling in the same water that once flowed in 20,000 Leagues Under the Sea!

The creek winds through pine, oak, and cypress forest and swamp, at times with a cathedral-like canopy of tangled branches. The tannic-stained water flows with just a slight current, and quiet paddlers often see white-tailed deer, wild hogs, and river otter along the creek, along with many species of waterfowl, such as wood ducks, ibis, ospreys, wood storks, and hawks. Even large (up to three feet) salamanders, called amphiumas, have been seen in the mud flats and thick vegetation along the banks.

The put-in is at the US17/92 bridge west of Kissimmee. From Orlando,

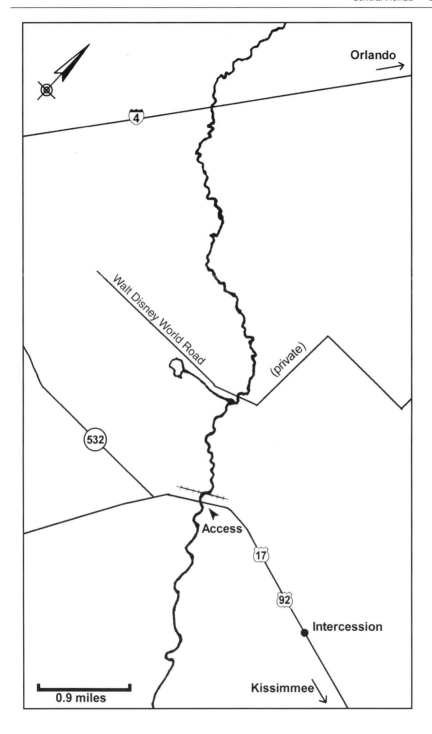

Orlando

4

Walt Disney World Road

(private)

532

Access

17

92

Intercession

0.9 miles

Kissimmee

take I-4 south to exit 24, go east on SR532 for four miles, turn left/northeast onto US17/92, and proceed a half mile to the third bridge. Or, from Kissimmee, take US17/92 west; the bridge is approximately three miles west of Intercession City. Parking is on the southeast side of the bridge, with a footpath leading to the creek.

Although it is possible to paddle several miles downstream during periods of high water, most paddlers head upstream/north, passing under a low railroad bridge and bicycle path.

The first mile of the trip winds though cypress swamp punctuated with cypress knees and deadfalls. This section calls for good paddling skills, and at low water you might encounter a few carry-overs.

The creek soon appears to dead-end against a grassy dike. On one map this skinny little overgrown jeep trail has the grandiose name of Walt Disney World Road. However, a narrow canal turns sharply left and leads to a small pond at the base of a water-control structure. A small dock on the right allows a portage around the dam.

The creek has been dredged wider for a quarter mile above the dam, but soon narrows and bears left again into its original course.

For the next several miles, the creek again winds through heavily canopied forest. For the most part, paddling is easiest on this section, although seasonal deadfalls may be encountered.

Eventually the creek narrows again and becomes shallower with increasing current, making paddling more difficult. A power line right-of-way clearing provides a good lunch spot, and if the water level allows, you can paddle further upstream to reach the I-4 overpass (no access from road). Most paddlers turn back prior to this point, however, satisfied that they have seen a piece of "real Florida" that the tourists in the Magic Kingdom just to the north never experience.

Destination 59: Sebastian Creek

Larry Reed

Miles: North Prong, upstream and return, 7 miles; South Prong, upstream and return, 9 miles

Average time: 3–4 hours each

Skill level: beginner

Current: light

Wind problems: open bay at beginning of North Prong; the South Prong is more sheltered

Emergency numbers: 911; Brevard County sheriff, (321) 264-5100 or -5201; Indian River County sheriff, (561) 569-0082

Rentals: Captain Hiram's Watercraft Rentals, 1606 Indian River Drive, Sebastian FL 32958, phone (561) 589-5560, e-mail hirams@sebastian.fl.us, website www.hirams.com; Donald MacDonald Park, CR 505, Sebastian FL 32958, phone (561) 589-0087

DeLorme page 96, section B-3

Official Florida canoe trail: no

Two-pronged Sebastian Creek empties into the Indian River Lagoon directly across from Sebastian Inlet with its beaches and great fishing.

The South Prong winds its way through high sandy bluffs covered with Australian pines on the northwest bank, with low estuarine hammocks on the east. As you go upstream against a usually light current, the banks become lower with numerous cabbage palms and an occasional oak festooned with cormorants and anhingas.

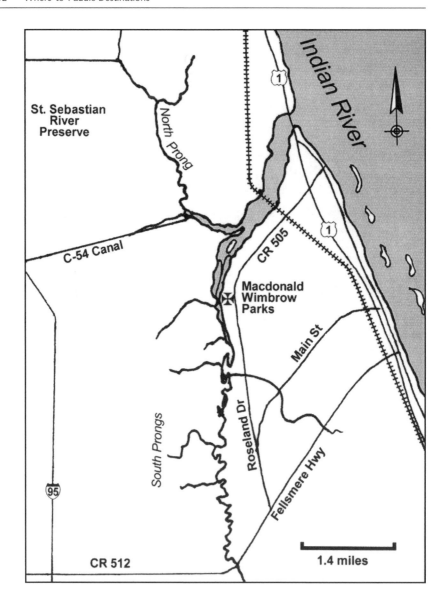

The creek narrows further and becomes winding, and the occasional house encountered in no way detracts from the excellent scenery. You'll eventually reach the CR512 bridge. No river access is available at this bridge at present, but there are plans to construct a canoe landing in the future. At this point, you may either continue upstream for several miles against a freshening current as the creek narrows even further, or turn and head downstream again.

The North Prong requires paddling westward across the baylike mouth of the creek. It is difficult on windy days, until you encounter the narrow entrance along the north bank just about the time a large water-control structure and canal come into sight to the west.

You'll wind upstream through scenic low hammocks and at times a tunnel-like canopy. Eventually you'll reach a canoe landing, which provides a good lunch spot and has access to a network of hiking and horseback riding trails in the St. Sebastian River Buffer Preserve.

The SSRBP has Bachman's sparrows from February to July, along with year-round brown-headed nuthatches, eastern bluebirds, swallow-tailed kites, wild turkeys, and quail. A colony of Florida scrub jays live on Scrub Jay Road. There are several colonies of red-cockaded woodpeckers.

Paddling the seven-mile round-trip on a windy day, along with a ten-mile hike through sand pine and scrub, leaves you mighty glad your tent awaits only a few yards from the takeout!

Both trips begin either at Donald MacDonald Park in Sebastian, two miles west of US1 on CR505 (12315 Roseland Road, phone (561) 589-0087), or at Dale Wimbrow Park, a half mile west (upstream) on CR505. Each has boat ramps, docks, and free parking. MacDonald Park has a nice campground located in a sand-pine forest near the creek. Sebastian Inlet State Park on the east side of the Indian River (9700 South A1A, Melbourne Beach FL 32951, phone (561) 589-9659) offers camping with more amenities.

St. Sebastian River Buffer Preserve is north of the C54 canal and west of the North Prong. HQ is at PO Box 350, Fellsmere FL 32948, phone (321) 953-5004. Hours are 8 A.M. to 5 P.M.

Destination 60: Terra Ceia Bay

Miles or average time: no limit, explore at your own pace

Skill level: beginner in no wind, intermediate when choppy

Current: tidal flow

Wind problems: yes, open waters

Emergency numbers: 911; Manatee County sheriff, (941) 747-3011

DeLorme page 90, section 3-D

Official Florida canoe trail: yes

Florida's newest official state canoe trail is Terra Ceia Bay and Emerson Point Conservation Park.

Charlie Hunsicker, ecosystems administrator for Manatee County, has been largely responsible for creating this park and canoe trail.

According to Charlie, you can paddle from Rattlesnake Key to I-275. Here are his directions: "From I-75, get off at exit 43, the Ellenton 301 exit. Go west. This becomes Tenth Street, and goes into Snead Island. From there, follow the signs to Emerson Point. The park and the canoe launch are on the north side." Charlie says the launch area is an old agricultural ditch that leads from the north side of the park to Terra Ceia Bay.

There are at least two Indian mounds in this area. The first, Partayant Indian Mound, is on park grounds, just west of the picnic area. Due south of this mound, across the Manatee River, is DeSoto Point, where some historians think Hernando DeSoto landed with his fleet in 1539. (Those of us who live at the top of Tampa Bay stoutly contend that he came all the way to Safety Harbor.) There is a park at DeSoto Point, and on weekends rangers and volunteers dress up like Spanish conquistadors.

The Madeira Bickel Mound is on the north side of Terra Ceia Bay. This was a heavily populated area back when the Spaniards arrived in the 1500s, and if you see a hump in the greenery, it could be an old Tocobaga midden, ceremonial mound, or house mound.

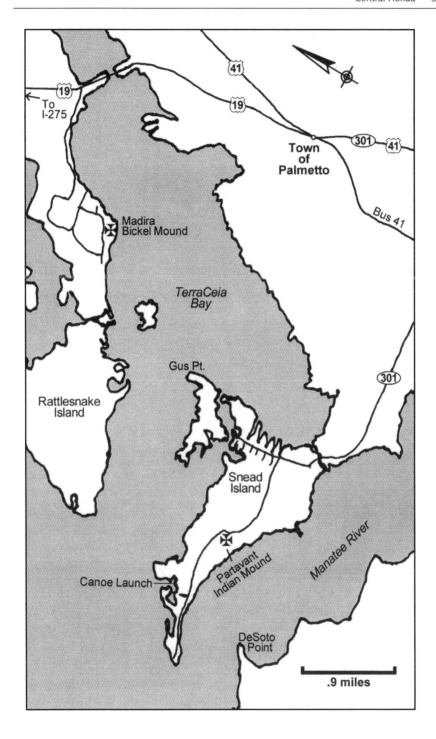

Town
of
Palmetto

Madira
Bickel Mound

TerraCeia
Bay

Gus Pt.

Rattlesnake
Island

Snead
Island

Canoe Launch

Partavant
Indian Mound

Manatee River

DeSoto
Point

.9 miles

To
I-275

Destination 61: Turkey Creek Sanctuary

Larry Reed and Arnie Diedrichs

Miles or average time: about 4 miles or 2–3 hours round-trip

Skill level: beginner

Current: light

Wind problems: mostly sheltered waters

Emergency numbers: 911; Brevard County sheriff, (321) 264-5201

Rentals: Nik's Boat Rental, Palm Bay Marina, 4350 Dixie Highway NE (on north side of US1 bridge over Turkey Inlet), Palm Bay FL 32905, phone (321) 723-0851

DeLorme page 88, section D-2

Official Florida canoe trail: no

Turkey Creek, located in the heart of Palm Bay, is one of Brevard County's paddling gems. Its lower portion flows through a series of estuarine hammocks interspersed with waterfront homes, but its upper section gives way to the junglelike growth and high sandy bluffs of the 113-acre Turkey Creek Sanctuary. This is a pleasant half-day paddle, counting lunch, a stroll around the boardwalk trail, and a visit to the sanctuary's interpretive center.

Begin at Captain Goode City Park in Palm Bay, which offers a new boat ramp, floating dock, rest rooms, and good parking. Head west to go upstream. After a half mile, an interesting fork opens to the left, which eventually rejoins the main channel. Turkey Creek winds through a series of braided channels here called the Willow Swamp, with residential areas on the north and south banks. This section is popular with manatees and ospreys.

The entire character of the creek changes dramatically as it passes under the Port Malabar Bridge 1.2 miles upstream and enters the sanctuary. The

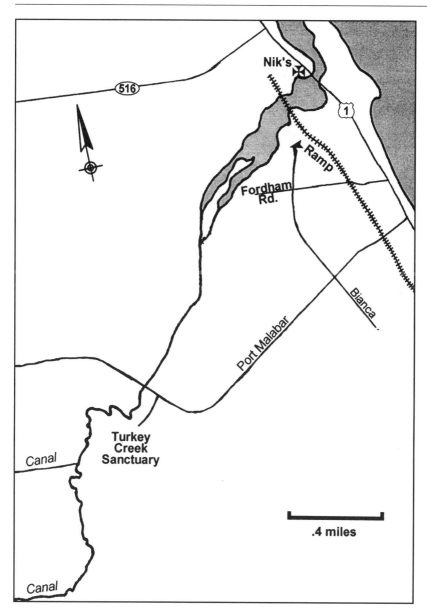

creek narrows and quickens under a thick tree canopy. This is the "real Florida," and a pleasant, quiet area to stop paddling and enjoy the sounds of nature as well as a respite from the sun. Although a few deadfalls may be encountered along this stretch at low water, most have been cut out of the way. Expect to see an occasional alligator, manatee, or otter in this area.

Farther upstream, twenty-foot-high sandy bluffs appear on the right bank, and a beautiful hardwood swamp on the left. The Turkey Creek Sanctuary Park's canoe landing is a mile farther. The covered pavilion at the landing is a nice place to enjoy lunch, and the boardwalk leads to the Margaret Hames Nature Center. The Florida Audubon Society owns the sanctuary, which is best known for more than twenty species of migratory warblers, plus all the usual wading birds. Some of the best bird viewing is along the jogging trails.

Another quarter mile upstream you'll come to a water-control structure. It is not possible to portage around it. The usual condition is mostly a gentle and pleasant flow. After heavy rains, novice paddlers should avoid this fast, narrow upper section. It is a hard paddle upstream—but a blast coming back!

Fishermen can expect to catch mostly sunfish, with an occasional bass. Very large gar lie motionless near the surface. At the brackish mouth of the creek, anglers find snook, sea trout, mangrove snapper, and sheepshead.

Directions: From US1 in Palm Bay, travel west on Port Malabar Boulevard for a quarter mile. After crossing the railroad tracks, turn right/north on Bianca Drive and go three-quarters of a mile to Captain Goode Park.

Turkey Creek Sanctuary is at 1518 Port Malabar Boulevard NE (behind the Community Center at 1502 Port Malabar Boulevard), phone (321) 952-3433. It is open every day of the year from 7 A.M. to sunset. For information on the sanctuary and Goode Park, contact the Palm Bay Parks and Recreation Department, 1502 Port Malabar Boulevard, Palm Bay FL 32905, (321) 952-3433.

The Turtle Coast Sierra Club, which meets on the fourth Thursday of each month in Melbourne, hosts a quarterly Turkey Creek cleanup. Some canoes are provided, and you need to bring old clothes, work gloves, and a rake. Contact them at (321) 984-0604 or www.sierraclub.org/chapters/fl/turtle-coast.

For a live view of the mouth of Turkey Creek, check the River Cam image at www.fl-fishing.com/cfml/river.cfm. Also try www.audubon-org/Destination/fl/indianriver/birdsites.htm.

Destination 62: Turnbull Creek

Laurilee Thompson

Miles or average time: 3 hours each way

Skill level: beginner

Current: slow, with tidal flux

Wind problems: yes, this is an open marsh area

Emergency numbers: 911; Volusia County sheriff, (904) 736-5961

Rentals: A Day Away Guided Kayak Tours, phone (321) 268-2655,
website www.nbbd.com/kayaktours

DeLorme page 81, section B-3

Official Florida canoe trail: no

Thin wisps of steam spiral up from the warm waters of the creek in the pre-dawn light. Patches of fog lie low over the marsh in the cool morning air. Silently I paddle, listening for the rustle of an elusive rail as it scurries through the dry grass. I pass a sora rail crouching on a willow limb. We lock eyes, but the bird never moves a muscle.

The rising sun turns the dew on the spiderwebs into sparkling diamonds. These shimmering jewels are all shapes, scattered throughout the marsh. Common yellowthroats flit about in the willows. A great blue heron takes to the air, then flies alongside, expressing with loud squawks his displeasure at my appearance. White ibis probe in the mud of the sandbars with their big orange bills, and a stealthy green heron crouches on a myrtle limb, waiting for his unsuspecting breakfast to swim by.

The sun burns the fog off and the air becomes warmer. A chattering king-fisher stays just in front of my boat, hovering like a hummingbird, then div-

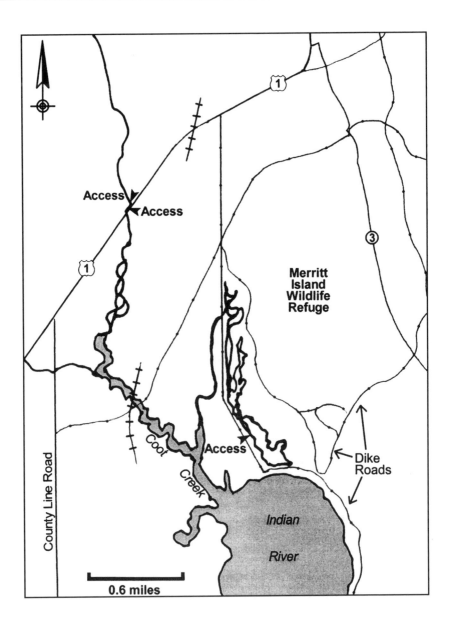

ing to snatch a minnow. Vultures circle lazily, riding the thermals. An occasional wood stork joins them as they wind higher and higher. A peregrine falcon sits on a dead palm snag, and a red-shouldered hawk screams nearby.

Thousands of robins awake in the red cedar hammocks. Tree swallows dive-bomb for insects over the marsh. Savannah sparrows and myrtle warblers flit and chip in the bushes, and a squadron of brown pelicans glides silently overhead. Around the next bend a flock of coots runs noisily on top of the water, trying to stay ahead of my boat.

The creek water becomes saltier. The myrtles, cattails, and willows give way to an unending sea of cordgrass. This is a pristine salt marsh, one of the few left in the Indian River Lagoon that has not been altered by man. It is one of the most relaxing paddles around. Hundreds of great southern white butterflies flutter by in their annual spring and fall migration.

A cormorant perches on an old sign and spreads his wings in the sun to dry. A flock of bluewing teal explode into the air from a hidden pond. An otter and her young frolic near the shore, then disappear through the grass as I approach. A great egret crosses my bow, and a tricolored heron takes off from a sandbar, squawking loudly in time with his wing beats.

As I near the Indian River the winding creek widens. An immature little blue heron stands silently on a log watching me glide by. Its pea green legs are the field mark for this snow white bird which will be steely blue a year from now. A flock of cormorants glide by, heading for their favorite fishing area near the mouth of the creek.

The water gets shallower, and occasionally I see a large redfish, head down and tail fin waving slowly above the water as it roots for blue crabs in the mud. A stingray explodes from the bottom, the undersides of its wings flashing white as it streaks across the grass flats.

When I leave the creek, I see dolphins playing in the river. They have a school of mullet cornered. A mullet jumps, followed by a leaping dolphin who snatches the hapless mullet in midair. A pelican fishes beside a young dolphin. The baby dolphin chases a mullet down, and the greedy pelican grabs it right in front of the dolphin. More gulls and terns dive noisily into the school of mullet that the dolphins are terrorizing. Beyond them, a raft of ducks floats out in the river.

Sadly I turn my boat toward the dike road and prepare myself for the trip back to civilization. Fiddler crabs scurry into their holes as I drag my boat up the dike, and a great blue heron protests my presence as he flaps slowly away.

Turnbull Creek is a serene escape back in time.

Getting there: From I-95, take exit 82, go east on SR5A. Go left/north on US1 approximately two miles to the small bridge just before the railroad overpass. Access is on the east side of the bridge.

It is possible to deadhead a vehicle on the dike road at the mouth of the river. From the launch area, head north on US1. Immediately after the railroad overpass, turn right/east on the dike road. Go two miles to an open area and park on the right side of the road.

Destination 63: Ulumay Wildlife Refuge

Larry Reed

Miles or average time: 6 miles or 2–3 hours round-trip

Skill level: beginner

Current: none

Wind problems: mixed open waters and sheltering banks

Emergency numbers: 911; Brevard County sheriff, (321) 264-5201

Rentals: A Day Away Guided Kayak Trips, phone (321) 268-2655

DeLorme page 88, section A-1

Official Florida canoe trail: no

Ulumay Wildlife Refuge is a wonderful paddling spot located on the south side of Merritt Island, in the town named Merritt Island. The area is a historically documented Indian settlement dating from the early eighteenth century.

The 437-acre wildlife sanctuary and bird rookery is just north of Kiwanis Island Park. This natural lagoon is surrounded by a man-made dike and crisscrossed with old mosquito control canals.

Local legend has it that Old Humpbacked Troll dwells under the hundred-foot fishing pier at the southwest corner of the park. You are more likely to see a wide variety of wading and migratory birds, including kingfishers, white and brown pelicans, wood storks, and even an occasional roseate spoonbill.

A hiking/bike trail extends around the perimeter of the refuge, and an observation tower is located a short distance inside. Sea kayakers will enjoy the paddling opportunities in the nearby Banana River.

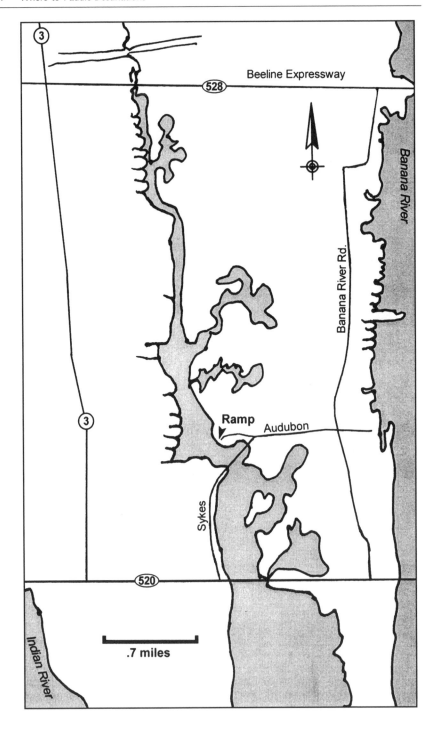

The canoe trail begins two hundred yards from the refuge entrance, to the right. It winds west, then north around the perimeter of the refuge. The natural and man-made canals and small bays tunnel through mangrove hammocks populated by a variety of waterfowl.

Stay close to the outer dike where the trail is poorly marked. At high tide you can explore the narrow channels that extend into the interior of the refuge. Keep an eye on the position of the sun, other distant landmarks, or a compass to keep your bearings.

After about three miles, you'll reach a small bay adjacent to the Beeline Causeway. A resident flock of roseate spoonbills frequents this area, especially in winter months. More adventurous paddlers can portage across the dike and into Sike's Creek for additional exploring; otherwise, further progress is thwarted as the waterway narrows and then disappears to the east.

Ulumay Refuge provides an easy and scenic paddle through a wildlife sanctuary in the midst of an urban environment. Its relatively short length and easy access make it well suited for a morning or afternoon trip.

Directions: From Beeline Expressway (SR528) on Merritt Island, turn south onto Banana River Drive and go almost three miles to a sharp left turn. Ulumay Refuge entrance (watch for the sign) is on the right, on the outside of a curve to the right. Alternatively, from Merritt Island Causeway (SR520), turn north just beyond Merritt Square Mall onto Sikes Creek Parkway and proceed one mile to refuge entrance on left.

For more information, contact the Brevard County Parks and Recreation Department, 591 Cone Road, Merritt Island FL 32952, phone (321) 455-1312.

Destination 64: Walk-in-the-Water to Kissimmee—A Four-Lake Paddle

Miles or average time: 4–7 hours, in three segments

Skill level: intermediate, with some pull-overs

Current: slow

Wind problems: very exposed open lakes

Emergency numbers: 911; Polk County sheriff, (863) 533-0344

Rentals: Lake Kissimmee State Park, 14248 Camp Mack Road, Lake Wales FL 33853, phone (863) 696-1112; Southland Scenic Water Tours, 5000 Fairmont Road, Lake Wales FL 33853, phone (863) 439-5898

DeLorme page 94, section B-1 to A-2

Official Florida canoe trail: no

Weohyakapka means "walk in the water." From this lake a series of winding creeks lead to three other lakes. If you wish, you can keep going and paddle up the Chain of Lakes to the town of Kissimmee and beyond.

Start at the boat ramp in the tiny town of Nalcrest, which is about ten miles east of Lake Wales. To drive to the access from Route 60, turn south on Walk in Water Road, then left/east on Oakwood or Pine Tree Drive to Lakefront Road.

Paddle for about fifteen minutes along the northern edge of Lake Weohyakapka and the settlement of Fedhaven, and turn up Weohyakapka Creek. It's about a two-hour paddle to Lake Rosalie.

Vicki Bailey, trip leader for the Florida Sport Paddling Club, wrote in the club newsletter, "Alongside the creek are the ruins of Sumica, once a turpen-

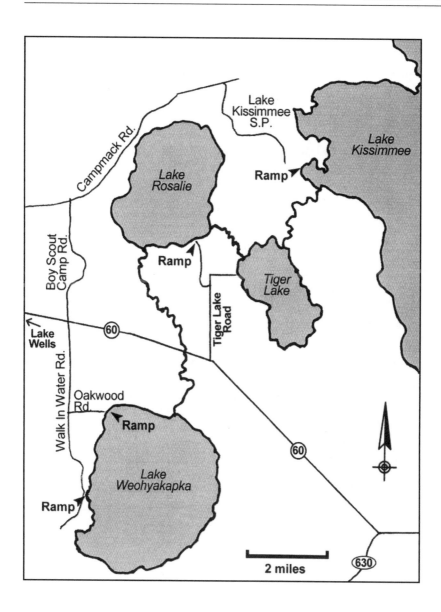

tine mill town. Polk County and SWWMD have agreed to buy 4,077 acres that surround this place and will designate it for recreation and preservation. It has 2.5 miles of frontage on Lake Walk-in-the-Water."

Once you get into Lake Rosalie, turn east and follow the south side of the lake to the boat ramp at the end of Rosalie Lake Road. (To deadhead a car at the Lake Rosalie ramp, drive .9 miles east of the Weohyakapka Creek bridge and turn north on Tiger Lake Road. Turn left onto Rosalie Lake Road. If you come to the abrupt right turn on Tiger Lake Road, you've passed Rosalie Lake Road.)

On Lake Tiger you can also launch or take out at Bud's Fish Camp. Rosalie Creek between Lakes Rosalie and Tiger Lake is short, and you can probably manage it in about twenty minutes.

Continue on by taking Tiger Creek at the northeast side of Lake Tiger. This opens up to Lake Kissimmee. Once on Kissimmee, skirt the west side of the lake until you sight a wooden observation tower. Follow the signs to the canal leading to the ramp at Lake Kissimmee State Park.

On weekends, visit the Cow Camp at the state park. This is two tiny lean-tos, a campfire, and a corral full of scrub cattle, where the rangers dress up like cow hunters in the late 1800s and pretend they don't know anything about modern life. It's only a short walk from the car, and there are benches, so it makes a nice end-of-trip visit.

This is a beautiful paddling trip, broken into enough small segments that you can stop when you're tired. If you have a big enough group, drop off a car at each landing.

Destination 65: Weedon Island

N.B.: *Trail is open only at high tide.*

Miles or average time: 4 miles or 2½ hours

Skill level: beginner

Current: weak inside mangroves, moderate in coves

Wind problems: only in open bayous

Emergency numbers: 911; Pinellas County sheriff, (727) 582-6200

Rentals: Sweetwater Kayaks, 1136 Pinellas Bayway, St. Petersburg FL 33715, phone (727) 906-0708; Weedon Island Canoe and Kayak Rental, 960 Weedon Drive, St. Petersburg FL 33702, phone (727) 570-9296

DeLorme page 91, section B-1

Official Florida canoe trail: no

Weedon Island lies on the west side of Tampa Bay. Its 1,500 acres are shaped like a slipper, with its toe pointing at St. Petersburg and its heel at McDill Air Force base in Tampa.

The area has a long history of human occupation. Some thirty mounds once dotted the high spine of the island. Most of these now lie under the road leading to the canoe ramp. Archeologists tell us that Indians from the Archaic and Pre-Archaic periods lived here from 10,000 B.C. to A.D. 1200. No one knows their own name for their tribe, but today they are referred to as the Tomokan and Minnesotan Indians, and they existed long before the Calusa, Timucuan, and Tocobaga cultures. Excavations of the mounds in 1923 revealed painted, stenciled pottery, along with 250 skeletons.

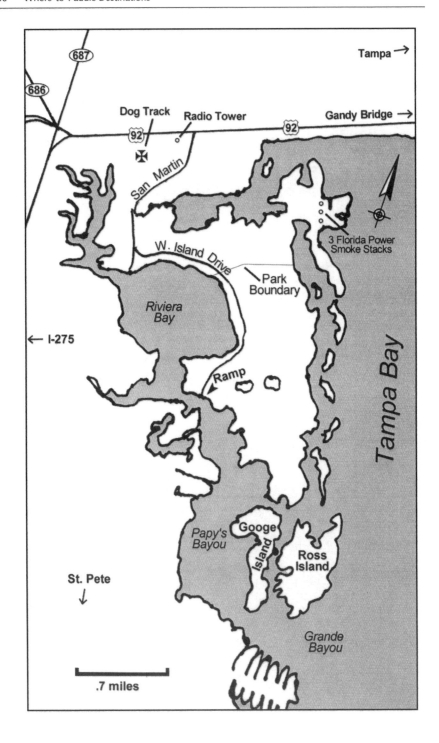

687

686

Tampa →

Dog Track   Radio Tower

Gandy Bridge →

92

92

San Martin

3 Florida Power
Smoke Stacks

W. Island Drive

Park
Boundary

Riviera
Bay

← I-275

Ramp

Tampa Bay

Papy's
Bayou

Googe
Island

Ross
Island

St. Pete
↓

Grande
Bayou

.7 miles

The island is named after Dr. Leslie Weedon, a young doctor and naturalist who acquired the island in 1898 as a weekend retreat. St. Petersburg's first airport was built here in 1930, and for years the old blimp hangar was the biggest structure in the county. Today the Weedon Island State Preserve is on the National Register of Historic Places.

Once you turn off San Martin into the preserve, the asphalt road is the only reminder that you're in the twenty-first century. The Tampa Bay Kayak Club maintains the canoe trail, using the old canals cut through the mangroves decades ago to give minnows access to mosquito larvae. These leafy tunnels become magical paths through acres of graceful mangrove trees. Tiny black crabs scuttle across the surrealistically arched red mangrove roots. Pencil-sized roots of black mangroves erupt out of the gray sands. Now and then a larger crab sitting high over your head will plop into the water beside your kayak.

Starting at the south end of the island, thirty-nine signs lead you clockwise around the mangrove jungles. Drop your kayak beside the hundred-foot pier, then move your vehicle to the parking area.

Shallow-draft kayaks are recommended, since most of the trail is only knee deep at high tide. If you have a canoe, be prepared to hop out and push now and then. It's also a good idea to have a short paddle along, since long kayak paddles are too wide for the narrowest tunnels. You might find yourself paddling with your hands, or pulling yourself along using roots and branches. On a rising tide the gentle current will waft you along with only a bit of steering needed.

After signpost 11, paddle silently. This open area is a favorite hangout for roseate spoonbills, leaping mullet, and hungry sheepshead.

If you want to paddle a bit more, stop at the rest rooms for a break, then hop back in your kayak and head right/west from the ramp, going under or around the pier. The bigger water to the west is Riviera Bay. Watch for moving dark shapes on the sandy bottom—those are southern stingrays, congregating for their annual summer spawning.

Another canoe trail at the north end of Weedon Island is maintained by the local Boy Scouts. It's on San Martin Boulevard, directly across from the back entrance to the Derby Lane Dog Track parking lot. This narrow channel, another mosquito ditch, leads east to the part of Tampa Bay just south of Gandy Boulevard and Gandy Bridge.

The entrance to Weedon Island is on the east side of the Derby Lane Dog Track, on Gandy Boulevard. For more information contact the Weedon Island Preserve headquarters at 1500 West Island Drive NE, St. Petersburg FL 33720-2756, phone (727) 579-8360.

Destination 66: Weeki Wachee River

Miles or average time: 4 hours upstream, 1½ hours downstream

Skill level: intermediate going up, beginner going down

Current: strong and steady

Wind problems: sheltered

Emergency numbers: 911; Hernando County sheriff, (352) 754-6830

Rentals: Weeki Wachee Canoe Rentals, 6131 Commercial Way (US19), Spring Hill FL 34606, phone (352) 597-0360; Weeki Wachee Marina, 7154 Shoal Line Boulevard (a block south of SR597 bridge), Spring Hill FL 34607, phone (352) 596-2852

DeLorme page 77, section D-1

Official Florida canoe trail: no

A first-magnitude spring, with a constant temperature of 74–77° and gushing more than a million gallons per minute, the Weeki Wachee runs clear and gorgeous. It begins beside US19 and ends nine miles later at the Gulf of Mexico.

For the first two-thirds of its length, the river winds through pure wilderness, then it skirts neat vacation houses and weedy canals on the north bank. Watch for red-shouldered hawks, manatees, mullet, and a covey of black vultures that sit like cartoon characters at one fork of the river.

I've solo paddled this river, starting at dawn on a weekday, with the red-winged blackbirds my only companions. I've also brought a group of thirty people in a flotilla, with a small powerboat hired to pull our string of fourteen canoes and kayaks from Rogers Park to the spring. (This is hilarious, but frowned upon by the residents. You also have to put your best paddlers at the

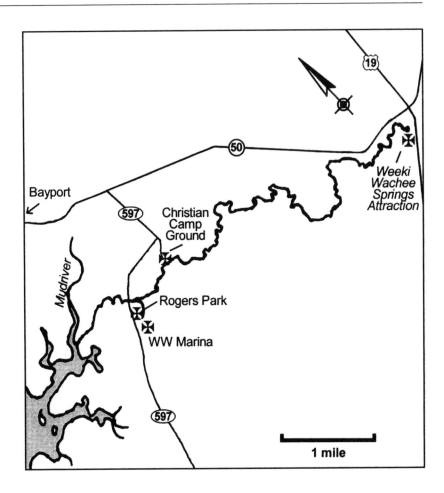

rear, because the line tends to straighten out, and they'll have to paddle hard
to get around corners.)

There are two swimming and picnicking beaches, marked by white sand
bluffs where the river makes right-angle turns.

The spring itself emerges from a house-sized pit inside Weeki Wachee attraction (phone (352) 596-2062). You can sit in air-conditioned comfort and
watch ladies wearing long spandex mermaid tails cavort underwater, gulping
air from a hose. There's a birds-of-prey show, a nice tall water slide at the tiny
bathing park, and two cruise boats that take tourists a short way downriver
to see pens of buffalo, rehabilitated pelicans, and a bit of wilderness.

At the two Weeki Wachee swimming beaches, the current swirls in a circle. Watch for nesting colonies of rare woodstorks. Lori Beese.

You can rent a canoe at the livery beside the Weeki Wachee attraction. If you'd like to do the river the old-fashioned way, launch at Rogers Park on SR597 and paddle upstream. Allow four hours to the springhead, and an hour and a half to get back again. Powerboats go all the way up and down the river, so be prepared to move over to give them room. An occasional pontoon boat bumbles up the river, scraping branches on each side, and you'll have to hug the banks to give one room to pass.

Watch for a colony of wood storks in the trees surrounding the wide pond where the tour boats from the attraction turn around. These birds appear for one or two years, then disappear. If you paddle to the sightseeing docks, you're not allowed to get out of your canoe, which is okay, since the only gators I've ever seen on the river hang out here. Be sure to wave at the tourists in the cruise boats, who think you're part of the show.

A second trip runs from Rogers Park out to Bayport on the Gulf of Mexico. This leg is very short and fast (I once churned it out in seven minutes) and essentially one-way, since the river is very fast and strong as it squeezes under the SR597 bridge. There's parking and access to the water at the Bayport end of SR50, so you can deadhead a car. If it's a windless day, you can paddle around the salt marshes, explore up Mud River, or head north to Pine Island at the end of SR595.

Two restaurants that are used to slightly damp patrons are Otters (phone (352) 597-9551) at the SR597 bridge and the Bayport Inn (phone (352) 596-1088) at the fork where SR50 and SR595 split.

Weeki Wachee Christian Camp (phone (352) 596-2326) is at the right-angle bend in SR597 north of the river. It's a popular tubing spot for youth groups (fee charged to use their beach), and it takes one hour to tube from there to Rogers Park.

Tourists only get a glimpse of this beautiful river. It's one of my favorite spots in all of Florida.

Destination 67: Wekiva River and Rock Springs Run

Miles or average time: 27 miles, in six segments ranging from 1 to 10 miles

Skill level: intermediate

Current: 2–4 mph; begins fast and slows at end

Wind problems: none in upper part; river widens drastically at its end

Emergency numbers: 911; Lake County sheriff, (352) 343-2101; Orange County sheriff, (407) 737-2400; Seminole County sheriff, (407) 330-6600; Volusia County sheriff, (904) 736-5961

Rentals: Katie's Landing, 190 Katie's Cove, Sanford FL 32771, phone (407) 628-1482; King's Landing, 5714 Baptist Camp Road, Apopka FL 32712, phone (407) 886-0859; Wekiva Marina, 1000 Miami Springs Drive, Longwood FL 32779, phone (407) 862-1500; Wekiva River Haven, 160 Wekiva Haven Trail, Sanford FL 32771, phone (407) 322-1909; Wekiva Springs State Park, 1800 Wekiva Circle, Apopka FL 32703, phone (407) 880-4110

DeLorme page 79, section B-3, to page 80, section B-1

Official Florida canoe trail: yes

Every week thousands of people motor down to central Florida, spend four days at Disney World, Epcot, Sea World, and Universal Studios, and then drive back home.

What they don't realize is that they've just passed up one of the prettiest rivers in the state of Florida, and it's only twenty miles from Mickey's back door.

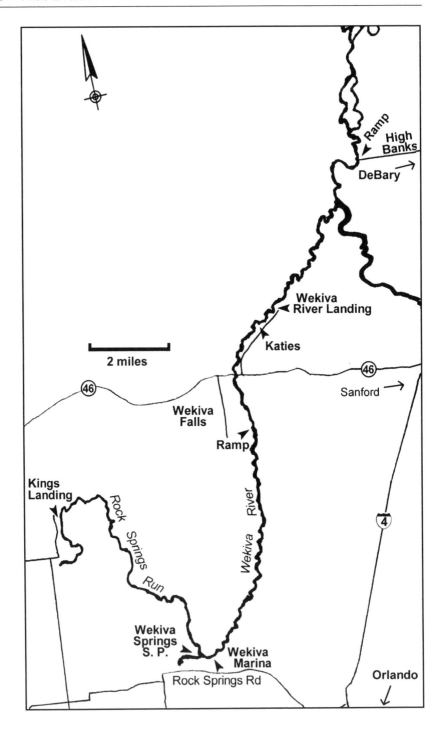

Rock Springs Run and the Wekiva River (pronounced wee-KIVE-ah) is a paddler's dream. It's easy to paddle and gorgeous. It's my favorite paddling spot in the entire state. It's busy on weekends, but twice on cool weekdays I've been the only human on the whole stretch.

Rock Springs Run is a narrow rivulet that flows over white sandy bottoms, surrounded by breathtaking gardens of floating water lettuce, giant horsetail, and native spider lilies. Huge marshes the size of football fields, thick with tall wild rice and yellow-flowered spatterdock, alternate with twenty-foot-wide tunnels shaded by water oak and cypress.

It's a wondrous, mysterious run, easy enough for beginners, yet with enough twists, turns, and ducking under mammoth fallen oaks to make it fun for advanced paddlers too.

Wildlife along the waterway is abundant, especially early in the morning and on weekdays when the river is almost deserted. Platter-sized cooter turtles stretch on sunny limbs. Flocks of speckled brown limpkins feed on the giant black apple snails slowly climbing up water lily stems to lay their clusters of pink bubble eggs.

Small alligators up to six feet are common. Larger ones are removed by the park service because of the number of people using the river. However, the St. Johns is only sixteen miles downriver, which isn't far for a gator to swim. Be prudent and swim only in the frequent areas of white sand bottoms.

Nine Indian middens show where Timucuan Indians once used the river as a seasonal camp. Said to be seven feet tall, the Timucuans had all disappeared two hundred years after the Spaniards came to Florida. The mounds, mostly composed of shells and other debris thrown away by the Indians for 7,500 years, are protected by law to preserve their record until trained archeologists can investigate them.

A large midden on Shell Island, about a half hour downstream from Wekiva Marina, is readily visible from the main channel. Also visible on the island are parts of an old river barge, a relic of the days when the Wekiva Steamship Line was practically the only way to travel through these roadless jungles.

There are two versions of the name: Wekiva and Wekiwa. Eddie Williford, the old man of the river, told me his great-uncle once asked Billy Bowlegs about the name. According to Eddie, the old Seminole Indian pulled his hands upwards and said, "WekiVA." Then he moved his hands outwards, in a flowing or pushing motion, and said, "WekiWA."

Other evidences of Florida's history are also visible during the trip. About a third of the way down Rock Springs Run, old railroad pilings mark the site of an 1870 logging operation. The crumbling stumps and hollow logs of huge cypress trees, up to sixteen feet in diameter, still dot the riverbank.

Upstream from Wekiva Marina you'll pass what's left of a large 1957 bridge. It's called the Bridge to Nowhere, since no roads were ever built to it. Days after it was built, local thieves stole the expensive aluminum railings to sell for scrap.

Until the parks system took over, anyone could build a cabin on the river. After a pitched legal battle, the squatters' cabins on the sixty-six islands were painted green, then numbered, then finally pulled down. The Wekiva Swamp north of the river is now an 8,750-acre state preserve.

Kelly Park, just south of King's Landing, is a fun place to take your kids tubing. A gushing hole the size of a card table spews a constant stream of 78° water. The spring flows down a tiny corridor into a central swimming area. Scoop up handfuls of gravel and look for fossil sharks' teeth, evidence that this part of Florida was underwater millions of years ago.

Rock Springs Run is probably best done with canoes and short river kayaks, since long ocean kayaks might have trouble making some of the sharp turns. Once you get onto the main Wekiva River, longer boats will be no problem.

> 1) King's Landing to Wekiva Marina, 9.5 miles or 2½ hours. From I-4 north of Orlando, take the SR436/Altamonte Springs exit. Drive north through Apopka. Turn right/north on SR435/Rock Springs Road. Go to the T-intersection and turn right/east on Baptist Church Road. Turn left/north at the end and follow the dirt road to King's Landing. This is the famous Rock Springs Run. When it joins the river, you can paddle upstream to the canoe concession in the state park or turn left/north and follow the current to the marina.
>
> 2) Wekiwa Springs State Park to Wekiva Marina, 1 mile or ½ hour. Every day 48 million gallons of crystal clear 72° water gush forth here to form the Wekiva River. A canoe concession lies just downstream of the wide swim basin.

3) Wekiva Marina to Wekiva Falls, 10 miles or 3½ hours. The canoe ramp at the marina is off a tiny canal downstream/north of the marina parking lot. Be wary of the well-fed raccoons that hang out across from Alexander's Restaurant. They are cute, but will bite.

You can also paddle four miles of the Little Wekiva River before it enters the regular Wekiva River. Ask at Katie's Landing about access.

4) Wekiva Falls to Katie's Landing, 1 mile or ½ hour. For decades the locals came to swim around the gushing pipe in the center of this deep basin. Today it's a retirement community, with no swimming.

5) Katie's Landing to Wekiva River Haven, 1 mile or ½ hour. To drive to Katie's Landing from Orlando, take I-4 east toward Sanford. Exit at SR46 and turn left/west. Go five miles to Wekiva Park Drive. Turn right and go one mile to the entrance to Katie's Landing. If you start at King's Landing, you'll paddle nine and a half miles on Rock Springs Run, then nine and a half miles on the Wekiva River, for a total of nineteen miles, or six to eight hours.

6) Wekiva River Haven to High Banks Landing, 5 miles or 1½ hours. The recommended route is to hug the west side of the river, then cross the St. Johns River between markers 91 and 92.

7) High Banks Road Landing. From the town of DeBary, head west on High Banks Road. The access is on the right/north side of the dead end.

You can also continue to Blue Springs and Hontoon Island (see destination 53). However, this stretch is wide, windy, and crowded with motorboats on the weekends. I don't think it's nearly as scenic as the upper part of the Wekiva River, and certainly not as pretty as Rock Springs Run.

I try to paddle Rock Springs Run a couple of times a year. If you can paddle only one waterway in Florida, make it this one.

Destination 68: Winter Haven Chain of Lakes

Miles or average time: no limit, explore at your own pace

Skill level: beginner

Current: weak

Wind problems: yes—open lakes

Emergency numbers: 911; Polk County sheriff, (863) 533-0344

DeLorme page 85, section D-2

Official Florida canoe trail: no

Winter Haven has two chains of lakes.

The north one has nine lakes, five boat ramps, one restaurant, and two boat lifts to navigate the different water levels.

The south chain has sixteen lakes, all connected by fifteen canals that range from 102 feet long to half a mile. It also has eight public boat ramps. This chain makes an interesting day's paddle, with the added feature that you can stop and have lunch at five different restaurants. The littlest body of water is Lake May at only 44 acres. The biggest is Lake Eloise, home of Cypress Gardens, at 1,160 acres.

Don't expect wilderness. Winter Haven seems to be 100 percent built out. The area is mixed economically. There are some beautifully kept homes under neatly trimmed oak trees set back from the water behind beautifully kept lawns. Then there are ramshackle shacks beside sprawling mobile home parks and orange groves. The Christmas boat parade is fun, and some very ingenious ways of lighting up boats are invariably on display.

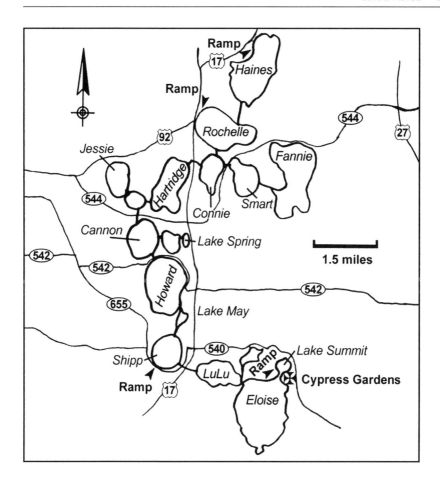

Do expect to encounter bass boats, all of which will display a bass fisherman's only two speeds—dead stop and full speed ahead. Polk County bills itself as the Largemouth Bass Capital of the World. Waterskiing is popular too. I've found the majority of boaters hereabouts to be considerate of their wake, but to be safe, stay next to the shore.

You can start at any of the ramps and paddle in any direction. I've started at Lake Summit, which is just north of Cypress Gardens, and simply taken every right turn.

There is a stone barrier or breakfront at Cypress Gardens, and you are not allowed to enter the little canal that winds through their always-blooming garden. But you can stay on the west side of the floating barrier and watch the water-ski shows. At dusk, they turn on more than a million Christmas tree lights wound through every bush and tree. There is also a laser light show projected on a spray of water. The announcer tells the crowd that the laser show is invisible from the back, but I saw it bright and clear.

The Cypress Gardens boat tour guides also tell tourists that there are more than 250 alligators on Lake Eloise, and that the biggest one ever taken out was seventeen feet long. This big fellow must have been around back in the 1930s when Jim Pope started Cypress Gardens. I've seen only five alligators in one day's hard looking—the biggest a measly seven feet—but maybe you'll luck out and find the other 245.

From the water, you'll pass dozens of access areas and ramps, but it's sometimes hard to tell which are private and which can be used by the general public. Here are the access spots I know about:

Lake Haines. The ramp on Lake Haines is at the end of Mosley Road.

Lake Rochelle. Access to Lake Rochelle is on the northwest corner, off US92/ SR600, which is named Lakeshore Highway.

Lake Shipp. To launch on Lake Shipp, head for the southwest corner, and Recker Highway. There's also a canoe-in, canoe-out restaurant on Lake Shipp called Harbor Side Restaurant.

Lake Lulu. A new dock will give boaters access to Chain o' Lakes Stadium, which is the spring training home of the Cleveland Indians.

This is a great set of lakes to explore on a day when you feel like "lily-dipping" or just paddling around.

Destination 69: Winter Park
Chain of Lakes

Miles or average time: no limit, paddle at your own pace

Skill level: beginner

Current: almost imperceptible

Wind problems: yes, on some open shores

Emergency numbers: 911; Orange County sheriff, (407) 737-2400

Rentals: Scenic Boat Tour, 312 East Morse Boulevard, Winter Park FL
32789, phone (407) 644-4056

DeLorme page 80, section D-2

Official Florida canoe trail: no

In the late 1800s, a lumber company harvesting the forests around north Orlando had a problem getting their cut logs to the railroad depot near Lake Virginia. The easiest way was by water, so two sluggish creeks between Lakes Osceola, Maitland, and Virginia were dug out just enough that low, narrow barges could get through.

These canals are just the right size for the pontoon boats run by the Scenic Boat Tour company, smaller powerboats, and your canoe or kayak. The end result is a fine paddling route. You can travel some twelve miles by water as you look over the City of Gracious Living.

While the tour boats can access only the three big lakes, you can paddle into all six: Virginia, Mizell, Osceola, Maitland, Nina, and Minnehaha.

The canals pass under low bridges that resemble drain pipes. Lush oaks, magnolias, bamboo, and banana trees overhang the water. Homeowners

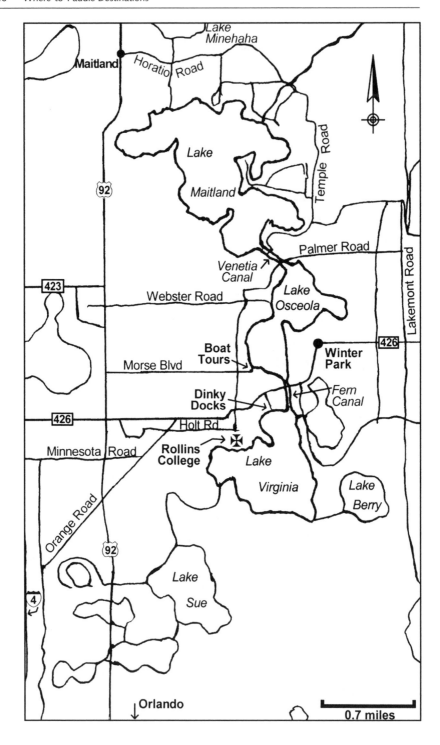

Old logging canals connect the lakes in Winter Park. Sandy Huff.

around the canals have dug little boat slips into their lawns for their own runabouts. Some of the boathouses have water doors with grilles at the bottom to keep out alligators. I suspect the few gators who accidentally stumble across these lakes would be interested in the boathouses only as a place to hide from all the water-skiers.

The Scenic Boat Tour has been in operation for fifty years. The captain points out Rollins College on Lake Virginia, the house of artist Albin Polasek on Lake Osceola, the Kraft Azalea Gardens on Lake Maitland, and the other fancy homes and gracious lawns that sweep back from the water. Building styles range from Italian Renaissance to Modern Cubic.

If you have your own boat, launch at the public ramp at Dinky Dock Boating Park, on Ollie Street across from the library on the northwest edge of Lake Virginia. Another public ramp is at Fort Maitland Park on US17/92, between Lake Avenue and Maitland Avenue in Maitland.

Fellow paddler Tim Egan says, "There is also a public ramp on Lake Baldwin, in Winter Park, near the old Naval Training Center. The ramp is located at Fleet Peeples Park on Lakemont Avenue, south of Glenridge Way."

The bigger lakes have almost constant water-skiers, but you can avoid them by staying inside the floating white buoys around the perimeter of each lake. There's a jump ramp just offshore from Rollins College Library, where we sat for half an hour and watched four water-skiers attempt to jump. Their takeoffs were terrific, but those wipeouts looked painful. We cheered when one teenager finally managed to land upright.

While you're in Winter Park, schedule an hour and $4 to visit the new building of the Morse Museum, built specifically to showcase glassware made by Louis Comfort Tiffany. They re-created a little chapel he designed for a World's Fair, which includes the ugliest hanging lamp ever made.

If you enjoy sculpture, make a stop at the free house and lawns of artist Albin Polasek, just south and around the bend from the Scenic Boat Tour dock.

Destination 70: Withlacoochee River (South)

Miles or average time: 90 miles, in twelve official sections for 84 miles

Skill level: beginner to intermediate

Current: slow

Wind problems: yes, in open, wide parts and lakes

Emergency numbers: 911; Citrus County sheriff, (352) 726-1121; Hernando County sheriff, (352) 754-6830; Marion County sheriff, (352) 732-8181; Pasco County sheriff, (352) 521-5100; Sumter County sheriff, (352) 793-0222

Rentals: Nobleton Canoe Rental, PO Box 265, Nobleton FL 34661, phone (352) 796-4343 or 1-800-783-5284; Shawnee Trail Campground, 2000 S. Bishop Point, Inverness FL 34450, phone (352) 344-3372 or 1-800-834-7595; Withlacoochee RV Park and Canoe Rental, PO Box 114 or 39847 SR575, Lacoochee FL 33537-0114, phone (352) 583-4778

DeLorme page 84, section A-1

Official Florida canoe trail: yes

My Cadette and Senior Girl Scouts were all excited about gathering their own food. They'd read *Stalking the Wild Asparagus* by Euell Gibbons and were enthusiastic outdoor cooks. During a weekend camping trip at the Girl Scout camp beside Silver Lake, they discovered the little nickel-sized clams living in the white sandy bottom of the Withlacoochee. Clam soup for supper, they declared.

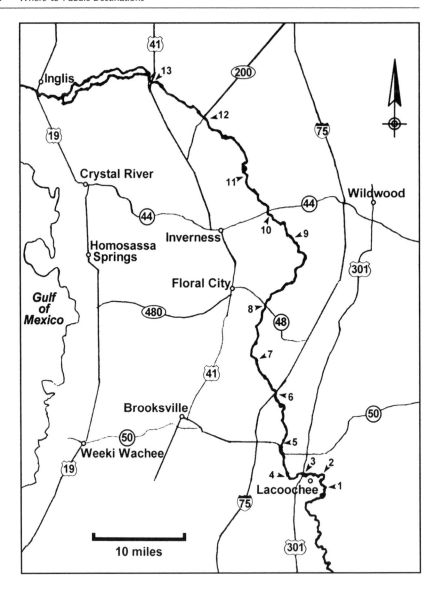

The problem was, these little twelve-to-sixteen-year-olds couldn't stay underwater in the waist-deep water. So they devised a new method. One would dive down and run her fingers through the sand, while another kid stood on her back to keep her underwater. I hastily stopped that unsafe practice, but they managed to gather more than a pint of the tiny clams.

At supper, they boiled the bivalves until the bits of meat floated free. With a bit of salt and butter it was delicious—if you ignored the layer of sand in the bottom of the pot.

Even if you're not into making clam soup, the Withlacoochee is a nice place to paddle. Remember, there are two Withlacoochee Rivers. This one is the south one. It has pretty scenery, great bass fishing, and good paddling.

The water is stained a winy red by tannic acid from tree roots. In the rainy season the river can get very high, and you'll see debris stuck in the treetops, deposited by floodwaters.

The "With" flows north, rising out of the Green Swamp and exiting a hundred miles later into the Gulf of Mexico about twenty miles west of Dunnellon. The official canoe trail stretches ninety miles, from Pasco County in the south to the Citrus/Marion County line in Dunnellon at the US41 bridge.

During its hundred miles, the river drains 2,090 square miles of land. The Indian name means "small big water." It was designated the Outstanding Florida Water in 1989.

The Florida Wildlife Commission recently opened up a new two-mile section at the head of the canoe trail. To get there from Lacoochee, head south on US301 through Trilacoochee. Turn left/east on Cummer Road, pass the railroad tracks, turn right on Main Line Road, and follow this to the river.

The FWC has put up a few signs, and there is a campsite at Low Bluff. About half a mile from the Coulter Hammock landing, the river opens up to Sawgrass Lake, which is a good place to watch for night herons and the elusive Florida clapper rail.

Beyond the end of the trail at Dunnellon, the Withlacoochee becomes Lake Rousseau, a long skinny lake formed by Inglis Dam. The lake was created to supply water to Inglis Locks, which were part of the ill-conceived Cross Florida Barge Canal. From the locks, the canal shoots straight as an arrow to the Gulf.

1) Coulter Hammock Recreation Area to CR575, 2 miles. Starting at US301, west of Lacoochee, go east on SR575 to Durden Road. Turn right/south. At the next stop sign, turn left onto Coit Road, which becomes Lacoochee Park Road. The recreation area is 2.5 miles down this road.

2) CR575 bridge to US301, 2 miles. This bridge is 1.2 miles northeast of Lacoochee.

3) US301 bridge to US98, 2 miles. From Trilacoochee, go 1.2 miles north to the river.

4) US98 bridge to SR50, 6 miles. From the town of Trilby, drive .7 miles north to the river. Peterson Park is closed, but there is a campground on the east side of the bridge that has access to the river.

5) SR50 to Silver Lake Recreation Area, 16 miles. From the SR50 bridge, twelve miles east of Brooksville, you paddle through the Croom Wildlife Management Area, part of the larger Withlacoochee State Forest. This section of the river starts off shallow, and deepens as you paddle. Silver Lake is seven miles downstream. Silver Lake Campground is a good place to stop for lunch, or to use as another access or takeout spot.

Cross under I-75, and watch for Hog Island Recreation Area on your right. A few houses appear on the banks. Evidently someone is feeding the great blue herons, because a flock hangs out in the backyard of one of the houses.

6) Silver Lake Recreation Area to SR476, 7 miles. Starting in Brooksville, drive east on SR50 one mile, then turn left/north on Rital-Croom Road, which is the first traffic light. Follow this east to the Silver Lake Recreation Area.

7) SR476 bridge to SR48, 9 miles. The SR476 bridge is a quarter mile east of Nobleton.

8) SR48 bridge to Carlson Landing, 11 miles. From Bushnell, head west on SR48. Pass I-75 and go eight miles to the river.

9) Carlson Landing to SR44, 4 miles. From the intersection of SR44 and CR470, drive south on CR470 for about two miles. Turn right/west for half a mile. Turn right/west at Gator Lodge, and go to ramp.

10) SR44 bridge to SR581, 6 miles. The access is in the town of Rutland, six and a half miles east of Inverness.

11) SR581 to SR200, 10 miles. From US41 in downtown Inverness, head north on SR581, which is Ella Avenue. Follow this seven miles to the boat ramp and Turner Fish Camp.

12) SR200 to US41, 15 miles. From the town of Hernando, go north on US200 for six and a half miles. Turn left/west beside a small convenience store. The county park will be on your right.

13) US41 bridge. Watch for the little wayside park in Dunnellon. There are a couple of old quarry sites along this section, but they might be hard

to spot in late summer when the morning glory, wild grape, and kudzu vines make living shields.

Just before you reach the takeout, the clear waters of the Rainbow River will come in from river right. The old photo of Dunns Bluff (see destination 28) was taken somewhere along this stretch. See if you can figure out where it is.

If you're into fishing, bring along your tackle and freshwater fishing license. Last year two twelve-pound bass were pulled out of the Withlacoochee. It's loaded with panfish too.

For bait, just run your toes through the white sand in the shallows. Those little clams make fine bait, and if you don't have any luck with fishing, you can always make soup.

Also try www8.myflorida.com/communities/learn/trails/canoe.

Area 4. The Lake Okeechobee Area

Destination 71: Braden River

Miles or average time: 5 hours round-trip

Skill level: beginner

Current: slow

Wind problems: only on high-wind days

Emergency numbers: 911; Manatee County sheriff, (941) 747-3011

Rentals: Florida Osprey Boat Tours, Bradenton FL 34208, phone (941) 745-9649; Ray's Canoe Hideaway, 1247 Hagle Park Road NE, Bradenton FL 34202, phone (941) 747-3909

DeLorme page 97, section A-2

Official Florida canoe trail: no

This is a lazy, leisurely paddle, and a favorite of the Florida Sport Paddling Club. You can make it a round-trip from Jiggs Landing (6106 Braden River Road, Bradenton FL 34203, phone (941) 756-6745) or end at Linger Lodge Fish Camp (7205 Linger Lodge Road, Bradenton FL 34202, phone (941) 755-2757).

From Jiggs, go left to head upriver, and stay with the left bank of the "reservoir" to follow the main river channel. The Braden River is wide between 63rd Street and Linger Lodge Road, but narrows under I-75. If it's a windy day, opt for a one-way trip in the direction that puts the wind at your back.

This sleepy little river has some rambunctious history. Civil War gunrunners were reputed to hide here, ducking into the numerous nooks and crannies to avoid Federal warships.

Legend says that Gaspar the Pirate and his cronies buried some of their loot here before heading back to Useppa Island down in Charlotte Harbor.

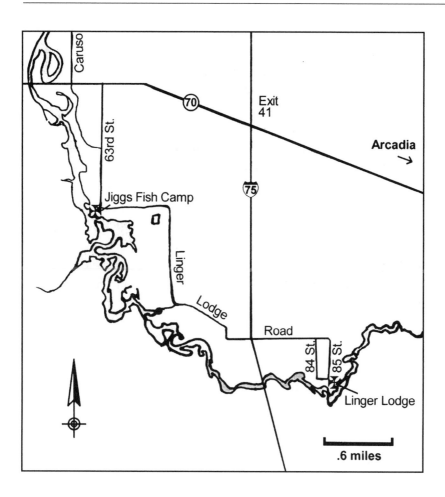

Gasparilla Day is celebrated in Tampa every February, when a couple of dozen Mystic Krewes—normally staid businessmen—dress up themselves and their pirate ships and invade the city. They throw strings of beads and chocolates wrapped as gold doubloons, and have a fine time.

It's about a two-hour paddle from Jiggs Landing to Linger Lodge Fish Camp, where you can have lunch at their rustic restaurant. The ramp has a sign that says it is closed to the public. "That's 'cuz nobody was paying the one-dollar ramp fee," said one resident of the RV park, "but call ahead and they'll be glad to make arrangements." From there you can either head back to Jiggs Landing or paddle upriver another two miles through a big housing area.

One group of paddlers reported seeing a wild sow with piglets. I never saw any hogs, but have passed through big flocks of diving or puddle ducks. The river has some really pretty stretches, and then some nice views of folks' backyards.

Destination 72: Estero River

Miles or average time: 7 miles

Skill level: beginner

Current: slow, tidal at Estero Bay

Wind problems: only at mouth of river and open bay

Emergency numbers: 911; Lee County sheriff, (941) 332-3456

Rentals: Estero Bay Boat Tours, 5231 Mamie Street SW, Bonita Springs FL 34134, phone (941) 992-2200; Estero River Tackle and Canoe Outfitters, 20991 South Tamiami Trail, Estero FL 33928, phone (941) 992-4050; Koreshan State Historic Site, 3850 Corkscrew Road, Estero FL 33928, phone (941) 992-9311

DeLorme page 111, section A-1

Official Florida canoe trail: yes

Back in 1869, a beautiful female angel appeared to Dr. Cyrus Teed and told him that the earth was actually hollow, we all lived on the inside, he would live forever, and he was to found a new religion called the Koreshan Unity.

Dr. Teed got together a congregation and moved it from Chicago to a jungle in southwest Florida. They brought a grand piano, Victorian loveseats, and tons of gear up the tiny Estero River.

On a nearby beach Dr. Teed set up a huge apparatus that conclusively proved that the earth is indeed concave, and we are living on the inside of our globe, not the outside. You can see a model of his gadget in the now air-conditioned Art Hall.

The Koreshans worked hard, with a bakery, a machine shop, concerts, and the unique idea that women were equal to men. Their fleet of thirteen boats

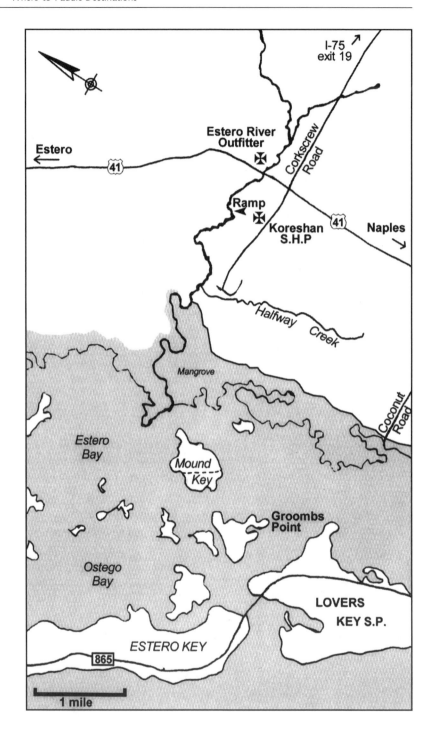

A religious sect that homesteaded beside the Estero River believed that the earth was hollow and we live inside. This gadget demonstrates the idea. Sandy Huff.

kept busy. Their wooden buildings were state of the art, with imported lumber and beautiful finishes. Their drama and music festivals brought visitors from miles around.

Today the two-hundred-member congregation is no more, but the old Koreshan State Historic Site is interesting to visit, and the beautiful Estero River is a joy to paddle. It's just off exit 19 on I-75.

The Estero (pronounced ess-TARE-oh) is a tidal river, and extends only a short distance east of US41. Heading upstream from the historical park makes an interesting hour-long round-trip before the river narrows down. The overhanging oaks are festooned with wild orchids and resurrection ferns. One May we picked ripe Surinam cherries from old bushes that overhang the water.

The longer trip is downstream. You'll pass housing developments for the first half an hour. Halfway Creek comes in from the south, and then you're in a thick mangrove forest that eventually opens into Estero Bay.

Once you emerge from the river's mouth, if there is no wind, head southwest to the huge island just ahead. This is Mound Key. Back in the 1500s it was the town of Calos, the capital of the entire Calusa Indian nation. The king, chief, or cacique was evidently also named Calos, and from this we get Carlos Bay, and St. Carlos. King Calos ruled a complex set of tributary tribes that sent tribute goodies from as far away as Miami.

From the north landing cove a dirt path runs southeast across the island to the south landing. Take mosquito repellent, in case you didn't already drown yourself in it during the mangrove paddle.

Archeologists have found three distinct mounds, a central canal, and many water courts. These water courts are a mystery. Opinions as to their purpose range from pretty landscaping, to sacred spots, to parking lots for dugout canoes. My favorite theory is that they were fish traps, where schools of mullet, redfish, and sea trout could be herded in and then kept alive to be used as needed. I think of them as Calusa convenience stores.

Back in A.D. 100, when humans first arrived, the island was flat, with no mounds. Of course, sea level was about three feet lower back then, so the island was much larger, and the bay was a bit shallower. In the next two thousand years, gatherers brought back so many oysters, clams, fish, deer, alligators, and other foods that the discarded shells and bones made huge mounds. The Indians were very well organized. When the Spaniards arrived in 1513, more than a thousand people lived in the man-made landings, water courts, ceremonial and residential mounds, and houses built on palm-trunk platforms.

The Calusas were completely uninterested in being subjugated by the short, narrow-minded, and smelly Spaniards, and practiced their own form of ethnic cleansing. Here, from the Calusa Coast Outfitters brochure, is an interesting paragraph that was written by the Spanish explorer Gonzalo Solís de Meras in 1567:

"The [ship] Adelantado entered the harbor and anchored near shore, for they could jump from the brigantine to land without wetting their shoes. More than 200 Spaniards from ships of the Indies that had been lost off the country of that Cacique [King Calos] for the past 20 years, had all been brought to him by his subjects. He and his father killed them all, sacrificing them to the Devil during their feasts and dances."

If you're interested in more archeology, you can take a guided tour with Calusa Coast Outfitters, Fish Tale Marina, 7225 Estero Boulevard, Fort Myers Beach FL 33931, phone (941) 418-5941.

The official end of the state canoe trail is across Estero Bay at Lover's Key Recreation Area, on SR865. Leave your car at the north parking lot before the cut to Estero Island. It's a long trip to deadhead a car, but useful if the wind or tides are unfavorable.

If it is windy, you have two options. Paddle back upstream on the Estero River to your put-in, since the current is no problem on the river. Or stick close to the eastern shore, and get out at the Coconut Road ramp on the mainland, about a seven-minute drive south of the put-in. To drive there from Koreshan Historic Site, head south on US41 and turn right/west on Coconut Road. There is access at the very end of Coconut, and you can leave a car there. Don't try to paddle across the bay during high winds.

Necessary equipment on this trip is insect repellent, water, and a compass.

Destination 73: Hickey Creek

Miles or average time: 4 miles round-trip

Skill level: intermediate

Current: slight in the creek, some in Caloosahatchee River when locks are open

Wind problems: only in the Caloosahatchee River

Emergency numbers: 911; Lee County sheriff, (941) 332-3456

DeLorme page 105, section C-2

Official Florida canoe trail: yes

This tiny canoe trail is only two miles up and two miles back. But it's a pretty stretch of twists and turns, and the clear, tea-colored water is full of bream, crappie, stumpknockers, and other panfish. I spotted three manatees blandly cruising down the center of the river. One of them had huge prop scars on her back, which evidently still hadn't taught her to stay out of the boating channels.

I had assumed that the town of Alva was named in honor of Thomas Alva Edison, whose house and lab is downstream in Fort Myers. But according to Nancy Musser at the Lee County Visitor and Convention Bureau, "It is named for a small white flower that once grew there. It was named by Captain Peter Nelson, the founder of the town, who is buried on Caya Costa in the small pioneer cemetery."

Alva looks like an old pioneer town, with tiny old wooden houses near the ramp area. The biggest building I saw in town was the elementary school.

To get to the Alva ramp, which is on the north side of the Caloosahatchee, take I-75 to exit 25 and go east on SR80 about eleven miles, then north on

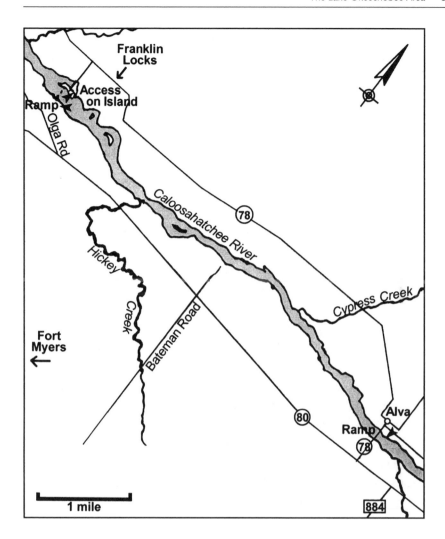

SR78 into Alva. As soon as you cross the SR78 bridge, turn right/east onto Pearl Street, go a couple of blocks, and you'll see the park and ramp on your right. Paddle downstream two miles to Hickey Creek.

If you'd rather paddle only downstream, launch at Alva and deadhead a car at the Franklin Locks. If you prefer paddling upstream, you can launch at the little ramp just south of the SR78 bridge over Telegraph Creek, paddle about a mile to the Caloosahatchee, then head upstream.

Another access point is the campground at the W. P. Franklin Locks, on the north side of the river. The turnoff is about a mile east of Telegraph Creek on SR78, at the south end of Franklin Lock Road. The volunteer lady running the registration desk said that if you pulled up into an empty campsite or a grassy area and slid your boat into the water, she wouldn't even charge a launch fee. And you have your choice of launching upstream or downstream from the locks.

A very steep ramp lies on the southwest side of the Caloosahatchee locks. From SR80, turn west/north onto Old Olga, and watch for Sessler Road heading north.

Guides at the Edison and Ford homes in Fort Myers (2350 McGregor Boulevard, Fort Myers FL 33901, phone (941) 334-3614) relate that Thomas Edison had two methods of keeping northern visitors out of his hair. He had the dining room built in the guest house, so after dinner he could go to bed without waiting for his guests to leave. And to keep them busy during the day, he sent them fishing up the Caloosahatchee.

Another local notable, Nelson Burroughs, was a military man who obviously left General Custer's unit *before* the battle of Little Big Horn. He made his fortune shipping live cattle from Fort Myers to Cuba. The main character in Patrick Smith's best-selling novel *A Land Remembered* may have been modeled after Burroughs. His restored mansion is at 2505 First Street, and the garden backs up to the Caloosahatchee.

"Hatchee" means river in Indian, so the name of the river is really River of the Calusas. People have lived and traveled here for thousands of years. You can be part of that parade.

Destination 74: Lake Okeechobee

Miles or average time: no limit, explore at your own pace

Skill level: beginner in low wind, intermediate in choppy water

Current: slight in rim canal when locks are operating, plus wind-generated

Wind problems: yes—open grassy areas

Emergency numbers: 911; Glades County sheriff, (863) 946-0100; Hendry County sheriff, (863) 983-1440; Palm Beach County sheriff, (561) 688-3000

DeLorme page 107, section B-1

Official Florida canoe trail: no

Okeechobee is a Seminole Creek Indian word that means "big water." The Big O is the second largest freshwater lake entirely inside the continental U.S., covering 730 square miles, or 467,200 acres.

This lake is famous for black bass, crappie, and catfish, so there are plenty of fishing boats. The western marshes of Lake O also produce many alligators during the September public waters hunt, so unless you go in right after the hunt when they have been scared away, you'll see lots of gators.

Instead of one spot to explore, I'm listing three different launch sites. All of them are on the south side of the lake.

The first trip starts at the west end, at Liberty Point campground (DeLorme page 107, section B-2). It's about two miles east of the Moore Haven lock and dam, off US27 on CR720. Once you launch, head for the back canal that runs along the shore. From there you can circle Observation Island and take the many cuts through the grassy areas that run north up to

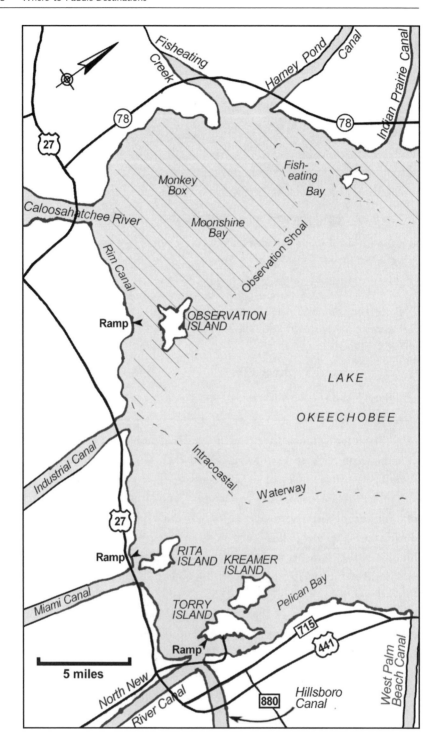

Moonshine Bay. In the spring and fall the flats are dotted white, pink, and gray with hundreds of wading birds.

The second place to launch is the public ramp at John Stretch Park, just to the west of the Miami Canal locks in the town of Lake Harbor (DeLorme page 107, section C-3). Look for the turnoff heading north from US27/SR80/SR25. The launch ramp is in a protected lane bordered by Rita Island on the north. This island is thumb-shaped, with a long "neck" that extends to the east. Paddling completely around the island takes a good four to six hours, and there are inside canals to explore.

The third paddling area is Torry Island (DeLorme page 108, section C-1). You can launch at Slim's Fish Camp or B. G. Campground. To get to the island from Belle Glade, follow CR880 northwest. Turn at the Community College, go over the rim canal bridge, and follow the signs. There's also an island to the west, right in between Torry and Rita Islands, that's mostly grass.

Now a bit of history. Some environmentalists moan that the Everglades and Lake O are the biggest man-made environmental disasters ever accomplished. Before Europeans arrived, the entire lower third of the state was the Everglades. The lake itself was a giant saucer, with no channels on the south-southwest side, so water oozed off in a wide, shallow sheet that took a year to reach Florida Bay. The 110-mile-wide Everglades supported millions of birds, huge numbers of animals, and a wide diversity of plants, including saw grass.

When Ponce de León arrived on the Florida east coast in 1513, the Tequesta Indians called it the Lake of Mayaime, and dugout canoes regularly traveled to what is now Miami.

The 1850 federal Swamp and Overflowed Lands Act gave the Everglades to the infant State of Florida, provided the state could drain it and make it "useful." From 1881 to 1884, "Ditch King" Hamilton Diston dug out channels to the Caloosahatchee River and other places. By the 1930s there were more than four hundred miles of canals, all ruler-straight, that diverted water in all directions.

The lake had a tiny dike around it. In 1926 a hurricane roared up past Miami and over the lake, killing 800 local farmers. In 1928 another hurricane pushed a wall of water over the southern shore of the lake. Some 2,400 people in South Bay and Clewiston died.

Now the 34-foot-high, 110-mile Herbert Hoover dike surrounds the lake. You can hike and bike along the top of the dike, and the views are good, if monotonous. Sugarcane fields stretch to the horizon. Clewiston has a Sugar Festival every April.

For an interesting look at the lives of the migrant laborers who toil here, read *Angel City* by Patrick Smith. And of course you've already read *Everglades, River of Grass* by Marjorie Stoneman Douglas. Her book started an entire ecological movement.

Every drop of runoff water is controlled by the U.S. Army Corps of Engineers, and it's a huge, multitentacled political issue. The lake averages 9 feet deep, with a maximum of 17 feet. The average diked depth of 14.5 feet is soon to be reduced to 13 feet, for some complex reason that involves water flow across the Glades. There are 1,100 square miles of leveed Everglades Agricultural Area, plus three Water Conservation Areas.

On some days, Lake Okeechobee seems deserted, with few animals and birds. But keep watching. Within an hour you'll probably spot a dozen species of wildlife, including river otters that bunch up along the shore.

Also watch for osprey—they're experts at diving in the shallow flats and bringing up huge bass. Anhinga and cormorants swim with just their long necks and tiny heads out of water.

Caracaras live here too. These giraffes of the hawk family have long orange legs, big creamy bills, orange faces, white cheeks, and a black crown. They mingle with vultures, so if you see a funny-looking bird among a crowd of low-slung black buzzards, it's a caracara.

The lake has a sizable population of manatees, but they're hard to see against the dark water, and impossible to spot if there's any chop at all. Many of them "lock through" the locks in the winter, searching for warm water.

Everything about this lake is big. Some forty species of fish live here. Fishermen periodically pull in huge prehistoric-looking "alligator gar."

Try a traditional catfish dinner at a local restaurant. Walt Reynolds, Clewiston resident, fishing expert, and professional fishing guide, recommends Lightsey's Seafood at Okee-Tantie Recreation Area, five miles west of Okeechobee City on Highway 78, on the north side of the lake. (You can contact Walt at 1650 Allen Road, Clewiston FL 33440, phone (941) 983-8692, e-mail walt@waltreynolds.com, or check out his website at www.waltrey-nolds.com.)

You can get a full-color map of the lake from South Florida Operations Office, 525 Ridgelawn Road, Clewiston FL 33440-5399, phone (941) 983-8101. The Clewiston Museum sells *The History of Lake Okeechobee,* which covers the famous flood that took out South Bay. Bill and Carol Gregware have written a very comprehensive *Guide to Lake Okeechobee.*

I like Lake Okeechobee. Once you get over the dike that circles the lake, there really is something to see and do.

Destination 75: Little Sarasota Bay

Miles or average time: no limit, explore at your own pace

Skill level: beginner for inshore paddling, more advanced for open waters

Current: tidal, plus Intracoastal channel crossings

Wind problems: mostly sheltered in the protected bays, can be extreme in the open Gulf

Emergency numbers: 911; Sarasota County sheriff, (941) 951-5800

Rentals: By the Bay Outfitters, 520 Blackburn Point Road, Osprey FL 34229, phone (941) 966-3937, website www.kayakflorida.com; Kayak Treks, 3667 Bahia Vista Street, Sarasota FL 34232, phone (941) 365-3892 or 1-800-656-3891, fax (941) 366-3891, website www.kayaktreks.com/info.html; Oscar Scherer State Recreation Area, 1843 South Tamiami Trail, Osprey FL 34229, phone (941) 483-5956

DeLorme page 97, section C-2

Official Florida canoe trail: no

It's hard to tell one bottle-nosed dolphin from another, so I was excited when the gray fin appeared just ten yards from my canoe. It had to be the famous friendly dolphin that had been amusing boaters around Little Sarasota Bay for the last decade. I was in the Intracoastal Waterway channel, just south of the Blackburn Point Road/Route 789 bridge that connects the upper end of Casey Key to the mainland.

However, when another fin showed up, and then another, I realized I was in the midst of a dolphin family. So maybe it wasn't the panhandling dolphin of local fame, but I was perfectly happy to share smiles with the three around

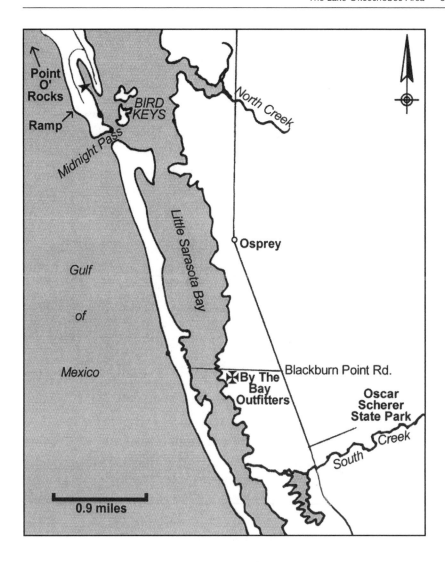

me. The magnificent frigate birds circling high overhead were icing on the cake.

Millionaire homes are sprouting left and right on Siesta and Casey Keys. Tiny cement-block houses are rapidly being replaced with multistoried mansions. The powdered-sugar sands of the beaches, great fishing, and gorgeous scenery are the attractions.

But for the paddler the long bay inside Siesta and Casey Keys is perfect.

There are still long stretches of mangroves dotted with egrets, herons, and cormorants. Your canoe or kayak gives you access to tiny nooks and crannies that seem as pristine as when the first Amerindians paddled their dugout canoes up the waterway.

Some two hundred species of birds live around Little Sarasota Bay and Oscar Scherer State Recreation Area. You can see oyster catchers with their bright red beaks, roseate spoonbills, and lots of pelicans, some treated and released by the Pelican Man on Longboat Key. The black birds shaped like the letter *M* circling far overhead are deservedly named magnificent frigate birds. They probably nest in the Dry Tortugas off Key West. The males have bright red throat pouches.

Heron Lagoon, on the south side of Bird Island, was once the main pass between Siesta Key and Casey Key, before a hurricane (which arrived at guess which hour) opened up Midnight Pass. Another storm closed this now-named Hurricane Pass (at guess which hour), giving us another example of the mighty power of Ma Nature.

The little inlet where the pass was is a lovely swimming hole. Bring your bathing suit for a dip here—the sands are soft and brilliant white, and the water a dozen shades of blue. Cars can't get too close to the point, so your only company will be other boaters.

If it's a perfectly calm day, go out Midnight Pass into the Gulf of Mexico, and head north to Turtle Beach. Further north is Point o' Rocks, a strange jumble of rocks, underwater caves, and coral formations. It's a favorite spot for snorkelers and divers, so bring along a mask and snorkel, tie your painter or towrope to your wrist, and hop overboard. You can also beach your boat on the sand and swim out to explore the rocks, but watch for current and make sure you can always get back to shore.

Parts of Bird Island, site of the Jim Neville Wildlife Preserve, are closed to motor craft. There's a boat ramp on the bay side of Route 789 on south Siesta Key, just about even with the island.

Little Sarasota Bay also has freshwater creeks to explore. Catfish Creek enters the north section of the bay, just east of Bird Island. Paddle into Catfish Creek, then quickly turn south into North Creek.

John Allaman, who runs By the Bay Outfitters, says, "A waterfall is reported in the lower reaches of this tributary which has not been accessible since the old Tamiami Trail/US41 bridge washed out in '39. Explore this for yourself, but watch out for the gators that inhabit the creeks."

John also runs Monday tours up to historic Spanish Point to see the Palmer House and Gardens. An old Indian mound and remains of the first white settlers' buildings are still visible.

In the south part of Little Sarasota Bay you can paddle up South Creek to Oscar Scherer State Recreation Area and swim in the freshwater lake. Watch your lunch—the scrub jays in this park are notorious for pilfering and will literally steal your lunch out of your hand.

Destination 76: Loxahatchee River

Miles or average time: 8 miles or 4–6 hours

Skill level: intermediate

Current: 2–3 mph, faster upstream, slow where the river broadens

Wind problems: only at the eastern half

Emergency numbers: 911; Jupiter Police, (561) 746-6201; Martin County sheriff, (561) 220-7000; Palm Beach County sheriff, (561) 688-3000

Rentals: Canoe Outfitters of Florida, 8900 West Indiantown Road, Jupiter FL 33478, phone (561) 746-7053, e-mail canoecof@aol.com, website www.canoes-kayaks-florida.com; Jonathan Dickinson State Park, 16450 SE Federal Highway (US1), Hobe Sound FL 33455, phone (561) 746-1466; Kayaks Etc., 1410 19th Place, Vero Beach FL 32896, phone (561) 794-9900 or 1-888-652-9257; Southern Exposure Sea Kayaks, 18487 SE Federal Highway, Tequesta FL 33469, phone (561) 575-4530

DeLorme page 109, section A-2

Official Florida canoe trail: yes, and a National Wild and Scenic River

The Loxahatchee is Florida's only National Wild and Scenic River, and was the first NWSR in the subtropics. This region was also important in the Seminole Wars. Here you'll see Florida as it existed in the days of Osceola and Billy Bowlegs.

Florida has fifteen animals on the endangered species list: Everglades kite, manatee, wood stork, osprey, scrub jay (I didn't have to look far—one swooped in and stole two potato chips), little blue heron, Louisiana or tricolored heron, yellow- and black-crowned night herons, red-cockaded wood-

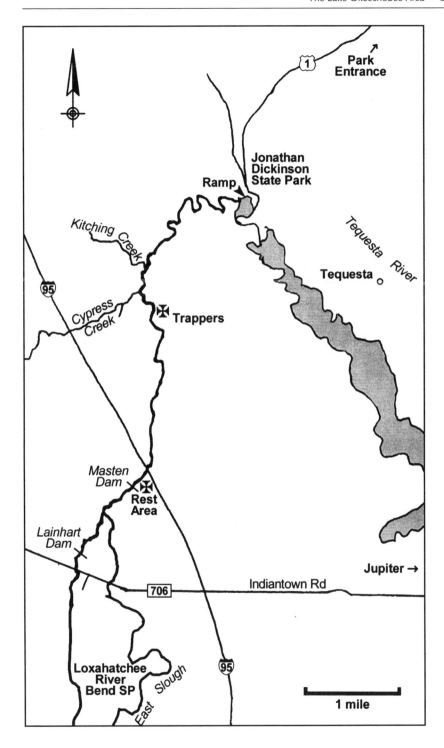

pecker, bald eagle, gopher tortoise, indigo snake, sandhill crane, and Florida panther. On one trip here I saw the first ten.

In character, it's really two completely different rivers.

The first half twists through a dense cypress jungle, with a fast current and enough maneuvering that you have to keep your head up to see what's ahead. The channel is crossed by fallen trees, and I've found there are always a couple of pull-overs, no matter what the water level. Old cypress trees line the banks, the coffee-colored water slipping around their head-high knees. Resurrection ferns and wild orchids fur the tops of the dark live oak branches.

Start at Riverbend Park, which is west of Jupiter on SR706/Indiantown Road. It's four and a half miles west of US1, and a mile west of Turnpike exit 116. From I-95, it's exit 59-B. Arrive early on weekends, because the number of paddlers is limited to lessen the impact on the river. Call the Ramp Master at (561) 746-7053 to check on launch times—she might suggest an appointment.

About ten minutes after you start, you will encounter Lainhart Dam, a low barrier with three openings that you can try to shoot. Or you can elect to use the carry-over ramp.

At 1.2 miles, or about a mile from Lainhart Dam, watch for the old Indian mound on the left. This area was inhabited either by a large number of Indians or by a small group that lived here for a long time. Archeologist Bill Steele of Palm Beach County has identified forty-six Indian sites "of great importance." He and his colleagues have also found where the first and second battles of the Loxahatchee were fought in one of the Seminole Wars. These locations were lost for over a century, which is easy to understand when you consider how hard it would be to mark such a location in the cypress jungle, and how poor the maps were back then.

Beyond this is the concrete Masten Dam. You can usually "shoot the vee" and paddle right through the wide opening. There are now rest rooms on the south side of Masten Dam.

You'll go under the Turnpike and I-95 at 1.5 miles. The saltwater intrusion starts about here, and will be much more evident by the time you get to Trapper Nelson's, which is right at the three-mile or halfway point of your trip.

You can either shoot the Loxahatchee River dam or take the ramp that goes around it. Watch for Trapper Nelson's cabin. Brian Faulk.

Plan a stop at Trapper Nelson's cabin. This is a good place for lunch, to get free water, and to stretch your legs. The *Loxahatchee Queen* cruise boat brings forty-four passengers at a time to visit this site. A ranger is usually available from Wednesday to Sunday to give a talk about this old homesteader, who had to smell to the high heavens. Nelson, who arrived in the 1930s, was called "the wild man of the Loxahatchee." The name of the river comes from the Indian words "lox" or "lowcha," meaning turtles, and "hatchee," meaning river. You'll still see dozens of turtles in the river but, according to legend, the homesteader caught and ate thousands of the things before he died in 1968.

It's easy to see why the old guy put his cabin where he did—it was the only high ground. Tidal influence is evident even this far up, and notice how saltwater intrusion is moving upstream as rising development sucks fresh water out of the underground aquifers.

East of Trapper Nelson's cabin, the river widens, slows down, and makes giant loops and circles as it changes into a saltwater mangrove estuary. Instead of fallen trees, watch for motorboats. If the wind is blowing, paddle from lee shore to lee shore.

You pass two smaller creeks coming in from the left that are fun to explore. The first is Cypress Creek at 5.3 miles, the other Kitching Creek at 6.6 miles. At about the 6.5-mile point, a narrow channel to the right will shortcut you across a big oxbow curve in the river—or you might want to paddle the oxbow, since we saw two flocks of ibis there. About the sixth left turn after the river widens, watch for an overhead power line. Just before it is a narrow channel to the left which leads to the takeout at Jonathan Dickinson Park.

The entrance to the park is off US1, five miles north of where SR706 crosses US1. There is an admission fee, plus a launch fee for the ramp.

This park is named for a Quaker merchant who was shipwrecked off Hobe Sound in 1696. Jonathan Dickinson, with his family and a few other survivors, made the long walk up the coast to St. Augustine, which was then the only settlement on the east coast of Florida. His fascinating story has been published under his own title: *Jonathan Dickinson's Journal, or God's Protecting Providence: Being the Narrative of a Journey from Port Royal to Philadelphia between August 23, 1696 and April 1, 1697.* It's at most Florida libraries under the call numbers FLA975.901 Dic. I also recommend *The Barefoot Mailman* by Theodore Pratt. Both of these books will give you a vivid picture of early Florida, and make you appreciate cars, air conditioning, and supermarkets.

The park has an observation tower on a bump of land called Hobe Mountain. This area was used as a radar operations training base during World War II. Before one trip the Florida Sport Paddling Club made there, tripmaster Nancy Doucette wrote, "Some of us may wish to paddle to the observation tower to almost watch the sunset. They kick you out of the tower when the sun actually sets."

If you put in at Riverbend Park around 9 or 10 A.M. and paddle slowly, you'll probably reach Jonathan Dickinson State Park around 3 P.M.

If you're starting at Jonathan Dickinson State Park, a short trip up Kitching Creek makes a nice round-trip paddle. If the wind kicks up and it is too rough to paddle, drive over to the Atlantic Coast at Blowing Rocks Preserve and watch the geysers coming out of the holes in the rocks.

A new section of the Loxahatchee is open now, according to Eric at Canoe Outfitters. He wrote at press time: "The old Loxahatchee East Slough is almost ready to paddle. This was filled and drained in the 1920s–30s for cattle and citrus. It has been restored and will be ready to float soon. It's about a six-mile loop. At first you will start at our launch, and paddle south/upstream about two miles to a cross over into the slough. Once you are in the slough, you paddle south and east for about three miles until you get to Indiantown Road. A small road is built to bring you back from there by van, about two hundred yards from our office, or you can hike that two hundred yards back if you like. Someday, if we can get the state to work with us, you will be able to paddle under the bridge at Indiantown, go all the way to the river, and then return back upstream to our launch site."

For more information, try the Palm Beach County Visitors Bureau at (561) 471-3995 or 1-800-833-5733.

Destination 77: Loxahatchee Slough

Miles or average time: 5.5 miles or 4–5 hours at Marshall Refuge

Skill level: beginner

Current: none

Wind problems: yes, very open area

Emergency numbers: 911; Palm Beach County sheriff, (561) 688-3000

Rentals: Loxahatchee Canoeing, PO Box 741714, Boynton Beach FL 33474-1714, phone (561) 733-0192 (call first); Loxahatchee Preserve Nature Center, 8264 Northlake Boulevard, West Palm Beach FL 33412, phone (561) 627-8831 (guided trips two Saturdays per month)

DeLorme page 115, section A-2

Official Florida canoe trail: no

Don't confuse what I'm calling Loxahatchee Slough with the Loxahatchee River (destination 76). The slough is a big swampy lake or wet prairie, and is the headwaters of the river of the same name. It is the remaining part of the Everglades that sits between Lake Okeechobee and the Atlantic Coast.

More than 250 kinds of birds frequent the area, along with a bunch of alligators and some good fishing.

The slough also catches runoff from the nearby sugar plantations. Another by-product of this nutrient-rich water is an overgrowth of cattails, and in very hot, dry weather, there is a proliferation of bright green water hyacinths and water lettuce. At this writing, all fishing is catch-and-release because of mercury contamination.

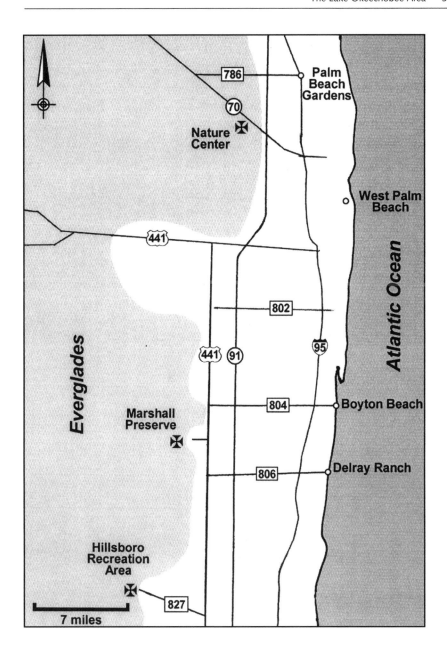

There are three separate places on the slough where you can go paddling.

1) The first is the Loxahatchee Preserve Nature Center, at the north end. We'll call this the Nature Center.

To get to the Nature Center, take I-95 to the Northlake Boulevard exit. Go west about four miles. About a mile past the intersection of Northlake Boulevard and the Beeline Expressway is the park entrance on the left/ south. The Visitor Center (phone (561) 627-8831) is open 8 A.M. to 4 P.M., with evening programs on Wednesdays.

Two Saturdays a month they host two- and three-hour guided canoe outings around the water catchment area. These are advertised as "lei- surely paced but of a moderate level of paddling difficulty." You must know how to swim, and youngsters under the age of six are not allowed. You can bring your own boat with advance reservations. The fee is $6, or $9 if you use their equipment. Plan to wear old clothes, and shoes that will stay on your feet in thick muck.

2) The second canoe trail is the Arthur R. Marshall Loxahatchee Na- tional Wildlife Refuge, 10216 Lee Road, Boynton Beach FL, 33437-4796, phone (561) 734-8303 (DeLorme page 115, section A-2). We'll call this the Marshall Refuge.

Their canoe trail is 5.5 miles, and takes four to five hours. After launch- ing at the ramp, paddle across the perimeter canal and go west. As Serena Rinker at the Refuge describes it, "The canoe trail is in the shape of a balloon on a string. You paddle the string for a quarter mile, then go around the circle."

To get to the Marshall Refuge, take I-95 to exit 44, Boynton Beach Boulevard/SR804. Turn west and go six or eight miles to the intersection of Boynton Beach Boulevard and US441/SR7. Go south/left about two miles. The Marshall Refuge entrance is on the west/right side of US441/ SR7 on Lee Road. An entrance fee of $5 per vehicle or $1 per pedestrian is charged.

3) The third place to paddle is Hillsboro Recreation Area, which is a public ramp twelve miles south and six miles west of the headquarters. To get to it from the Refuge headquarters, head south on US441 and turn right/west on SR827 (Loxahatchee Road) west of Deerfield Beach. Go about six miles to the dead end.

I first visited here when the Hillsboro Recreation Area launch ramp was an old fish camp, and shot a photo of my middle kid pulling in a nice bass.

In the last decade the wildlife numbers have tripled. About half a mile from the ramp we paddled past a family of otters. Raptors are common, with red-shouldered hawks plentiful. Limpkins and black-necked stilts tip-toe around the clumps of spatterdock. One German tourist family excitedly pointed out "ein grosser Alligator"—one big alligator—but it turned out to be a little five-footer.

Whichever part of the slough you visit, you'll come away with a better understanding of the vast Everglades that once stretched from Kissimmee to Florida Bay.

For more information, try Palm Beach County Chamber of Commerce at 1-800-544-PALM. Also try http://loxahatchee.fws.gov/sitemap/sitemap.asp.

Destination 78: Manatee River (Upper)

Miles or average time: 5 miles

Skill level: beginner

Current: slow, but varies with rainfall and outfall from Lake Manatee

Wind problems: little

Emergency numbers: 911; Manatee County sheriff, (941) 747-3011

Rentals: Ray's Canoe Hideaway, 1247 Hagle Park Road NE, Bradenton FL 34202, phone (941) 747-3909 or 1-888-57-CANOE.

DeLorme page 91, section D-3

Official Florida canoe trail: yes

Don't confuse the upper part of the Manatee River with the Little Manatee River (destination 54), which is further north.

The Manatee River opens into the wide and windy bay that separates Palmetto and Bradenton. Only five miles due east of busy I-75 the river narrows down, and is usually slow and placid. You can launch from any of the access points listed here and paddle easily upstream and down, so you won't need to deadhead a car.

Like most rivers, it runs high in the rainy season. During the dry season, shoals and deadfalls and sandbars make it a more strenuous trip. Water is released from the Lake Manatee Dam on no predictable schedule or logic that I've been able to discern. You can check both the dam openings and the water level by calling the dam office during office hours at (941) 746-3020.

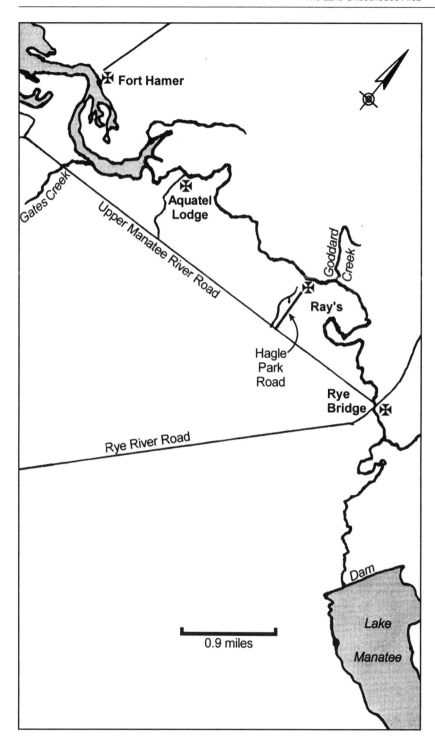

Fort Hamer

Gates Creek

Aquatel
Lodge

Upper Manatee River Road

Goddard Creek

Ray's

Hagle
Park
Road

Rye
Bridge

Rye River Road

Dam

Lake

Manatee

0.9 miles

1) Rye Road Bridge to Ray's Canoe Hideaway, 2.5 miles. To reach Rye Road Bridge from I-75, take exit 42 in Bradenton and head east on SR64, the Bradenton-Arcadia Road. After about four miles, or just after the big bend to the southeast, turn left/north onto Rye Road. You'll find the bridge right where Upper Manatee River Road comes in from the west.

2) Ray's Canoe Hideaway to Aquatel Lodge, 2.5 miles. From the Rye Road Bridge, head west on Upper Manatee River Road for one mile. Turn north on Hagle Park Road and follow it to the river. This is the end of the official canoe trail.

3) Aquatel Lodge to Fort Hamer, 2 miles. Again starting at the Rye Road Bridge, head west for two miles on the Upper Manatee River Road. Turn north on Aquatel Road, which takes you to Aquatel Lodge.

Downstream about .4 miles from Aquatel Lodge the river opens up to wide salt marshes. Hug the right/north bank to explore Gamble Creek. Keep going left/west to continue on to the Fort Hamer Manatee County boat ramp. There's another boat ramp on the left/south bank, about half-way to Fort Hamer, just before Gates Creek.

4) Fort Hamer. If there's no wind, and if it's a weekday so the motorboat traffic has thinned out, Fort Hamer is another place to start your paddling expedition. You can head east and hug the north bank to get to Gamble Creek.

Or go west into the open river to find some prime spots for wading birds during the May and October migration periods. There are several islands and crooked coves, so take your bearings often so you don't get lost. This may sound silly, but during low tide you might be sitting below the level of the marsh grasses, and it's hard to see where you are in this big tangled area. If you are in doubt, follow a motorboat. This open area is a great fishing site, with plentiful snook, redfish, and mullet.

To get to Fort Hamer, take exit 43 off I-75 and head northeast on US301 for 5.5 miles. At the bend where US301 turns north, turn south on Fort Hamer Road and go to the end.

For more information, contact the Bradenton Area Visitors Bureau, PO Box 1000, Bradenton FL 34207, phone (941) 729-9177, or e-mail them at gulfisl@bhip.infi.net.

Destination 79: Matlacha Island

Miles or average time: no limit, explore at your own speed

Skill level: beginner to advanced intermediate, depending on the current and wind

Current: little in mangrove lanes, strong tides in Matlacha Pass, Charlotte Harbor, and Caloosahatchee River

Wind problems: little inside mangroves, lots in open bays

Emergency numbers: 911; Lee County sheriff, (941) 332-3456

Rentals: Gulf Coast Kayak, Matlacha Marina, 3922 NW Pine Island Road, Matlacha FL 33993, phone (941) 283-1125, fax (941) 283-7034 (ask about full and new moon trips too); Tropic Star Cruises, 1835 Main Street, Bokeelia FL 33922, phone (941) 283-1125; Useppa Island, PO Box 640, Bokeelia FL 33922, phone (941) 283-5255

DeLorme page 104, section D-2

Official Florida canoe trail: no

Matlacha (pronounced mat-lah-SHAY) is a tiny island between Fort Myers and Little Pine Key. It sits squarely in Matlacha Pass Aquatic Preserve, inside a national wildlife refuge.

Protected by the offshore islands of Captiva and Sanibel, Pine Island has no white sandy beaches. It does have 54,000 acres of protected waters, and is an important nursery for local fish and marine animals. For a century trophy fish have been taken from these waters, and the big charter boats that roar out of Boca Grande Pass are searching for billfish.

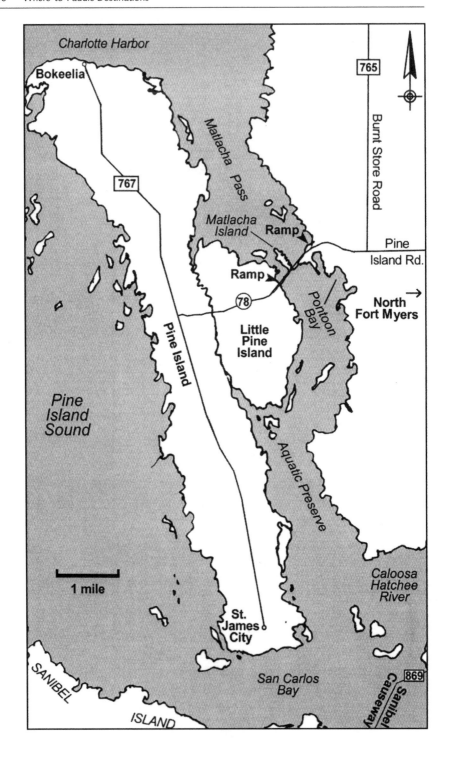

Old woodcut of Federal gunboat. Pirates like Jose Gaspar had plenty of hiding places around Charlotte Harbor. University of South Florida archives.

The attractions for paddlers are the maze of mangrove islets, tiny creeks that run to hidden lakes, and secret nooks. The shallow sun-warmed waters and grass flats are ideal for a kayak.

We took a guided kayak trip with Gulf Coast Kayak and saw about two dozen different species of birds, including a big flock of roseate spoonbills, ospreys, three kinds of herons, and two kinds of egrets. Underwater were mullet, redfish, and a mystery fish that made a monster wake as it kept darting ahead of my hull.

Humans have been here for thousands of years. Galt Island was a Calusa religious center, with mounds, canals, and a large population. Several modern houses are built on old Indian shell mounds. A scandal erupted years ago when a northerner bought the last untouched shell mound and secretly bulldozed off the top five or six feet—the part likely to have the most artifacts—so he could build a house. The archeology societies are still furious.

An ongoing archeology dig is run by University of Florida personnel, and you can see a replica of a mound (unbulldozed) at the Museum of the Islands at 5728 Sesame Drive, Bokeelia FL 33922, phone (941) 283-1525.

Pedro Menéndez de Avilés is supposed to have visited Pine Island in 1565, searching for his shipwrecked son. He built a fort named San Anton, but the exact site is in dispute. Some history buffs claim that it was at Mound Key, farther south (see destination 72).

Pirates raised strongholds at Boca Grande, Useppa Island, and Gasparilla Island. After Gaspar, Bru Baker, and Blackbeard paid off their pirate crews, where do you think the men hid their treasure? The many niches and coves would have been perfect for rowboats to steal up to in the dead of night. Federal gunboats had a terrible time finding the pirates or their small boats in the tangled waterways. Legend says a chest was dug up on Useppa Island. The Boca Grande Library has century-old books in its open stacks that discuss where and how the pirates hid their loot. It's fun to try to think like a pirate and imagine hiding places.

Tidal currents can be fierce in this long pass. If you venture too far south, you'll get out into San Carlos Bay, which is the mouth of the Caloosahatchee River. Paddle too far north, and you'll be in the open Charlotte Harbor area. If you're feeling adventuresome, you can circle seventeen-mile-long Pine Island, about a forty-mile round-trip.

At the north end of Pine Island is the sleepy little village of Bokeelia, cut off from the big island by Hog Creek. The current is strong here, so be careful. Launch your kayak or canoe and explore the hidden nooks that surround Matlacha. It's a wonderful way to spend a day.

For more information, contact the Lee County Visitor and Convention Bureau, 2180 West First Street, Suite 100, Fort Myers FL 33901, phone (941) 338-3500, website www.leeislandcoast.com.

Destination 80: Myakka River

Miles or average time: go at your own pace; 12 miles total, depending on water levels

Skill level: beginner at the upper lake, intermediate above it; portaging can be necessary in low water and at the weir

Current: wildly variable with rainfall

Wind problems: wildly variable in the open lake

Emergency numbers: 911; Sarasota County sheriff, (941) 951-5800

Rentals: Canoe Country Outfitters, phone (941) 545-4554; Economy Tackle, 6018 South Tamiami Trail, Sarasota FL 34231, phone (941) 922-9671, e-mail hurxthal@netsrq.com; Grande Tours, PO Box 281, Placida FL 33946, phone (941) 697-8825; Myakka Outpost, Myakka River State Park, 13207 SR 72, Sarasota FL 34241, phone (941) 923-1120; Snook Haven Fish Camp, 5000 East Venice Avenue, Venice FL 34292, phone (941) 485-7221; Venice Campground, 4085 East Venice Avenue, Venice FL 34292, phone (941) 488-0850, website www.campvenice.com

DeLorme page 97, section B-3

Official Florida canoe trail: no

Myakka River State Park is one of the oldest parks in Florida, and the largest, with 45 square miles or 28,875 acres, plus an 8,000-acre new addition.

The Myakka River runs for sixty-six miles, from a distant swamp to Charlotte Harbor. Fourteen miles of the river run through the park. The Florida Wild and Scenic stretch of the river runs for thirty-four miles, from the north Sarasota County line to the Charlotte County line.

You can stay in the old palm-log cabins built by the Civilian Conservation

Corps during the Depression (call (941) 361-6511 for reservations), ride the world's largest airboats, fish for bass and crappie, hike more than forty miles of trails, watch a video at the Visitors Center, or sit in on the wintertime nature talks at the campfire circle or the log pavilion.

The big airboats *Gator Gal* and *Myakka Maiden* hold seventy-two passengers each. Tickets are $7, and during the winter season there are four tours a day. There is also a tram that runs January through May, so tourists can view the myriad animals, birds, and alligators.

Paddling in this park is not for the faint of heart. There are alligators—herds of them. Many of them are babies, which means that, one, their moms are very close by and, two, their dads are lurking somewhere too.

On the other hand, the birding is great. More than thirteen thousand birds were spotted during a recent Christmas bird count. Ducks are plentiful. Migratory birds stop here, so you'll see different species every time you visit.

Hydrilla has been introduced into this waterway, probably stuck to the props of motorboats or even (horrors) on a canoe. The amount of weed in the water column fluctuates according to the herbicide treatment, the season, and how hungry the Nile perch are the week you're there. When it is thick, you might have trouble getting through it. Call the park to check on paddling conditions.

Most folks paddle Upper Myakka Lake, a fairly strenuous six-mile round-trip. Put in at the concession and ramp at the south side of the lake and paddle to Lower Myakka Lake and back.

During low water, you might have to portage over the weir at the south end of Upper Myakka Lake, across exposed shoals, or around hyacinth jams. The river north of the Upper Lake is not accessible during low water.

Park naturalist Paula Benshoff says, "The current is usually nonexistent or swift, depending on the time of year. It is very difficult to paddle against the current when the water levels are very high. And there can be wind problems. My husband has had to walk the entire way back along the river, towing the canoe, on a windy day."

Lower Myakka Lake is in the 7,500-acre wilderness preserve. Motorboats are restricted to no-wake speeds. Only thirty people a day are allowed in, whether walking or paddling, so arrive early. Ranger Robert says, "This is a LONG trip for ANY level canoeist, and they need to get a permit to go south of SR72 on the river."

At the west end of the lower lake, outside the park limits, you'll pass a 150-foot-deep sinkhole, which is loaded with fish. Below the park two springs come up from deep caverns—Little Salt Spring and Warm Mineral Spring.

Adventuresome paddlers have also done the twenty-three-mile paddle to Snook Haven Fish Camp and beyond to Charlotte Harbor.

Fifty-year-old Snook Haven is a venerable institution. According to its not-very-serious menu, a Tarzan movie called *Revenge of the Killer Turtles* was made there. Some of the turtles escaped, you see, and you must watch for them to come swinging through the trees to drop into your canoe. I keep meaning to call Blockbuster Video and ask for that movie.

To get to Myakka River State Park from Sarasota, take exit 37 off I-75.

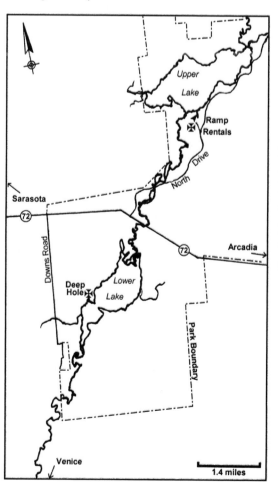

Drive east on SR72 for nine miles. The park entrance is on the left. Note that the north entrance is open only on weekends and holidays.

For more information, plus current river conditons, contact Myakka River State Park, 13207 SR72, Sarasota FL 34241, phone (941) 361-6511, website www.myakka.sarasota.fl.us.

Destination 81: Naples Nature Center

> Miles or average time: 2 hours, paddle at your own pace
>
> Skill level: beginner in narrow creek, intermediate if windy in bay
>
> Current: tidal
>
> Wind problems: some, further downstream as river opens up
>
> Emergency numbers: 911; Collier County sheriff, (941) 774-4434
>
> Rentals: Naples Nature Center, 1450 Merrihue Drive, Naples FL 34102, phone (941) 262-0304
>
> DeLorme page 111, section C-1
>
> Official Florida canoe trail: no

This is not a high adventure trip, but a pleasant way to spend two hours in the Naples area.

You'll be paddling in a small creek that runs mostly in a housing area, with a small bit of motorboat traffic as you get further down the Gordon River. The river opens onto Naples Bay, which is really a long, skinny waterway that stretches north and south. Most of the waterway is sheltered from the wind.

Canoes and kayaks may be rented at the Naples Nature Center. The administration building is on Merrihue Drive, off 14th Avenue N, off Goodlette-Frank Road, between Caribbean Gardens and the post office. The Naples Nature Center is run by the Conservancy of Southwest Florida, the people who also run Briggs Nature Center at Rookery Bay (destination 89). They've installed a little dock in among the mangroves and buttonwoods of the creek. Rental fees are $11 for two hours for members, $13 for nonmem-

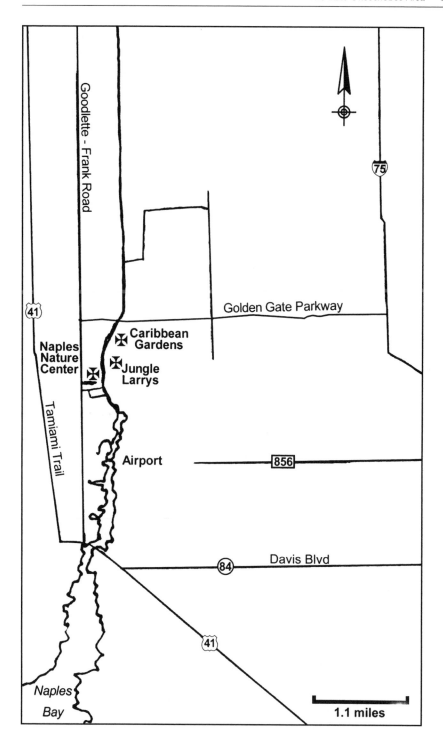

bers, additional time $5 an hour. Children have to be age eight or older. Rentals start at 9:30 A.M. and you must be back by 4 P.M. from November to April, and back by 1 P.M. from May to October. Only canoes rented from the Nature Center can be launched from their dock.

Ed Duklewski, dockmaster, describes it this way, "You start in a little mangrove-bordered lagoon, and take a mangrove-lined channel out to the Gordon River. There are a few Brazilian pepper trees mixed in too. Stay on the right-hand side and you can go as far as City Dock, which is about Fourteenth Street. If you turn upstream, you can go as far as the Golden Gate Canal and the dam."

For more information on the Conservancy of Southwest Florida, try www.conservancy.org. For more tourist information on the Naples area, try www.naples.net/travel/conservmap.html.

Destination 82: Orange River

Miles or average time: 3.5 miles southeast, 1.5 miles northwest to Caloosahatchee River

Skill level: beginner in creek, advanced beginner for river

Current: slight except during rainy seasons; tidal influence

Wind problems: none on creek

Emergency numbers: 911; Lee County sheriff, (941) 332-3456

Rentals: Manatee Canoes (November–April) at Coastal Marine Mart, 5605 Palm Beach Boulevard, Fort Myers FL 33919, phone (941) 694-0486, website www.manateeworld.org; Manatee Park (November–March), 10901 Palm Beach Boulevard, Fort Myers FL 33905, phone (941) 432-2004, website www.lee-county.com/parks&rec

DeLorme page 105, section C-1

Official Florida canoe trail: no

The Orange River is just five miles west of Hickey Creek (destination 73), but it has easier access. The two runs are quite similar. Hickey Creek runs through a marshy area and is upstream/east of the W. P. Franklin Locks, while the Orange River is more sheltered, downstream/west of the locks, and more tunnely, with overhanging trees and lots of Spanish moss (some of it in your teeth).

Nancy Musser, with the Lee County Visitor and Convention Bureau, told me, "I've heard that the residents along the Orange River don't want the river designated a Florida Canoe Trail, therefore the county has given up on plans to offer any other public access to the Orange River."

Lee County Manatee Park, which is the easiest access to the river, is di-

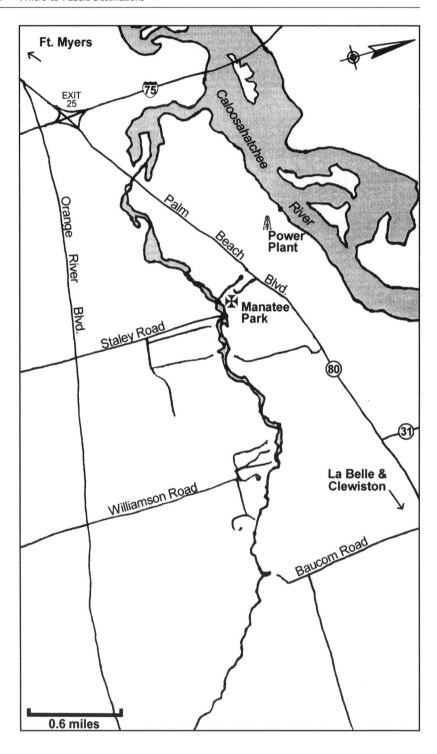

The Orange River is a favorite hangout for manatees. Sandy Huff.

rectly across the street from the FPL power plant on SR80, and immediately west of the Forestry Service lookout tower. The tall red-and-white-barred smokestack of the power plant is visible at odd moments during the entire trip, and makes a good reference point. However, the stacks will be changed to smaller ones in 2003.

Parking at Manatee Park is self-serve. You buy a ticket from a machine (75 cents per hour or $3 per day) and stick it on your windshield. There are two loading-zone parking places for unloading your boat. The wheelchair-accessible dock itself is often underwater during high tides, and gets very slippery.

The Visitor Center in the park is open from November through March. They rent two-person kayaks, and have a gift shop and manatee info. The park gates close automatically at night. When you arrive, check the closing times posted at the gate to make sure your car doesn't get locked inside. The park hours are 8 A.M. to 5 P.M. October to March, and 8 A.M. to 8 P.M. April to September. Kayak rental hours are 9 A.M. to 3 P.M. daily, at $8 per hour.

You have your choice of direction once you paddle out of the tiny put-in "ditch." You can turn right and head downstream to the confluence of the Orange and Caloosahatchee Rivers. You'll pass Manatee Marina, which has the Manatee Canoes rental livery from November through early April and a picturesque bunch of old boat sheds and rickety docks.

Or you can turn left and head upstream for three and a half miles. The Orange River is a hot spot for manatees in the winter. Watch for their noses poking up for about four seconds, then plopping back underwater.

I've paddled only a short distance upstream on the Orange before it started raining and we turned back. In that short distance we passed two small alligators, a dozen cattle egrets, and one tree dotted with wood storks.

The river runs mostly through cow pastures, huge stands of Brazilian pepper trees, beautiful live oaks, and assorted brush. In the early morning one whole bank was festooned with the white blossoms of moonflowers, which are a type of morning glory.

This looks like a prime fishing creek, with plenty of forage for bass and some deep holes that look perfect for tarpon. I wished I'd brought fishing tackle.

Destination 83: Peace River

Miles or average time: 61 miles, in nine official segments ranging from 1 to 23 miles

Skill level: beginner

Current: slow, except during the rainy season

Wind problems: only in open straight stretches

Emergency numbers: 911; Polk County sheriff, (863) 533-0344; Fort Meade Police (863) 285-1100; Hardee County sheriff, (863) 773-0304; Bowling Green Police, (863) 375-35499; Wauchula Police, (863) 773-3265, DeSoto County sheriff, (863) 993-4700; Arcadia Police, (863) 993-4660

Rentals: Canoe Outpost, 2816 NW County Road 661, Arcadia FL 34266, phone (863) 494-1215 or 1-800-268-0083, e-mail canoefla@desoto.net, website www.canoeoutpost.com; Canoe Safari, 3020 NW County Road 661, Arcadia FL 34266, phone (863) 494-7865 or 1-800-262-1119, website www.canoesafari.com; Peace River Canoes, 2184 East Main Street, Wauchula FL 33873, phone (863) 773-6370

DeLorme page 93, section B-1, to page 98, section C-3

Official Florida canoe trail: yes

I once came around a bend of the Peace and surprised a herd of cows standing at the edge of the river. They stampeded away in a thunder of muddy hooves (okay, it was a flop-plop, not a thunder).

There are two versions of how the river got its name. First is the old Spanish name Rio de la Paz marked on a 1544 map. The next version says the river was originally named Tallackchopo, which means cow peas, and the early settlers changed it to Peace. I've looked for cow peas along this river for years and never found any. The fact that I don't know what a cow pea looks like might have something to do with that.

Around the middle third of the last century, barges steamed up and down the river, scooping up the phosphate gravel for fertilizer. Becky Bragg of Canoe Outpost says, "Rafts of logs, especially cypress, were floated to sawmills, so the different timbers you see on the bottom and jutting out of banks are either old phosphate docks or logs that broke loose from the rafts."

This is another great river for finding sharks' teeth. Anytime you come across a bed of gravel, hop out of your boat and closely examine handfuls of gravel. The pure black triangular teeth are mostly the size of your little fingernail, but now and then you'll find one as wide as your palm. Plan ahead and take a zip-shut bag or plastic medicine vial to hold them in, instead of always storing them in your cheek like a hamster.

There are also fossilized bits of palm bark, plus skate mouth plates. To me they look like cockroach eggs, all evidence for what I've believed for years: that (1) this area was once a Miocene, Pliocene, and Pleistocene seabed and (2) yes, cockroaches are indeed the dominant species on earth.

Bragg says, "What are commonly found in the river are the bones and teeth of mammoth, mastodon, three-toed horse, camel, rhino, saber-tooth tiger—we're talking about the big boys!"

The canoe trail is well kept, with fallen trees cleared out enough that you don't have to strain getting around or over them. Every June Becky Bragg organizes a big river cleanup—you can get a free T-shirt, trash bags, and use of a canoe if you preregister. Most access points have no trash pickup, so put your trash in your car until you find a real garbage can.

1) Fort Meade to CR657, 3 miles. The official trail starts at the Fort Meade Recreational Park ramp beside the US98 bridge, about a mile east of SR17.

A quick history lesson: Fort Meade was an actual fort, built by Lieutenant George G. Meade, who went on to become the commanding general of the Union Army in the Civil War. Stonewall Jackson was here as a first lieutenant.

The fort saw action from 1849 to 1858 in one of the Seminole Wars, when the river was the dividing line between Indian territory to the east and white settlers on the west.

There are three islands in this stretch, and the main current usually goes on the east side of each island.

2) CR657 to CR664, 7 miles. From the center of town in Fort Meade, take US17 two miles south and go left/east on Berquist Road to CR 657/ Mount Pisgah Road. Go right/southeast one mile to the bridge.

3) CR664/County Line Road to CR664A, 2 miles. Chuck McIntire, park manager for the Paynes Creek State Historic Site, says, "In my personal opinion, the section between Bowling Green (#3) and Zolfo Springs (#8) is the prettiest. I predict that within the next couple of years this section will be designated an Outstanding and Scenic Waterway."

4) CR664A/Lake Branch to CR664A, 2 miles. In Bowling Green, turn east on Main Street/Lake Branch Road. Go two miles to Paynes Creek State Historic Site (phone (863) 375-4717) on the right.

Sonny Norris, of the Central Florida Paddlemasters, says, "Put your two dollars in a drop box if the ranger is not there. Follow the road until you come to a parking lot and rest room with a hundred-yard asphalt footpath on the right.

"Transport your boat and equipment to the wooden steps to the creek. A canoe/kayak cart is a good idea. Launch and go left downstream. The creek will dump into the Peace River."

Paynes Creek State Historic Site is an old fort that was in service only from 1849 to 1850. It was built because four hothead Seminoles got trigger-happy and ambushed U.S. soldiers. Seminole leaders had already banished one of the men, and after the ambush the tribe turned the others over to the U.S. Government. Unfortunately Federal troops were already en route, ready to gun down any "Injuns." The ensuing string of forts, built every ten miles from the Manatee River on the Gulf Coast to the Indian River on the Atlantic Coast, probably had more to do with opening up the interior of Florida than any other action in that century.

The park is open every day, year round. It closes at sundown. There is overnight parking at the park, but you cannot camp on the grounds. You can camp on private property near the park, with advance permission from the landowners. A list of these kind souls is kept at the park office, with the canoe liveries, and at the Hardee County Chamber of Commerce (phone (863) 773-6967).

5) CR664A to Crews Park, 2 miles.

6) Crews Park to SR652, 1 mile. Crews Park is on the northwest side of the SR636 bridge. Bragg told me this bridge is called Bloody Bucket—you'll have to ask her why. There are rest rooms at the park.

7) SR652 bridge to Pioneer City County Park in Zolfo Springs, 5 miles. The ramp is on the southeast side of the river. No rest rooms.

Our Girl Scout troop did this section as part of a river cleanup day. The banks are wild and tangled. I understand there is a lot of wildlife, but we didn't see any. While the kids have been known to be completely silent during dawn paddles, and often sneak up on turtles and otters with the stealth of Red Indians, this was not one of their zip-lip days. The full lyrics of "Ninety-Nine Bottles of Pop" plus three hours of nonstop giggling made sure that every living creature on the river knew we were coming.

We did, however, fill five garbage bags with floating trash. A passing wildlife officer in his powerboat noticed the full bags and stopped to thank the girls. He ended up getting stuck with the bags, and was thoroughly grilled on career opportunities in his field.

8) Pioneer City Park to Gardner, 23 miles. Twenty-one left turns. The park is on the northwest side of the intersection of US17 and SR64 in Zolfo Springs. It has rest rooms, a public boat ramp, and camping for a fee.

This is a popular stretch for canoe camping, but stay on the west bank. No stopping on either side until you are past the yellow cabin on river right, about five or six miles from Zolfo. The Peace River Ranch owns both sides of the river, and warns everyone to stay on the west bank. The east bank is patrolled.

9) Gardner to Arcadia, 16 miles. Going south from Zolfo Springs on US17, turn right/west on the continuation of SR665. Gardner boat ramp is a public ramp with no rest rooms. South of the ramp is the Canoe Outpost for Gardner. This is for Outpost customers only, with no public access. From Gardner to Brownville there is no camping.

There is one additional access point at Brownville Park, which is west of Brownville beside the Brownville Bridge, on Brownville Street, about a mile and a half west of US17. This is a county boat ramp, with no rest rooms. Camping is allowed at the bridge and the boat ramp at the east.

There once was another site about three miles downriver. But it is a private boat ramp, and evidently some paddlers were obnoxious and wore out their welcome. Don't plan to stop there.

Canoe Outpost has another private access at Oak Hill, five miles south of Brownville. From Oak Hill to Arcadia is five miles. Camping is possible at the railroad trestle just north of Arcadia.

10) SR70 bridge, 1.5 miles west of US17 in Arcadia. This is the end of the official canoe trail. The DeSoto Park ramp is on the northwest side of the bridge. It has no rest rooms. By river, you'll pass Canoe Safari and Canoe Outpost on river right about two miles before the bridge.

11) It is possible to continue downstream fifteen more miles to the

DeSoto Marina and Charlotte Harbor, but Bragg warns, "We avoid send-
ing canoes south of Arcadia because of all the personal water craft, airboats, and limited camping or stopping places."

If you do continue, the next takeout is seven miles downstream, at
Nocatee. There is a tiny area for camping south of the island and a pump
on river right, three miles from Arcadia. Otherwise the banks are privately
owned and camping is not allowed.

For more information, try the Fort Meade Chamber of Commerce, PO Box
91, Fort Meade FL 33841, phone (863) 285-8253; Central Florida Visitors
Bureau, 600 North Broadway #300, Bartow FL 33830, phone 1-800-828-
POLK (7655); Har-
dee County Cham-
ber of Commerce,
209 South Sixth Av-
enue, Wauchula FL
33873, phone (863)
773-6967.

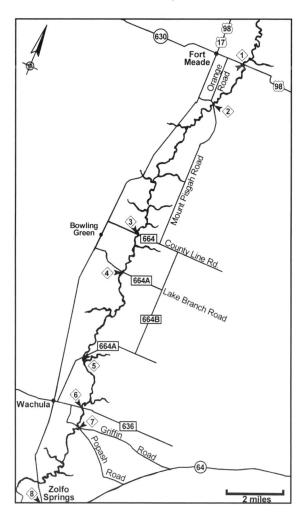

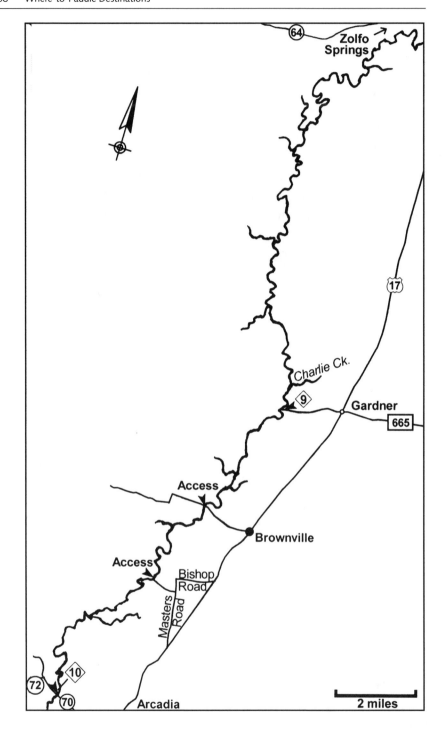

Area 5. South Florida and the Keys

Panama City

Tallahassee

Jacksonville

Orlando

Tampa

Naples

Miami

Destination 84: Big Pine Key and the Back Country

Miles or average time: no limits, paddle at your own pace

Skill level: beginner

Current: strong tidal flow between islands

Wind problems: yes, very open, unsheltered waters

Emergency numbers: 911, Monroe County sheriff, (305) 292-7075

Rentals: Cayo Carbie Kayak Rentals, 1018 Truman Avenue, Key West FL 33040, phone (305) 296-4115; Florida Bay Outfitters, 104050 Overseas Highway, Key Largo FL 33037, phone (305) 451-3018, www.kayakfloridakeys.com; Adventures Charters & Tours, 6810 Front Street, Key West FL 33040, phone (305) 296-0362, www.keywestadventures.com; Jigs Bait & Tackle, MM 33, Big Pine Key FL 33043, phone (305) 872-1040; Keys Kayaks, MM 17, Sugarloaf Key FL 33042, phone (305) 745-6635, e-mail keykayak@netrox.net; Reflections Kayaks, PO Box 431714, Big Pine Key FL 33043, phone (305) 872-2896, www.mindspring.com/~pad-dler/; Scarlet Ibis Canoe Tours and Rentals, MM 27, Big Pine Key FL 33043, phone (305) 872-9314, e-mail canoetours@aol.com, website http://keys-kayak-canoe-tours.com/canoe.htm; Summerland Kayaks, MM 24.1, Summerland Key FL 33042, phone (305) 745-2726

DeLorme page 124, section C-1

Official Florida canoe trail: no

Whoops. I'd misjudged the tide. The current rushing under the tiny bridge on Duck Key was ferocious. I leaned over to push myself along the seawall,

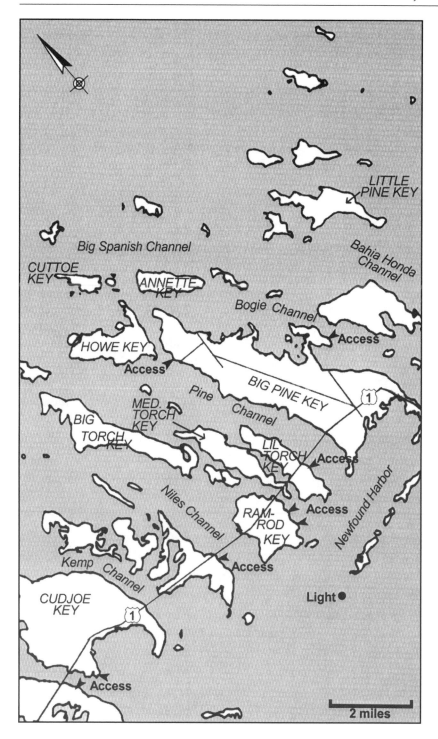

and promptly capsized. As I gathered up my hat, lunch, and other gear, I overheard another kayaker sigh, "Sandy's dumped over *again*."

The Florida Keys have been called Florida's string of scenic pearls. The scenery is gorgeous. Miles of shallow, glittering warm waters shimmer in uncountable shades of blue. Dark green islets dot the horizon beneath a vast sky.

The Keys stretch for 150 miles, from the southern tip of Florida to Key West. The remains of ancient coral reefs, these rocky paths show cross patterns of brain coral, sea fans, and shells.

You can paddle all up and down the string of Keys. One of my favorite spots is about two-thirds of the way to Key West, in a cluster of islands called the Back Country. The smaller keys are entirely mangroves, while the larger islands support a unique forest of hardwood trees, such as gumbo-limbo, that manage to root themselves in the porous coral rock. Many of the keys have interior lakes, and a few crocodiles even hide in the more isolated nooks.

Instead of regular addresses, businesses and houses are marked by their position on US1. Mile Markers start at zero in Key West. Driving time from Miami to Big Pine Key is two and a half to three hours.

Except for a narrow ribbon of land fronting US1, which is called the Overseas Highway down here, the Back Country keys are uninhabited. Most of them lie inside overlapping wildlife refuges.

Tremendous volumes of water flow through the channels during the tidal changes. However, with reasonable care you'll find plenty of places to explore without straining your shoulder muscles.

Markus Godula, who runs Scarlet Ibis Tours on Big Pine Key, says, "Our tides can be strong, but most are not. Typically the water is calm and shallow. If it is a windy day, we'll find the 'lee side' of one of our large islands to protect you. The water depth is not more that nine feet in most channels, and an average depth of one to two feet on the flats. It's amazing how many large fish species live in these shallows, including tarpon, bonefish, permit, sharks, and snapper. There are also tropical fish, lobster, crabs, rays, sponges, and so much more.

"The mangrove islands are one of the main reasons that our area is so vastly different from the rest of Florida. Our mangrove islands have 'mangrove caves' that you can travel through and are very interesting themselves. We are more in the Caribbean Basin than the mainland, and have some species of animals that are only found between Big Pine and Key West, such as the reef gecko. Several migrating species of birds from the surrounding Caribbean islands, including the Bahamian swallow, come only to Big Pine to nest."

Probably the most famous animals are the stunted deer that have adapted to the sparse grass and foliage on the islands. Markus says, "The Key deer are a miniature subspecies of the Virginia whitetail deer that have adapted to island life and are on the endangered list. A full-grown eight-point buck is barely twenty-six inches high at the shoulder. Most people mistake them for dogs at first. The fawns are tiny, and very cute."

You might see deer swimming between islands. If you do, leave them strictly alone. The rangers and local residents of Big Pine Key are extremely protective of their tiny charges.

Don't expect big city life. As Markus says, "Key West is an interesting arty town about thirty miles to the south. It's considered party central."

Markus has even found a quick way to get paddlers out to the more secluded islands. "We put the canoes on special racks we've built into our Jonboat and motor you back to the pristine areas away from the normal routes. Besides your boat, paddle, PFD, and a small anchor, we provide a map, a plastic bird card, and a cell phone."

Even if you can only get out on the water for a couple of hours, paddling the Back Country is a terrific experience. And if you do capsize, I can attest that the water is nice and warm.

Destination 85: Blackwater and Royal Palm Hammock Creeks

Miles or average time: 13.6 miles

Skill level: beginner

Current: slow, some tidal influence at Gulf

Wind problems: mostly sheltered, but three open bays

Emergency numbers: 911; Collier County sheriff, (941) 774-4434

Rentals: Collier-Seminole State Park, 20200 East Tamiami Trail, Naples FL 34114, phone (941) 394-3397

DeLorme page 110, section C-2

Official Florida canoe trail: yes

Don't even think about paddling here in the summer. The temperature can reach 106°, and the rangers wear full mosquito suits when they go outside. Ranger Nicolette Makruski says, "The best time to paddle this area is November through January, when the mosquito population is at its lowest."

Blackwater Creek lies near the Ten Thousand Islands just east of Marco Island. Royal Palm Hammock is named after the rare Florida royal palms. The Collier comes from Barron Collier, who started designing this park in 1942, plus the Seminole Indians who live nearby. The park encompasses 6,430 acres, and the canoe trail leads through an array of habitats, from swamp to mangrove mazes.

A huge "walking dredge" at the park demonstrates how much work was involved when the Tamiami Trail/US41 was built in the 1920s. It is now a National Historical Mechanical Engineering Landmark.

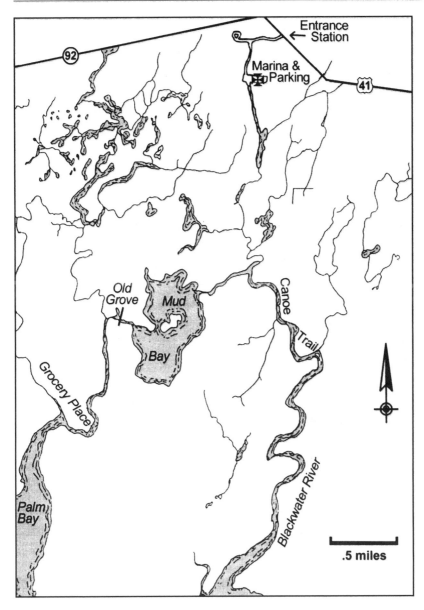

A sightseeing pontoon boat (phone (941) 642-8898, www.floridaever-gladestours.com/index.htm) leaves from the park. You can find $1-off coupons for this in any of the little tourist giveaway magazines at nearby gas stations and hotel lobbies. But it is a short trip, and you'll see far more, from anhinga birds to zebra butterflies, as you paddle the canoe trail.

Collier-Seminole State Park has a few rental canoes, and an easy-to-read map. Only a few canoes per day are allowed on the 13.6-mile loop trail, so arrive early. Register a trip plan before taking off. When I was there, the ranger on duty suggested we carry a compass and asked if we knew how to read it. I've been lost in the Ten Thousand Islands before, so I made sure to get a map and watch for the signposts, especially in the bigger lakes and the bay.

The whole trip is a loop, so you leave and return via the park marina. You start by heading south. At marker 47 you'll leave Blackwater River and head west down a narrow channel. Cross Mud Bay, continue south to skirt the east shore of Palm Bay and the north shore of Blackwater Bay, then head north on Blackwater River. The river varies in width, and the water level fluctuates according to the tides. Motorboat access to the park is up the Blackwater River, from marker 13 on.

Look up now and then to spot wood storks. These black-headed giant ibis ride the thermal currents, circling higher than any other bird. At low tide the exposed sandbars and mud flats attract sandpipers, plovers, stilts, and other tiny birds that dig for succulent tidbits in the sand.

You'll certainly see belted kingfishers. They must be territorial, as we noticed kingfishers sitting on the power lines beside the highway every 1.4 miles. Also watch for white-crowned pigeons and smooth-billed anis, refugees from the Bahamas.

An extremely rare Florida crocodile was spotted here a few years ago, so if you see what looks like an alligator, check for a pointed snout—it might be a croc.

The trees in the tropical hammock are species found in the West Indies and the Yucatan. Watch for the "tourist tree," the gumbo-limbo, which has red, peeling skin. There are strangler figs, ferns, Jamaica dogwoods, and sabal palms in addition to the royal palms.

For information, contact Collier-Seminole State Park, 20200 East Tamiami Trail, Naples FL 34114, phone (941) 394-3397.

Destination 86: Blackwater Sound

Miles or average time: unlimited

Skill level: beginner to intermediate, depending on wind

Current: tidal flats

Wind problems: yes

Emergency numbers: 911; Monroe County sheriff, (305) 292-7075

Rentals: Florida Bay Outfitters, 104050 Overseas Highway, Key Largo FL 33037, phone (305) 451-3018, website www.pennekamp.com/fbout; Island Waterworks, 51 Garden Cove Drive, Key Largo FL 33037, phone (305) 453-4131, e-mail waterworks@pennekamp.com

DeLorme page 122, section C-3

Official Florida canoe trail: no

Biologists are mystified by a subspecies of diamondback terrapin that lives here. These little palm-sized turtles live by the dozen on certain islets, and completely ignore other keys that look identical to human eyes. They often burrow so deep in the mud that even when you see one, it is hard to identify. Watch for a little head about the size of a walnut to pop out of the water, then dive back down. If you see one, you'll probably see several more.

Blackwater Sound is an interesting place to explore. The wide, shallow grass flats are a major nursery area for many species of fish. Wading birds dot the shallows at low tide.

Several parts of this bay are deep enough for powerboats, so stick to the edges and avoid the channel of the Intracoastal. At low tides a kayak is the ideal craft, since it can skim over mere inches of water and, with its lower gunwale, is not knocked around by winds.

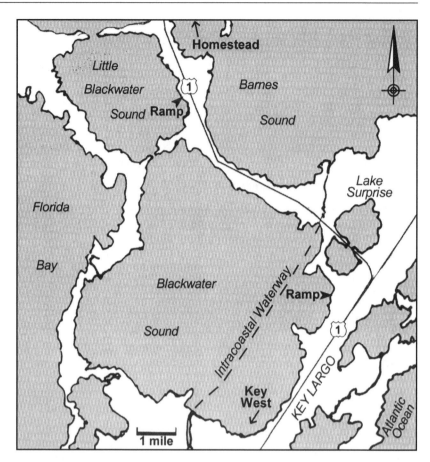

During calm weather, you can see every blade of grass and each tiny hermit crab on the bottom. In fact, the slower you go, the more life you'll see. Take along a mask and snorkel, and slip overboard to meet these little creatures face to face. Make sure you have a long bow line or painter so you can tow your kayak behind you as you explore.

You probably won't see any American crocodiles around Key Largo. There are said to be only fifty-eight left in the wild, and they lurk up in the hidden creeks and mangrove mazes.

The west side of Key Largo is completely different from the east side, where you'll find the headquarters for John Pennekamp Coral Reef State Park.

Old Florida Bay is fascinating. Try to imagine it as John James Audubon found it more than a century ago. Take along a bird book, count the cars that zoom over US1, or just poke around.

Destination 87: Dania Wetlands

Miles or average time: no limit, paddle at your own speed

Skill level: beginner

Current: slight tidal flow

Wind problems: little, mostly sheltered

Emergency numbers: 911; Broward County sheriff, (954) 831-8900

Rentals: Ann Kolb Nature Center, West Lake Park, 751 Sheridan
Street, Hollywood FL 33019, phone (954) 926-2480

DeLorme page 115, section D-3

Official Florida canoe trail: no

Anthony Meola told me about this trip. He said, "I'm new to paddling, but I
have a spot in the Dania-Hollywood area that I have been exploring and I
love it. It is the wetlands of West Lake Park. I put in right off the road on
Dania Beach Boulevard, just west of the Intracoastal bridge. There you have
the option to paddle in the park through West Lake, and there are four
marked trails that can be followed to the Ann Kolb Nature Center, or to the
dry land off West Lake Park.

"Your other option is to paddle into the Intracoastal, under the Dania
Bridge, behind the old Seafare Marina, and you can drag or carry your boat a
short distance right to the ocean surf. Any way you go, it's a safe, easy paddle
with lots of scenery."

Broward County has fourteen parks, about half of them involving water.
West Lake Park, and the Ann Kolb Nature Center, are part of a 1,500-acre
mangrove preserve named after the late county commissioner who was a
staunch advocate of conservation. It's open during daylight hours, usually 8

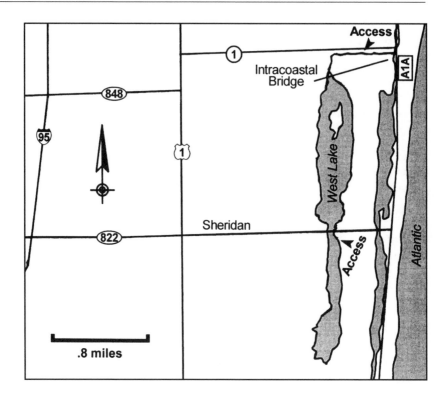

A.M. to 6 P.M. in the winter, and 8 A.M. to 7:30 P.M. in the summer. Call (954) 926-2480 for details.

A thirty-two-foot tourist boat provides forty-minute narrated tours through the preserve, and the park now advertises five trails. Paddled and electric-motor are the only craft allowed—no internal combustion engines.

Canoe and kayak rentals are available at the marina on the south side of Sheridan Street.

Directions to the park: Take the Sheridan Street/CR822 exit off I-95. Head east past Federal Highway, which is US1. West Lake Park's entrance is on the south/right side of the road. The Ann Kolb Nature Center is half a mile east of the entrance, on the north/left side.

Also try www.co.broward.fl.us/pri02302.htm.

Destination 88: Marco Island

Miles or average time: no limit, take your own time

Skill level: beginner

Current: mild tidal flows

Wind problems: yes, in very open bays

Emergency numbers: 911; Collier County sheriff, (941) 774-4434

Rentals: Beach Sports, 571 South Collier Boulevard, Marco Island FL 34145, phone (941) 642-4282; Tiger Tail Beach Rentals, 480 Hernando Drive, Marco Island FL 34145, phone (941) 642-8414

DeLorme page 110, section C-1

Official Florida canoe trail: no

Marco Island takes up twenty-four square miles, being roughly six miles long by six and a half miles wide. It is interlaced with a hundred miles of canals and two hundred of seawall, installed in 1965 by the Deltona Corporation. The resulting waterside homes are interesting to ogle, and nature lovers have only to paddle due north to meet miles of mangrove shorelines.

The Calusa Indians left several mounds in this area. One is in the tiny fishing settlement of Goodland, east of Marco Island. Another, named Indian Hill, is on the southeast corner of Marco Island, and at fifty-eight feet is the highest point in southwest Florida. The famous Marco Cat statue was discovered in Old Marco, at the northwest end of Marco Island. The original is now at the Smithsonian, but a replica is at the Collier County Museum in Naples.

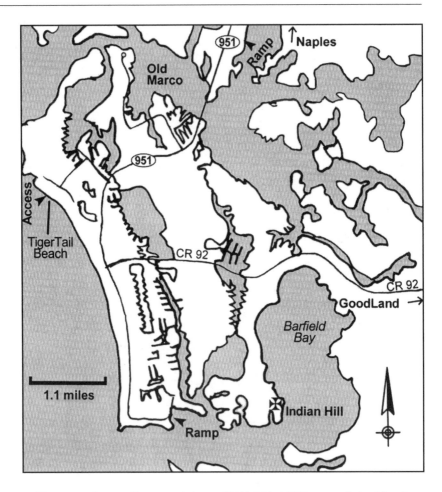

You can take a trolley tour (phone (941) 394-1600) around the island, or get the self-guided map from the Chamber of Commerce and save ten dollars. But I believe Marco Island is best seen from water level.

There are three places to launch.

1) Tiger Tail Beach on the southwest side of the island is especially popular with paddlers. The lagoon is open to the winds, but a long sandbar called Sanddollar Island breaks up most of the waves. The offshore areas consist of sand, sea grass, and pebbly ground. Best of all, there are no mosquitoes. Two long strips of protected dunes behind the beach are roped off as bird rookeries.

Tony Smith, who runs Tiger Tail Rentals, will tell you in his cheerful Cockney accent that this is the best place in the whole world to paddle. He has six sit-on-top kayaks, but can stock more with advance notice.

"Right this minute I can see two thousand least and royal terns, some plovers, and lots more birds," he said. "This is a natural beach, not one of the man-made ones. We have no noisy internal-combustion vehicles, but only electric, paddle, pedal, and sail boards."

To get to Tiger Tail Beach, enter Marco Island on SR951, also called North Collier Boulevard. Turn right/west on either Tigertail Court or Kendall Drive, then left/south on Hernando Drive, which dead-ends at the beach.

2) The north end of the island has a public launch ramp on SR951 coming into Marco.

3) At the southeast end of the island, there's a public ramp at Caxambas Pass Park on South Collier Boulevard.

You'll pass more marinas, fish camps, bait stores, and other places to launch just by driving along the bayside roads on the way to Old Marco, or to Goodland on SR92. North Barfield Drive, which connects all the finger lands on the inland side of the island, is fun to either drive, skate, bike, or paddle by, since the homes there are a mixture of plain and fancy.

Ponce de León landed at Caxambas Pass around 1513, and named the island San Marco. He thought the high sand dunes behind the beaches were foothills, and declared that all of Florida was mountainous. For the next century sailors stopped at the springs for fresh water, but few ventured past the intimidating barrier of mangroves and swampland to reach the mainland.

Those sailors were in big, clumsy boats. Your canoe or kayak can take you past huge hotels, quiet residential canals, bald eagle nests, sheltered lagoons, and primitive jungles.

For more information, contact the Collier County Visitor Information office at (941) 262-6141, or Marco Island Chamber of Commerce at (941) 394-7549.

Destination 89: Rookery Bay

Miles or average time: 2.5 miles or 1½ hours

Skill level: intermediate

Current: tidal creeks

Wind problems: yes, in exposed bays

Emergency numbers: 911; Collier County sheriff, (941) 774-4434

Rentals: Conservancy Briggs Nature Center, 401 Shell Island Road, Naples FL 34113, phone (941) 775-8569 or 755-7566 or 775-8845

DeLorme page 111, section D-1

Official Florida canoe trail: no

I'd expected silence, but life hummed all around us. Distant splashes denoted feeding redfish, jumping mullet, and skittering minnows. A male osprey *keerow'd* overhead, clutching a fish in his talons. He stopped on a tall dead stump to nibble at the head of the fish, then presented the properly subdued meal to the female guarding their nest of tangled sticks.

Thanks to some intelligent planning, Rookery Bay National Estuarine Research Reserve now covers 13,000 acres. The sanctuary is teeming with wildlife, especially early in the morning. It's a fantastic birding location. You'll see roseate spoonbills and other wading birds, as well as ospreys and bald eagles.

Feeding manatees snort and blow in the deeper channels. Three mullet almost jumped into my boat, chased by an unseen predator. We followed the dark head of a sea turtle until it disappeared around a bend.

Briggs Nature Center, part of the Conservancy, is located six miles north of Marco Island. To get there from I-75, take exit 15, travel south about 2½ miles on SR951, and turn right/west on Shell Island Road.

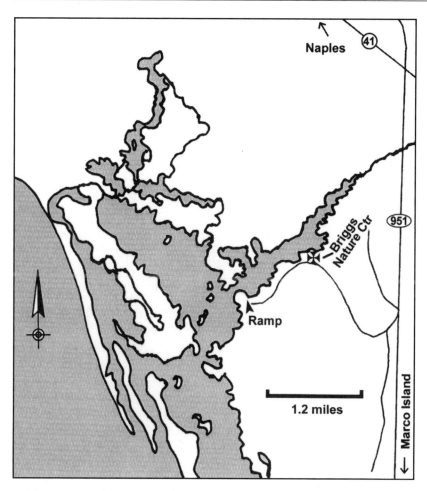

The canoe trail starts at the boat ramp at the end of Shell Island Road. You can launch your own canoe or kayak there. Canoes are not rented on windy days. The trail is well marked and easy to follow. Stretches of shady mangrove tunnels open into frequent hidden lakes. Capsizing is not a worry, since most of the canoe trail is only thigh deep.

There's supposed to be another Calusa Indian mound in the area, but I haven't found it yet. What we did encounter were two prancing reddish egrets, a dozen spoonbills, a tiny islet covered with egrets, a great horned owl hooting from a dead tree, and an indignant kingfisher that followed us for fifty feet, scolding us for invading his territory. When we finally drifted past his invisible boundary, he flew back to an overhanging branch, satisfied that he'd protected his kingdom for another day.

Destination 90: West Lake

Miles or average time: 7.7 miles or 4–5 hours

Skill level: intermediate

Current: gentle tidal drifts

Wind problems: on windy days, stay away

Emergency numbers: 911; Monroe County sheriff, (305) 292-7075

Rentals: Everglades International Hostel and Canoe Rental, 20 SW 2nd Avenue, Homestead FL 33034, phone (305) 248-1122; Flamingo Lodge, 1 Flamingo Lodge Highway, Homestead FL 33034, phone (941) 695-3101

DeLorme page 121, section C-3

Official Florida canoe trail: no, but it is part of Everglades National Park

Several years ago, a female alligator built her nest so close to the Flamingo Highway that she slept with her chin on the asphalt. Rangers had to cordon off the area to keep her from being run over. She has moved away now, so you can get into West Lake again.

There are seven canoe trails in the Flamingo area: Nine Mile Pond Loop, Noble Hammock Trail, Hells Bay Trail, Florida Bay, Bear Lake Canal, Mud Lake Loop, and West Lake Trail. Information on all of these is available at Everglades National Park visitor centers.

My favorite trail is West Lake. Narrow mangrove-lined canals lead from one lake or bight to another, like beads on a string. Early morning and low tide are the best times to see wildlife. A large colony of roseate spoonbills live

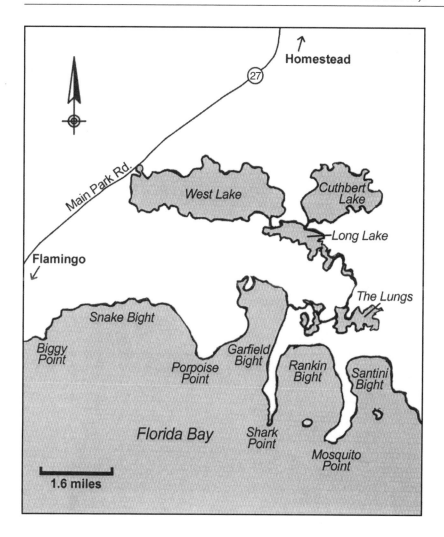

in this area, and I saw a flock of four dozen of these lovely pink birds beside Alligator Creek. You might even spot a rare American crocodile.

West Lake is closed to boats with motors over 5.5 hp, and no motors at all are allowed from the east end of the lake to Garfield Bight.

To get here from Homestead/Florida City, drive west on SR27, which is the first traffic light south of the Turnpike terminus. Follow the Everglades National Park signs to the entrance gate. There is a $10 entrance fee, plus a $5 ramp fee to use the concrete ramp at Flamingo Lodge. Make sure you gas up around US1, since it is forty miles to the lodge.

The West Lake ramp is on the south side of the road, 2.8 miles south of the bend where SR27/9336 changes from due south to southwest; if you get to Flamingo, you've gone seven miles too far south.

Do take a compass, a GPS, a map, mosquito repellent, and water. The canals are easy to follow, but watch for landmarks, since it is easy to get turned around in the Ten Thousand Islands area.

Keep a good distance from any mound of dead grass you pass. That mother alligator might be nesting again.

Destination 91: Wilderness Waterway

Miles or average time: 99 miles or 10 days

Skill level: intermediate, and strong arms will help

Current: very strong in river mouths, plus strong tidal flows

Wind problems: yes, in open bays

Emergency numbers: 911; Monroe County sheriff, (941) 292-7075

Rentals: Everglades National Park, 40001 SR 9336, Homestead FL 33034-6733, phone (305) 242-7700, website www.nps.gov/ever/; Flamingo Visitor Center or Gulf Coast (Everglades City) Visitor Center, PO Box 120, Everglades City FL 34139, phone (941) 695-3311; Florida Bay Outfitters, 104050 Overseas Highway (MM 104), Key Largo FL 33037, phone (305) 451-3018, website www.pennekamp.com/fbout; North American Canoe Tours, 107 Camellia Street, Everglades City FL 34139, phone (941) 695-4666

DeLorme page 116, section B-2, to page 121, section C-2

Official Florida canoe trail: no, but a National Park trail

If you don't have eleven or twelve days available for the entire trip, at least take a day to paddle around either end of this wonderful trail. You can tour Chokoloskee Bay, visit Sandfly Island constructed by the Calusa Indians, or go bird-watching along a canoe trail at Flamingo (destination 90).

If you have the time, do the whole trip. This is the experience of a lifetime.

The Wilderness Waterway follows the lower tip of the Florida peninsula. The tangle of mangrove islands, twisting creeks, hidden bays, and shallow, hot-water grass flats is called the Ten Thousand Islands, but it should really

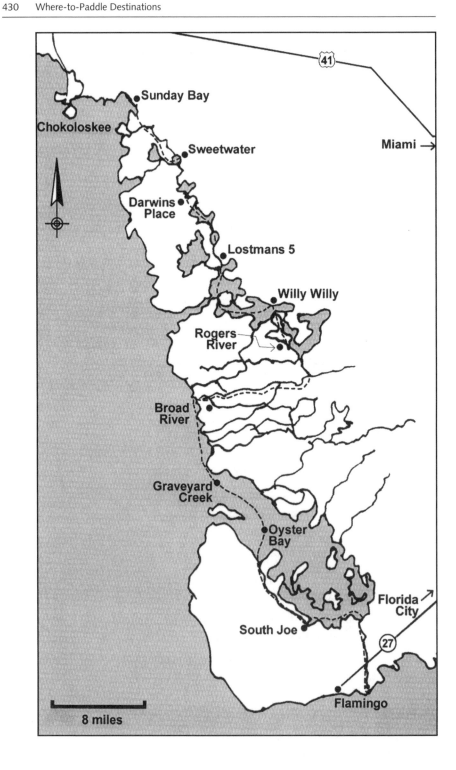

be named the One Zillion Islands. There are no cliffs, huge trees, or fancy
rock formations. Instead, you'll see a hundred miles of low mangrove forests,
deserted beaches, and vast, shallow bays.

When John James Audubon first visited in 1832, huge flocks of birds
waded, fed, and bred here. Then Europeans arrived. You've heard the story of
the plume hunters who wiped out whole colonies of birds. The word "egret"
comes from the French *aigrette*, meaning plume.

It is hard to imagine how the early settlers survived the heat and bugs.
Read *Lost Man's River* by Peter Matthiessen to get a glimpse of these lawless,
grudge-holding pioneers.

Everglades National Park still has many problems. Pollution from the two
and a half million people who populate the east coast is creeping into the
water table. On busy weekends you can barely find a place to park your car at
Flamingo Lodge. In summer the mosquitoes and gnats are so bad that you
can't buy a permit because nobody is around to sell you one.

But from November to May, this is one of the most magical and complex
tours you can make by boat. In fact, going by canoe or kayak is the only way
to get back inside some of these secret coves.

This is where the great blue heron and the reddish egret show up in their
rare white phases. Watch for a white-crowned pigeon, the trademark bird of
the Keys. Some four hundred kinds of birds have been spotted here, plus
alligators, manatees, ospreys, yellow sulfur butterflies, bald eagles, and the
fifty-eight lonely crocodiles left in Florida.

Plan and equip your trip with care. This ninety-nine-mile, ten-day paddle
is strongly influenced by weather, seasons, governmental restrictions, and
your own paddling ability. A medium-sized kayak with internal storage is
probably the vessel of choice.

Err on the side of caution. If storms are forecast, cancel your trip. The trail
leads across open bays, and the combination of waves, wind, tidal currents,
oyster bars, and unprotected campsites is a guarantee of a wet and miserable
week. We had one cold, rainy day, and were never so delighted to see the sun
come back out. You can call the Miami weather report at (305) 661-5065,
check the long-term forecast on TV, listen to radio channel 1, or ask the rangers and canoe rental people, who make it their business to know the weather
forecasts.

The wide, warm bays of the Upper Keys are nursery areas for dozens of species. The fishing is great too. Courtesy of Visit Florida.

I guarantee you'll get lost at least once. Practice how to use your maps, GPS, radio, and cell phone before you hit the water. Tide charts and a detailed nautical map are for sale at the Visitor Center. The Gulf Coast and Flamingo Ranger Stations monitor channel 16. And there's an emergency twenty-four-hour dispatch station at Park HQ at (305) 242-7740. You could also flag down a passing motorboat and use their radio.

The National Park Service has built forty-seven campsites, each big enough for six to sixty people. Some thirty-one of them have self-contained toilets. There are three kinds of camps: (1) roofed wooden platforms called chickees (these sleep six, but four people would be more comfortable), (2) sites on open beaches, and (3) inland high ground, sometimes on old Indian mounds.

Since you can't use stakes on a wooden chickee or in loose sand, use a self-supporting tent, and tie it to the chickee posts or even a stunted tree in case of wind. Extra rope and bungee cords are handy for three-way-tying your canoe or kayak, hoisting your food overhead to keep it away from raccoons, lashing a tarp over your gear when it rains, making a sunshade for lunch stops, and the like.

You'll also need a gallon of water a day per person, insect repellent, insect netting or netting suits, several trash bags, a trowel for digging cat holes if you're in a spot with no toilet, toilet paper, eleven days' worth of no-refrigeration food in zip-shut plastic bags, a tie-on sun hat, paddling gloves, long-sleeved shirt and long, loose pants for sun and insects, sunscreen, toe-covering shoes for oyster beds, polarized sunglasses, rain gear, swimsuit, inflatable mattress, sleeping bag or sheet bag, fire starters, a tiny Spider camp stove with utensils, two tarps, biodegradable soap, and the thirty other indispensable things listed in the camping chapter at the beginning of the book.

Everglades raccoons are the most aggressive I've ever met. Adult coons can open an ice chest in seconds, gnaw through milk jugs to lap up your extra water, and even slit open tents—with people in them! They'll hop right into your beached boat looking for food. Store your food inside your battened-down kayak compartment or a strapped-shut ice chest. Be liberal with the black pepper spray.

The bigger campsites have room for more than one party, and you'll develop new friendships with other boaters traveling in the same direction. Unfortunately, at one middle camp, a bunch of drunks from two powerboats rip-roared past midnight. We discussed siccing the local raccoons on them.

Here's a trip plan I used several years ago. We took the inside route from Chokoloskee to Flamingo, only paddling along the exposed beach to Shark Point and Graveyard Creek on day seven. Your trip will probably differ, depending on tides, wind, and other campers.

We tried to start paddling shortly after dawn each day. The goal was to arrive at the next campground in the early afternoon. That gave us four or five extra hours of daylight in case the winds or tides were against us or we got lost. Most days we arrived in time to pitch camp and then explore the local area before supper. We discussed how we could spend the night sitting up in a canoe if we got very, very lost. These discussions usually degenerated into completely batty scenarios involving "cordon black" meals, inventive uses for mosquito netting, and strange potty arrangements.

> Day 0: Before your trip: Get your $10 back-country permit from a ranger at the visitor center. Drop off a car at Flamingo Visitor Center, about a three-hour drive from Chokoloskee. Hang around the campground, canoe rental station, or boat ramp and eavesdrop when the experts give advice.
>
> Day 1: Launch very early at Chokoloskee. Paddle 11 miles to Sunday Bay chickee, with a stop at Lopez River chickee for lunch. Erect tent. Repack your canoe or kayak now that you know what gear can be put away out of reach.
>
> Day 2: Get up at dawn. Paddle 8.5 miles to Sweetwater chickee.
>
> Day 3: Paddle 11.5 miles to Plate Creek, with a lunch stop at Darwin's Place.
>
> Day 4: Paddle 11.5 miles to Willy Willy ground camp.
>
> Day 5: Short day. Paddle 3.6 miles to Roger's River chickee.
>
> Day 6: Paddle 11.5 miles to Broad River ground campsite.
>
> Day 7: Paddle 9 miles to Graveyard Creek ground site. Tell ghost stories until midnight.
>
> Day 8: Paddle 10 miles to Oyster Bay chickee.
>
> Day 9: Paddle 10 miles to South Joe River chickee.
>
> Day 10: Paddle the last 11 miles to Flamingo, with a portage over the dam at Buttonwood Canal. Celebrate!

William G. Truesdale's book on the Wilderness Waterway goes over the route thoroughly, and is available at the visitor centers. Read Brad Manley's excellent account of his ten-day trip at www.paddlefl.com/destinations/glades/glades.htm.

Conclusion

Does this book include *all* the places to canoe and kayak in Florida? Absolutely not. It only gives you a good start. Now that you've been introduced to paddling, you will find yourself scrutinizing every canal, river, pond, and lake for places to launch and explore. You'll peer past superhighways, glitzy condominiums, and sprawling malls in search of hidden glints of water.

You will realize that paddling is not only an inexpensive way to travel, it is truly a magic carpet, an entry to a seldom seen part of Florida that most people never experience. You will see birds and animals in their native, natural homes, and brush past lush plants that arrived in Florida during the last ice age.

If you think you have a lot to learn, you are not alone. Don't be afraid to ask questions. The people who run the canoe liveries not only love to paddle but are eager to share their knowledge of local waterways. If you want company, join a paddling club for an extra-special trip.

Every time you step into your boat, you are transformed. You are no longer an office worker or teacher but an explorer. Imagine yourself as the first Indian to paddle the upper reaches of Tampa Bay, or a Spanish conquistador intent on finding the Fountain of Youth, or even a grizzled riverboat captain making his thousandth steamboat trip up the Silver River. In modern times, you can watch the space shuttle blast into the heavens from Cape Canaveral.

Florida is surrounded and laced with water. For diversity and year-round paddling adventure, our state can't be beat. This book is a mere introduction to the many places you can explore by boat.

Grab your paddle and go!

Appendix 1: Paddling Clubs

Paddling clubs provide instant friends—fellow paddlers who know the ropes, will pitch in to help load gear, and provide good companionship. It's also nice to have someone else plan a trip—where to put in and take out, where to park the cars, where to pitch camp, and so on. Most clubs ask that you do your part and plan a trip yourself now and then.

Clubs are also a good way to find used equipment for sale, and advice on which equipment is the best.

If you're worried about legal liability as a trip leader, the 1997 Volunteer Protection Act, Public Law 105-19, gives you a legal umbrella. You are not at fault if you act in good faith, and to the best of your personal abilities. This act does not cover gross negligence, reckless misconduct, or harm caused by your misoperation of a licensed vehicle. It is still advisable to have some form of liability insurance, such as is offered by the ACA membership.

Clubs are often the brainchild of one good organizer, and if this person moves or drops out, the club may decline. Your local canoe shop probably knows about nearby paddling clubs, and may even sponsor one. Brad Manley at Paddle Florida! also keeps up an online list. Check his information at www.paddlefl.com. Or run a web search using the keywords canoe+club+fl.

- American Canoe Association, Inc., 7432 Alban Station Boulevard, Suite B-226, Springfield VA 22150, phone (703) 451-0141, fax (703) 451-2245, e-mail acadirect@aol.com, website www.aca-paddler.org. Established in 1880, this venerable group puts out two publications: the newsletter *American Canoeist* and *Paddler* magazine. You can order instructional videos, join trips, and read up on technique. Membership in the ACA is required by several clubs for insurance purposes. The $15 registration fee is good value, and if you become a life member for $500 you get a free laminated wood paddle. They also have an on-line magazine at www.aca-paddler.org/paddler.
- American Whitewater Association, PO Box 636, Margaretville NY 12455, phone (845) 586-2355, e-mail whiteh2o@catskill.net. This watchdog or-

ganization strives to keep more waterways open for paddling. Dues are
$25 individual, $35 family. Florida really doesn't have any white water,
with only one real rapid on the Suwannee, but if you'd like to go further
with your paddling, this group knows the places to go.

- Apalachee Canoe Club, PO Box 4027, Tallahassee FL 32315.
- Buzzard Flapper Canoe Club, e-mail greg@buzzardflapper.com, website
www.buzzardflapper.com. This group is centered in Georgia, and makes
forays into Florida and Alabama.
- By the Bay Outfitters, proprietor John Allaman, e-mail bythebay@home.
com, has trips and canoe tours.
- Citrus Paddling Club, Route 1, Box 415, Floral City FL 32636.
- Coastal Kayaking Association, St. Marys GA, e-mail epitt@gate.net.
- Coconut Kayakers, PO Box 3646, Tequesta FL 33469.
- Emerald Coast Paddlers, PO Box 2424, Fort Walton Beach FL 32549,
phone (904) 678-4159, e-mail kayaks@emeraldcoast.com or alexg2@aol.
com. This active group has found many places to paddle around the panhandle. One newsletter listed thirty-nine upcoming trips. Dues are $10 a
year for singles, $15 for families.
- Florida Competition Paddlers Association, contact G. Williams, 1725
Georgia Avenue NE, St. Petersburg FL 33703, phone (727) 525-7588, or
Larry Frederick, phone (352) 495-9846, e-mail LFred@ibm.net. The
members like to paddle fast, and stage a couple of events every month. A
sample would be a twelve-mile race down the Weeki Wachee River, or
eight miles of the Suwannee. Annual dues are $15 a year for a single, $20
for a family or business membership.
- Florida Professional Paddlesports Association. Your local canoe livery is
probably already a member. They try to set professional standards for
safety, equipment, PR, conservation, business practices, education, and
trip planning.
- Florida Sea Kayaking Association, contact Bruce Meier, 3068 North Mer-
lin Drive, Jacksonville FL 32257, e-mail kayakers@hotmail.com, website
www.jacksonville.net/~didecker/fska.htm. This club has officers and members in Tallahassee, Central Florida, Miami, Fort Myers, and Jacksonville.
They sponsor clinics, paddling instruction, and many trips.

- Florida Sport Paddling Club, contact Heminger, 3835 Malec Circle, Sarasota FL 34233. One of the oldest paddling clubs in the state, they have trips almost every weekend and usually plan a big trip each summer. Dues are $15 individual, $20 family. ACA membership is advised, or participants will be charged $5 per outing.
- Kayak Treks, 1239 Beneva Road South, Sarasota FL 34232, phone (941) 365-3892 or 1-800-656-3891, e-mail kayakgide1@aol.com, website www.kayaktreks.com. This may not be exactly a club, but owner Bob organizes monthly guided trips, picnics, competitions, games, and moonlight cruises around the Sarasota area. E-mail him and ask to be put on his list of addresses to receive his electronic newsletters. He gives a discount if you bring your own boat. He also sells boats and equipment on consignment and takes trade-ins.
- King's Landing Canoe Club, 5714 Baptist Camp Road, Apopka FL 32712, phone (407) 886-0859.
- Marion County Aquaholics Paddlers Group, PO Box 1138, Citra FL 32113, phone (352) 595-7009, e-mail fralick@atlanta.net.
- Mugwump Canoe Club, 9025 Sunset Drive, Miami FL 33173.
- Open Ocean Canoeing, Fort Lauderdale. Member John Gage says, "Just walk up to 600 South Seabreeze, Fort Lauderdale, any Saturday morning, and go canoeing." You can contact him at d02224c@dcfreenet.seflin.lib.fl.us.
- Seminole Canoe & Kayak Club, 4619 Ortega Farms Circle, Jacksonville FL 32210, phone (904) 778-8621.
- Sierra Club, Florida Chapter, 214 North 17 Street, Fernandina Beach FL 32034-2608, or 462 Fernwood Road, Key Biscayne FL 33149, website www.sierraclub.org/chapters/fl/outings.html. The Sierra Club has chapters all over the state. They run canoe trips, hikes, biking, nature walks, birding walks, and more.
- Silent Otters Paddling Club, 28608 NW 142 Avenue, High Springs FL 32643, phone (904) 454-1082, e-mail ObLaDi4me@aol.com. The Otters are centered around High Springs. Their home waterway is the Santa Fe River. They meet the second Thursday of each month.
- Space Coast Paddlers, PO Box 360193, Melbourne FL 32936, phone (407) 773-4664.

- Southwest Florida Paddling Club, Marty Walker, phone (941) 936-3028, e-mail marty@cyberstreet.com.
- Suwannee Paddlers, 1512 Cambridge Drive, Cocoa FL 32922. Bill Logan, who wrote *Canoeing and Camping the 213 miles of the Beautiful Suwannee River,* organizes weekend paddle trips. Check them out at www.canoe-suwannee.com.
- Tampa Bay Sea Kayakers, 765 24 Avenue N, St. Petersburg FL 33704, phone (727) 898-2907. This group erected and maintains the trail signs at Weedon Island in St. Pete.
- West Florida Canoe Club, PO Box 17203, Pensacola FL 32522, phone (904) 932-3756.
- Wilderness Trekkers, 8611 Bay View Court, Orlando FL 32836- 6309, e-mail wildtreker@aol.com, website www.geocities.com/~wild-trek/. Organizers Kim and Dave Lippey describe Wilderness Trekkers as a nonprofit organization formed by people who enjoy hiking, canoeing, camping, and backpacking in the wilderness. It is organized and operated for and by its members, with no paid staff. With more than a thousand members in seven states, the organization puts people with the same outdoor interests in touch with each other through free impromptu activities, educational and recreational activities, and seminars. Membership is $15 a year for singles, $20 for a family. Kim also posts photos from her past trips on her website, which give you a good idea of what to expect on the waterway.

Finding a Local Club near You

There is no club in the list that's near your house? Look in the Yellow Pages under "Canoes, rental" and ask if they know of a club. If they don't, think about organizing one of your own.

For ideas on how to run your own club, contact the American Canoe Association, and talk to several people in other clubs listed above. Find out what makes trips enjoyable, how to get the word out about your new group, and legal liability (this mostly consists of having a signed roster and ACA membership, and not drinking).

Besides canoe and kayak clubs, there are many organizations that are devoted to conservation and preservation, from Audubon to Swiftmud. One such is Current Problems Inc., PO Box 753, Alachua FL 32616, phone (352) 472-2920, on the web at www.currentproblems.org.

Cyber Clubs, E-zines, and On-Line Information

- *Paddle Florida! Online Canoeing and Kayaking Guide,* www.brainee.com/ paddlefl/Destinations.htm or www.paddlefl.com. Brad Manley publishes an e-zine (on-line magazine) with "descriptions of Florida rivers and waterways for canoeists and kayakers." If you're thinking of tackling a specific river, check *Paddle Florida!* to see if there's a nice recent description of the river in his index. If you have been on a terrific paddling adventure, write up a description of the trip and send it in to Brad at paddlefl@brainee. com. Brad stays in touch with many liveries, conservation groups, and policymakers, so he's active in keeping our rivers and waterways in top shape for paddlers.
- *Florida Outdoors.* Another on-line canoe and kayak magazine, they are at www.florida-outdoors.com. Their index covers: Canoe and Kayak Safety, Vessel Registration, Canoes and Kayaks for Florida, Paddling Along the River, Paddling Products, Tides, Where to Canoe/Kayak, Instruction, and FAQ (Frequently Asked Questions).
- *Suwannee River E-zine.* Bill Logan not only has a book out about the Suwannee, he has a nice home page about the river. He also organizes trips on various sections of this and other rivers, and invites anyone interested to come along. He does ask for reservations so he'll know how many to expect, and limits the size of each group. For big groups, he brings along an extra Coleman stove, big pots, special latrines, and such. Check his latest newsletter at www.canoe-suwannee.com.

Appendix 2: Suggested Reading

Your trips will be safer and more enjoyable if you have a few references on
hand. Here are the ones that I use:

Maps

- DeLorme's *Florida: Atlas and Gazetteer* (Yarborough, Maine: DeLorme,
  128 pages, $19.95). So many Florida paddlers use DeLorme's book of
  maps that I've keyed the locations of each paddling destination to this
  atlas.

  The index is on the back cover, showing which pages cover which sections of the state. The maps show boat ramps, museums, recreation areas,
  theme parks, bicycle routes, fishing piers, historic sites, campgrounds, the
  Florida Trail, golf courses, springs, and of course the official state canoe
  trails. The scale is 1:150,000, or one inch to 2.4 miles. If all the maps were
  laid out, the mosaic would measure 17.5 feet wide by 15.5 feet high. It's
  available at drug and discount stores, or you can order a copy at 1-800-
  452-5931 or www.delorme.com.

  This book's only drawback is its ungainly size (11" x 15"). Ordering a
  cover is a good idea, since my last three editions got wrinkled fast.
- U.S. Geological Survey topographical maps. For vendors of these detailed
  maps, look under "Maps and Charts" in your Yellow Pages. You can also
  write to: U.S. Geological Survey, Map Information Office, Washington DC
  20242.

Bird Watching

- *The Sibley Guide to Birds,* by David Sibley (New York: Knopf, 544 pages,
  $35.00). Comprehensive coverage of North American birds, with detailed
  paintings of male and female birds at various ages.
- *Stokes Field Guide to Birds: Eastern Region,* by Donald and Lillian Stokes
  (Boston: Little, Brown, 471 pages, $17.95). Photos and a write-up about

each bird are on the same page. A quick index is on the inside of the covers, and the edge of each page is color coded so you can instantly flip to all the ducks, shorebirds, warblers, or whatever.

- *Field Guide to the Birds of North America,* 3d ed., by Jon L. Dunn (Washington, D.C.: National Geographic Society, 480 pages, $21.95). Instead of photos, this book has color paintings, and birds of a type are shown on the same page, which makes identifying them easier. Its stitched binding holds up to repeated use.
- *Florida's Fabulous Waterbirds,* by photographer Winston Williams. Gorgeous photos of fifty-five bird species, plus tidbits of information about their habits. Available at $9.95 at bookstores and tourist spots, or from World Wide Printing, PO Box 24339, Tampa FL 33623.

Florida Animals

- *National Audubon Society Field Guide to Florida* (New York: Knopf, 447 pages, $19.95). Brad Manley, who publishes the on-line paddling magazine *Paddle Florida!,* recommends this. "It covers birds, animals, trees, wildflowers, insects, weather, and more," he says. "It replaces a stack of other guides in the field."
- *Harper and Row's Complete Field Guide to North American Wildlife, Eastern Edition,* by Henry Hill Collins. Using drawings instead of photos, this 714-page guidebook touches on most of the birds, mammals, reptiles, amphibians, fish, mollusks, and other life that you might run across while paddling. It's out of print now, but try used-book vendors in your area, or web sources like www.alibris.com.

State Parks

The State of Florida puts out a good booklet listing the 150 state parks throughout the state. For a free copy, call (850) 488-9872 or 1-800-529-5329 and ask for Document #500, or try www.dep.state.fl.us/parks.

Appendix 3: Glossary

abeam—directly away from the center of the boat at a right angle to the bow-stern line

aft—in or toward the stern

ahead—in front of the boat

amidships—in or toward the middle of the boat

astern—behind the boat

beam—the width of the boat at its widest part

bow—the front part of the boat

bowman—the paddler at the front of the boat

deadheading—the practice of leaving cars at both ends of a run, usually done by dropping off the boats at the launch spot, moving all the cars to the takeout spot, then bringing the drivers back in one vehicle, which stays at the launch site and is picked up after the trip

forward—in or toward the bow

gunwale, pronounced gunnel here in the South—finishing strip at the upper edge of a boat's side

leeward—the downwind side of the boat or shoreline

logjam—an obstruction caused by fallen trees or other obstacles

port—when facing forward, the left side of the boat

starboard—when facing forward, the right side of the boat

stern—the back end of the boat

sternman or steersman—the paddler at the back of the boat

strainer—an obstruction in the channel, usually fallen trees, where water can flow freely but a boat cannot pass

thwart—a lateral bar or other stiffening support that stretches from gunwale to gunwale

windward—the direction from which the wind is blowing; also the side of the boat that the wind hits first

Appendix 4: Florida State Parks with Canoe Rentals

Anastasia State Recreation Area
Big Lagoon State Recreation Area
Blackwater River State Park
Blue Spring State Park
Bulow Plantation Ruins State Historic Site
Collier-Seminole State Park
Dead Lakes State Recreation Area
DeLeon Springs State Recreation Area
Econfina River State Park
Faver-Dykes State Park
Florida Caverns State Park
Fort Cooper State Park
Gold Head Branch State Park
Guana River State Park
Hillsborough River State Park
Hontoon Island State Park
Hugh Taylor Birch State Recreation Area
Ichetucknee Springs State Park
Indian Key State Historic Site
John Pennekamp Coral Reef State Park
John U. Lloyd Beach State Recreation Area
Jonathan Dickinson State Park
Koreshan State Historic Site
Lake Griffin State Recreation Area
Lake Kissimmee State Park
Lake Louisa State Park
Lake Manatee State Recreation Area
Little Manatee River State Recreation Area
Little Talbot Island State Park

Long Key State Recreation Area
Lower Wekiva River State Preserve
Maclay State Gardens
Manatee Springs State Park
Myakka River State Park
Ochlockonee River State Park
O'Leno State Park
Oleta River State Recreation Area
Oscar Scherer State Park
Paynes Prairie State Preserve
Rock Springs Run State Reserve
Silver River State Park
Stephen Foster State Folk Culture Center
St. Joseph Peninsula State Park
Suwannee River State Park
Three Rivers State Recreation Area
Tomoka State Park
Waccasassa Bay State Preserve
Wekiwa Springs State Park

Appendix 5: Florida's Official State Canoe Trails

The Florida Department of Environmental Protection, Office of Greenways and Trails, has designated thirty-nine official canoe trails around the state. These have been chosen for beauty, moderate ease of paddling, and accessibility. The Terra Ceia canoe trail might be added shortly to this list. A full-color brochure is available by calling toll-free 1-877-822-5208, or you can access their website at www8.myflorida.com/communities/learn/trails/canoe.

Alafia River
Aucilla River
Blackwater River
Blackwater River/Royal Palm Hammock Creek
Bulow Creek
Chipola River
Coldwater Creek
Econfina Creek
Econlockhatchee River
Estero River
Hickory Creek
Hillsborough River
Historic Big Bend Saltwater Paddling Trail
Holmes Creek
Little Manatee River
Loxahatchee River
Manatee River (Upper)
Ochlockonee River (Lower) (not in this book)
Ochlockonee River (Upper)
Peace River
Pellicer Creek
Perdido River

Pithlachascotee River

Santa Fe River

Shoal River

Sopchoppy River

Spruce Creek

St. Marys River

Suwannee River (Lower)

Suwannee River (Upper)

Sweetwater/Juniper Creeks

Tomoka River

Wacissa River

Wakulla River

Wekiva River/Rock Springs Run

Withlacoochee River (North)

Withlacoochee River (South)

Yellow River

Guest Authors

Arnie Diedrichs loves water and has paddled much of Florida's east coast by canoe.

For *Jean Faulk,* exploring the Hillsborough River is a daily task. She and her family run Canoe Escape Outfitters in Thonotosassa, Florida.

A systems analyst with a major computer firm, *Bryce Huff* spends most of his free time hiking with his dog or accompanying his mother, Sandy, on canoe expeditions.

John Phillips has used his military background to prepare for his paddling expeditions. He tries to paddle the Suwannee annually.

Larry Reed is a dedicated paddler and has explored most of central Florida by water.

Nancy Scharmach is the executive director of the Florida Outdoor Writers Association. Her first kayaking experience at Matlacha (egged on by Sandy) led her to buy her own kayak, and she has now explored dozens of Florida waterways.

Laurilee Thompson runs A Day Away livery in Titusville. She is active in the east coast paddling community and is part owner of a seafood restaurant.

Contributors

Writing this book has been a lesson in humility.

Two years ago, Dan Spinella and I chatted during a Florida Outdoor Writers Association conference. Dan mentioned that he was an editor with University Press of Florida and was looking for someone to write a "where to" book on canoeing and kayaking in Florida.

I cockily said that I was an expert, having at that time paddled some fifty-five rivers around Florida. Plus I'd taught canoeing for the American Red Cross for years. And as an outdoor and travel writer, I had almost 800 published articles under my belt, with probably two-thirds of them written about Florida destinations. "I know this state like the back of my hand," I bragged.

Was that a dumb statement!

The gaps in my memory were the size of Lake Okeechobee. My notes left out practical items like ramp locations and driving directions. Instead, I remembered that dew-spangled spiderweb that stretched completely across a stream, or the time we saw the herd of pigs, or the morning I caught a huge catfish before breakfast.

No problem, I blithely thought. I'd just look at a map. So I whipped out five sets of maps—and found to my dismay that none of them agreed. And I still didn't remember which side of the bridge that particular ramp was on, or the name of the outfitter who rented us kayaks when we'd left our own canoes at home, or how many hours it took to paddle all the way up to the head of that gorgeous spring.

I made many trips back to rivers I'd paddled for years, checking on details and trying out new spots (the count is now up to sixty-eight waterways that I've paddled, with numberless coves, creeks, and little bays that weren't big or interesting or safe enough to put into this book). Still, there are endless details in a book of this nature. Having zip and area codes change meant that my twenty-plus years of files, records, Rolodex numbers, and even my own old articles needed to be updated too.

Joe Faulk, owner of Canoe Escape at the Hillsborough River outside Tampa (see destination 52), suggested letting the livery operators and other experts lend a hand.

When I called for help, dozens of people responded. My paddling partners shared stories, hints, secret put-ins, and easy-to-reach haul-outs. They and others pitched in with advice, proofreading, critiquing drafts of chapters, putting captions on maps, letting me copy newsletter reports, or loaning photos for the book. Then there were all the people whose names I never learned—operators of fish camps, media liaisons at convention and visitor bureaus, professional PR people, fish biologists, wildlife rangers, FWC officers, park rangers, canoe manufacturers, passing paddlers, fishermen, and bait and tackle salespeople who cheerfully answered questions, pointed downstream, and made life easier.

If the advice and directions are right, thank the experts who patiently corrected my faulty memory. They've been super.

They include:

John Allaman, Gail Allen, Arbie Arbuthnot, Bill Aucoin, Vicki Bailey, Barbara at Hidden Ranch, Carol Beal, Cuma Beirne, Paula and Perry Benshoff, Wes Biggs, Roseann Bosclair, Dick Bowles, Becky Bragg, Wendy Brenner, Joe Brocato, Earl and Betty Brubaker, "High Sheriff" Hardy Bryant, Teddy Buell, Leila Bugenhagen, Hoagie Carmichael, Arnie Diedrichs, the Doucettes, Ed Duklewski, Carolyn and Bill Eaton, Tim Egan, Bob and Barbara Epstein, Joe, Jean, and Brian Faulk, Mark and Liz Godula, Peggy and Bill Goldberg, Nancy Hamilton, Roger and Dorothy Harbster, Tiffany Hardy, Don Hastings, Paul and Carl Hegner, Marty Hoffman, Chris Hofgren, "Big Al" Hubbard, M. Hugendorf, Charlie Hunsicker, Bob Huttemeyer, Walt Jennings, John Kiseda, Jutta Kohl, Dyane Koskela, Gloria Kuchinskas, Gobby Kuhn (look what you started!), Arlene Lane, Frank and Jan Lapniewski, Doris Leeper, Chris Linhoff, Kim Lippy, Nicolette and Ed Makruski, Brad Manley, Chuck McIntire, Anthony Meola, Jim Miller, Reed Miller, Lawson Mitchell, Frank and Kathy Morello, Frank and Jean Mueller, Nancy Musser, Sonny Norris, Laura Patterson, John Phillips, Pat and Jim Pochurek, Rosemary Potter, Joe Quimby, Larry Reed, SarahBeth and Clint Reeves, Walt Reynolds, Serena Rinker, Duke Rountree, Esther Sanborn, Frank Sargeant, Nancy Scharmach, Robin Smillie, Linda Smith, Rodney Smith, Tony Smith, Chris Thoemke,

Chad Thompson, Laurilee Thompson, Candace Tinkler, Pam Traas, Cheryl Twining, Bob and Loree Van Leer, Jim Wagner, Shelley Whiting, Sandy Wieher, Joanne Williams, Marty Williamson, Eddie Williford, *all* the Windlasses, Sofia Zander, and—

In the family: son Bryce, who not only is my paddling companion but took over the mapmaking chores; daughter Teresa, my organizer and administrative assistant; daughter Wendy and our three grandkids, Logan, Sean, and Kira, who let me use my own computer now and then; and especially my ever patient boat-loader, message-relayer, and resolute landlubber, my husband, Bill.

Index

This book is written by a grandmother!

A prizewinning photojournalist, Sandy Huff has published more than 800 articles in more than a hundred magazines and newspapers. She specializes in travel and outdoor articles, and is a member of the National League of American Penwomen and the Florida Outdoor Writers Association.

But she'd rather talk about her paddling experiences. Or about the bird colony she monitors near her home in Safety Harbor, Florida. Or the best way to cook freshwater mussels. Or how to get a loaded canoe across a log-jam. Or about the time she capsized right beside a bull alligator. (Ask her about the five bull gators she bagged from a canoe.)

Sandy grew up in Miami, the gateway to the Everglades, where she spent many a day exploring the beaches, canals, and sawgrass swamps. She discovered the midstate lakes and streams when attending church camps. In high school she joined a scuba diving club and spent fascinated hours face to face with moray eels, sting rays, and manatees. In college, her marine biology professor arranged for his students to ride along on research vessels and all-night shrimp boats, and Sandy developed the best saltwater aquarium in town. When she transferred to the University of Florida for her B.S. degree, then went on to UNC–Chapel Hill for an M.A., she managed to find time to tube, paddle, snorkel, sail, and powerboat every body of water she could find.

When her three kids came along, Sandy organized a traveling Girl Scout troop. Somehow, most troop excursions involved getting wet. With other adults she paddled across the Okeefenokee Swamp, got lost in the salt-marsh rivers around Cape Canaveral, and got swept down the Suwanee. Over the years she's paddled over sixty of Florida's major rivers, and innumerable miles of shoreline.

As a Red Cross canoe instructor, she taught hundreds of people the basics of paddling. She learned kayak basics at Nantahala Outdoor Center in North Carolina. She is currently certified as a sailing instructor for U.S. Sailing, and is past captain of Windlasses, a women's sailing club.

Has she done it all? Not on a bet. "There's so much water, and so many places in Florida that can only be explored in a small boat," she says. "And remember, you don't have to be Hercules to be a successful paddler. If a pudgy woman with no upper body strength like me can do it, then anybody can. With a few tricks of the trade, getting onto the water is easy, and the paddling itself is a joy. Have a ball!"